THE OFFICIAL
PRICE GUIDE TO ®
Royal Doulton

BY
RUTH M. POLLARD

EDITOR
THOMAS E. HUDGEONS III

SECOND EDITION

THE HOUSE OF COLLECTIBLES, INC., ORLANDO, FLORIDA 32809

ACKNOWLEDGEMENTS

For his valuable assistance in pricing and identification the author would like to thank: Fred Dearden, Trenton, NJ, for allowing us to photograph his extensive collection. Mr. Dearden loves to share his knowledge that took years to accumulate and has helped the novice and advanced collector to find their wants. He can also assist in the buying and selling of a single piece or a entire collection. If you would like to avail yourself of his expertise in the area of identification, or for in-depth information concerning Royal Doulton, just write: Mr. Fred S. Dearden, P.O. Box 3622, Trenton, NJ 08629.

We would also like to acknowledge, for their contributions in pricing and identification, the following:

Ms. Lillian Rosenbaum
59er Antiques
San Diego, CA

Mr. Ed Pascoe
Pascoe And Soloman Inc.
New York, NY

Mr. Robert Fortune
Ashtabula Antiques Importing Co. Ltd.
Ashtabula, OH

Ms. Ann Cook
private collector

PHOTOGRAPHIC RECOGNITION

Cover and Color Section Photograph: Photographer — Marc Hudgeons, Orlando, FL 32809.
Color Separations: World Color, Ormond Beach, FL 32074.

Published by: The House of Collectibles, Inc.
Orlando Central Park
1900 Premier Row
Orlando, FL 32809
Phone: (305) 857-9095

Printed in the United States of America

Library of Congress Catalog Card Number: 80-81289

ISBN: 0-87637-355-4 / Paperback

TABLE OF CONTENTS

IMPORTANT NOTICE

Products listed or shown were originally manufactured by Royal Doulton Tableware (Holdings) Limited and distributed in the Untied States by Royal Doulton. Ruth M. Pollard is an independent dealer who is no way connected with Royal Doulton Tableware (Holdings) Limited and/or Royal Doulton, which claim and reserve all rights under the trademark and copyright laws with respect to each of the products listed or shown. The products are listed or shown with the permission of Royal Doulton.

ABOUT THE AUTHOR

Mrs. Pollard has been a dealer in limited editions and collectibles for over twenty-five years. She was owner of Beru's, Inc., a store designed with the collector in mind for eleven years, and recently sold in order to devote more time to writing and traveling. She is the editor of the American Artist Print Price Trends for a national magazine.

She is a past charter member of the National Association of Limited Edition Dealers and the American Limited Audubon Society; President of the Irvington Businessmen's Association in Indianapolis for two terms.

She was awarded Dealer of the Year award by Frame House Gallery for outstanding sales and advertisement in 1973 and the President's Cup in 1977 for her continuing efforts in behalf of both dealer and collector in the limited edition print field.

Ruth M. Pollard

The author welcomes any comments, corrections or additions which will either be answered personally or used in any future updating of this price guide. Please write:
Ruth M. Pollard
P.O. Box 39038
Indianapolis, IN 46239

INTRODUCTION TO ROYAL DOULTON

The world of collecting has expanded into territories unknown to hobbyists as recently as ten or even five years ago. Each passing year brings fresh groups of "collectibles" into the ranks of acknowledged hobbies — many of them of recent manufacture, little artistic quality, or questionable historical significance. Amidst the vast changes constantly occuring in the collectibles market, it is reassuring that the traditional hobbies have lost none of their lustre. Quite the reverse. The multitude of newcomers into the sphere of collecting, and the explosion of new ideas, seems only to enhance the position of classic collectors' items. That has been true of Old Master oils, American federal furniture, and certainly of fine porcelain. Quality has been admired and actively collected for at least six centuries in the western hemisphere, long before it was even manufactured in our part of the world. The early fascination of Europeans with Chinese ceramics was later transferred to that of Sevres, Meissen, and Chelsea. Today the lover of fine porcelain has literally the world at his feet, able to choose from the finest productions of the Orient, the Old World (that is, Europe), and the New. The works of Ohio and New Jersey potters of the 19th and early 20th century have justifiably laid a claim on the collector's attention. But among this boundless array, this panorama of fine art wrought from clay and fused with enamel and glaze, the productions of England's Royal Doulton Pottery hold an unrivaled position. No other ceramic ware of the 20th century, with the possible exception of the Goebel Hummel figurines, is as universally sought and esteemed. And certainly in the variety of types and designs, in artistic merit, and in the obvious significance of its more monumental pieces, Royal Doulton stands alone.

We should recognize at the outset that pottery manufacturers have always — since the days of Johann Boettger at Meissen — kept an eye toward the collector. While collecting in the formal sense was quite a different matter in the 18th and even the 19th centuries, nevertheless sales to collectors accounted for a large share of business. Very little of the deluxe hardpaste ware f Sevres, Meissen or other historic potteries had a real utilitarian purpose. Some of it COULD be used at the table or for other purposes; but such items were much in the minority, and they were bought primarily by persons who had intentions only of admiring them. Porcelain was luxury merchandise for the luxury classes. It was purchased by those who wished to surround themselves in beautiful things, and these individuals were the direct ancestors of the modern "collector." Consequently, the directors of porcelain factories seldon thought in terms of what might appeal to the mass populace, or what was really needed in the home. They attempted instead to devise pieces that would enchant the eye, pieces of such unquestioned visual magnetism that they would be bought — at high prices — by persons who could easily live without them.

This state of affairs promoted, in fact demanded, strict obedience to quality. Bitter rivalries existed among the porcelain manufacturers, not only at home but abroad, as a result of export. Such rivalries were fully in force when Royal Doulton launched into operation, and continued many years thereafter. It was a matter of foregone conclusion that the public had taste, and could tell the good from the not-so-good. This was repeatedly borne out by the fact that companies producing the finest work enjoyed the most prosperity. The fight in those days was to make the best porcelain and the most original porcelain. Gradually, while the battle carried on, it changed direction. In the 20th century, and more especially in the present generation, we have witnessed a situation that can bring only alarm to the more serious porcelain collector.

The population of collectors grew to staggering numbers, slowly enveloping more and more sectors of the general population. Whereas the early collectors had been connoisseurs (chiefly, at any rate) with some education in the arts and a large purse to accompany it, those of the later generations included many who admired fine works but could not afford them. Thus, a market was opened up for cut-rate art and decorations: things which had the suggestion of fine quality but sold at much lower sums. The success in marketing merchandise of this type, which of course included porcelain, let to its immense proliferation. Output was increased and production methods speeded up, using materials of lower grade and artisans of marginal skill. Gang labor was employed in the Orient, by firms supplying porcelain to the West, to insure the fastes prodution at breast minimum expense. Then, beginning around the 1950's and becoming more pronounced thereafter, we were introduced to the *instant* collectible. Collecting had become so widespread that it offered unlimited opportunities to manufacturers. If the public wanted "collectors' items," why not lead them away from the antiques shops, the art galleries, and the auction rooms, into the gift shops and novelty stores? Billions of dollars were being spent on collectors' items, and manufacturers felt it was their due to acquire some of this wealth.

Thus we have arrived at a point today in the 1980's where the picture is not entirely pretty, for anyone to whom porcelain represents a valued art form. A jungle of wares now parades across the market, much of it masquerading as "collectors' items," most of it shabby compared to the great porcelain of the world. In a sense it has dulled the glamor of porcelain collecting as a respected, noble hobby. But cream *does* rise, and this is one tussle in which weight of numbers does not, and cannot, bring victory. Royal doulton carries on today, no less aristocratic than in the days of Britain's far-flung colonial empire. Its modern works are not mere shadows of their illustrious ancestors, as is the case with so many other porcelain factories, but rightful heirs. Like a royal bloodline they have carried on, oblivious to the ruin around them. Compare at random any Royal Doulton creations of the 1970's or 1980's with those originating prior to World War I; or even those from Victoria's reign. At once you notice the same sprightly originality; the same beguiling play of imagination; the same dedication to purity of line and correctness of color. Royal Doulton has not played the game of "catch the collector." It has continued to place quality foremost in its operations; and in so doing, it has not only drawn an increasing number of collectors to its products, but a far larger percentage of those worthy to call themselves *collectors.*

Though Doultons are distributed internationally, they are still far from common compared to the works of nearly all other potteries. For works in current production, the retail prices are justifiably high; thus the owner of even a single prized work (let alone a whole collection) has something which carries an authentic exclusivity. It will never be plentiful because it is not manufactured in large quantity. Thus, Doultons hold a position today — in this chaotic world of fast-buck enterprising — roughly parallel to that of the most prestigeous French and German hardpaste ware in the 18th century. It is the porcelain bought by those who admire the best, and have developed their tastes to the degree of recognizing and appreciating the best. The difference of course is that the porcelain "war" of 200 years ago is now over. Rival factories of the 1980's have neither the inclination, nor ability, to compete against Royal Doulton on its terms. They have fallen off by the wayside, leaving this firm as the sole survivor of its species.

So far as the out-of-production specimens are concerned, we need hardly comment on their fate in the antiques shops and public auction sales. Many of them, despite more recent origins and somewhat output, outsell the "name" porcelain of the 1700's. An out-of-production Doulton has fully the status, on the collector market, of a Hemingway first edition or a Reverse tea service. Though scarcity for its own sake has never seduced the connoisseurs of fine porcelain, there is a genuine scarcity factor at work here. With ceramic objects the rate of loss through the years is inevitably high. Consider also that Great Britain, where Doultons originate, was destructively bombed during World War II. While the loss of collectors' items was overlooked amid the loss of life, both were heavy. Any Doulton produced before that time, and taken out of production before or shortly after the War, is automatically quite scarce. And on the subject of scarcity, institutional collecting must likewise be mentioned. This is obviously not a factor in the gimmicky collectibles spoken of above, most of which would be quite out of place in a respectable museum. But many museums are actively collecting Doultons, some by direct purchase and others through bequest, or by a combination of both means. While the specimens in museums count among those in existence, they are nevertheless off the market for all practical purposes, thereby increasing the scarcity of those yet in circulation.

For the private collector or hobbyist, Royal Doultons are almost automatically more appealing than even the best works of Georgian and Regency potters. While the old porcelain of the 18th and 19th centuries has equal charm, physical beauty, and historical intrigue, it is lacking one significant ingredient possessed by Royal Doultons: namely, a reliable record of production. We simply do not know, and probably never will know, the year-by-year production activities of the old European potteries. A work can be identified as Meissen of Frankfurt or Sevres but beyond this bare knowledge, it is often impossible to learn anything else about it. Most times the date of manufacture must be guessed at, and the guesses, even amongst informed collectors, can cover a span of 20, 30 or more years. One is not aware, in the majority of instances, who designed the work, who molded it, or who enameled it. Nor can it be said with any degree of certainly whether the piece represents a first of later editin, or whether it was made in this size exclusively or in various sizes. As far as production figures are concerned, it is hopeless to gather information on the old porcelains. Their original output can only be estimated by the quanitities now in existence; and even this is very far from a precise science, as the numbers in existence cannot be tabulated without a worldwide census of collectors, dealers, investors, museums, and other owners. Thus the rarity of any given example is judged, very roughly, by the numbers that have gone through the auction sale rooms within recent years. So imprecise is the knowledge of rarity, in connection with early porcelain, that it becomes almost a negligible factor in the desirability or value. With Royal Doultons a much different situation is presented. Its works are superbly catalogued, thanks to the factory's use of serial numbering systems. The people behind the scenes are known — known not just as vague names in a ledger, but through full biographical data. Almost any question which can be asked about the background or a work is answerable (and will find most of the answers in this book). There is no shroud of mystery. This not only aids the collector in learning more fully about each piece in his possession, it likewise establishes paths for specialist collecting. One can, for example, direct his intentions to works released before World War I; or during the Twenties or Thirties; or those of certain modelers, etc. The possibilities as you will quickly discover are numerous.

Royal Doultons have always possessed a somewhat magical attraction, and this has intensified with the passage of time. We often hear of them referred to as "relics of history," which is certainly appropriate; but even this attempt to explain their appeal is inadequate. A great deal of the history of the British Isles is incorporated in the works of Doulton, in figures of its kings and queens, knights, sea captains, adventurers, and even occasionally its scroundrels. But there is also much of the literature and folklore of Britain captured in its products, and (perhaps most interestingly of all) the social history of its daily life. Doultons are literally a record of British history and thought, a mirror of its people stretching back centuries.

Here, perhaps, lies the core of their popularity — the fact that Doulton themes are not inventions or flights of fancy, but reflections of real people and real life. Glamor takes a back seat to reality when the situation demands it. The Gardener Character Jug (D6630) is not a pretty face, but an aesthetically appealing creation and a faithful one. This is hardly an historical celebrity or character from a novel, but the laboring gardener who kept neat the grounds at noble estates was surely a significant cog in the wheel of British history. If he was not a familiar figure at court or in the company of princes, he was abundantly familiar to the average populace of the 18th and 19th centuries. He was the next door neighbor, the sage philosopher at the coffeehouse, the amateur poet; and, unlike folk of the middle working classes, he had at least a nodding acquaintence with the immortals of his time. he was a solid part of Old Britain, perhaps ignored in the history books, but not in Royal Doulton porcelain.

The charm of works like The Gardener, and others in the Doulton line, is closely woven with the sentimentally and traditions of Britain. it is the stuff of novels and dreams. The collector in 20th century America needs only a spark of imagination to transport himself — via Doultons — to the age of knights in armor, to the quaint mustiness and clutter of Dickens' "Old Curiosity Shop," to the shell-riddled decks on which Admiral Nelson stood and repulsed the enemy's attacks. Doultons have a timelessness because so many of their subjects are timeless: vignettes out of history, often captured more dramatically in the plastic art or porcelain than by the writer's pen or even the photographer's camera. The famous characters are known well to everyone from school days and the pages of history books. But you have undoubtedly met most of the others, too, in the pages of novels or in motion pictures or theatrical plays. "The Old Salt," "The Lawyer," and "The Night Watchman," to name three more jugs, are "types." They pop up everywhere. A casual excursion through the writings of Sir Walter Scott, Dickens, or any of the greats of British literature will acquaint anyone with them. Each work is not only a conversation piece (certainly an overused term!) but a vehicle for thought and daydreaming. So much of the pleasure in owning Doultons is in their clear link to romantic, colorful, dramatic times and traditions. "The Night Watchman" is not merely a designer's concept for porcelain, but an actual person. He patrolled the streets of London for several centuries, carrying a lantern and bell. He also carried something which not many citizens owned — a timepiece. In his rounds he announced the hour, and often interspersed his announcements with notices on the weather: "One of the clock and a chill frosty wind." Thus as a collection of Royal Doultons grows, it becomes a framework of British history, fitting in a piece here and a piece there — a king, a pretender to the throne, a pirate, several men-in-the-street, and so on. It is quite a cast.

The historical characters — that is, individuals from the history books rather that "types" representing a profession — are very numerous in the Doulton arsenal. They are uniformly well modeled, whether as jugs or statuettes, and without any doubt can be enjoyed as creations of the potter's art. Anyone who has attaines some familiarity with British history will find them immensely more engaging, however. The portraiture in all instances is extremely faithful, even in cases where some slight license is taken for satrical or dramatic effect. This in itself is not a feat to be taken lightly. The camera was developed only in the 1830's and portrait photography was not commonplace until the late 1850's. All previous likenesses were preserved in oil on canvas, in some print medium such as copper engraving or mezzotint, in drawings, or in sculpture. Individuals of rank such as royalty were of course frequently depicted in portraiture, and there is no difficulty finding suitable portraits to use as models. But for many of the historical characters immortalized by Royal Doulton, very scant pictorial record exists. Such matters as the color and style of hair, the presence of absence of a beard or mustache, and other features, can often be settled only by the most exhaustive research — when then can be settled at all. Many rare old portraits have been used by Doulton factory, as well as shreds of miscellaneous information gleaned from books, newspapers, old letters and other sources.

The Doulton collector knows that not only do his proud possessions boast a noble heritage, but that he himself can point to a line of worthy predecessors. Doultons have been actively collected for a very long time, and their enthusiasts have included the loftiest levels of society. You will find today in the English country estates, many of which are now thrown open to the public for a small admission charge, arrays of Doultons bought and placed there by a duke or earl in the 1800's or early 1900's. The reputation of Doultons, plus their reflection of British history, has long rendered them a favorite "collectible" of the nobility.

It is precisely this "Britishness" which attracts so many American buyers. America, it is true, has had a colorful history of its own; but the characters unique to british history are unique indeed, to the point that their attraction is well beyond national boundaries. Even the British criminals — amptly included among Doulton's array — were memorable characters. Dick Turpin, the highwayman, set the model for Old West stage rustlers of the 19th century. It was said of Turpin that his penchant for thievery flourished to the final moments of his life, and that he picked the pocket of the hangman while on the gallows. Turpin and other of his brood were gentlemen thieves who spoke and acted like aristocrats — and they cut aristocratic figures in porcelain.

Henry VIII is of course included in the doulton entourage, along with his six wives (two of whom were executed, to make way for their successors). The fact that one of the executed wives, Ann Boleyn, is said to have returned as a ghost and continues to haunt the Tower of London (the place of her beheading in the 16th century), is just another in the myriad of historical sidelights and fantasies which add interest to the Doulton creations.

Separating fact from fiction has long been a challenge for the historian, and of course the porcelain maker cannot hope to fare any more successfully. In the case of character jug D6375 we have a representation of a person who was unquestionably real flesh-and-blood, but whose life has been entangled largely in fable. This is Dick Whittington, "thrice Lord Mayor of London" as the old rhyme goes. He was indeed Lord Mayor of London three separate times in the 13th century, but his chief claim to historical fame — rising from rags to riches through the sale of a common house cat — is open to question. As a youth, Whittington's only possession was a cat, as the legend goes. The master of the house, in which Whittington served as a stable boy, was involved in the export business. It was his custom to allow his servants to include any of their personal possessions, in the cargos he assembled for export. Whatever price they fetched, upon reaching a foreign port, went to the owner of the article. Whittington tried his luck by including his cat among one of the parcels, though everyone declared it to be worthless. But it happened that the boat called at an Asian port, and that the Sultan was in desperate need of a cat to rid his palace of mice. So Whittington received a fortune in jewels, in exchange for it.

The more you know of the stories behind each piece, the better you will recognize the significance of small details. For example in D6375, Dick Whittington's eyes are turned to one side and he carries a melancholy expression. this refers to another line in the old rhyme or ballad, "Turn back, Dick Whittington." After serving as Lord Mayor of London, Whittington decided to leave the city; but while walking along the road he heard the sound of "bow bells," and turned around, returning to his native city. "Bow bells" is the archaic English name for "church bells," so called because of a medieval church named St. Mary-le-Bow.From this church also derives "Marylebone," the name of a street in present-day London.

Many more pages could be written, of the trappings of history and legend intermingled in Royal Doultons. The collector will soon enough discover plenty of them for himself, and these will lead him inevitably to others. Even sometimes against one's will, the avid collector of Doultons becomes an amateur historian.

Since the publication of the first edition of THE OFFICIAL PRICE GUIDE TO ROYAL DOULTON, the lingering economic slump has forced down the values on many collectors' items. Collectors should be heartened by the price reports in this edition, which shows that the market for Royal Doulton has held its own and in many instances advanced. Certainly the future outlook appears bright. More dealers are adding Doultons to their inventories, and the competition from private hobbyists is likewise on the increase. A period of adjustment may be needed before the pace of late 1970's price advances returns, however. The rapid price increases of that era were caused in some measure by investor buying, which, because of the economic conditions of the present time, are no longer as substantial. It is likely that the coming years will witness either a return of peak investor activity or, failing that, the investor void will be filled by growth of private collecting. While it is far from the intent of the editors to make recommendations, the buying opportunities which now exist may not be available in the future.

The collector who wishes to be fully informed of the Doulton market will want to keep in touch with specialist dealers; review the advertisements appearing in weekly collector newspapers; check the auction catalogues; and, of course, enroll for membership in Royal Doulton's "International Collectors' Club." This British-based organization, sponsored by Doulton, has an American branch office to expidite its dealings with American collectors. It publishes a very useful newsletter, with announcements of new products, factory events, personalities, and much collector data. Details on membership will be found elsewhere in this book.

Good collecting, good luck, and welcome to a world which has held the rapt attention of hobbyists for several generations.

HISTORY OF ROYAL DOULTON

Though the Doulton firm has roots well back into history, admiration for fine pottery had already been long established, before it came upon the scene. In addition to manufacturing terra-cotta or earthenware for all manner of household use, civilizations of the ancient world also worked pottery into artistic forms. Pottery sculptures, the forerunners of modern porcelain figureware, were made thousands of years ago and were almost universal in their production; countless numbers have turned up in pre-Columbian ruins of America. The earliest specimens were not, however, cast from molds, but made freehand by the modeler and thus could not be precisely duplicated. Nor did they possess a lustrous finish or bright enameling. They were largely left in the basic earth color (reddish) with, sometimes, painted decorations on a portion of the surface. This was firmly believed to be the highest state to which earthenware could reach. Eventually, the western world established communication with China, and was very surprised to find that the Chinese manufactured a far superior type of ceramic: hard, smooth, glossy, and beautifully enameled. It soon acquired the name Chinaware, and became the rage of Europe. By the 1400's it was being imported in very large quantities. The difference in quality between Chinaware and European pottery was so great that demand for the latter dwindled. So, understandably, European potters tried to duplicate the imported product. But for many years the technique of making true porcelain remained a secret. It did not become known until the early 18th century, when porcelain began to be made at Meissen in Prussia. The "secret" was the use of a special clay. Though strenuous efforts were made to keep the formula in Prussian hands, porcelain was soon thereafter manufactured in far-flung parts of the continent. Apparently some workers at the Meissen pottery went out and sold the "secret."

Both table and figureware were produced by the earliest potteries, of which Sevres in France (owned by the French government) gained acknowledged leadership. By about 1750 porcelain had become a rage all over Europe. The domestic works won even greater popularity than their Oriental predecessors of centuries earlier — but, interestingly enough, this fresh wave of interest brought old Chinese porcelains back into favor, too. From the mid to late 1700's everyone was buying porcelain and arraying it in all corners of their homes. Being in fashion meant having porcelain everywhere, and for a while nearly all other forms of art were taking a backseat. Where bronze figures had stood, porcelain went up in their place. The porcelain explosion had its effect on other industries, too. It proved a boon to the furniture trade; purchases of glass-fronted cabinets, for showing figureware, multiplied.

The colorfulness of porcelain was mainly responsible for working up this public fervor. Other statues and figures seemed dull by comparison. Of course the manufacturers made certain that a steady flow of new designs was always coming into the market, to satisfy the voracious appetite of buyers. New factories produced a prodigious amount, from one end of Europe to the the other and into Britain as well. Rivalry was extremely potent. Many copies and outright counterfeits were made of the Sevres designs and works of other successful potters. But most manufacturers showed plenty of their own imagination. They turned out classical subjects, whimsical, sets of monkeys playing musical instruments, gorgeously costumed young ladies, intricately detailed carriages in porcelain, and series of portraits of celebrated persons. Even after this first wave of porcelain fever subsided, the portraits of famous individuals continued. In the early 1800's you could get porcelain statuettes of Napoleon in every conceivable size and pose. In Britain, of course, they did not sell as well as figures of Admiral Nelson and Wellington.

It was essentially the revival of this faddish popularity in figureware that brought Doulton into prominence, in the late 19th century, though by then the firm was long established. The Victorians loved porcelain, and the late Victorians — from about 1880 to 1900 — loved it most of all. By then, ideals of interior decoration had drastically changed. Interiors popular in the 18th century found little favor any longer. But the Victorians had developed a collecting sense, and liked to crowd their rooms to the fullest with whatever seemed decorative or curious. This was true of all economic brackets right down the line, from royalty to day laborer: the more you stuffed into a home, the better it supposedly looked. Porcelain became one of the favorite "stuffers," and admittedly many of its owners knew very little about it from an aesthetic point of view. They "bought what they liked," and often were ignorant of manufacturers. At the same time, prestigeous firms like Doulton were gathering a clientele of more serious owners, who awaited each new release. Some very outstanding collections were made at that time, even though the individuals assembling them would have objected to being called "hobbyists."

For the history of Doulton pottery we must reach back before discovery of porcelain making in Europe, into the 17th century. As we have said, the successful commercial sale of Oriental wares had prompted potters to strive for reasonably faithful imitations. One of these was John Dwight of Fulham, a small country village just outside London. In very remote times, long before John Dwight, Fulham had gotten its name from being a center of pottery making; "fuller" was the Old English word for potter. But that was just earthenware — reddish, made for functional household use. John Dwight wanted to manufacture porcelain. Or, if he could not exactly do that, at least manufacture something more dazzling than earthenware, in hopes of sending it down the river to London and making his fortune. There was a fair chance of doing this; the public of 300 years ago was not likely to know the difference between real porcelain and a close facsimile of it. After much struggle and experiment Dwight produced a white stoneware with lustrous finish. It was not really porcelain, but a better imitation of it than any other Englishman had made up to that time. Bubbling with excitement and a dream of vast riches, Dwight applied to Charles II for a patent in 1671 and received it. In his patent application Dwight assured the king that he had "discovered the mystery of transperent earthenware," and perhaps he really believed he had. A second patent was applied for and granted in 1684, when Dwight claimed to have made improvements on his original discovery and could now produce wares identical to those of Persia, China, and other nations. Of course there was more behind all of this than met the eye. Even if the government was fully aware that Dwight did NOT possess the secret of making true porcelain, it was to the royal advantage for his efforts to be successful. A national market for domestic potters — good, bad or indifferent — would reduce the onslaught of importations and, at the same time, reduce the flow of British sterling out of the country. Not to mention the fact that if "Dwightware" gained enough reputation, it could be exported all over Europe and prove an excellent source of tax revenue for the crown.

Dwight did prosper. He eventually was running a string of factories in Fulham and was, unquestionably, the town's leading citizen. As far as his works are concerned, their modeling was better than their finishing. Dwight restrained himself from putting out cascades of small inexpensive figures, which probably would not have suited the tastes of that era. Instead he stayed mainly with grand concepts, producing large stoneware busts and classical statuary similar in design to bronzes and marbles. Made in limited numbers, they have become quite rare. Some are found in museums.

It was a start. It put Fulham squarely on the map as Britain's pottery capitol, if not one of the more important centers in all Europe. It proved that the public was not so snobbish about pottery that it would reject anything non-Oriental. Most of all it sent scores of other potters to work, trying to cash in on Dwight's success and, if possible, coming up with a finer grade of ware.

During the following century, numerous major developments occurred in pottery making. After the discovery of porcelain's "secret" at Meissen, doom was spelled for potters who turned out anything less. So, in the 18th century, a succession of old established potteries swung over to porcelain, while a much greater number of new ones came on the scene to manufacture it. It was a helter-skelter time. Many poor potters succeeded in obtaining substantial funding from investors. Nearly every pottery was, at that time, backed to the hilt by investors, to whom porcelain seemed as promising a venture as did the horseless carriage in the 1890's. Despite the overwhelming success of the porcelain trade in general, many investors lost heavily by backing potteries that were badly run or snuffed out by local competition.

Staffordshire became the unrivaled leader in figureware, of all the British potteries. Its figures were not usually as delicate or colorful as those of continental European makers, but had charm and originality and perfectly satisfied the buying public. By the late 1700's every British pottery works was getting its inspiration, if not directly pirating, from Staffordshire. Sometimes the copies did better than the originals, but there was really nothing to be done. Not many potters considered a trip to court worthwhile.

Porcelain popularity was still riding very high in England when John Doulton was born, in 1793. The native manufacturers had received a boost from the French Revolution, which had reduced export from France and aided sales of British ware. Doulton's place of birth was Fulham — not far from Dwight's pottery, which was still in operation. Many youths from the region were automatically apprenticed to the pottery trade, as was John Doulton, simply because it was there. Scores became potters who, had they been born somewhere else, would never have ventured into the business. Craft apprenticeship was the usual route for children of middle-class families in that time. It began usually at age 12 after several years of classroom education, in which the rudiments of spelling, mathematics, penmanship and the classics were learned. As these were not likely to be of great use in later life their study was not carried beyond that point. Doulton went for apprenticeship to Dwight's in 1805 and remained there until reaching age 19 in 1812. It was a tumultuous age: Britain facing the "Napoleonic problem" at home and making preparations for another war with the rebel Americans. The economy was not in good condition (it got even worse later). Yet the market for porcelain had been so firmly established by then that, good times or bad, the trade went on with no really serious hindrance.

John Doulton, like other apprentices, was worked to the bone at Dwight's. He wasn't treated as anything special because he wasn't anything special: just another local youth born under the smoke-belching kilns of Fulham, who came and went through the potteries. Most of them ended up as journeymen and some dropped out before reaching that stage, to run away from home. The braver ones who could stand the intense heat, the filth-riddled air, and the 12-hour working days of apprentices for seven or eight years ended up as masters. John Doulton was one of these. But even those who successfully completed their apprenticeship had an uncertain future. They were not automatically guaranteed a position at the factory where they served, and it was always questionable whether employment could be found elsewhere. Times of economic stress made things especially risky. There were really more master potters than demand for them. Some had to swallow their pride and take up menial posts in pottery factories, hoping for a brighter day. Others tried to buck the tide and set up their own works; but this was very costly and carried a high risk factor.

John Doulton did not work for Dwight's after filling out his apprenticeship. He went to Lambeth, another small English village known for pottery, and was employed by the Vauxhall works. This had been a successful organization some years earlier but had struck on lean times because of the owner's death. It was then being run by his widow, Martha Jones. In 1815 Doulton, then 22, and with three years under his belt at Vauxhall, bought a partnership in the factory for 100 pounds sterling. The partnership gave him one-third ownership, the other two-thirds being in the hands of Mrs. Jones and another partner named John Watt. There were no grandiose plans at that time of conquering the porcelain trade. It was essentially a small business, evident by the fact that 100 pounds could buy a third of it. It is difficult to translate one hundred pounds sterling of 1815 into modern money, but a rough estimate would place it in the range of $15,000 in 1982 spending power. This would make the whole business worth only about $45,000 in today's money. Other potteries of that time were worth much, much more. Vauxhall did mostly local marketing. It probably did no continental trade whatsoever. And even locally it could certainly not compete on even terms with the major factories. But the owners were optimistic. Doulton showed no small genius for modeling. With just a little luck, in the way of an improved economy, Vauxhall could possibly expand.

But the economy did not improve. It went totally sour. Demand for all types of luxury articles was collapsing, and most factories producing such articles collapsed with it. In 1820, after five years of struggling to keep out of red ink, Mrs. Jones threw in the towel. She withdrew from Vauxhall. Doulton and Watt, faced with the choice of closing the doors or going it along, decided to go it alone. Things improved markedly thereafter. The early 1820's was a period of significant growth for the company. Watt and Doulton proved amicable partners. Watt handled the business end while Doulton ran factory operations. Though Doulton is rightly given credit for the firm's success, Watt tends to be unfairly overlooked. But the fact is that good pottery, even great pottery, could not sell itself. Behind each flourishing factory was a director with marketing skills, and in the case of Vauxhall this was John Watt. Agencies had to be set up and an advertising program mounted. Doulton, busy with modeling and overseeing the workers, could not have handled this himself. Thanks to Watt the Vauxhall products gained distribution through the kingdom. Little was it expected, then, that in the future Doulton would conquer other lands too.

The firm's line in this era differed considerably from what we now familiarly recognize as "Doulton." That, of course, stands to reason, because public taste in the 1820's would not have supported the kind of wares sold by Doulton in the 1900's. Though the market for porcelain was working down to the upper middle class (a millionaire businessman, if not from a titled family, was "upper middle class"), it was still basically a socially elite clientele, most of whom had very established ideas on what good porcelain was all about. A large part of the trade — not only of Doulton and Watt's but most potters — was in garden ornaments. These creations, usually of huge size, brought in a good profit. They were considered chic but later eras of collectors have not taken quite the same view of them. Doulton and Watt did, however, make Toby Jugs, though not in such diverse variety as in the 20th century. The firm also did a thriving trade in commercial packing jars, sold in wholesale lots to pharmacists and food processors. Later, decorative flasks were added to the line, and in general the passing years brought more experimentation and a broadening of the company's scope.

In 1826 the firm acquired a new headquarters, on High Street in Lambeth — not far from historic Lambeth Palace, built in the middle ages. It was a smart place to move to. Growing tourism brought many art-minded visitors to Lambeth Palace, and most of them stopped in to see the "famous pottery just down the street." Naturally, examples of the factory's work were on sale (every pottery had a showroom and made sales on the premises). A drawing by Thomas Wakeman, made around the time of Queen Victoria's ascent, shows the factory's exterior and a general view of the street. By this time the factory was known as Lambeth Pottery; the name appears boldly several times on the building facade. This was not a typical-looking factory, or at least not what Americans think of as an old-time factory. It had more the appearance of a gentlemen's country estate and probably had served that function in earlier ages. The building was made entirely of stone, in a U-shape; that is, the entrance was recessed well off the street. At the front was a tall stately iron gate, leading into a sculpture garden. The gateposts were surmounted with huge likenesses of eagles, and there were various embellishments on the building itself: classical urns along the roof fronting, and a sculptured coat of arms rising high over the door. There was also a flagstaff, but at the time of Wakeman's sketch no flag was flying. A large gas lamp hung out front. The windows were barred with iron, and shuttered (as was the common style). A hoist with block-and-tackle is seen at one of the upper windows, with a platform to convey packed goods to the street below (where they would be loaded on carts). It was an impressive scene, spoiled by only one detracting element: a big smokestack rising out of the factory, which must have fouled the air for miles around. A man in an apron is seen at the gate, apparently an employee, though he could merely be engaged in painting the gate (the view is too distant to tell). Such was the Lambeth Pottery in the late 1830's — and so, essentially, was it to remain a long while.

Henry Doulton, John's son, joined the staff in 1835 at age 15. He had been primed for a university education but saw no reason why he should not start as early as possibly to learn the business he would eventually inherit. John Doulton is said to have worked to the same capacity he himself had been worked at Dwight's two decades before. To the surprise of nearly everyone, but maybe not of his father, Henry Doulton acquired a skill for pottery making. It was Henry who expanded the firm in the mid to later Victorian era, putting Doulton squarely on top of the porcelain trade. Henry was well-schooled in art and not only knew artistic porcelain when he saw it (or made it), but was attuned to the artistic tastes of the public. It was rare for a porcelain works to be commanded by someone with real artistic bent. Most factories depended for artistic guidance on their artists and modelers, who might be extremely talented but not necessarily in touch with what will *sell*. Over and beyond this, Henry Doulton was a go-getter and a big thinker, who thought unceasingly of expansion. In 1877 he bought out a factory in Burslem, England, previously used by the firm of Pinder, Bourne and Co. Five years later the name was changed to Doulton and Co. It was here that most of the firm's figureware was made in the later 19th century and thereafter.

Doulton's had become one of Britain's major industrial enterprises. Its works had enormous influence, not only on other potteries of the time, but in setting styles and shaping public tastes. Henry Doulton became SIR Henry Doulton in 1887, thanks to his contributions to the artistic and commercial life of his country. This was the first time a potter had received knighthood; it was rare for tradespeople of any sort, whom royalty traditionally held to be a lower order of humans. There was no doubt by this time that Doulton ruled the pottery trade. But that was the feather that made its cap noble indeed.

In the later 1800's, homes of anyone who sought to be in style had Doultons. They were featured at exhibitions and found their way into museums. Such individuals as the Vanderbilts, Whitneys, Astors and other titans of American commerce stocked their homes with Doultons. It was unquestionably the thing to have.

But even in this rather late era, with the factory greatly expanded and its output growing almost daily, Doultonware was essentially different in character from that of today. It was still very 19th century with heavy emphasis on vases and ornaments of all kinds, rather than the small decorative figures of our time. The philosophy of all pottery makers leaned toward interior decor. The age had not quite arrived when potters catered to *collectors,* or persons who might, even if not concerned with interior decoration as a whole, purchase wares simply for the enjoyment of owning them. When that fateful line was crossed, as it was soon thereafter, the modern era of Doulton began.

A change in direction began to occur in the years immediately preceding World War I. Doulton's was still doing very well. Wares of the same general character as those of the later 1800's were being produced, and were selling — mostly to the same class of buyers who had been purchasing them all along. But fresh winds were blowing and it appeared certain that the future of fine porcelain would go in avenues much different than those of Victoria's day. Charles Noke, the firm's art director, lobbied in favor of diversification. Collecting enthusiasm was strong for the old Staffordshire figures of the 18th century. These were being sold for high prices in antiques shops and at the auction rooms, and written up in books. Obviously there was a market to be tapped here. If the public was willing to buy fine old Staffordshire figures for big prices, wouldn't it buy equally fine modern figures for lower prices? This was the gist of Noke's reasoning and it made sense. In 1913 Doulton introduced a series of small models into its line, thus beginning the HN series (named for the firm's head colorist, Harry Nixon). It was also in 1913 that the name became Royal Doulton, inspired in part by a visit from George V and Queen Mary to the Burslam factory. The queen was enchanted with the new small figures and her approval of them virtually assured their commercial success.

So, for all practical purposes, the year 1913 serves as the dividing line between "old Doulton" — which obviously is of collector interest, too — and the objects covered in this book.

Before the year was out, Royal Doulton had placed 40 character figurines on the market. The project was well orchestrated and the public was receptive, but world affairs got in the way. In 1914 World War I broke out. The war naturally had far-reaching effects on the porcelain industry, as it made foreign distribution difficult or impossible. Even the domestic trade was sharply reduced. Less than a dozen new numbers were added to the HN line in 1914, and even fewer in 1915. But the output of new additions rose in 1916, and it became evident at that point that the series had found great favor. The war's conclusion saw greatly stepped-up production. Most of these early designs were retained until 1938, on the eve of the next war. Despite being manufactured for 20 or more years, however, they were never excessively common. Distribution in those days was not as extensive as it became later. Also, the fact that a model was listed as "in production" for a long stretch of years did not necessarily mean it was manufactured every one of those years. Certainly, the majority of low-number HN figures, discontinued in 1938, went for lengthy periods of non-production. Their present-day scarcity is ample testimony of that fact — levels of scarcity which even the current retail prices do not fully reflect. Then, of course, there was the attrition factor: specimens that were damaged or otherwise lost. Considering their ages and the fact that some went through two World Wars, the percentage destroyed is possibly higher than most writers have recognized. German blitz bombings of Britain, during the early part of World War II, leveled homes, shops, and warehouses. Artworks of all kinds perished at an appalling rate, and naturally anything as fragile as porcelain stood no chance at all.

During the 1920's Royal Doulton enjoyed exceptional success, thanks to growing international popularity of the HN models and also — in part — to good times in general. The twenties saw healthy economies in most nations. During this decade the HN series was vastly expanded. Not only were many more figures added, but a greater variety in types, with considerable experimentation and even some daring along the way. But the public, even though it was comprised of few actual collectors in those days, never cried "enough!" People were buying Royal Doultons for interior decor or just out of attraction to them, yet still the volume of buying was sufficient to make a success of nearly every figure. Quite a bit of what was produced in this hectic decade could be classified as Art Deco, though it was the British rather than American style of Art Deco . . . which tended to be slightly more theatrical.

No one would ever suggest that Royal Doultons mirror the times in which they were created, since history and fantasy are often prime ingredients — and these are timeless. But, occasionally, they have done just that. Figures of *The Bather* sold during the liberal-minded '20's were a nude study. In the 1930's the figure continued in production, but a swing toward conservatism prompted the factory to add a painted-on bathing suit. Today, of course, matters of this type are no consideration in choosing subjects for the factory's line.

The golden twenties encouraged Royal Doulton to believe that it had a winning formula in which no major changes would be necessary for long into the future. But the decade ended on a crushing note with America's financial crisis. Soon all of the western world lay mired in economic ruin, and all industries were threatened. In a way, the HN series proved Royal Doulton's salvation. If the company's line had been structured along 1890 or even 1910 principles, consisting mostly of large expensive works for the wealthy, things would have gone very badly indeed. But by having these troops of modestly-priced wares, Royal Doulton did not lose its whole clientele. In fact it probably gained some new customers, among the formerly rich who suddenly found themselves in reduced circumstances. Still, of course, the ground-shocks were too severe to just keep forging ahead under the old plan. The factory recognized, early in the Depression, that it must diversify, and must produce items of even lower cost than the standard HN line. So in 1932 the now-familiar series of miniature figures was introduced. At first the firm's miniatures carried regular HN numbers, but later were given M numbers (and, eventually, taken off the number scheme altogether). These miniatures perfectly suited the needs and pocketbooks of the glum '30's — they were cheery and spoiled no ones budget. It was also at this time that Royal Doulton began issuing Limited Editions, another very significant step. The firm likewise gave greater attention to its miscellaneous wares in the '30's, in the wise belief that one's eggs should not, in dangerous times, be all in one basket. And in this fashion it not only rode out the dismal '30's in praiseworthy style, it generated considerable fresh collecting interest in its products, which has carried on to the present time.

World War II was another bleak period, but after the war Royal Doulton went into full gear at a pace surpassing anything in the company's history. Collecting enthusiasm boomed, spurred on by the fact that so many early HN's had been discontinued in 1938. This gave collectors two targets at which to aim their sights: the in-production figures (of which there were still plenty, and more coming all the time), and the scarcer obsolete ones. This was exactly the "push" needed to get the Royal Doulton hobby going. Antique dealers had, prior to 1938, hesitated to stock the HN figures because, despite their obvious collector appeal, they fell into the category of currently made merchandise. After World War II, the older HNs began appearing in antique shops in a vast abundance. And as other figures were discontinued, collectors looked to the antique trade to supply them, too, just as the situation is today. Prices were of course a mere fraction of what they have now become.

In recent years Royal Doulton has further displayed its versatility with such series as the *Dancers of the World* and *Soldiers of the Revolution,* showing that it has no intention of allowing tradition to get in the way of new inventiveness. Surely an exciting future for the company and the fans of its products is in store.

THE DESIGNERS

The success of any manufacturer of artistic porcelain depends in large measure on its designers and artists — the individuals who create each design and the working models for them, which are sculpted in clay. It is often said that Royal Doulton has been fortunate over the years in claiming some of the outstanding talent in the field. But good fortune alone played only a partial role; most of Royal Doulton's skilled minds and hands would not have felt at home in any lesser factory.

Royal Doulton's designers and artists deserve more attention than they have received — and more than we, unfortunately, can give in a book which is essentially a value guide. The serious collector realizes that no degree of manufacturing talent can turn a mediocre model into a public favorite, when the finished work goes on sale. In a company such as Royal Doulton, a high standard is always required; and so is, at the same time, imaginatively designing that does not merely repeat what has been done in the past. Thus, experimentation is always a necessity, and designers and artists must constantly bring a high level of quality to their experimental efforts. The ratio of success is not 100%. Some extremely worthy models fail to become popular, or as popular as others. Then, too, public taste changes periodically, and a porcelain maker must be ever aware of the times. What Doulton produced at different times in the 19th century might not have sold at other times; but it was right for its era. It not only suited the "mode," but often made the mode, as Doulton was at the forefront of porcelain's great renaissance for interior decoration.

Certainly, any methodical collector looks beyond size and color and first visual impression. The decorativeness of Doultons should not blot out the fact that they are, unquestionably, important works of sculpture, and gems of creative design.

The following paragraphs give some brief information on the more noteworthy of Doulton's artists and designers.

GEORGE TINWORTH. George Tinworth's influence on the factory — and on porcelain making in general — is well recognized. Tinworth had a very successful career as an independent sculptor in Victorian Britain in addition to his work with Doulton. Born in 1843, he grew up in the dawning years of one of the more memorable classical revivals. Heroic sculptures after the Greek manner were strongly in demand when Tinworth began his career, and he received many commissions for such works. Some of his productions, showing warriors, gladiators, etc., were of immense size. At the same time, and probably for a refreshing change of pace, he also sculpted small figures of children and animals. These were often in a slightly humorous vein. Some of Tinworth's models were cast at Doulton's. They enjoyed great popularity, and Tinworth gained a reputation in Britain on a par with that of John Rogers in America — though the "Tinworths" were much smaller physically. A number of Tinworth's models provided inspiration for Doulton's artists. But his most significant connection with the firm came through his set of *Merry Musicians,* a group of Huck Finn type of children playing various instruments. Charles Noke, Doulton's art director at the time, was interested in having Tinworth carry this concept much further. This was prevented by Tinworth's death, which occurred just as Doulton was launching its series of Fancy Character Figurines. Nevertheless his influence is apparent in many of the early additions to the HN series.

LESLIE HARRADINE. Leslie Harradine was born in 1887 and came to Doulton as an apprentice modeler at age 15. His great creativity proved a driving force in the organization and resulted in many imaginative creations. Harradine was responsible for a number of the character jugs issued in the early 1900's, including Sam Weller, Pickwick, Sairey Gamp and Micawber. His personal tastes in modeling ran strongly in the direction of figureware, but the firm's trade then consisted heavily of vases and garden ornaments, so his talents were directed toward them as well. In 1912, when still very young and on the threshhold of an apparently bright career, Harradine decided that factory life did not appeal to him. He bought a farm in Canada and refused all offers to return to Doulton's. An arrangement was worked out, however, whereby Harradine would model figures in clay and ship them across the Atlantic, for use in the Doulton line if they won approval. In this fashion Doulton gained some of its most popular models. Harradine's figures included Polly Peachum, The Goose Girl, Contentment, and many others. For nearly 40 years Harradine sent off models to Doulton. He died in 1965, aged 78.

RICHARD GARBE. Richard Garbe worked at Royal Doulton during the 1930's and created many of its Limited Editions of that era, such as Spirit of the Wind, Beethoven, Salome, and Lady of the Snows. He also modeled wall-masks. Garbe had the important distinction of being instructor in sculpture at London's Royal College of Art. The letters "RA," often shown after his name, signify Royal Artist.

CHARLES NOKE. Charles Noke was Art Director of Doulton's for many years, in the late 19th and early 20th centuries. He had previously been with Worcester, a rival factory, and joined Doulton in 1889. To Noke belongs credit for shaping Doulton into its present form, for he conceived the idea of Fancy Character Figures and instituted the HN series. Noke was extremely partial to figureware and even before the HN series he was adding figures (some of them of immense size) to the Doulton line. He was originally a modeler.

MARGARET M. DAVIES. Peggy Davies, as she is more familiarly known, has been responsible for designing and modeling many of Royal Doulton's postwar creations. She joined the firm in 1939 just as the war was beginning. Trade was naturally curtailed by the war, and Peggy's home was damaged by German air raids. But she continued her interest in art, and after the war became a very successful independent sculptress. Though not employed by Doulton thereafter, she executed many works for the firm on a contract arrangement, in her own studios. Her Royal Doultons have included Lady Musicians, Figures of Williamsburg, and the much-heralded Dancers of the World, in which each piece has a low limited number of just 750 specimens.

ERIC GRIFFITHS. A sculptor of considerable skill and reputation, Eric Griffiths is noted for his masterful Soldiers of the Revolution series. His early background was in industrial sculptoring. Griffiths now serves as Head of Sculpture for Royal Doulton.

MARY NICOLL. Mary Nicoll contributed many works to the HN series during the 1960's and 1970's, until her death in 1974. Her figures were mainly "general types" rather than historical or fictional characters. They included a number of nautical types, in which she had a special interest.

HOW ROYAL DOULTONS ARE MADE

While some collectors may be uninterested in the technical details of how Royal Doultons are made, it is well to realize (at the least) that quality standards differ greatly from one porcelain factory to another. Simply making porcelain is not, in itself, mysterious or difficult; or even very expensive. But making it well, to a consistent level of perfection, requires skilled, dedicated workers, and a factory atmosphere that encourages quality by not stressing volume output. This is quite the exception, rather than the rule, in 20th century porcelain making. In most factories, even those which issue signed works and try to build international reputations, the production steps are rushed; or the work suffers from faulty or uncreative designing. Fine porcelain is born out of a balanced combination of imaginative, purposeful designing, and careful execution. Both the workers and their products must be screened, and rejection given to those not measuring up. The belief that fine porcelain is a lost art, that the levels of achievement recorded by (for example) Staffordshire in the 18th century are beyond duplication, is mistaken. The overall quality of ceramic wares produced throughout the world has steadily declined; but this has been by plan, not by any decline in human skill. *Most* manufacturers have aimed at a larger and larger market, and have reduced selling prices to appeal to the masses. This means shortcuts in production and an inevitable loss of quality. When a factory resolves to keep a high standard, nothing stands in the way of old-time excellence. Anyone who owns Royal Doultons knows that they stand comparison with the predecessors of 200 years ago.

Each item entering the Royal Doulton line begins with an idea, which must be transferred into a model. Usually the idea or concept is worked up by one of the factory's artists. But the matter of getting ideas for Royal Doultons is more complex than it might sound. A number of important criteria must be met, and potential works that fall short of meeting any of these criteria never get off the drawing board. A work must be compatible with products already in the line, but not closely similar. These decisions are not always easy to arrive at. For example, the line already includes many characters from the novels of Dickens, which have been well received. Should this be interpreted to mean that the public would welcome more and more Dickens characters (there is an inexhaustable supply), or would it be just as receptive to characters from other Victorian writings, such as those of Thackeray or Melville? Many considerations must be weighed before giving the "go" to any new design. The design must be capable of being rendered with real visual appeal. It must be decorative enough or interesting enough to stand on its own merits — not to serve exclusively as an addition to a collection of Royal Doulton. It need not be pretty in the traditional sense — not many of the Toby or character jugs are — but it must be captivating. It cannot be just another number in a list.

After settling on a design concept, the usual procedure is for various sketches to be made on paper, showing different poses or attitudes. The possible variations of poses and props with any design are endless, but normally the artist has something special and definite in mind. He does not need to experiment with numerous possibilities. These original sketches, which would be of great interest for collectors, hardly ever get into circulation, as they seldom leave the factory. There is always a danger that they might be utilized by a rival manufacturer.

The next step is to transfer this sketched idea to a working model. Working models must be the exact size of the future porcelain models, and alike them in every respect. In coin designing, the artist may work on a large model and have his design transferred (by sophisticated machine) to a tiny die. With ceramics this is not possible. The working model must be fashioned as a carbon copy — in everything but enameling — of what the actual model is intended to be.

The working model is a clay sculpture. Soft non-hardening clay is used, so it can easily be removed from the mould after the model has set. The clay of the finished models is quite a different substance. Its ingredients are selected to provide maximum hardness (as in old Chinese porcelain), purity, and the gleaming surface translucence so admired in fine ceramic ware. The Royal Doulton clays are strictly of local composition, made from native materials in the tradition of British potters of the Georgian era. China clay (kaolin), Cornish stone (well powdered) and calcined bone ash are the chief components. The term "stoneware," not used very often any longer but still applicable, was not an adman's idea of a name that would draw attention; real ground stone was, and is, used. Stone is not used for the purpose of providing ruggedness, but rather hardness — the quality that gives fine porcelain a distinctive "ring" when tapped with a spoon handle. Each ingredient is inspected to assure proper texture and quality, and blended together at the factory according to rigid procedures.

When the working model has won final approval, it is submerged into plaster of paris for a cast to be taken. This cast will be a faithful image, in reverse, of the model: that is, everything raised on the model will be recessed on the cast and vice-versa. The cast cannot of course be used "as is," for actual casting of the finished porcelain figures, since it would be impossible to remove them from the cast. This seemingly hopeless problem is easily solved by cutting up the cast — actually sawing it — into numerous smaller casts, each one representing a component of the model. There is no standard number of parts into which a cast is cut, nor any standard way of cutting. This is determined by the individual model and its intricacies. The more detailing, the more parts into which the cast must usually be divided. In casting porcelain from the molds, each casting is a separate operation: an arm is done, then a portion of body, and so on. Clay slip (liquid clay) is poured into the molds and left to remain for a certain specified time, so it becomes perfectly set but not overset. When hardened, they are assembled into figures, another exacting operation, then dried. The drying procedure is important because water has been used in mixing the ingredients, and it is desirable to eliminate as much of it as possible. Cracking in the kiln may occur otherwise, or the figure could develop surface bubbles or other blemishes. The model then makes its so-called "biscuit trip" through the firing oven or kiln, heated up to as much as 1,240 degrees Centigrade. It is called the "biscuit trip" because the figure emerges white and unglazed, and if sold in that state would be called biscuitware. But of course it has not as yet completed its manufacturing process.

Upon coming from the kiln the figure has shrunk somewhat, because of drying, which compacts the material. A figure that enters the kiln at 6 inches high will emerge less than 5½″. This of course must be taken into account when the original master model is sculpted. Fortunately the degree of shrinkage can be foretold very closely, thus enabling the modeler to gauge just how oversized his working model must be.

If the figure is intended to be highly translucent, which is the case with most Royal Doultons, it is then dipped into a vat of liquid glaze, which has about the consistency of buttermilk and a very similar appearance. The glaze is not clear but white, with a hint of pink. However when the figure is fired again in the kiln, it emerges with a crystal-like coating over the entire surface. It is still of course in a solid color, and now passes to the enameling department for painting. In porcelain factories, "paint" is always referred to as "enamel." Royal Doulton takes pride, and justly so, in the fact that all its enameling is done by hand. This may not carry much weight with the general public, who finds "hand painted china" on the trinket shelves in variety shops, selling for a few dollars. These inexpensive hand-painted wares are produced by gang labor, where wages are very low and no degree of skill is expected. The work is not only sloppy, but often unfinished; and extremely uninspired, to say the least. Royal Doultons are enameled by qualified artisans, who operate at a leisurely pace. There is no watering down of enamel to make it stretch. This is why the colors are always bold and vibrant. The color scheme for each model is worked out in advance and must be rigidly adhered to. Of course there are minor variations, especially in models requiring very intricate detailing, but this is regarded as adding to their charm. Staffordshire figures of the Golden Age showed variations in enameling, too.

After painting, groups of specimens representing the same model pass along to the factory's inspectors. They are now in the finished state ready for release to distributors, but any that are deemed to be unsatisfactory will be culled at this point. In this phase of its operations Royal Doulton is meticulous indeed. If a model has not been fused together perfectly, if there is any defect in the glaze or problem with the enameling, it will not be released. Thanks to their expertise, the inspectors will notice tiny faults that would go undetected by most observers.

When you buy a Royal Doulton, you have truly bought the end result of much effort on the parts of many talented and concerned individuals.

TRADEMARK IDENTIFICATION AND DATING

The prospective buyer, when locating what appears to be a Royal Doulton figure, must ask, "Is it actually a Doulton?" "How can I tell?" "And are there any clues to the year or general era of production?"

Porcelain markings have a reputation of being confusing, to the point where some individuals, faced with the interpretations of marks, cry uncle and go off into another hobby. In the realm of British porcelain this situation does not exist. Potential collectors and buyers of Royal Doulton learn, through brief study, that they are not up against a stone wall in the matter of markings. There are questions which remain unanswered in the history of Doulton's markings, however, those questions concern pottery lines dated prior to the line of production represented in this book.

The figures listed in this book — that is, Fancy and Character Figures or statuettes as collectors often term them — are all in the HN or M series. Remember just those prefixes, and you are on the road to identifying a Royal Doulton from the work of a rival potter.

Doulton has always stamped his wares. In the 1850's the familiar marking was a terse "DOULTON, LAMBETH." It gave the manufacturer's name and location as shown in illustrations 1-6.

1

2

3

4

5

6

After expansion in 1877 the backstamps refered to their factories accordingly, Lambeth or Burslem. The coronet was added at the Burslem factory, 1886, to designate the appointment of Henry Doulton as potter to H.R.H., the Prince of Wales. The word "England" was added after 1891 and in 1902 the Royal Warrant by King Edward VII allowed the use of the world "Royal in identifying Doulton Products. The marking system became more detailed through the years and arrived at its present form in which the lion and crown are emblematic of the firm's wares, illustrations 7-12.

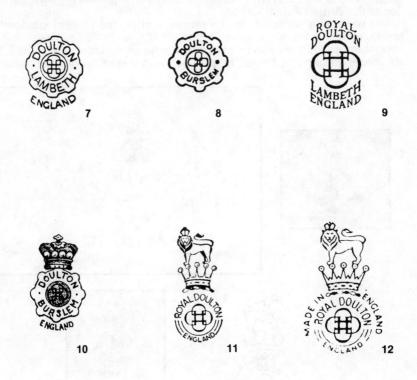

The HN numbering system was instituted in 1913, the letters HN being the initials of Doulton's chief colorist, Harryd Nixon. This might be an indication that nobody, at the time, really foresaw the extent to which the HN series would grow. The plan was to have this HN prefix on every model, followed by a serial number, and, in addition, the official name of the model. At first the model names were applied by hand, then later were stamped. Occasionally specimens turn up which bear the model name lack the series number.

Additionally, many bear the wording "POTTED BY DOULTON & CO.," also hand lettered. And of course they carry the Royal Doulton Lion and Crown symbol, which even at that time, was being affixed by stamping. All fine bone china products, 1928-current, show the words "BONE CHINA" on figures, animals and other non-table items.

Each specimen also bears the artist's signature, and USUALLY a rectangle impressed into the material, enclosing a number. No official explantion has been given of this marking, but it may designate the mold number. Then, there is the "RD. NO.," which is simply the figure's registration number at the British Patent Office.

The beginning collector may be thrown a bit by the style of stamped lettering used by Royal Doulton in the 1950's and 1960's, which closely resembles script. This was used to give the figures addded charm, as if they HAD been lettered by hand. The practice was thereafter discontinued.

13

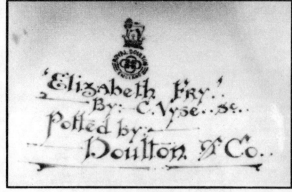

14

15

16

17

18

Revisions of lettering styles naturally created a situation in which identical figures do not always bear identical markings. This is a useful aid in dating. Illustration #17 shows the current marking of "THE BALLOON MAN," the same figure pictured in Illustration #18. In this case the numbering is alike but the style of lettering different. You will find examples of the same figures — with the same names — bearing *different numbers.* At first this is perplexing, until one learns that Royal Doulton changes the series number whenever it makes revisions in a figure's color scheme. In the factory's view, new coloration means a new figure, and a new number is assigned. This can happen to the same figure any number of times. *Kate Hardcastle* exists with numbers HN1718, HN1719, HN1734, HN1919 and HN2028. If a date appears, impressed into the mold, this can be taken to signify the date of that model's introduction to the line. These dates are found on older figures only and, even then, only occasionally. Molds for HN564, *Parson's Daughter,* carried a dating of 3-1-31. This work remained in the line from then until 1949. When reading these dates, it is important to remember that the British (as Europeans generally) give the DAY before the MONTH. Thus, 3-1-31 is not March 1, 1931, as Americans would write it, but January 3, 1931.

In general the HN series runs in sequence, and the numerical order roughly indicates the chronological order in which figures were issued. In the absence of other evidence, it is usually safe to assume that of any two figures, the one whose number is lower was issued first. The exception is where numbers are intentionally set aside, for figures that will be issued years in the future, for the purpose of giving figures in a set consecutive numbers. This is a general practice among makers of fine porcelain.

The M series comprises miniature figures 4½″ tall. It was introduced in 1932. Some of the works in this series are reduced versions of HN figures, changed in nothing but size. Others were created created expressly for the M series and have no HN counterpart. When Royal Doulton began this series, the M prefix was not used. The early miniatures carried HN numbers and were serialized as part of the regular HN series. The last miniatures to carry HN numbers appeared in 1949. Today, *numbering has been abandoned* for the minature figures; they now bear only the model name. They are of course readily identified by the standard Royal Doulton markings. Some of the earliest miniatures are marked "DOULTON" or "DOULTON C.," but those in current production have the same stamping as the HN figures.

WINSTON CHUPCHILL
PRIME MINISTER
OF GREAT BRITAIN
— 1940 —

Royal Doulton marks its special series and editions with backstamp information which is unique and identifies that item or series. The following backstamps represent Dickensware, plates, limited edition figures and Rouge Flambe. Dickensware was first introduced in 1908 and the range of subject matter constantly expanded. A brown backstamp was used until 1930 and from 1931 to 1960 the backstamp was black. The Winston Churchill and Cliff Cornell backstamps are examples of limited editions. The Rouge Flambe trademarks vary. Sometimes all marks are found on one piece and often only one marking will be found along with the traditional Royal Doulton emblem.

By reviewing the illustrations in this book, the subject of trademarks and numbering should become thoroughly clear.

INVESTING IN ROYAL DOULTON

With so much attention turned toward investment in art objects, there is inevitably the question: what kinds of investment potential are offered by Royal Doulton products? If I collect intelligently, can I expect to recoup my expenditure, or realize a profit? If I wish to approach collecting from an investment standpoint, is any special strategy to be used?

At this point, the level of pure investment buying of Royal Doulton is still low compared to pure collector buying. But this in itself may be misleading, as it depends upon the definition of "pure collector buying." We can safely assume that "pure *investor* buying" is done by persons whose aesthetic interest in the material is slight, and who mainly want to speculate for financial gain. Some of these individuals are buying Royal Doulton because they want a dressy investment, something that looks pretty while sitting around maturing in value. In any case they are not collectors. But we could not, on the other hand, say that "pure collector buying" is motivated entirely by hobbyist interest. In this day and age (if in no other), very few hobbyists, no matter how dedicated, will buy anything expensive if it represents a financial risk. The "pure collector" may not think first and foremost of turning a profit. But without the assurance of going with an established winner, many collectors might hesitate.

Based on world economic conditions, the state of investments in general, and opportunities offered by investing in art objects, it would strongly appear that investment buying of Royal Doulton will increase. If 10% of current sales are made to investors (a rough guess — and the figure is probably much higher for items in the $1,000-up range), this is likely to rise to 20% within a year or two. It would seem doubtful that the concentration of investment activity on Royal Doulton will ever equal that of postage stamps, coins, or oil paintings — for reasons that have nothing to do with its investment potential. It is simply a matter of the nature of the materials. Stamps and coins attract great throngs of investors because they can be easily stored in a bank deposit box or even hidden in the home. Oil paintings cannot be so easily stored, but many investors — especially new ones — feel that they carry great prestige value, but the public at large has not awakened to this as yet.

The "track record" of Royal Doulton on the market is favorable for investment in most respects. Of the thousands of items listed in this book, excluding of course those of very recent manufacture, the vast majority have registered strong upward value increases during the 1970's and into the eighties. Their rate of increase has been sufficient to return a profit for anyone who purchased them a decade ago or even, in some cases, more recently.

There is every likelihood that, even at the present levels of price, Royal Doulton will bring profits to MOST of those who buy today.

If you intend to collect, and especially if you intend to spend large sums for some of the more valuable works, we would not hesitate to say that your money is safe. Barring some broad economic calamity, there is little danger that Doulton will not continue its forward surge on the market. There is virtually no danger of a reversal in prices. If you buy as a collector, for the pleasure and satisfaction of owning superior porcelain, this is certainly ample assurance for you. You will have objects of sparkling merit and no worry of suddenly discovering that the market is under and your treasures are going at 10¢ on the dollar.

If you have any thoughts about investing, purposely for the aim of making money, then we would suggest that you look into the picture more deeply. Investing is not a hobby but a business. It must be undertaken with certain procedural rules in mind. And you must become thoroughly familiar with the Royal Doulton market, before making any decisions of what pieces to buy.

If you invest, you will probably be buying at retail and selling at wholesale — not a very attractive proposition, but one which does not rule out success. You will be purchasing from dealers and in most instances paying sums in the neighborhood of those stated in this book. When you sell, you will most likely be selling to dealers, perhaps the same ones from whom you bought. A dealer buying a Royal Doulton — any Royal Doulton — from the public does not pay the current retail value. His percentage of discount, often referred to as a "commission," depends on the item, its price range, his circumstances, and other factors. In-production items are bought by dealers at larger discounts than discontinued pieces. The dealer already has the opportunity, with in-production items, of ordering from the distributor and getting an automatic discount. He will buy from you only if he can buy cheaper than from his supplier — and that could mean cleaving the retail value in half. Discontinued items are of course more appealing to a dealer, and he may pay 70% of his selling price for them. It is very rare for a dealer to pay more than 70%, because of the expense now required to run a business.

Successful investing is not simply a matter of selling for more than you paid. The length of "holding" time, and inflation's pace during the holding period, must be taken into account. Investments, of any kind, are not considered successful unless they yield an increase in buying power. The value of money is eternally decreasing, so it is quite possible (depending on circumstances) to sell for more than you paid and end up worse than you began — by having more money but less buying power. To give a simplified example, say that inflation decreases the value of money by 50% over a five-year period. If you invest $1,000 at the beginning of this five-year period, and sell the investment for $1,300 five years later, you appear to have made $300. But in fact the $1,300 received has less buying power than your original $1,000 at the time you invested it. You would need to get $1,500 just to break even. Anything over $1,500 would be a clear profit.

As we said, this is a simplified example. Inflation fluctuates. But it never ceases to be a factor in investments of any kind.

Anyone setting out to invest in 1982 would probably be safe in assuming that inflation will average around 10% annually in the next five or six years. The question then becomes: do Royal Doultons have favorable investment qualities in that kind of economic situation? Faced with a stiff rate of inflation, and the inevitable dealer's commission when you sell, would it still be possible to realize a profit?

Much depends of course on the scale of growth in the collector market, which is hard to foresee. The late seventies and early eighties saw remarkable growth, and at this point there is no reason to believe it will cease. Competition for Royal Doulton's discontinued models is almost certain to intensify, in the hobbyist community. The question mark is whether investment buyers will come into the field in really large numbers, bringing greater competition. If they do, prices could double in two or three years, or even in a shorter time. Royal Doulton has unimpeachable investment credentials, among collector's items. It has the established reputation of being a favorite of collectors and connoisseurs for many years. There is the further impetus of its works being released in limited quantities, not nearly enough to "go around" to all interested parties. This is particularly true of the discontinued models, which were manufactured when Royal Doulton collecting was on a small scale compared with the present day.

Our advice for those who choose to invest in Royal Doulton would be to concentrate mainly on the discontinued models, and be very selective about buying. Nobody can effectively look into the future and foretell collecting patterns that might develop. But what has happened in the past, and what is happening in this market at the present time, should point investors in the correct directions. Character and Toby Jugs have come in for enormous collector popularity in the U.S. within recent years. The older items in these series appear to be underpriced, based on current availability and interest. It is not difficult to tell why. Many collectors are simply uninformed about the relative scarcity of one model vs. that of another, and some are not even aware that the older models have been discontinued. To a certain extent the market as it stands today is suffering from a lack of buyer education, which an investor could possibly use to his advantage. Most enthusiasts of Royal Doulton are still buying what they like, for their own personal reasons. This is not unusual with highly decorative material, which has appeal to the non-collecting general public as well as hobbyists. A certain proportion of sales will probably always be made that way. But in time, likely a short time, relative scarcity is sure to become a more potent force with buyers than it is today. The discontinued models, even though they started out with MUCH lower selling prices than current releases, should (if this hobby follows other hobbies) leave the current works far behind in price. We are already beginning to see an indication of this, but values have a great deal of adjusting to do before becoming equitable all around.

Though we could be mistaken on this score, our feeling is that the very costly models (such as Princess Badoura) are NOT among the most attractive for financial investment. For one thing they might prove a bit more difficult to sell when the time comes, since some dealers hesitate to make that large an investment unless they have a waiting customer. But our main reason for not recommending the cream of Royal Doulton's current line is simply that they're out of range for most collectors. The majority of new hobbyists going into Royal Doulton collecting will be concentrating on models in a lower price category, and it is these which *could* score very quick price leaps. The pieces selling for thousands of dollars are not as likely to receive a rush of buying activity, though they should climb steadily in value. You stand very little danger of losing money on them, but we see only a slim chance of gaining a satisfactory investment profit on such works.

If you buy Royal Doultons for investment, we suggest that you keep a close watch on the market. It would be inadvisable to buy, and then put them away to mature without monitoring the market. The hobby magazines and newspapers carry many ads, in each issue, for buying and selling Royal Doultons. These should be checked as a matter of routine by investors. It is quite possible that you might find, soon after making a purchase, a "wanted" ad for the very item, placed by a collector who will pay you a profit. Keep in mind that the availability of discontinued models varies throughout the country. What you find in your area may not turn up in some distant part of the country. Sometimes a collector searching for a particular model will gladly pay more than the usual retail value. This is why the sums quoted in this book are intended as guides only — there are no firm prices because the price in every transaction hinges on circumstances. In this kind of situation you could do much better by selling early, and taking what may appear a very small profit, rather than waiting until years in the future.

Of course there is the strong possibility that if you DO get into investing, you will sooner or later get into dealing as well. Selling to a dealer and taking less than the current retail value may seem unappealing to you, compared to the opportunity of advertising your Doultons and possibly doing much better on them. Many of the selling ads in hobby papers are placed by investors, or collector-investors. This is by far the best way to reach the public, and there is nothing frightening about selling to collectors and thereby acting as a dealer. You may hit upon some good buying contacts in this fashion, too. If a Doulton collector has switched direction along the way — if he started with animal and bird models but is now into character jugs — he will usually be willing to "trade in" his unwanted pieces below the current retail value. Opportunities will present themselves to work out very favorable transactions, if you keep up-to-date on values.

If you invest, keep a record of your investments with the date of each purchase and the amount paid. If you want to speculate in the new limited editions, get them as soon as they come out. You should, normally, count on holding limited editions for at least five years before selling, but there will sometimes be the chance to sell at a good profit in less time.

CARE AND REPAIR

The question is sure to come up, among readers of this book, of what to do about cleaning and repair. As stated earlier, we advocate a careful storage program, which, if pursued, should make it unnecessary to ever face the task of repair. In answer to those who wonder about buying damaged Doultons and mending them, our opinion is that this is useless, and generally results in financial loss. It is quite correct that damaged specimens can be bought from dealers at a bare fraction of the standard market prices. Anyone handy with a gluepot may automatically start making mental calculations, and assume he can, with a few deft strokes, turn a $25 buy into $100. Sadly it cannot be done. It if could, the dealer would do it himself and charge $100. Once a Doulton has been damaged by breakage (meaning any component snapped off), it rates as a "second," even if very skillfully repaird. There is of course the possibility of selling such an item to a buyer unaware of the defect; but this is quite dishonest, and a practice to which no serious collector would care to stoop. You may be curious why a damaged and well-repaird Doulton is worth just a fraction of the normal value, even though the repaired area is not conspicuous and all else is well. It is simply because mint state specimens are not difficult to get. The majority of the market ARE mint state, which of course is not the situation with coins, postage stamps, or antiques in general. Even when drastically reduced in price they are considered, by some dealers, to be unsalable.

If you have the misfortune of having a Doulton break on you, while in your possession, then of course it should be repaired rather than simply discarded. It can serve as a second or "gap filler" while you await the acquisition of another; and you may find that you learn to live with it, and do not seek to replace it after all. Whether or not a specimen can be successfully repaired depends on the nature of the fracture. In cases of shattering, which will occur if Doultons are dropped on marble or concrete floors, ragged bits of all sizes are sprayed about and there is really no hope of repair. Droppage on a wood floor generally results merely in a clean localized break, such as the handle popping off a jug (while droppage on a carpeted floor may, depending on the point of impact, cause no harm at all). Look first to see if tiny pieces at the points of breakage are missing, as they often are. If you are dealing with two intact pieces that have merely separated, there is no great problem getting them back together. Apply some rubber cement lightly with a brush to the areas that will be fitted together, let it dry slightly for a minute or two, then bring the pieces together and press gently. If you have used fast-drying cement, it should not be inconvenient to hold the sections until fully dry. Otherwise, it may be necessary to use some kind of clamping device, which will need to be improvised from rubber bands or whatever is available. Obviously a metal clamp will do more harm than good. If you do not trust your own dexterity, a restorer of antiques can do the job — and it will come out looking good. But you will be charged for it, and since you have already lost money with the item breaking, you may not care to lose any more. A restorer will usually apply a bit of enamel to the jointure, to conceal the least sign of what has occurred. In terms of salvaging the specimen's cash value, this procedure works better on ancient pottery.

Your Doultons may require a cleaning periodically. There are no hard fast rules about this. You need not clean them if you feel you'd rather not, but this display appeal is certainly diminished when the surface luster and enameling have been dulled. Many dealers automatically do a clean-up job on any Doultons they acquire, to improve their appearance and enhance their sales appeal. But quite a few do not, and you may purchase a specimen that has never been cleaned in any way. The surface is likely to be dusty, and this will brush away effortlessly with a plain cloth — giving the impression that you have cleaned the figure. Sadly you have not. Underneath this "topsoil" is the ingrained grime, which is probably so evenly distributed that it cannot really be notices — UNLESS you compare the figure against a clean one. This can be removed and should be removed, but carefully. You will first of all want to soak the figure for a few minutes in plain lukewarm water, neither hot or cold, submerging it fully. This softens the grime and leads the way for Step Two, which is soaking (also for several minutes) in a bath of lukewarm sudsy water. Do not use bleach or any potent washing liquid; ordinary hand soap worked up into a frothy lather is safest. After this stage is completed, the item is returned to clean water for a rinsing. In nine cases out of 10, this is all that will be necessary to achieve a good cleaning. When you meet with an obstinately dirty Doulton, as you will occasionally, the same general procedure is used, but is repeated several times, and the length of soaking time in sudsy water is lengthened. Be cautious about heating up the water as this could be damaging to the enamel. Greyish streaks that remain after a thorough cleaning should be baked in. This is not uncommon with porcelain.

HOW TO USE THIS BOOK

The Official Price Guide to Royal Doulton presents the Royal Doulton market as it exists at the time of publication. It is intended as a guide to both values and identification, and as a general introduction to Royal Doultons as collectors' items.

Royal Doulton has been the subject of voluminous writings over the years, but there has not been any official market guide until now. *The Official Price Guide to Royal Doulton* is the product of extensive analyzation of the world market. For collectors, dealers, investors, museum directors and others interested in Royal Doulton, an authoritative work of this nature was long overdue. Updated editions will be issued each year, including all the new factory releases, revised prices to reflect the current market, and (when possible) fresh research into the history of Royal Doulton and its creations.

No one should find any difficulty in using the book. The HN series, which of course comprises the majority of the book (as it does the Royal Doulton line), is listed both numerically and alphabetically. The numerical list is given first, and records all the HN figures from the outset of this series to the present, along with their dates of introduction and discontinuance. In the alphabetical list which follows, a brief description is given, along with any pertinent collector information as space allows. Because of the great number of figures to be listed, text has been held to a necessary minimum. CURRENT RETAIL SELLING PRICES ARE GIVEN IN BOTH THE NUMERICAL AND ALPHABETICAL SECTIONS. You may, therefore, check prices in either section, as they will be the same for any given figure. Following the listings for HN figures are those for other items in the factory's line, each grouped by type of item. The introductory pages explain the trademarks, dating, and collecting approaches, and a background on the company and technical production methods as well.

THE PRICES IN THIS BOOK

The prices shown in this book represent average retail selling prices. Collectors' items invariably sell at different prices under different circumstances, and this is true of Royal Doultons. Price *ranges* are given for all the out-of-production items (those in current production are listed at the factory's suggested retail selling figures). These have been compiled from dealers' catalogues, auction sale results, magazine advertisements, and other sources. Virtually every sale of Royal Doultons in recent months, excepting of course private sales that create no record, has been evaluated in arriving at our prices. Hence we can confidently state that these prices are as accurate, in reflecting the current market, as it is possible to be. Still, we urge the reader to keep in mind that sales at lower or higher prices can and DO occur, for various reasons. At auction sales, particularly, the average prices on any collectors' items are not necessarily the prices for which they sell. A dealer may intentionally price an item higher because, in his opinion, the collector demand is sufficient to warrant a higher sum. Another dealer could price the same item below the market average, because (possibly) he is more interested in making a quick sale at low profit. There are many reasons for price variations, which will become clearer to the collector as he acquires experience buying and sees at first-hand how the trade operates.

When you sell TO a dealer, the sum received will of course be less than the average retail price. A buying offer of 60-70% of the retail price is considered fair in most cases, for out-of-production Doultons. Works still in production do not bring this high a percentage of the retail value, when sold to a dealer. Watch the buying ads in collector periodicals and you may find offers of 80%, 90% or full market value for certain Royal Doultons. (Prices for 1983 releases were not available for this publication.)

RECOMMENDED READING

Doulton Pottery, Parts I and II by Richard Dennis
The Doulton Lambeth Wares by Desmond Eyles
Royal Doulton 1815-1965 by Desmond Eyles
Royal Doulton Figures by Desmond Eyles and Richard Dennis
Royal Doulton Character & Toby Jugs by Desmond Eyles
The Doulton Story by Paul Atterbury and Louise Irvine
Limited Edition Loving-Cups and Jugs by Richard Dennis
Doulton Flambe Animals by Jocelyn Lukins
Royal Doulton Figurines and Character Jugs by Katherine Morrison McClinton
Royal Doulton Series Ware by Louise Irvine
Doulton Stoneware Pottery by Richard Dennis
Royal Doulton Figurines by Chilton Press

NUMERICAL LISTINGS OF "HN," "M" AND "K" MODEL NUMBERS

This series, the brainchild of C. J. Noke, began in 1913. Noke, Royal Doulton's Art Director, felt that small figures in a modest range of price would be appealing to the public. The company had of course produced figures prior to that time, but not as part of a standard series. The Fancy and Character Figures are designated by the HN prefix to their series numbers, and are often referred to simply as "HN figures." Subjects included in this series are highly diversified, representing the works of many different artists at different time periods. They lend themselves well to topical collecting. Basically they can be divided into three rough groups: historical characters; fictional characters; and (for want of a better term) general types. Historical characters are kings, queens, or other individuals taken from history, such as Nell Gwynn and Sir Walter Raleigh. Fictional characters are best exemplified by the Dickens characters. General types, by far the largest of the groups, consist of tradespeople, pretty ladies in flowing gowns, and so on. In recent years the HN series has included sub-series, such as the Middle Earth characters. The letters HN are the initials of Harry Nixon, who was the factory's chief colorist when the series began.

The HN series is added to every year and the volume of new additions is growing. To date the numeration system has reached HN 2928 (a likeness of Admiral Lord Nelson in the Ships' Figureheads sub-series). This does not mean, however, that 2,928 figures bearing the HN prefix exist. Some numbers have been reserved for figures not yet issued (later additions to sub-series). Others are simply skipped numbers, assigned to figures that were intended for release but, for one reason or other, never reached production.

The M series came about mainly because of the financial depression of the 1930's. Royal Doulton introduced a line of reduced-size Fancy and Character Figures in 1932, intended for the strained budgets of the time. This series has the M prefix letter. It proved popular and was retained even when times improved. These are smaller versions of the standard HN models, which may differ slightly in detail or painting, as well as original designs.

In the following pages, the HN figures are listed numerically, followed by a numerical listing of M figures. These listings include ALL objects bearing those prefix letters, even those which belong to sub-series of their own. The numerical listings are provided for quick easy reference. More detailed information on these works is contained in the alphabetical listings, elsewhere in this book. Occasionally, a Doulton may be found which carries a number but not a name. In these situations the numerical listing will serve to identify it. NOTE: Prices shown in the numerical listings are the same as those in the alphabetical listings, and are repeated for the sake of convenience.

Over the years Royal Doulton has issued many figurines of wildlife. The majority, while carrying HN prefix numbers, were grouped into a sub-series of their own. Some were issued as part of the regular HN Fancy and Character Figures series, and will be found in the main body of HN listings.

In addition to these HN figures of animals and birds, the factory has also produced a K series of MINIATURE figures of animals and birds.

In this section, the HN Animal and Bird figures are listed NUMERICALLY, followed by a NUMERICAL listing of the K (miniature) Animal and Bird figures. These numerical listings are then in turn followed by PRICED AL-PHABETICAL LISTINGS. There is a single priced alphabetical section, in which BOTH the HN and K figures are integrated.

The collector should bear in mind that these works include some which are limited, and some which are not limited. Royal Doulton has not followed any standard approach in issuing them.

The Chatcull Range series, inaugurated in 1940, was named after the estate of its artist, Joseph Ledger. A very important series was the Art Sculptures of Robert Jefferson, begun in 1974. These were MOSTLY limited editions, and limited to small production. The "Jeffersons," as collectors often call them, are not only handsome artworks but precise in their ana-tomical detailing and coloration — perhaps the finest of all wildlife porce-lains.

"HN" NUMERICAL LISTINGS OF FANCY AND CHARACTER FIGURES

	Date	Price Range	
HN 1			
☐ Darling (1st version)	1913-1928	1000.00	1150.00
HN 2			
☐ Elizabeth Fry.....................	1913-1938	4000.00	4500.00
HN 3			
☐ Milking Time	1913-1938	3000.00	3500.00
HN 4			
☐ Picardy Peasant (female)...........	1913-1938	1500.00	2000.00
HN 5			
☐ Picardy Peasant (female)...........	1913-1938	1500.00	2000.00
HN 6			
☐ Dunce	1913-1938	2750.00	3000.00
HN 7			
☐ Pedlar Wolf	1913-1938	2000.00	2500.00
HN 8			
☐ The Crinoline	1913-1938	1300.00	1450.00
HN 9			
☐ The Crinoline	1913-1938	1300.00	1450.00
HN 9A			
☐ The Crinoline	1913-1938	1300.00	1450.00
HN 10			
☐ Madonna of the Square	1913-1938	1450.00	1600.00
HN 10A			
☐ Madonna of the Square	1913-1938	1350.00	1500.00
HN 11			
☐ Madonna of the Square	1913-1938	1450.00	1700.00
HN 12			
☐ Baby..........................	1913-1938	2050.00	2200.00
HN 13			
☐ Picardy Peasant (male)	1913-1938	1950.00	2000.00
HN 14			
☐ Madonna of the Square	1913-1938	1450.00	1700.00

	Date	Price Range	
HN 15			
☐ The Sleepy Scholar	1913-1938	**1650.00**	**1800.00**
HN 16			
☐ The Sleepy Scholar	1913-1938	**1550.00**	**1700.00**
HN 17			
☐ Picardy Peasant (male)	1913-1938	**1850.00**	**2000.00**
HN 17A			
☐ Picardy Peasant (female)..........	1913-1938	**1850.00**	**2000.00**
HN 18			
☐ Pussy.........................	1913-1938	**2400.00**	**2600.00**
HN 19			
☐ Picardy Peasant (male)	1913-1938	**1600.00**	**1850.00**
HN 20			
☐ The Coquette	1913-1938	**2500.00**	**3000.00**
HN 21			
☐ The Crinoline	1913-1938	**1300.00**	**1450.00**
HN 21A			
☐ The Crinoline	1913-1938	**1250.00**	**1400.00**
HN 22			
☐ The Lavender Woman	1913-1938	**1750.00**	**2000.00**
HN 23			
☐ The Lavender Woman	1913-1938	**1750.00**	**2000.00**
HN 23A			
☐ The Lavender Woman	1913-1938	**1750.00**	**2000.00**
HN 24			
☐ Sleep	1913-1938	**2000.00**	**2250.00**
HN 24A			
☐ Sleep	1913-1938	**2200.00**	**2400.00**
HN 25			
☐ Sleep	1913-1938	**2500.00**	**2800.00**
HN 25A			
☐ Sleep	1913-1938	**2500.00**	**2800.00**
HN 26			
☐ The Diligent Scholar	1913-1938	**1750.00**	**2000.00**
HN 27			
☐ Madonna of the Square	1913-1938	**1650.00**	**1800.00**
HN 28			
☐ Motherhood	1913-1938	**1750.00**	**2000.00**
HN 29			
☐ The Sleepy Scholar	1913-1938	**1450.00**	**1600.00**
HN 30			
☐ Motherhood	1913-1938	**2250.00**	**2500.00**
HN 31			
☐ The Return of Persephone	1913-1938	**4000.00**	**5000.00**
HN 32			
☐ Child and Crab	1913-1938	**1600.00**	**1800.00**
HN 33			
☐ An Arab	1913-1938	**1600.00**	**1800.00**
HN 34			
☐ Moorish Minstrel	1913-1938	**2000.00**	**2200.00**

	Date	Price Range	
HN 35			
☐ Charley's Aunt(1st version)	1914-1938	700.00	800.00
HN 36			
☐ The Sentimental Pierrot.	1914-1938	1750.00	1900.00
HN 37			
☐ The Coquette	1914-1938	2500.00	3000.00
HN 38			
☐ The Carpet Vendor (1st version)	1914-1938	2750.00	3000.00
HN 38A			
☐ The Carpet Vendor (1st version)	1914-1938	2750.00	3000.00
HN 39			
☐ The Welsh Girl	1914-1938	2500.00	2750.00
HN 40			
☐ A Lady of the Elizabethan Period (1st version).	1914-1938	1750.00	2000.00
HN 40A			
☐ A Lady of the Elizabethan Period (1st version).	1914-1938	1750.00	2000.00
HN 41			
☐ A Lady of the Georgian Period	1914-1938	2000.00	2300.00
HN 42			
☐ Robert Burns.	1914-1938	3000.00	3500.00
HN 43			
☐ A Lady of the Time of Henry VI	1914-1938	2750.00	3250.00
HN 44			
☐ A Lilac Shawl	1915-1938	1250.00	1500.00
HN 44A			
☐ A Lilac Shawl	1915-1938	1250.00	1500.00
HN 45			
☐ A Jester (1st version)	1915-1938	1250.00	1500.00
HN 45A			
☐ A Jester (2nd version).	1915-1938	1250.00	1500.00
HN 45B			
☐ A Jester (2nd version).	1915-1938	1250.00	1500.00
HN 46			
☐ The Gainsborough Hat	1915-1938	1100.00	1200.00
HN 46A			
☐ The Gainsborough Hat	1915-1938	1100.00	1200.00
HN 47			
☐ The Gainsborough Hat	1915-1938	1100.00	1200.00
HN 48			
☐ Lady of the Fan.	1916-1938	1650.00	1800.00
HN 48A			
☐ Lady with Rose	1916-1938	1650.00	1800.00
HN 49			
☐ Under the Gooseberry Bush	1916-1938	1250.00	1500.00
HN 50			
☐ A Spook.	1916-1938	1100.00	1200.00
HN 51			
☐ A Spook.	1916-1938	1250.00	1400.00

	Date	Price Range	
HN 51A			
☐ A Spook	1916-1938	**1250.00**	**1400.00**
HN 51B			
☐ A Spook	1916-1938	**1250.00**	**1400.00**
HN 52			
☐ Lady of the Fan	1916-1938	**1650.00**	**1800.00**
HN 52A			
☐ Lady with Rose	1916-1938	**1650.00**	**1800.00**
HN 53			
☐ Lady of the Fan	1916-1938	**1650.00**	**1800.00**
HN 53A			
☐ Lady of the Fan	1916-1938	**1650.00**	**1800.00**
HN 54			
☐ Lady Ermine	1916-1938	**1250.00**	**1500.00**
HN 55			
☐ A Jester (2nd version)	1916-1938	**1300.00**	**1500.00**
HN 56			
☐ The Land of Nod	1916-1938	**1750.00**	**2000.00**
HN 56A			
☐ The Land of Nod	1916-1938	**2000.00**	**2300.00**
HN 56B			
☐ The Land of Nod	1916-1938	**1750.00**	**2000.00**
HN 57			
☐ The Curtsey	1916-1938	**1500.00**	**1750.00**
HN 57A			
☐ The Flounced Skirt	1916-1938	**1650.00**	**1800.00**
HN 57B			
☐ The Curtsey	1916-1938	**1500.00**	**1750.00**
HN 58			
☐ A Spook	1916-1938	**1250.00**	**1400.00**
HN 59			
☐ Upon her Cheeks she Wept	1916-1938	**1500.00**	**1600.00**
HN 60			
☐ Shy Anne	1916-1938	**1500.00**	**1700.00**
HN 61			
☐ Katharine	1916-1938	**1500.00**	**1700.00**
HN 62			
☐ A Child's Grace	1916-1938	**1400.00**	**1600.00**
HN 62A			
☐ A Child's Grace	1916-1938	**1500.00**	**1700.00**
HN 63			
☐ The Little Land	1916-1938	**2000.00**	**2500.00**
HN 64			
☐ Shy Anne	1916-1938	**1500.00**	**1600.00**
HN 65			
☐ Shy Anne	1916-1938	**1550.00**	**1700.00**
HN 66			
☐ The Flounced Skirt	1916-1938	**1650.00**	**1800.00**
HN 66A			
☐ The Curtsey	1916-1938	**1550.00**	**1700.00**

	Date	Price Range
HN 67		
☐ The Little Land	1916-1938	**1750.00 2000.00**
HN 68		
☐ Lady with a Rose	1916-1938	**1650.00 1800.00**
HN 69		
☐ Pretty Lady	1916-1938	**1250.00 1500.00**
HN 70		
☐ Pretty Lady	1916-1938	**1250.00 1500.00**
HN 71		
☐ A Jester (1st version)	1917-1938	**1250.00 1500.00**
HN 71A		
☐ A Jester (1st version)	1917-1938	**1250.00 1500.00**
HN 72		
☐ An Orange Vendor	1917-1938	**950.00 1100.00**
HN 73		
☐ A Lady of the Elizabethan Period (1st version).	1917-1938	**1800.00 2000.00**
HN 74		
☐ Katharine	1917-1938	**1650.00 1800.00**
HN 75		
☐ Blue Beard (1st version)	1917-1938	**2550.00 3000.00**
HN 76		
☐ Carper Vendor (2nd version)	1917-1938	**3000.00 3500.00**
HN 77		
☐ The Flounced Skirt	1917-1938	**1650.00 1800.00**
HN 78		
☐ The Flounced Skirt	1917-1938	**1650.00 1800.00**
HN 79		
☐ Shylock	1917-1938	**2500.00 2750.00**
HN 80		
☐ Fisherwomen	1917-1938	**3000.00 3500.00**
HN 81		
☐ A Shepherd (1st version)	1918-1938	**2250.00 2500.00**
HN 82		
☐ The Afternoon Call	1918-1938	**2250.00 2500.00**
HN 83		
☐ The Lady Anne	1918-1938	**2750.00 3000.00**
HN 84		
☐ A Mandarin (1st version)	1918-1938	**2250.00 2500.00**
HN 85		
☐ Jack Point	1918-1938	**2000.00 2200.00**
HN 86		
☐ Out for a Walk	1918-1936	**2250.00 2500.00**
HN 87		
☐ The Lady Anne	1918-1938	**2750.00 3000.00**
HN 88		
☐ Spooks	1918-1936	**1400.00 1650.00**
HN 89		
☐ Spooks	1918-1936	**1400.00 1650.00**

	Date	Price Range	
HN 90			
☐ Doris Keene as Cavallini (1st version)	1918-1936	2000.00	2500.00
HN 91			
☐ Jack Point	1918-1938	2000.00	2250.00
HN 92			
☐ The Welsh Girl	1918-1938	2500.00	2750.00
HN 93			
☐ The Lady Anne	1918-1938	2750.00	3000.00
HN 94			
☐ The Young Knight	1918-1936	2750.00	3250.00
HN 95			
☐ Europa and the Bull	1918-1938	3000.00	3500.00
HN 96			
☐ Doris Keene as Cavallini (2nd version)	1918-1938	2250.00	2500.00
HN 97			
☐ The Mermaid	1918-1936	650.00	750.00
HN 98			
☐ Guy Gawkes	1918-1949	1300.00	1500.00
HN 99			
☐ Jack Point	1918-1938	2000.00	2250.00
HN 100 — HN 299 ANIMAL AND BIRD MODELS			
HN 300			
☐ The Mermaid	1918-1936	850.00	1000.00
HN 301			
☐ Moorish Piper Minstrel	1918-1938	2750.00	3000.00
HN 302			
☐ Pretty Lady	1918-1938	1350.00	1600.00
HN 303			
☐ Motherhood	1918-1938	2250.00	2500.00
HN 304			
☐ Lady with Rose	1918-1938	1650.00	1800.00
HN 305			
☐ A Scribe	1918-1936	1100.00	1200.00
HN 306			
☐ Milking Time	1913-1938	2750.00	3000.00
HN 307			
☐ The Sentimental Pierrot	1918-1938	1750.00	1900.00
HN 308			
☐ A Jester (2nd version)	1918-1938	1250.00	1500.00
HN 309			
☐ A Lady of the Elizabethan Period (2nd version)	1918-1938	1750.00	2000.00
HN 310			
☐ Dunce	1918-1938	2750.00	3000.00
HN 311			
☐ Dancing Figure	1918-1938	3500.00	4000.00
HN 312			
☐ Spring (1st version) The Seasons	1918-1938	1500.00	1800.00
HN 313			
☐ Summer (1st version) The Seasons . .	1918-1938	1650.00	1800.00

HN 314	Date	Price Range	
☐ Autumn (1st version) The Seasons ...	1918-1938	1200.00	1400.00
HN 315			
☐ Winter (1st version) The Seasons	1918-1938	1500.00	1800.00
HN 316			
☐ A Mandarin (1st version)	1918-1938	2250.00	2500.00
HN 317			
☐ Shylock	1918-1938	2500.00	2750.00
HN 318			
☐ A Mandarin (1st version)	1918-1938	2250.00	2500.00
HN 319			
☐ A Gnome	1918-1938	1000.00	1200.00
HN 320			
☐ A Jester (1st version)	1918-1938	1250.00	1500.00
HN 321			
☐ Digger (New Zealand)..............	1918-1938	1250.00	1500.00
HN 322			
☐ Digger (Australian)	1918-1938	1250.00	1500.00
HN 323			
☐ Blighty.........................	1918-1938	1250.00	1500.00
HN 324			
☐ A Scribe.......................	1918-1938	1100.00	1200.00
HN 325			
☐ Pussy..........................	1918-1938	2450.00	2650.00
HN 326			
☐ Madonna of the Square	1918-1938	1650.00	1800.00
HN 327			
☐ The Curtsey....................	1918-1938	1550.00	1700.00
HN 328			
☐ Moorish Piper Minstrel	1918-1938	2750.00	3000.00
HN 329			
☐ The Gainsborough Hat	1918-1938	1100.00	1200.00
HN 330			
☐ Pretty Lady	1918-1938	1450.00	1600.00
HN 331			
☐ A Lady of the Georgian Period	1918-1938	2000.00	2300.00
HN 332			
☐ Lady Ermine	1918-1938	1450.00	1750.00
HN 333			
☐ The Flounced Skirt	1918-1938	1550.00	1700.00
HN 334			
☐ The Curtsey....................	1918-1938	1450.00	1600.00
HN 335			
☐ Lady of the Fan..................	1919-1938	1650.00	1800.00
HN 336			
☐ Lady with Rose	1919-1938	1700.00	1800.00
HN 337			
☐ The Parson's Daughter	1919-1938	800.00	900.00
HN 338			
☐ The Parson's Daughter	1919-1938	800.00	900.00

	Date	Price Range	
HN 339			
☐ In Grandma's Days (A Lilac Shawl)...	1919-1938	1250.00	1500.00
HN 340			
☐ In Grandma's Days (A Lilac Shawl)...	1919-1938	1250.00	1500.00
HN 341			
☐ Katherine	1919-1938	1250.00	1500.00
HN 342			
☐ The Lavender Woman	1919-1938	1650.00	1800.00
HN 343			
☐ An Arab	1919-1938	1750.00	2000.00
HN 344			
☐ Henry Irving as Cardinal Wolsey	1919-1949	2000.00	2500.00
HN 345			
☐ Doris Keene as Cavallini (2nd version)	1919-1949	2750.00	3000.00
HN 346			
☐ Tony Weller (1st version)	1919-1938	1800.00	2000.00
HN 347			
☐ Guy Fawkes	1919-1938	1250.00	1400.00
HN 348			
☐ The Carpet Vendor (1st version)	1919-1938	1750.00	2000.00
HN 349			
☐ Fisherwomen	1919-1968	2750.00	3000.00
HN 350			
☐ The Carpet Vendor (1st version)	1919-1938	3000.00	3500.00
HN 351			
☐ Picardy Peasant (female)	1919-1938	3000.00	3250.00
HN 352			
☐ The Gainsborough Hat	1919-1938	1750.00	2000.00
HN 353			
☐ Digger (Australian)	1919-1938	1350.00	1600.00
HN 354			
☐ A Geisha (1st version)	1919-1938	2250.00	2500.00
HN 355			
☐ Dolly	1919-1938	1250.00	1500.00
HN 356			
☐ Sir Thomas Lovell	1919-1938	1500.00	1700.00
HN 357			
☐ Dunce	1919-1938	2750.00	3000.00
HN 358			
☐ An Old King	1919-1938	1150.00	1300.00
HN 359			
☐ Fisherwomen	1919-1938	3000.00	3500.00
HN 360 NO DETAILS AVAILABLE			
HN 361			
☐ Pretty Lady	1919-1938	1450.00	1600.00
HN 362			
☐ In Grandma's Days	1919-1938	1550.00	1700.00
HN 363			
☐ The Curtsey	1919-1938	1600.00	1700.00

	Date	Price Range	
HN 364			
☐ Moorish Minstrel	1920-1938	**2750.00**	**3000.00**
HN 365			
☐ Double Jester	1920-1938	**2750.00**	**3250.00**
HN 366			
☐ A Mandarin (2nd version)	1920-1938	**1400.00**	**1550.00**
HN 367			
☐ A Jester (1st version)	1920-1938	**1400.00**	**1500.00**
HN 368			
☐ Tony Weller (1st version)	1920-1938	**1800.00**	**2000.00**
HN 369			
☐ Cavalier (1st version)	1920-1938	**2100.00**	**2400.00**
HN 370			
☐ Henry VIII (1st version)	1920-1938	**2350.00**	**2600.00**
HN 371			
☐ The Curtsey.....................	1920-1938	**1650.00**	**1800.00**
HN 372			
☐ Spooks	1920-1936	**1400.00**	**1650.00**
HN 373			
☐ Boy on a Crocodile	1920-1938	**4000.00**	**4500.00**
HN 374			
☐ Lady and Blackamoor (1st version) ..	1920-1936	**2500.00**	**2700.00**
HN 375			
☐ Lady and Blackamoor (2nd version) ..	1920-1938	**2500.00**	**2700.00**
HN 376			
☐ A Geisha (1st version)	1920-1938	**2300.00**	**2500.00**
HN 377			
☐ Lady and Blackamoor (2nd version) ..	1920-1938	**2500.00**	**2700.00**
HN 378			
☐ An Arab	1920-1938	**1500.00**	**1750.00**
HN 379			
☐ Ellen Terry as Queen Catherine	1920-1949	**2750.00**	**3000.00**
HN 380			
☐ A Gnome	1920-1938	**1000.00**	**1200.00**
HN 381			
☐ A Gnome	1920-1938	**1000.00**	**1200.00**
HN 382			
☐ A Mandarin (1st version)	1920-1938	**2250.00**	**2500.00**
HN 383			
☐ The Gainsborough Hat	1920-1938	**1050.00**	**1200.00**
HN 384			
☐ Pretty Lady	1920-1938	**1450.00**	**1600.00**
HN 385			
☐ St. George (1st version)	1920-1938	**4500.00**	**5000.00**
HN 386			
☐ St. George (1st version)	1920-1938	**4500.00**	**5000.00**
HN 387			
☐ A Geisha (1st version)	1920-1938	**2250.00**	**2500.00**
HN 388			
☐ In Grandma's Days...............	1920-1938	**1650.00**	**1800.00**

	Date	Price Range	
HN 389			
☐ The Little Mother (1st version).......	1920-1938	2500.00	2700.00
HN 390			
☐ The Little Mother (1st version).......	1920-1938	2500.00	2700.00
HN 391			
☐ A Princess.....................	1920-1938	2750.00	3000.00
HN 392			
☐ A Princess.....................	1920-1938	2750.00	3000.00
HN 393			
☐ Lady Without Bouquet.............	1920-1938	2000.00	2500.00
HN 394			
☐ Lady Without Bouquet.............	1920-1938	2000.00	2500.00
HN 395			
☐ Contenment	1920-1938	1850.00	2000.00
HN 396			
☐ Contenment	1920-1938	1850.00	2000.00
HN 397			
☐ Puff and Powder.................	1920-1938	2000.00	2200.00
HN 398			
☐ Puff and Powder.................	1920-1938	2000.00	2200.00
HN 399			
☐ Japanese Fan...................	1920-1938	1450.00	1600.00
HN 400			
☐ Puff and Powder.................	1920-1938	2000.00	2200.00
HN 401			
☐ Marie (1st version)	1920-1938	2250.00	2500.00
HN 402			
☐ Betty (1st version)...............	1920-1938	2000.00	2250.00
HN 403			
☐ Betty (1st version	1920-1938	2000.00	2250.00
HN 404			
☐ King Charles	1920-1951	1750.00	2000.00
HN 405			
☐ Japanese Fan...................	1920-1938	1250.00	1500.00
HN 406			
☐ The Bouquet	1920-1938	1500.00	1700.00
HN 407			
☐ Omar Khayyman and the Beloved ...	1920-1938	3500.00	4000.00
HN 408			
☐ Omar Khayyman (1st version)	1920-1938	2250.00	3000.00
HN 409			
☐ Omar Khayyman (1st version)	1938-1938	2250.00	3000.00
HN 410			
☐ Blue Beard (1st version)...........	1920-1938	3000.00	3500.00
HN 411			
☐ A Lady of the Elizabethan Period (1st version).....................	1920-1938	2000.00	2500.00
HN 412			
☐ A Jester (1st version)	1920-1938	1350.00	1300.00

	Date	Price Range	
HN 413			
☐ The Crinoline	1920-1938	**1700.00**	**1950.00**
HN 414			
☐ The Bouquet	1920-1938	**1550.00**	**1700.00**
HN 415			
☐ Moorish Minstrel	1920-1938	**2750.00**	**3000.00**
HN 416			
☐ Moorish Piper Minstrel	1920-1938	**2750.00**	**3000.00**
HN 417			
☐ One of the Forty (1st version)	1920-1938	**1100.00**	**1200.00**
HN 418			
☐ One of the Forty (2nd version)	1920-1938	**1100.00**	**1200.00**
HN 419			
☐ Omar Khayyam and the Beloved.....	1920-1938	**3500.00**	**4000.00**
HN 420			
☐ A Princess.......................	1920-1938	**2750.00**	**3000.00**
HN 421			
☐ Contentment.....................	1920-1938	**1500.00**	**1700.00**
HN 422			
☐ The Bouquet	1920-1938	**1550.00**	**1700.00**
HN 423			
☐ One of the Forty (3rd and 8th version)	1921-1938	**450.00**	**500.00**
HN 424			
☐ Sleep	1921-1938	**2000.00**	**2200.00**
HN 425			
☐ The Goosegirl	1921-1938	**2750.00**	**3000.00**
HN 426			
☐ A Jester (1st version)	1921-1938	**1250.00**	**1500.00**
HN 427			
☐ One of the Forty (9th version)	1921-1938	**1100.00**	**1200.00**
HN 428			
☐ The Bouquet	1921-1938	**1550.00**	**1700.00**
HN 429			
☐ The Bouquet	1921-1938	**1550.00**	**1700.00**
HN 430			
☐ A Princess.......................	1921-1938	**2750.00**	**3000.00**
HN 431			
☐ A Princess.......................	1921-1938	**2750.00**	**3000.00**
HN 432			
☐ Puff and Powder	1921-1938	**2000.00**	**2200.00**
HN 433			
☐ Puff and Powder	1921-1938	**2000.00**	**2200.00**
HN 434			
☐ Marie (1st version)	1921-1938	**2250.00**	**2500.00**
HN 435			
☐ Betty (1st version)...............	1921-1938	**2000.00**	**2250.00**
HN 436			
☐ The Goosegirl	1921-1938	**2500.00**	**3000.00**
HN 437			
☐ The Goosegirl	1921-1938	**2500.00**	**3000.00**

	Date	Price Range	
HN 438			
☐ Betty (1st version)................	1921-1938	**2000.00**	**2250.00**
HN 439			
☐ Japanese Fan....................	1921-1938	**1500.00**	**1600.00**
HN 440			
☐ Japanese Fan...................	1921-1938	**1500.00**	**1600.00**
HN 441			
☐ The Parson's Daughter	1921-1938	**850.00**	**950.00**
HN 442			
☐ In Grandma's Days...............	1921-1938	**1650.00**	**1800.00**
HN 443			
☐ Out for a Walk...................	1921-1938	**2250.00**	**2500.00**
HN 444			
☐ A Lady of the Georgian Period	1921-1938	**2100.00**	**2300.00**
HN 445			
☐ Guy Fawkes	1921-1938	**1250.00**	**1400.00**
HN 446			
☐ A Jester (1st version)	1921-1936	**1350.00**	**1500.00**
HN 447			
☐ Lady with Shawl	1921-1936	**3250.00**	**3500.00**
HN 448			
☐ The Goosegirl	1921-1936	**2750.00**	**3000.00**
HN 449			
☐ Fruit Gathering	1921-1938	**2750.00**	**3000.00**
HN 450			
☐ A Mandarin (3rd version)	1921-1938	**1500.00**	**1750.00**
HN 451			
☐ An Old Man	1921-1938	**2250.00**	**2500.00**
HN 452 NO DETAILS AVAILABLE			
HN 453			
☐ The Gainsborough Hat	1921-1938	**1250.00**	**1400.00**
HN 454			
☐ The Smiling Buddha..............	1921-1938	**1250.00**	**1400.00**
HN 455			
☐ A Mandarin (2nd version)	1921-1938	**1750.00**	**2000.00**
HN 456			
☐ The Welsh Girl	1921-1938	**2500.00**	**2700.00**
HN 457			
☐ Crouching Nude	1921-1938	**1100.00**	**1300.00**
HN 458			
☐ Lady with Shawl	1921-1938	**3000.00**	**3500.00**
HN 459			
☐ Omar Khayyman and the Beloved ...	1921-1938	**3500.00**	**4000.00**
HN 460			
☐ A Mandarin (3rd version)	1921-1938	**2250.00**	**2500.00**
HN 461			
☐ A Mandarin (3rd version)	1921-1938	**2250.00**	**2500.00**
HN 462			
☐ Woman Holding Child	1921-1938	**2000.00**	**2200.00**

	Date	Price Range	
HN 463			
☐ Polly Peachum (1st version)	1921-1949	600.00	700.00
HN 464			
☐ Captain MacHeath	1921-1949	750.00	850.00
HN 465			
☐ Polly Peachum	1921-1949	500.00	600.00
HN 466			
☐ Tulips	1921-1938	1600.00	1700.00
HN 467			
☐ Doris Keane as Cavallini			
(1st version)	1921-1936	2000.00	2200.00
HN 468			
☐ Contentment	1921-1938	1750.00	2000.00
HN 469			
☐ The Little Mother (1st version)	1921-1938	1750.00	2000.00
HN 470			
☐ Lady and Blackamoor (2nd version) . .	1921-1938	2500.00	2700.00
HN 471			
☐ Katharine	1921-1938	2000.00	2500.00
HN 472			
☐ Spring (1st version) The Seasons	1921-1938	1500.00	1800.00
HN 473			
☐ Summer (1st version) The Seasons . .	1921-1938	1650.00	1800.00
HN 474			
☐ Autumn (1st version) The Seasons . . .	1921-1938	1300.00	1400.00
HN 475			
☐ Winter (1st version) The Seasons	1921-1938	1500.00	1800.00
HN 476			
☐ Fruit Gathering	1921-1938	2650.00	2800.00
HN 477			
☐ Betty (1st version)	1921-1938	2500.00	3000.00
HN 478			
☐ Betty (1st version)	1921-1938	2500.00	3000.00
HN 479			
☐ The Balloon Seller	1921-1938	2250.00	2500.00
HN 480			
☐ One of the Forty (10th version)	1921-1938	800.00	900.00
HN 481			
☐ One of the Forty (11th version)	1921-1938	1100.00	1200.00
HN 482			
☐ One of the Forty (12th version)	1921-1938	1100.00	1200.00
HN 483			
☐ One of the Forty (11th version)	1921-1938	1100.00	1200.00
HN 484			
☐ One of the Forty (12th version)	1921-1938	1100.00	1200.00
HN 485			
☐ Lucy Lockett (1st version)	1921-1949	800.00	900.00
HN 486			
☐ The Balloon Seller	1921-1938	1500.00	1700.00

HN		Date	Price Range	
HN 487				
☐ Pavlova		1921-1938	1500.00	1700.00
HN 488				
☐ Tulips.		1921-1938	1500.00	1700.00
HN 489				
☐ Polly Peachum (2nd version)		1921-1938	400.00	500.00
HN 490				
☐ One of the Forty (1st version)		1921-1938	1100.00	1200.00
HN 491				
☐ One of the Forty (11th version)		1921-1938	1100.00	1200.00
HN 492				
☐ One of the Forty (12th version)		1921-1938	1100.00	1200.00
HN 493				
☐ One of the Forty (10th version)		1921-1938	1100.00	1200.00
HN 494				
☐ One of the Forty (2nd version)		1921-1938	1100.00	1200.00
HN 495				
☐ One of the Forty (1st version)		1921-1938	1100.00	1200.00
HN 496				
☐ One of the Forty (13th version)		1921-1938	1100.00	1200.00
HN 497				
☐ One of the Forty (10th version)		1921-1938	1100.00	1200.00
HN 498				
☐ One of the Forty (2nd version)		1921-1938	1100.00	1200.00
HN 499				
☐ One of the Forty (10th version)		1921-1938	1100.00	1200.00
HN 500				
☐ One of the Forty (13th version)		1921-1938	1100.00	1200.00
HN 501				
☐ One of the Forty (1st version)		1921-1938	1100.00	1200.00
HN 502				
☐ Marie (1st version)		1921-1938	2250.00	2500.00
HN 503				
☐ Fruit Gathering		1921-1938	2500.00	3000.00
HN 504				
☐ Marie (1st version)		1921-1938	2250.00	2500.00
HN 505				
☐ Marie (1st version)		1921-1938	2250.00	2500.00
HN 506				
☐ Marie (1st version)		1921-1938	2250.00	2500.00
HN 507				
☐ Pussy.		1921-1938	2400.00	2600.00
HN 508				
☐ An Orange Vendor		1921-1938	1000.00	1100.00
HN 509				
☐ Lady of the Fan		1921-1938	1650.00	1800.00
HN 510				
☐ A Child's Grace		1921-1938	1650.00	1800.00
HN 511				
☐ Upon her Cheeks she Wept		1921-1938	1500.00	1600.00

	Date	Price Range	
HN 512			
☐ A Spook	1921-1938	**1250.00**	**1400.00**
HN 513			
☐ Picardy Peasant (female)	1921-1938	**1750.00**	**2000.00**
HN 514			
☐ The Welsh Girl	1921-1938	**2500.00**	**2700.00**
HN 515			
☐ Lady with Rose	1921-1938	**1650.00**	**1800.00**
HN 516			
☐ The Welsh Girl	1921-1938	**2500.00**	**2700.00**
HN 517			
☐ Lady with Rose	1921-1938	**1650.00**	**1800.00**
HN 518			
☐ The Curtsey	1921-1938	**1650.00**	**1800.00**
HN 519			
☐ The Welsh Girl	1921-1938	**2500.00**	**2700.00**
HN 520			
☐ The Welsh Girl	1921-1938	**2500.00**	**2700.00**
HN 521			
☐ An Orange Vendor	1921-1938	**1000.00**	**1100.00**
HN 522			
☐ Upon her Cheeks she Wept	1921-1938	**1500.00**	**1600.00**
HN 523			
☐ Sentinel	1921-1938	**4500.00**	**5000.00**
HN 524			
☐ Lucy Lockett	1921-1938	**850.00**	**950.00**
HN 525			
☐ The Flower Seller's Children	1921-1949	**650.00**	**750.00**
HN 526			
☐ The Beggar (1st version)	1921-1949	**600.00**	**700.00**
HN 527			
☐ The Highwayman	1921-1949	**700.00**	**800.00**
HN 528			
☐ One of the Forty (1st version)	1921-1938	**1100.00**	**1200.00**
HN 529			
☐ Mr. Pickwick (1st version)	1922-	**45.00**	**60.00**
renumbered as miniature	1932-		
HN 530			
☐ The Fat Boy (1st version)	1922-	**45.00**	**60.00**
renumbered as miniature	1932-		
HN 531			
☐ Sam Weller	1922-	**45.00**	**60.00**
renumbered as miniature	1932-		
HN 532			
☐ Mr. Micawber (1st version)..........	1922-	**45.00**	**60.00**
renumbered as miniature	1932-		
HN 533			
☐ Sairey Gamp (1st version)	1922-	**45.00**	**60.00**
renumbered as miniature	1932-		

	Date	Price Range	
HN 534			
☐ Fagin	1922-	**45.00**	**60.00**
renumbered as miniature	1932-		
HN 535			
☐ Pecksniff (1st version)	1922-	**45.00**	**60.00**
renumbered as miniature	1932-		
HN 536			
☐ Stiggins	1922-	**45.00**	**60.00**
renumbered as miniature	1932-		
HN 537			
☐ Bill Sykes	1922-	**45.00**	**60.00**
renumbered as miniature	1932-		
HN 538			
☐ Buz Fuz	1922-	**45.00**	**60.00**
renumbered as miniature	1932-		
HN 539			
☐ Tiny Tim.......................	1922-	**45.00**	**60.00**
renumbered as miniature	1932-		
HN 540			
☐ Little Nell	1922-	**45.00**	**60.00**
renumbered as miniature	1932-		
HN 541			
☐ Alfred Jingle	1922-	**45.00**	**60.00**
renumbered as miniature	1932-		
HN 542			
☐ The Cobbler (1st version)	1922-1939	**1100.00**	**1200.00**
HN 543			
☐ The Cobbler (1st version)	1922-1938	**1200.00**	**1300.00**
HN 544			
☐ Tony Weller (2nd version)...........	1922-	**45.00**	**60.00**
renumbered as miniature	1932-		
HN 545			
☐ Uriah Heep (1st version)............	1922-	**45.00**	**60.00**
renumbered as miniature	1932-		
HN 546			
☐ The Artful Dodger	1922-	**45.00**	**60.00**
renumbered as miniature	1932-		
HN 547			
☐ The Curtsey....................	1922-1938	**1450.00**	**1600.00**
HN 548			
☐ The Balloon Seller	1922-1938	**800.00**	**900.00**
HN 549			
☐ Polly Peachum (2nd version)	1922-1949	**450.00**	**500.00**
HN 550			
☐ Polly Peachum (1st version)	1922-1949	**500.00**	**600.00**
HN 551			
☐ The Flower Seller's Children	1922-1949	**450.00**	**500.00**
HN 552			
☐ A Jester (1st version)	1922-1938	**1350.00**	**1500.00**

	Date	Price Range	
HN 553			
☐ Pecksniff (2nd version)	1923-1939	400.00	500.00
HN 554			
☐ Uriah Heep (2nd version)	1923-1939	400.00	500.00
HN 555			
☐ The Fat Boy (2nd version)	1923-1939	400.00	500.00
HN 556			
☐ Mr. Pickwick (2nd version)	1923-1939	400.00	500.00
HN 557			
☐ Mr. Micawber (2nd version)	1923-1939	400.00	500.00
HN 558			
☐ Sairey Gamp (2nd version)..........	1923-1939	400.00	500.00
HN 559			
☐ The Goosegirl	1923-1938	2750.00	3000.00
HN 560			
☐ The Goosegirl	1923-1938	2750.00	3000.00
HN 561			
☐ Fruit Gathering	1923-1938	2500.00	3000.00
HN 562			
☐ Fruit Gathering	1923-1938	2500.00	3000.00
HN 563			
☐ Man in Tudor Costume	1923-1938	1400.00	1750.00
HN 564			
☐ The Parson's Daughter	1923-1949	350.00	400.00
HN 565			
☐ Pretty Lady	1923-1938	1450.00	1600.00
HN 566			
☐ The Crinoline	1923-1938	1250.00	1400.00
HN 567			
☐ The Bouquet	1923-1938	1550.00	1700.00
HN 568			
☐ Shy Anne	1923-1949	1450.00	1600.00
HN 569			
☐ The Lavendar Woman	1924-1928	1150.00	1300.00
HN 570			
☐ Woman Holding Child	1923-1938	2000.00	2200.00
HN 571			
☐ Falstaff (1st version)	1923-1938	700.00	800.00
HN 572			
☐ Contentment....................	1923-1938	1750.00	2000.00
HN 573			
☐ Madonna of the Square	1913-1938	1650.00	1800.00
HN 574 NO DETAILS AVAILABLE			
HN 575			
☐ Falstaff (1st version)	1923-1938	700.00	800.00
HN 576			
☐ Madonna of the Square	1923-1938	1650.00	1800.00
HN 577			
☐ The Chelsea Pair (female)	1923-1938	700.00	800.00

	Date	Price Range	
HN 578			
☐ The Chelsea Pair (female)	1923-1938	**700.00**	**800.00**
HN 579			
☐ The Chelsea Pair (male)	1923-1938	**725.00**	**800.00**
HN 580			
☐ The Chelsea Pair (male)	1923-1938	**725.00**	**800.00**
HN 581			
☐ The Perfect Pair	1923-1938	**1000.00**	**1100.00**
HN 582			
☐ Grossmith's "Tsang Ihang" Perfume . of Tibet (also called "Tibetian Lady")	1923-Unknown	**650.00**	**700.00**
HN 583			
☐ The Balloon Seller	1923-1949	**500.00**	**600.00**
HN 584			
☐ Lady with Rose	1923-1938	**1650.00**	**1800.00**
HN 585			
☐ Harlequinade	1923-1938	**850.00**	**950.00**
HN 586			
☐ Boy with Turban	1923-1938	**550.00**	**650.00**
HN 587			
☐ Boy with Turban	1923-1938	**550.00**	**650.00**
HN 588			
☐ Girl with Yellow Frock	1923-1938	**1350.00**	**1500.00**
HN 589			
☐ Polly Peachum (1st version)	1924-1949	**500.00**	**600.00**
HN 590			
☐ Captain MacHeath	1924-1949	**750.00**	**850.00**
HN 591			
☐ The Beggar (1st version)	1924-1949	**650.00**	**750.00**
HN 592			
☐ The Highwayman	1924-1949	**700.00**	**800.00**
HN 593			
☐ Nude on Rock	1924-1938	**950.00**	**1000.00**
HN 594			
☐ Madonna of the Square	1924-1938	**1650.00**	**1800.00**
HN 595			
☐ Grief..........................	1924-1938	**900.00**	**1000.00**
HN 596			
☐ Despair	1924-1938	**1400.00**	**1650.00**
HN 597			
☐ The Bather (1st version)	1924-1938	**900.00**	**1000.00**
HN 598			
☐ Omar Khayyam and the Beloved.....	1924-1938	**3500.00**	**4000.00**
HN 599			
☐ Masquerade (male, 1st version)	1924-1949	**750.00**	**800.00**
HN 600			
☐ Masquerade (female, 1st version)....	1924-1949	**750.00**	**800.00**
HN 601			
☐ A Mandarin (3rd version)	1924-1938	**2250.00**	**2500.00**
HN 602 NO DETAILS AVAILABLE			

	Date	Price Range	
HN 603a			
☐ Child Study	1924-1938	**275.00**	**325.00**
HN 603b			
☐ Child Study	1924-1938	**300.00**	**350.00**
HN 604a			
☐ Child Study	1924-1938	**300.00**	**350.00**
HN 604b			
☐ Child Study	1924-1938	**300.00**	**350.00**
HN 605a			
☐ Child Study	1924-1938	**300.00**	**350.00**
HN 605b			
☐ Child Study	1924-1938	**300.00**	**350.00**
HN 606a			
☐ Child Study	1924-1949	**300.00**	**350.00**
HN 606b			
☐ Child Study	1924-1949	**300.00**	**350.00**
HN 607 NO DETAILS AVAILABLE			
HN 608			
☐ Falstaff (1st version)	1924-1938	**700.00**	**800.00**
HN 609			
☐ Falstaff (1st version)	1924-1938	**700.00**	**800.00**
HN 610			
☐ Henry Lytton as Jack Point	1924-1949	**800.00**	**900.00**
HN 611			
☐ A Mandarin (3rd version)	1924-1938	**2000.00**	**2500.00**
HN 612			
☐ Poke Bonnett	1924-1938	**1350.00**	**1500.00**
HN 613			
☐ Madonna of the Square	1924-1938	**1650.00**	**1800.00**
HN 614			
☐ Polly Peachum (1st version)	1924-1938	**600.00**	**700.00**
HN 615			
☐ Katharine	1924-1938	**1650.00**	**1800.00**
HN 616			
☐ A Jester (1st version)	1924-1938	**1350.00**	**1500.00**
HN 617			
☐ A Shepherd (1st version)	1924-1938	**1750.00**	**2000.00**
HN 618			
☐ Falstaff (2nd version)	1924-1938	**700.00**	**800.00**
HN 619			
☐ Falstaff (1st version)	1924-1938	**700.00**	**800.00**
HN 620			
☐ Polly Peachum (2nd version)	1924-1938	**450.00**	**500.00**
HN 621			
☐ Pan on Rock	1924-1938	**1100.00**	**1200.00**
HN 622			
☐ Pan on Rock	1924-1938	**1100.00**	**1200.00**
HN 623			
☐ An Old King	1924-1938	**1300.00**	**1500.00**

	Date	Price Range	
HN 624			
☐ Lady with Rose	1924-1938	**1650.00**	**1800.00**
HN 625			
☐ A Spook	1924-1938	**1250.00**	**1400.00**
HN 626			
☐ Lady with Shawl	1924-1938	**3000.00**	**3500.00**
HN 627			
☐ A Jester (1st version)	1924-1938	**1350.00**	**1500.00**
HN 628			
☐ The Crinoline	1924-1938	**1350.00**	**1500.00**
HN 629			
☐ The Curtsey	1924-1938	**1650.00**	**1800.00**
HN 630			
☐ A Jester (2nd version)	1924-1938	**1350.00**	**1500.00**
HN 631			
☐ Fisherwomen	1924-1938	**3000.00**	**3500.00**
HN 632			
☐ A Shepherd (1st version)	1924-1938	**1750.00**	**2000.00**
HN 633			
☐ A Princess	1924-1938	**2750.00**	**3000.00**
HN 634			
☐ A Geisha (1st version)	1924-1938	**2250.00**	**2500.00**
HN 635			
☐ Harlequinade	1924-1938	**1150.00**	**1300.00**
HN 636			
☐ Masquerade (male, 1st version)	1924-1938	**1000.00**	**1250.00**
HN 637			
☐ Masquerade (female, 1st version)	1924-1938	**1000.00**	**1250.00**
HN 638			
☐ Falstaff (1st version)	1924-1938	**700.00**	**800.00**
HN 639			
☐ Elsie Maynard	1924-1949	**800.00**	**900.00**
HN 640			
☐ Charley's Aunt (1st version)	1924-1938	**900.00**	**1000.00**
HN 641			
☐ A Mandarin	1924-1938	**1100.00**	**1200.00**
HN 642			
☐ Pierrette (1st version)	1924-1938	**900.00**	**1000.00**
HN 643			
☐ Pierrette (1st version)	1924-1938	**900.00**	**1000.00**
HN 644			
☐ Pierrette (1st version)	1924-1938	**800.00**	**900.00**
HN 645			
☐ One of the Forty (12th version)	1924-1938	**1100.00**	**1200.00**
HN 646			
☐ One of the Forty (11th version)	1924-1938	**1100.00**	**1200.00**
HN 647			
☐ One of the Forty (2nd version)	1924-1938	**1100.00**	**1200.00**

HN 648	Date	Price Range	
☐ One of the Forty (1st version)	1924-1938	1100.00	1200.00
HN 649			
☐ One of the Forty (13th version)	1924-1938	1100.00	1200.00
HN 650			
☐ Crinoline Lady (miniature)	1924-1938	550.00	650.00
HN 651			
☐ Crinoline Lady (miniature)	1924-1938	550.00	650.00
HN 652			
☐ Crinoline Lady (miniature)	1924-1938	550.00	650.00
HN 653			
☐ Crinoline Lady (miniature)	1924-1938	550.00	650.00
HN 654			
☐ Crinoline Lady (miniature)	1924-1938	550.00	650.00
HN 655			
☐ Crinoline Lady (miniature)	1924-1938	550.00	650.00
HN 656			
☐ The Mask	1924-1938	850.00	950.00
HN 657			
☐ The Mask	1924-1938	850.00	950.00
HN 658			
☐ Mam'selle	1924-1938	850.00	950.00
HN 659			
☐ Mam'selle	1924-1938	900.00	1000.00
HN 660			
☐ The Welsh Girl	1924-1938	2500.00	2750.00
HN 661			
☐ Boy with Turban	1924-1938	500.00	600.00
HN 662			
☐ Boy with Turban	1924-1938	500.00	600.00
HN 663			
☐ One of the Forty (12th version)	1924-1938	1100.00	1200.00
HN 664			
☐ One of the Forty (10th version)	1924-1938	1100.00	1200.00
HN 665			
☐ One of the Forty (13th version)	1924-1938	1100.00	1200.00
HN 666			
☐ One of the Forty (2nd version)	1924-1938	1100.00	1200.00
HN 667			
☐ One of the Forty (11th version)	1924-1938	1100.00	1200.00
HN 668			
☐ The Welsh Girl	1924-1938	2500.00	2700.00
HN 669			
☐ The Welsh Girl	1924-1938	2500.00	2700.00
HN 670			
☐ The Curtsey	1924-1938	1450.00	1600.00
HN 671			
☐ Lady Ermine	1924-1938	1650.00	1800.00
HN 672			
☐ Tulips	1924-1938	1550.00	1700.00

HN 673	Date	Price Range	
☐ Henry VIII (1st version)	1924-1938	2350.00	2600.00
HN 674			
☐ Masquerade (female, 1st version)	1924-1938	700.00	800.00
HN 675			
☐ The Gainsborough Hat	1924-1938	1350.00	1500.00
HN 676			
☐ Pavlova	1924-1938	1500.00	1700.00
HN 677			
☐ One of the Forty (1st version)	1924-1938	1100.00	1200.00
HN 678			
☐ Lady with Shawl	1924-1938	3250.00	3500.00
HN 679			
☐ Lady with Shawl	1924-1938	3250.00	3500.00
HN 680			
☐ Polly Peachum (1st version)	1924-1949	600.00	700.00
HN 681			
☐ The Cobbler (2nd version)	1924-1938	600.00	700.00
HN 682			
☐ The Cobbler (1st version)	1924-1938	700.00	800.00
HN 683			
☐ Masquerade (male, 1st version)	1924-1938	700.00	800.00
HN 684			
☐ Tony Weller (1st version)	1924-1938	1650.00	1800.00
HN 685			
☐ Contentment	1923-1938	1900.00	2000.00
HN 686			
☐ Contentment	1924-1938	1900.00	2000.00
HN 687			
☐ The Bather (1st version)	1924-1949	675.00	775.00
HN 688			
☐ A Yeoman of the Guard	1924-1938	950.00	1050.00
HN 689			
☐ A Chelsea Pensioner	1924-1938	1250.00	1400.00
HN 690			
☐ A Lady of the Georgian Perod	1925-1938	2150.00	2300.00
HN 691			
☐ Pierrette (1st version)	1925-1938	1250.00	1500.00
HN 692			
☐ Sleep	1925-1938	2050.00	2200.00
HN 693			
☐ Polly Peachum (1st version)	1925-1949	600.00	700.00
HN 694			
☐ Polly Peachum (2nd version)	1925-1949	400.00	500.00
HN 695			
☐ Lucy Lockett (2nd version)	1925-1949	650.00	750.00
HN 696			
☐ Lucy Lockett (2nd version	1925-1949	650.00	750.00
HN 697			
☐ The Balloon Seller	1925-1938	800.00	900.00

	Date	Price Range	
HN 698			
☐ Polly Peachum (3rd version, miniature)	1925-1949	400.00	500.00
HN 699			
☐ Polly Peachum (3rd version, miniature)	1925-1949	400.00	500.00
HN 700			
☐ Pretty Lady	1925-1938	1500.00	1750.00
HN 701			
☐ The Welsh Girl	1925-1938	2500.00	2700.00
HN 702			
☐ A Lady of the Georgian Period	1925-1938	2150.00	2300.00
HN 703			
☐ Woman Holding Child	1925-1938	2000.00	2200.00
HN 704			
☐ One of the Forty (2nd version)	1925-1938	1100.00	1200.00
HN 705			
☐ The Gainsborough Hat	1925-1938	1100.00	1200.00
HN 706			
☐ Fruit Gathering	1925-1938	2500.00	3000.00
HN 707			
☐ Fruit Gathering	1925-1938	3000.00	3500.00
HN 708			
☐ Shepherdess (1st version, miniature) .	1925-1948	650.00	750.00
HN 709			
☐ Shepherd (1st version, miniature)	1925-1938	550.00	650.00
HN 710			
☐ Sleep	1925-1938	2050.00	2200.00
HN 711			
☐ Harlequinade	1925-1938	850.00	950.00
HN 712			
☐ One of the Forty (11th version)	1925-1938	1100.00	1200.00
HN 713			
☐ One of the Forty (12th version	1925-1938	1100.00	1200.00
HN 714			
☐ One of the Forty (10th version)	1925-1938	1100.00	1200.00
HN 715			
☐ Proposal (lady)	1925-1938	950.00	1000.00
HN 716			
☐ Proposal (lady)	1925-1938	950.00	1000.00
HN 717			
☐ Lady Clown	1925-1938	1300.00	1450.00
HN 718			
☐ Lady Clown	1925-1938	1300.00	1450.00
HN 719			
☐ Butterfly	1925-1938	700.00	800.00
HN 720			
☐ Butterfly	1925-1938	700.00	800.00
HN 721			
☐ Pierrette (1st version)	1925-1938	900.00	1000.00

	Date	Price Range	
HN 722			
☐ Mephisto	1925-1938	1350.00	1500.00
HN 723			
☐ Mephisto	1925-1938	1500.00	1600.00
HN 724			
☐ Mam'selle	1925-1938	900.00	1000.00
HN 725			
☐ The Proposal (male)	1925-1938	950.00	1000.00
HN 726			
☐ A Victorian Lady	1925-1938	350.00	400.00
HN 727			
☐ A Victorian Lady	1925-1938	350.00	400.00
HN 728			
☐ A Victorian Lady	1925-1952	300.00	350.00
HN 729			
☐ The Mask	1925-1938	850.00	950.00
HN 730			
☐ Butterfly	1925-1938	800.00	900.00
HN 731			
☐ Pierrette (1st version)	1925-1938	900.00	1000.00
HN 732			
☐ Pierrette (1st version)	1925-1938	900.00	1000.00
HN 733			
☐ The Mask	1925-1938	850.00	950.00
HN 734			
☐ Polly Peachum (2nd version)	1925-1949	450.00	500.00
HN 735			
☐ Shepherdess (2nd version)	1925-1938	1500.00	1750.00
HN 736			
☐ A Victorian Lady	1925-1938	450.00	500.00
HN 737 NO DETAILS AVAILABLE			
HN 738			
☐ Lady Clown	1925-1938	1300.00	1450.00
HN 739			
☐ A Victorian Lady	1925-1938	650.00	750.00
HN 740			
☐ A Victorian Lady	1925-1938	450.00	500.00
HN 741			
☐ A Geisha (1st version)	1925-1938	2250.00	2500.00
HN 742			
☐ A Victorian Lady	1925-1938	450.00	500.00
HN 743			
☐ Woman Holding Child	1925-1938	2050.00	2200.00
HN 744			
☐ The Lavender Woman	1925-1938	1750.00	2000.00
HN 745			
☐ A Victorian Lady	1925-1938	450.00	500.00
HN 746			
☐ A Mandarin (1st version)	1926-1938	2250.00	2500.00

	Date	Price Range	
HN 747			
☐ Tulips..........................	1925-1938	**1550.00**	**1700.00**
HN 748			
☐ Out for a Walk...................	1925-1936	**2350.00**	**2500.00**
HN 749			
☐ London Cry, Strawberries..........	1925-1938	**900.00**	**1000.00**
HN 750			
☐ Shepherdess (2nd version)........	1925-1938	**1500.00**	**1750.00**
HN 751			
☐ Shepherd (3rd version)............	1925-1938	**1500.00**	**1750.00**
HN 752			
☐ London Cry, Turnips and Carrots....	1925-1938	**900.00**	**1000.00**
HN 753			
☐ The Dandy......................	1925-1938	**1100.00**	**1250.00**
HN 754			
☐ The Belle.......................	1925-1938	**1150.00**	**1250.00**
HN 755			
☐ Mephistopheles and Marguerite.....	1925-1949	**1350.00**	**1500.00**
HN 756			
☐ The Modern Piper.................	1925-1938	**1650.00**	**1800.00**
HN 757			
☐ Polly Peachum (3rd version)........	1925-1949	**350.00**	**400.00**
HN 758			
☐ Polly Peachum (3rd version)........	1925-1949	**350.00**	**400.00**
HN 759			
☐ Polly Peachum (3rd version)........	1925-1949	**350.00**	**400.00**
HN 760			
☐ Polly Peachum (3rd version miniature)......................	1925-1949	**350.00**	**400.00**
HN 761			
☐ Polly Peachum (3rd version miniature)......................	1925-1949	**350.00**	**400.00**
HN 762			
☐ Polly Peachum (3rd version miniature)......................	1925-1949	**350.00**	**400.00**
HN 763			
☐ Pretty Lady.....................	1925-1938	**1450.00**	**1600.00**
HN 764			
☐ Madonna of the Square............	1925-1938	**1650.00**	**1800.00**
HN 765			
☐ The Poke Bonnet.................	1925-1938	**1500.00**	**1600.00**
HN 766			
☐ Irish Colleen....................	1925-1938	**1650.00**	**1800.00**
HN 767			
☐ Irish Colleen....................	1925-1938	**1650.00**	**1800.00**
HN 768			
☐ Harlequinade Masked.............	1925-1938	**1350.00**	**1450.00**
HN 769			
☐ Harlequinade Masked.............	1925-1938	**1350.00**	**1450.00**

	Date	Price Range	
HN 770			
☐ Lady Clown	1925-1938	1300.00	1450.00
HN 771			
☐ London Cry, Turnips and Carrots	1925-1938	900.00	1000.00
HN 772			
☐ London Cry, Strawberries	1925-1938	900.00	1000.00
HN 773			
☐ The Bather (2nd version)	1925-1938	900.00	1100.00
HN 774			
☐ The Bather (2nd version)	1925-1938	900.00	1100.00
HN 775			
☐ Mephistopheles and Marguerite	1925-1949	1350.00	1500.00
HN 776			
☐ The Belle	1925-1938	1250.00	1350.00
HN 777			
☐ Bo-Peep (1st version)	1926-1938	1250.00	1350.00
HN 778			
☐ Captain (1st version)	1926-1938	1250.00	1400.00
HN 779			
☐ A Geisha (1st version)	1926-1938	2250.00	2500.00
HN 780			
☐ Harlequinade	1926-1938	850.00	950.00
HN 781			
☐ The Bather (1st version)	1926-1938	800.00	900.00
HN 782			
☐ The Bather (1st version)	1926-1938	800.00	900.00
HN 783			
☐ Pretty Lady	1926-1938	1450.00	1600.00
HN 784			
☐ Pierette (1st version)	1926-1938	900.00	1000.00
HN 785			
☐ The Mask	1926-1938	850.00	950.00
HN 786			
☐ Mam'selle	1926-1938	900.00	1000.00
HN 787			
☐ A Mandarin (1st version)	1926-1938	2250.00	2500.00
HN 788			
☐ Proposal (lady)	1926-1938	900.00	1000.00
HN 789			
☐ The Flower Seller	1926-1938	600.00	700.00
HN 790			
☐ The Parson's Daughter	1926-1938	550.00	600.00
HN 791			
☐ A Mandarin (1st version)	1926-1938	2250.00	2500.00
HN 792			
☐ The Welsh Girl	1926-1938	2550.00	2700.00
HN 793			
☐ Katharine	1926-1938	1650.00	1800.00
HN 794			
☐ The Bouquet	1926-1938	1550.00	1700.00

	Date	Price Range	
HN 795			
☐ Pierrette (2nd version, miniature)	1926-1938	650.00	750.00
HN 796			
☐ Pierrette (2nd version, miniature)	1926-1938	650.00	750.00
HN 797			
☐ Moorish Minstrel	1926-1949	2150.00	2300.00
HN 798			
☐ Tête-á-Tête (1st version).	1926-1938	1150.00	1300.00
HN 799			
☐ Tête-á-Tête (1st version).	1926-1938	1150.00	1300.00
HN 800 — HN 1200 ANIMAL AND BIRD MODELS			
HN 1201			
☐ Hunts Lady	1926-1938	1100.00	1200.00
HN 1202			
☐ Bo-Peep (1st version)	1926-1938	1050.00	1200.00
HN 1203			
☐ Butterfly	1926-1938	900.00	1000.00
HN 1204			
☐ Angela	1926-1938	675.00	850.00
HN 1205			
☐ Miss 1926	1926-1938	2050.00	2200.00
HN 1206			
☐ The Flower Seller's Children	1926-1949	450.00	500.00
HN 1207			
☐ Miss 1926	1926-1938	2050.00	2200.00
HN 1208			
☐ A Victorian Lady	1926-1938	450.00	500.00
HN 1209			
☐ The Proposal (male)	1926-1938	900.00	1000.00
HN 1210			
☐ Boy with Turban	1926-1938	500.00	600.00
HN 1211			
☐ Quality Street	1926-1938	1100.00	1200.00
HN 1212			
☐ Boy with Turban	1926-1938	550.00	650.00
HN 1213			
☐ Boy with Turban	1926-1938	500.00	600.00
HN 1214			
☐ Boy with Turban	1926-1938	500.00	600.00
HN 1215			
☐ The Pied Piper	1926-1938	800.00	900.00
HN 1216			
☐ Falstaff (1st version)	1926-1949	700.00	800.00
HN 1217			
☐ The Prince of Wales	1926-1938	1450.00	1600.00
HN 1218			
☐ A Spook	1926-1938	1250.00	1400.00
HN 1219			
☐ Negligeé	1927-1938	1100.00	1200.00

HN 1220	Date	Price Range	
☐ Lido Lady	1927-1938	1000.00	1100.00
HN 1221			
☐ Lady Jester (1st version)	1927-1938	1350.00	1500.00
HN 1222			
☐ Lady Jester (1st version)	1927-1938	1350.00	1500.00
HN 1223			
☐ A Geisha (2nd version)	1927-1938	900.00	1000.00
HN 1224			
☐ The Wandering Minstrel	1927-1938	1350.00	1500.00
HN 1225			
☐ Boy with Turban	1927-1938	500.00	600.00
HN 1226			
☐ The Huntsman (1st version).	1927-1938	1350.00	1500.00
HN 1227			
☐ The Bather (2nd version)	1927-1938	900.00	1000.00
HN 1228			
☐ Negligeé	1927-1938	1100.00	1200.00
HN 1229			
☐ Lido Lady.	1927-1938	1100.00	1200.00
HN 1230			
☐ Baba	1927-1938	600.00	650.00
HN 1231			
☐ Cassim (1st version).	1927-1938	550.00	600.00
HN 1232			
☐ Cassim (1st version).	1927-1938	550.00	600.00
HN 1233			
☐ Susanna	1927-1938	1100.00	1200.00
HN 1234			
☐ A Geisha (2nd version)	1927-1938	900.00	1000.00
HN 1235			
☐ A Scribe	1927-1938	1100.00	1200.00
HN 1236			
☐ Tête-à-Tête (2nd version)	1927-1938	650.00	750.00
HN 1237			
☐ Tête-à-Tête (2nd version)	1927-1938	650.00	750.00
HN 1238			
☐ The Bather (1st version)	1927-1938	900.00	1000.00
HN 1239 - HN 1241 ANIMAL and BIRD MODELS			
HN 1242			
☐ The Parson's Daughter	1927-1938	550.00	600.00
HN 1243			
☐ Baba	1927-1927	600.00	650.00
HN 1244			
☐ Baba	1927-1938	600.00	650.00
HN 1245			
☐ Baba	1927-1938	600.00	650.00
HN 1246			
☐ Baba	1927-1938	600.00	650.00

	Date	Price Range	
HN 1247			
☐ Baba	1928-1938	600.00	650.00
HN 1248			
☐ Baba	1927-1938	600.00	650.00
HN 1249			
☐ Circe	1927-1938	1200.00	1400.00
HN 1250			
☐ Circe	1927-1938	1200.00	1400.00
HN 1251			
☐ The Cobbler	1927-1938	600.00	700.00
HN 1252			
☐ Kathleen	1927-1938	800.00	850.00
HN 1253			
☐ Kathleen	1927-1938	800.00	850.00
HN 1254			
☐ Circe	1927-1938	1200.00	1400.00
HN 1255			
☐ Circe	1927-1938	1200.00	1400.00
HN 1256			
☐ Captain MacHeath...............	1927-1949	700.00	800.00
HN 1257			
☐ The Highwayman	1927-1949	600.00	700.00
HN 1258			
☐ A Victorian Lady	1927-1938	450.00	500.00
HN 1259			
☐ The Alchemist...................	1927-1938	1550.00	1750.00
HN 1260			
☐ Carnival	1927-1938	1500.00	1650.00
HN 1261			
☐ Sea Sprite (1st version)	1927-1938	600.00	650.00
HN 1262			
☐ Spanish Lady	1927-1938	900.00	1000.00
HN 1263			
☐ Lady Clown	1927-1938	1300.00	1450.00
HN 1264			
☐ Judge and Jury	1927-1938	3000.00	3500.00
HN 1265			
☐ Lady Fayre	1928-1938	550.00	650.00
HN 1266			
☐ Ko-Ko..........................	1928-1949	650.00	750.00
HN 1267			
☐ Carmen (1st version)	1928-1938	750.00	850.00
HN 1268			
☐ Yum-Yum.......................	1928-1938	650.00	750.00
HN 1269			
☐ Scotch Girl	1928-1938	1350.00	1500.00
HN 1270			
☐ The Swimmer	1928-1938	1100.00	1200.00
HN 1271			
☐ The Mask.......................	1928-1938	950.00	1050.00

	Date	Price Range	
HN 1272			
☐ Negligeé	1928-1938	1100.00	1200.00
HN 1273			
☐ Negligeé	1928-1938	1100.00	1200.00
HN 1274			
☐ Harlequinade Masked	1928-1938	1350.00	1450.00
HN 1275			
☐ Kathleen	1928-1938	800.00	850.00
HN 1276			
☐ A Victorian Lady	1928-1938	350.00	400.00
HN 1277			
☐ A Victorian Lady	1928-1938	350.00	400.00
HN 1278			
☐ Carnival	1928-1938	1400.00	1550.00
HN 1279			
☐ Kathleen	1928-1938	800.00	850.00
HN 1280			
☐ Blue Bird	1928-1938	650.00	750.00
HN 1281			
☐ Scotties	1928-1938	1100.00	1200.00
HN 1282			
☐ The Alchemist	1928-1938	1550.00	1750.00
HN 1283			
☐ The Cobbler (2nd version)	1928-1949	600.00	700.00
HN 1284			
☐ Lady Jester (2nd version)	1928-1938	750.00	850.00
HN 1285			
☐ Lady Jester (2nd version)	1928-1938	750.00	850.00
HN 1286			
☐ Ko-Ko	1938-1949	600.00	750.00
HN 1287			
☐ Yum-Yum	1928-1939	650.00	750.00
HN 1288			
☐ Susanna	1928-1938	1100.00	1200.00
HN 1289			
☐ Midinette (1st version)	1928-1938	1500.00	1600.00
HN 1290			
☐ Spanish Lady	1928-1938	900.00	1000.00
HN 1291			
☐ Kathleen	1928-1938	850.00	950.00
HN 1292			
☐ A Geisha (2nd version)	1928-1938	900.00	1000.00
HN 1293			
☐ Spanish Lady	1928-1938	900.00	1000.00
HN 1294			
☐ Spanish Lady	1928-1938	900.00	1000.00
HN 1295			
☐ A Jester (1st version)	1928-1949	900.00	1000.00
HN 1296			
☐ Columbine (1st version)	1928-1938	700.00	800.00

	Date	Price Range	
HN 1297			
☐ Columbine (1st version)	1928-1938	700.00	800.00
HN 1298			
☐ Sweet and Twenty (1st version)	1928-1969	225.00	275.00
HN 1299			
☐ Susanna	1928-1938	1100.00	1200.00
HN 1300			
☐ Carmen (1st version)	1928-1938	800.00	900.00
HN 1301			
☐ Gypsy Woman with Child	1928-1938	2250.00	2400.00
HN 1302			
☐ Gypsy Girl with Flowers	1928-1938	2250.00	2400.00
HN 1303			
☐ Angela	1928-1938	950.00	1100.00
HN 1304			
☐ Harlequinade Masked	1928-1938	1350.00	1450.00
HN 1305			
☐ Siesta	1928-1938	1350.00	1500.00
HN 1306			
☐ Midinette (1st version)	1928-1938	1500.00	1600.00
HN 1307			
☐ An Irishman	1928-1938	1150.00	1250.00
HN 1308			
☐ The Moor	1928-1938	1500.00	1750.00
HN 1309			
☐ Spanish Lady	1928-1938	900.00	1000.00
HN 1310			
☐ A Geisha (2nd version)	1929-1938	800.00	900.00
HN 1311			
☐ Cassim (2nd version)	1929-1938	700.00	800.00
HN 1312			
☐ Cassim (2nd version)	1929-1938	700.00	800.00
HN 1313			
☐ Sonny	1929-1938	600.00	700.00
HN 1314			
☐ Sonny	1929-1938	600.00	700.00
HN 1315			
☐ Old Balloon Seller	1929-	185.00	
HN 1316			
☐ Toys	1929-1938	1200.00	1500.00
HN 1317			
☐ The Snake Charmer	1929-1938	1000.00	1100.00
HN 1318			
☐ Sweet Anne	1929-1949	200.00	250.00
HN 1319			
☐ Darling (1st version)	1929-1959	150.00	200.00
HN 1320			
☐ Rosamund (1st version)	1929-1938	1500.00	2000.00
HN 1321			
☐ A Geisha (1st verson)	1929-1938	2250.00	2500.00

	Date	Price Range	
HN 1322			
☐ A Geisha (1st version)	1929-1938	2250.00	2500.00
HN 1323			
☐ Contentment....................	1929-1938	1550.00	1700.00
HN 1324			
☐ Fairy	1929-1938	850.00	950.00
HN 1325			
☐ The Orange Seller................	1929-1949	900.00	1000.00
HN 1326			
☐ The Swimmer	1929-1938	1300.00	1400.00
HN 1327			
☐ Bo-Peep (1st version)	1929-1938	1050.00	1200.00
HN 1328			
☐ Bo-Peep (1st version)	1929-1938	1050.00	1200.00
HN 1329			
☐ The Swimmer	1929-1938	1300.00	1400.00
HN 1330			
☐ Sweet Anne.....................	1929-1949	325.00	375.00
HN 1331			
☐ Sweet Anne.....................	1929-1949	300.00	350.00
HN 1332			
☐ Lady Jester (1st version)	1929-1938	1250.00	1350.00
HN 1333			
☐ A Jester (2nd version).............	1929-1949	1350.00	1500.00
HN 1334			
☐ Tulips.........................	1929-1938	1550.00	1700.00
HN 1335			
☐ Folly..........................	1929-1938	1600.00	1750.00
HN 1336			
☐ One of the Forty (11th version)	1929-1938	1100.00	1200.00
HN 1337			
☐ Priscilla	1929-1938	500.00	600.00
HN 1338			
☐ The Courtier	1929-1938	1200.00	1350.00
HN 1339			
☐ Covent Garden	1929-1938	1000.00	1200.00
HN 1340			
☐ Priscilla	1929-1949	325.00	375.00
HN 1341			
☐ Marietta.......................	1929-1949	700.00	800.00
HN 1342			
☐ The Flower Seller's Children	1929-	395.00	
HN 1343			
☐ Dulcinea	1929-1938	900.00	1050.00
HN 1344			
☐ Sunshine Girl	1929-1938	1400.00	1500.00
HN 1345			
☐ A Victorian Lady	1929-1949	250.00	300.00
HN 1346			
☐ Iona	1929-1938	2500.00	3000.00

	Date	Price Range	
HN 1347			
☐ Moira	1929-1938	2750.00	3000.00
HN 1348			
☐ Sunshine Girl	1929-1938	1400.00	1500.00
HN 1349			
☐ Scotties	1929-1949	1500.00	1600.00
HN 1350			
☐ One of the Forty (11th version)	1929-1949	1100.00	1200.00
HN 1351			
☐ One of the Forty (1st version)	1920-1949	1100.00	1200.00
HN 1352			
☐ One of the Forty (1st version)	1929-1949	1100.00	1200.00
HN 1353			
☐ One of the Forty (2nd version)	1929-1949	1100.00	1200.00
HN 1354			
☐ One of the Forty (13th version)	1929-1949	1100.00	1200.00
HN 1355			
☐ The Mendicant	1929-1938	350.00	400.00
HN 1356			
☐ The Parson's Daughter	1929-1938	475.00	550.00
HN 1357			
☐ Kathleen	1929-1938	800.00	850.00
HN 1358			
☐ Rosina	1929-1938	750.00	850.00
HN 1359			
☐ Two-A-Penny	1929-1938	1200.00	1300.00
HN 1360			
☐ Sweet and Twenty (1st version)	1929-1938	450.00	500.00
HN 1361			
☐ Mask Seller	1929-1938	650.00	700.00
HN 1362			
☐ Pantalettes	1929-1938	350.00	400.00
HN 1363			
☐ Doreen	1929-1938	900.00	1000.00
HN 1364			
☐ Rosina	1929-1938	750.00	850.00
HN 1365			
☐ The Mendicant	1929-1969	300.00	350.00
HN 1366			
☐ The Moor	1930-1949	1500.00	1750.00
HN 1367			
☐ Kitty	1930-1938	1000.00	1100.00
HN 1368			
☐ Rose	1930-	65.00	
HN 1369			
☐ Boy on Pig	1930-1938	900.00	1000.00
HN 1370			
☐ Marie (2nd version)	1930-	65.00	
HN 1371			
☐ Darling (1st version)	1930-1938	275.00	325.00

	Date	Price Range	
HN 1372			
☐ Darling (1st verson)	1930-1938	**275.00**	**325.00**
HN 1373			
☐ Sweet Lavender	1930-1949	**225.00**	**275.00**
HN 1374			
☐ Fairy	1930-1938	**850.00**	**950.00**
HN 1375			
☐ Fairy	1930-1938	**750.00**	**850.00**
HN 1376			
☐ Fairy	1930-1938	**650.00**	**750.00**
HN 1377			
☐ Fairy	NOT ISSUED		
HN 1378			
☐ Fairy	1930-1938	**550.00**	**650.00**
HN 1379			
☐ Fairy	1930-1938	**550.00**	**650.00**
HN 1380			
☐ Fairy	1930-1938	**850.00**	**950.00**
HN 1381 - HN 1386 FAIRIES — NOT ISSUED			
HN 1387			
☐ Rose.........................	1930-1938	**250.00**	**300.00**
HN 1388			
☐ Marie (2nd version)..............	1930-1938	**250.00**	**300.00**
HN 1389			
☐ Doreen........................	1930-1938	**700.00**	**800.00**
HN 1390			
☐ Doreen........................	1929-1938	**700.00**	**800.00**
HN 1391			
☐ Pierrette (3rd version).............	1930-1938	**1000.00**	**1100.00**
HN 1392			
☐ Paisley Shawl (1st version)	1930-1949	**300.00**	**350.00**
HN 1393			
☐ Fairy	1930-1938	**650.00**	**750.00**
HN 1394			
☐ Fairy	1930-1938	**550.00**	**650.00**
HN 1395			
☐ Fairy	1930-1938	**750.00**	**850.00**
HN 1396			
☐ Fairy	1930-1938	**550.00**	**650.00**
HN 1397			
☐ Gretchen	1930-1938	**650.00**	**700.00**
HN 1398			
☐ Derrick........................	1930-1938	**600.00**	**700.00**
HN 1399			
☐ The Young Widow	1930-1930	**1250.00**	**1500.00**
HN 1400			
☐ The Windmill Lady	1930-1938	**1550.00**	**1700.00**
HN 1401			
☐ Chorus Girl	1930-1938	**1650.00**	**1800.00**

	Date	Price Range	
HN 1402			
☐ Miss Demure.....................	1930-1975	225.00	275.00
HN 1403			
☐ The Old Huntsman	NOT ISSUED		
HN 1404			
☐ Betty (2nd version)	1930-1938	500.00	600.00
HN 1405			
☐ Betty (2nd version)	1930-1938	500.00	600.00
HN 1406			
☐ The Flower Seller's Children	1930-1938	550.00	650.00
HN 1407			
☐ The Winner	1930-1938	3000.00	3500.00
HN 1408			
☐ John Peel	1930-1937	2750.00	3000.00
HN 1409			
☐ Hunting Squire	1930-1938	2000.00	2500.00
HN 1410			
☐ Abdullah	1930-1938	950.00	1150.00
HN 1411			
☐ Charley's Aunt (2nd version)	1930-1938	1375.00	1425.00
HN 1412			
☐ Pantalettes	1930-1949	350.00	400.00
HN 1413			
☐ Margery	1930-1949	400.00	450.00
HN 1414			
☐ Patricia	1930-1949	550.00	650.00
HN 1415 NO DETAILS AVAILABLE			
HN 1416			
☐ Rose..........................	1930-1949	150.00	200.00
HN 1417			
☐ Marie (2nd version)	1930-1949	250.00	300.00
HN 1418			
☐ The Little Mother (2nd version)	1930-1938	1100.00	1200.00
HN 1419			
☐ Dulcinea	1930-1938	1000.00	1150.00
HN 1420			
☐ Phyllis	1930-1949	550.00	650.00
HN 1421			
☐ Barbara	1930-1938	750.00	850.00
HN 1422			
☐ Joan..........................	1930-1949	450.00	550.00
HN 1423			
☐ Babette	1930-1938	500.00	600.00
HN 1424			
☐ Babette	1930-1938	550.00	650.00
HN 1425			
☐ The Moor	1930-1949	1500.00	1750.00
HN 1426			
☐ The Gossips	1930-1949	500.00	750.00

	Date	Price Range	
HN 1427			
☐ Darby	1930-1949	375.00	425.00
HN 1428			
☐ Calumet	1930-1949	1050.00	1150.00
HN 1429			
☐ The Gossips	1930-1949	525.00	575.00
HN 1430			
☐ Phyllis	1930-1938	700.00	800.00
HN 1431			
☐ Patricia	1930-1949	550.00	650.00
HN 1432			
☐ Barbara	1930-1938	775.00	875.00
HN 1433			
☐ The Little Bridesmaid (1st version) . . .	1930-1951	175.00	225.00
HN 1434			
☐ The Little Bridesmaid (1st version) . . .	1930-1949	225.00	275.00
HN 1435			
☐ Betty (2nd version)	1930-1938	500.00	600.00
HN 1436			
☐ Betty (2nd version)	1930-1938	500.00	600.00
HN 1437			
☐ Sweet and Twenty (1st version)	1930-1938	400.00	450.00
HN 1438			
☐ Sweet and Twenty (1st version)	1930-1938	450.00	500.00
HN 1439			
☐ Columbine (1st version)	1930-1938	700.00	800.00
HN 1440			
☐ Miss Demure	1930-1949	350.00	400.00
HN 1441			
☐ Child Study	1931-1938	350.00	400.00
HN 1442			
☐ Child Study	1931-1938	350.00	400.00
HN 1443			
☐ Child Study	1931-1938	350.00	400.00
HN 1444			
☐ Pauline	1931-1938	400.00	450.00
HN 1445			
☐ Biddy	1931-1938	300.00	350.00
HN 1446			
☐ Marietta	1931-1949	700.00	800.00
HN 1447			
☐ Marigold	1931-1949	450.00	500.00
HN 1448			
☐ Rita	1931-1938	600.00	700.00
HN 1449			
☐ The Little Mistress	1931-1949	500.00	550.00
HN 1450			
☐ Rita	1931-1938	600.00	700.00
HN 1451			
☐ Marigold	1931-1938	450.00	500.00

	Date	Price Range	
HN 1452			
☐ A Victorian Lady	1931-1949	250.00	300.00
HN 1453			
☐ Sweet Anne	1931-1949	325.00	375.00
HN 1454			
☐ Negligeé	1931-1938	1100.00	1200.00
HN 1455			
☐ Molly Malone	1931-1938	1350.00	1500.00
HN 1456			
☐ Butterfly	1931-1938	800.00	900.00
HN 1457			
☐ All-A-Blooming	1931-Unknown	900.00	1000.00
HN 1458			
☐ Monica	1931-1949	200.00	250.00
HN 1459			
☐ Monica	1931-Unknown	200.00	250.00
HN 1460			
☐ Paisley Shawl (1st version)	1931-1949	400.00	450.00
HN 1461			
☐ Barbara	1931-1938	750.00	850.00
HN 1462			
☐ Patricia	1931-1938	550.00	650.00
HN 1463			
☐ Miss Demure	1931-1949	350.00	400.00
HN 1464			
☐ The Carpet Seller	1931-1969	400.00	450.00
HN 1464A			
☐ The Carpet Seller	1969-Unknown	375.00	425.00
HN 1465			
☐ Lady Clare	1931-1938	650.00	750.00
HN 1466			
☐ All-A-Blooming	1931-1938	1000.00	1100.00
HN 1467			
☐ Monica	1931-	100.00	
HN 1468			
☐ Pamela	1931-1938	750.00	850.00
HN 1469			
☐ Pamela	1931-1938	650.00	750.00
HN 1470			
☐ Chloe	1931-1949	300.00	350.00
HN 1471			
☐ Annette	1931-1938	375.00	425.00
HN 1472			
☐ Annette	1931-1949	425.00	475.00
HN 1473			
☐ Dreamland	1931-1938	1850.00	2000.00
HN 1474			
☐ In the Stocks (1st version)	1931-1938	1300.00	1500.00
HN 1475			
☐ In the Stocks (1st version)	1931-1938	1000.00	1250.00

	Date	Price Range	
HN 1476			
☐ Chloe	1931-1938	300.00	350.00
HN 1477 NO DETAILS AVAILABLE			
HN 1478			
☐ Sylvia.........................	1931-1938	700.00	800.00
HN 1479			
☐ Chloe	1931-1949	275.00	325.00
HN 1480			
☐ Newhaven Fishwife	1931-1938	1350.00	1500.00
HN 1481			
☐ Dreamland	1931-1938	1850.00	2000.00
HN 1482			
☐ Pearly Boy (1st version)	1931-1949	350.00	400.00
HN 1483			
☐ Pearly Girl (1st version)	1931-1949	350.00	400.00
HN 1484			
☐ Jennifer	1931-1949	500.00	550.00
HN 1485			
☐ Greta	1931-1953	300.00	350.00
HN 1486			
☐ Phyllis	1931-1949	650.00	750.00
HN 1487			
☐ Suzette	1931-1950	325.00	375.00
HN 1488			
☐ Gloria.........................	1932-1938	900.00	1000.00
HN 1489			
☐ Marie (2nd version)	1932-1949	250.00	300.00
HN 1490			
☐ Dorcas........................	1932-1938	450.00	500.00
HN 1491			
☐ Dorcas........................	1932-1938	450.00	500.00
HN 1492			
☐ Old Lavender Seller	1932-1949	600.00	700.00
HN 1493			
☐ The Potter	1932-	325.00	
HN 1494			
☐ Gwendolen	1932-1938	775.00	850.00
HN 1495			
☐ Priscilla	1932-1949	500.00	600.00
HN 1496			
☐ Sweet Anne....................	1932-1967	225.00	275.00
HN 1497			
☐ Rosamund (2nd version)	1932-1938	800.00	1000.00
HN 1498			
☐ Chloe..........................	1932-1938	350.00	400.00
HN 1499			
☐ Miss Demure...................	1932-1938	400.00	450.00
HN 1500			
☐ Biddy	1932-1938	300.00	350.00

	Date	Price Range	
HN 1501			
☐ Priscilla	1932-1938	500.00	600.00
HN 1502			
☐ Lucy Ann	1932-1951	300.00	350.00
HN 1503			
☐ Gwendolen	1932-1949	700.00	800.00
HN 1504			
☐ Sweet Maid (1st version)	1932-1938	900.00	1000.00
HN 1505			
☐ Sweet Maid (1st version)	1932-1938	900.00	1000.00
HN 1506			
☐ Rose.	1932-1938	250.00	300.00
HN 1507			
☐ Pantalettes	1932-1949	450.00	500.00
HN 1508			
☐ Helen	1932-1938	750.00	900.00
HN 1509			
☐ Helen	1932-1938	750.00	900.00
HN 1510			
☐ Constance.	1932-1938	1500.00	1700.00
HN 1511			
☐ Constance.	1932-1938	1500.00	1700.00
HN 1512			
☐ Kathleen	1932-1938	700.00	800.00
HN 1513			
☐ Biddy	1932-1951	200.00	250.00
HN 1514			
☐ Dolly Vardon	1932-1938	700.00	800.00
HN 1515			
☐ Dolly Vardon	1932-1949	800.00	900.00
HN 1516			
☐ Cicely.	1932-1949	1100.00	1200.00
HN 1517			
☐ Veronica (1st version)	1932-1951	300.00	350.00
HN 1518			
☐ The Potter	1932-1949	425.00	475.00
HN 1519			
☐ Veronica (1st version)	1932-1938	400.00	450.00
HN 1520			
☐ Eugene	1932-1938	650.00	750.00
HN 1521			
☐ Eugene	1932-1938	650.00	750.00
HN 1522			
☐ The Potter	1932-1949	425.00	475.00
HN 1523			
☐ Lisette	1932-1938	900.00	1000.00
HN 1524			
☐ Lisette	1932-1938	900.00	1000.00
HN 1525			
☐ Clarissa (1st version)	1932-1938	625.00	700.00

HN 1526	Date	Price Range	
☐ Anthea......................	1932-1938	550.00	650.00
HN 1527			
☐ Anthea......................	1932-1949	600.00	700.00
HN 1528			
☐ Bluebeard (2nd version)	1932-1949	1000.00	1100.00
HN 1529			
☐ A Victorian Lady	1932-1938	400.00	450.00
HN 1530			
☐ The Little Bridesmaid	1932-1938	200.00	250.00
HN 1531			
☐ Marie (2nd version)	1932-1938	250.00	350.00
HN 1532			
☐ Fairy	1932-1938	550.00	650.00
HN 1533			
☐ Fairy	1932-1938	550.00	650.00
HN 1534			
☐ Fairy	1932-1938	550.00	650.00
HN 1535			
☐ Fairy	1932-1938	550.00	650.00
HN 1536			
☐ Fairy	1932-1938	550.00	650.00
HN 1537			
☐ Janet (1st version)	1932-	125.00	
HN 1538			
☐ Janet (1st version)	1932-1949	275.00	325.00
HN 1539			
☐ A Saucy Nymph	1933-1949	275.00	325.00
HN 1540			
☐ 'Little Child so Rare and Sweet'	1933-1949	425.00	475.00
HN 1541			
☐ 'Happy Joy, Baby Boy'	1933-1949	300.00	350.00
HN 1542			
☐ 'Little Child so Rare and Sweet'	1933-1949	375.00	425.00
HN 1543			
☐ 'Dancing Eyes and Sunny Hair'......	1933-1949	300.00	350.00
HN 1544			
☐ 'Do you Wonder where Fairies are that Folk Declare Have Vanished' ...	1933-1949	300.00	350.00
HN 1545			
☐ 'Called Love, a Little Boy, almost Naked, Wanton, Blind, Cruel now, and then as Kind'	1933-1949	325.00	375.00
HN 1546			
☐ 'Here a Little Child I Stand'	1933-1949	325.00	375.00
HN 1547			
☐ Pearly Boy (1st version)	1933-1949	400.00	450.00
HN 1548			
☐ Pearly Girl (1st version)	1933-1949	375.00	425.00

HN 1549	Date	Price	Range
☐ Sweet and Twenty (1st version)	1933-1949	350.00	400.00
HN 1550			
☐ Annette	1933-1949	450.00	500.00
HN 1551			
☐ Rosamund (2nd version)	1933-1938	450.00	500.00
HN 1552			
☐ Pinkie.	1933-1938	450.00	500.00
HN 1553			
☐ Pinkie.	1933-1938	450.00	500.00
HN 1554			
☐ Charley's Aunt (2nd version)	1933-1938	1200.00	1350.00
HN 1555			
☐ Marigold	1933-1949	450.00	500.00
HN 1556			
☐ Rosina	1933-1938	500.00	600.00
HN 1557			
☐ Lady Fayre	1933-1938	750.00	850.00
HN 1558			
☐ Dorcas.	1933-1952	350.00	400.00
HN 1559			
☐ Priscilla	1933-1949	400.00	500.00
HN 1560			
☐ Miss Demure	1933-1949	350.00	400.00
HN 1561			
☐ Willy-Won't He	1933-1949	500.00	550.00
HN 1562			
☐ Gretchen	1933-1938	700.00	800.00
HN 1563			
☐ Sweet and Twenty (1st version)	1933-1938	450.00	500.00
HN 1564			
☐ Pamela	1933-1938	650.00	750.00
HN 1565			
☐ Lucy Ann	1933-1938	325.00	375.00
HN 1566			
☐ Estelle	1933-1938	800.00	900.00
HN 1567			
☐ Patricia	1933-1949	650.00	750.00
HN 1568			
☐ Charmain	1933-1938	500.00	600.00
HN 1569			
☐ Charmain	1933-1938	500.00	600.00
HN 1570			
☐ Gwendolen	1933-1949	675.00	750.00
HN 1571			
☐ Old Lavender Seller	1933-1949	600.00	700.00
HN 1572			
☐ Helen	1933-1938	650.00	800.00
HN 1573			
☐ Rhoda	1933-1949	575.00	650.00

	Date	Price Range	
HN 1574			
☐ Rhoda	1933-1938	500.00	550.00
HN 1575			
☐ Daisy	1933-1949	250.00	300.00
HN 1576			
☐ Tildy	1933-1938	700.00	800.00
HN 1577			
☐ Suzette	1933-1949	500.00	550.00
HN 1578			
☐ The Hinged Parasol	1933-1949	400.00	500.00
HN 1579			
☐ The Hinged Parasol	1933-1949	400.00	500.00
HN 1580			
☐ Rosebud (1st version)..............	1933-1938	600.00	700.00
HN 1581			
☐ Rosebud (1st version)..............	1933-1938	600.00	700.00
HN 1582			
☐ Marion	1933-1938	700.00	800.00
HN 1583			
☐ Marion	1933-1938	700.00	800.00
HN 1584			
☐ Willy-Won't He	1933-1949	350.00	400.00
HN 1585			
☐ Suzette	1933-1938	500.00	600.00
HN 1586			
☐ Camille	1933-1949	650.00	700.00
HN 1587			
☐ Fleurette	1933-1949	625.00	700.00
HN 1588			
☐ The Bride (1st version)	1933-1938	750.00	850.00
HN 1589			
☐ Sweet and Twenty (2nd version)	1933-1949	225.00	275.00
HN 1590 - HN 1597 WALL MASKS			
HN 1598			
☐ Clothilde	1933-1949	600.00	700.00
HN 1599			
☐ Clothilde	1933-1949	600.00	700.00
HN 1600			
☐ The Bride (1st version)	1933-1949	650.00	750.00
HN 1601 - HN 1603 WALL MASKS			
HN 1604			
☐ The Emir	1933-1949	900.00	1000.00
HN 1605			
☐ The Emir	1933-1949	900.00	1000.00
HN 1606			
☐ Falstaff (1st version)	1933-1949	700.00	800.00
HN 1607			
☐ Cerise	1933-1949	300.00	375.00
HN 1608 - HN 1609 WALL MASKS			

HN 1610	Date	Price Range	
☐ Sweet and Twenty (2nd version)	1933-1938	275.00	325.00
HN 1611 · HN 1614 WALL MASKS			
HN 1615			
☐ BOOK END, MICAWBER		350.00	400.00
HN 1616			
☐ BOOKEND, TONY WELLER		350.00	400.00
HN 1617			
☐ Primroses	1934-1949	525.00	575.00
HN 1618			
☐ Maisie	1934-1949	475.00	525.00
HN 1619			
☐ Maisie	1934-1949	475.00	525.00
HN 1620			
☐ Rosabell	1934-1938	900.00	1000.00
HN 1621			
☐ Irene..........................	1934-1951	450.00	500.00
HN 1622			
☐ Evelyn	1934-1949	700.00	850.00
HN 1623			
☐ BOOK END, PICKWICK		350.00	400.00
HN 1624			
☐ NO DETAILS AVAILABLE			
HN 1625			
☐ BOOKEND, SAIREY GAMP		350.00	400.00
HN 1626			
☐ Bonnie Lassie	1934-1953	275.00	325.00
HN 1627			
☐ Curly Knob	1934-1949	525.00	575.00
HN 1628			
☐ Margot........................	1934-1938	700.00	800.00
HN 1629			
☐ Grizel	1934-1938	550.00	650.00
HN 1630 WALL MASK			
HN 1631			
☐ Sweet Anne....................	1934-1938	300.00	400.00
HN 1632			
☐ A Gentlewoman	1934-1949	675.00	775.00
HN 1633			
☐ Clemency	1934-1938	650.00	750.00
HN 1634			
☐ Clemency	1934-1949	650.00	750.00
HN 1635			
☐ Marie (2nd version)	1934-1949	250.00	300.00
HN 1636			
☐ Margot........................	1934-1938	700.00	800.00
HN 1637			
☐ Evelyn	1934-1938	850.00	950.00
HN 1638			
☐ Ladybird	1934-1949	900.00	1000.00

	Date	Price Range	
HN 1639			
☐ Dainty May	1934-1949	400.00	450.00
HN 1640			
☐ Ladybird	1934-1938	900.00	1000.00
HN 1641			
☐ The Little Mother (2nd version)	1934-1949	900.00	1000.00
HN 1642			
☐ Granny's Shawl	1934-1949	400.00	500.00
HN 1643			
☐ Clemency	1934-1938	650.00	750.00
HN 1644			
☐ Herminia	1934-1938	850.00	950.00
HN 1645			
☐ Aileen	1934-1938	750.00	850.00
HN 1646			
☐ Herminia	1934-1938	900.00	1000.00
HN 1647			
☐ Granny's Shawl	1934-1949	350.00	400.00
HN 1648			
☐ Camille	1934-1949	600.00	675.00
HN 1649			
☐ Sweet and Twenty (1st version)	1934-1949	450.00	500.00
HN 1650			
☐ Veronica (1st version)	1934-1949	500.00	550.00
HN 1651			
☐ Charmain	1934-1938	700.00	800.00
HN 1652			
☐ Janet (1st version)	1934-1949	300.00	350.00
HN 1653			
☐ Margot.......................	1934-1938	700.00	800.00
HN 1654			
☐ Rose.........................	1934-1938	250.00	300.00
HN 1655			
☐ Marie (2nd version)	1934-1938	250.00	300.00
HN 1656			
☐ Dainty May	1934-1949	300.00	350.00
HN 1657			
☐ The Moor	1934-1949	1500.00	1750.00
HN 1658 - HN 1661 WALL MASKS			
HN 1662			
☐ Delicia	1934-1938	550.00	650.00
HN 1663			
☐ Delicia	1934-1938	550.00	650.00
HN 1664			
☐ Aileen	1934-1938	850.00	950.00
HN 1665			
☐ Miss Winsome	1934-1949	600.00	700.00
HN 1666			
☐ Miss Winsome	1934-1938	650.00	750.00

HN 1667	Date	Price Range	
☐ Blossom	1934-1949	700.00	800.00
HN 1668			
☐ Sibell	1934-1949	600.00	700.00
HN 1669			
☐ Anthea......................	1934-1938	600.00	700.00
HN 1670			
☐ Gillian	1934-1949	700.00	800.00
HN 1671 - HN 1676 WALL MASKS			
HN 1677			
☐ Tinkle Bell	1935-	75.00	
HN 1678			
☐ Dinky Doo	1934-	65.00	
HN 1679			
☐ Babie	1935-	75.00	
HN 1680			
☐ Tottles	1935-1975	110.00	150.00
HN 1681			
☐ Delicia	1935-1938	600.00	700.00
HN 1682			
☐ Teresa	1935-1949	800.00	900.00
HN 1683			
☐ Teresa	1935-1938	900.00	1000.00
HN 1684			
☐ Lisette	1935-1938	900.00	1000.00
HN 1685			
☐ Cynthia	1935-1949	500.00	600.00
HN 1686			
☐ Cynthia	1935-1949	500.00	600.00
HN 1687			
☐ Clarissa (1st version)	1935-1949	675.00	750.00
HN 1688			
☐ Rhoda	1935-1949	550.00	650.00
HN 1689			
☐ Calumet......................	1935-1949	875.00	975.00
HN 1690			
☐ June.........................	1935-1949	450.00	500.00
HN 1691			
☐ June.........................	1935-1949	350.00	400.00
HN 1692			
☐ Sonia	1935-1949	650.00	750.00
HN 1693			
☐ Virginia	1935-1949	650.00	750.00
HN 1694			
☐ Virginia	1935-1949	650.00	750.00
HN 1695			
☐ Sibell	1935-1949	600.00	700.00
HN 1696			
☐ Suzette	1935-1949	400.00	450.00

	Date	Price Range	
HN 1697			
☐ Irene........................	1935-1949	500.00	575.00
HN 1698			
☐ Phyllis	1935-1949	750.00	850.00
HN 1699			
☐ Marietta.....................	1935-1949	900.00	1000.00
HN 1700			
☐ Gloria.......................	1935-1938	1000.00	1100.00
HN 1701			
☐ Sweet Anne..................	1935-1938	300.00	400.00
HN 1702			
☐ A Jester (1st version)	1935-1949	900.00	1000.00
HN 1703			
☐ Charley's Aunt (3rd version)	1935-1938	800.00	900.00
HN 1704			
☐ Herminia	1935-1938	850.00	950.00
HN 1705			
☐ The Cobbler (3rd version)..........	1935-1949	550.00	600.00
HN 1706			
☐ The Cobbler (3rd version)..........	1935-1949	275.00	325.00
HN 1707			
☐ Paisley Shawl (1st version)	1935-1949	525.00	575.00
HN 1708			
☐ The Bather (1st version)	1935-1938	1250.00	1450.00
HN 1709			
☐ Pantalettes	1935-1938	500.00	600.00
HN 1710			
☐ Camilla	1935-1949	700.00	800.00
HN 1711			
☐ Camilla	1935-1949	700.00	800.00
HN 1712			
☐ Daffy Down Dilly................	1935-1975	275.00	325.00
HN 1713			
☐ Daffy Down Dilly................	1935-1949	475.00	525.00
HN 1714			
☐ Millicent	1935-1949	1050.00	1150.00
HN 1715			
☐ Millicent	1935-1949	1050.00	1150.00
HN 1716			
☐ Diana.......................	1935-1949	300.00	375.00
HN 1717			
☐ Diana.......................	1935-1949	300.00	375.00
HN 1718			
☐ Kate Hardcastle	1935-1949	600.00	650.00
HN 1719			
☐ Kate Hardcastle	1935-1949	650.00	700.00
HN 1720			
☐ Frangcon....................	1935-1949	650.00	750.00
HN 1721			
☐ Frangcon....................	1935-1949	650.00	750.00

	Date	Price Range	
HN 1722			
☐ The Coming of Spring	1935-1949	1250.00	1400.00
HN 1723			
☐ The Coming of Spring	1935-1949	1250.00	1400.00
HN 1724			
☐ Ruby	1935-1949	300.00	350.00
HN 1725			
☐ Ruby	1935-1949	300.00	350.00
HN 1726			
☐ Celia	1935-1949	750.00	850.00
HN 1727			
☐ Celia	1935-1949	750.00	850.00
HN 1728			
☐ The New Bonnet	1935-1949	525.00	575.00
HN 1729			
☐ Vera	1935-1938	500.00	600.00
HN 1730			
☐ Vera	1935-1938	500.00	600.00
HN 1731			
☐ Daydreams	1935-	155.00	
HN 1732			
☐ Daydreams	1935-1949	275.00	325.00
HN 1733 WALL MASK			
HN 1734			
☐ Kate Hardcastle	1935-1949	650.00	750.00
HN 1735			
☐ Sibell	1935-1949	800.00	850.00
HN 1736			
☐ Camille	1935-1949	700.00	800.00
HN 1737			
☐ Janet (1st version)	1935-1949	300.00	350.00
HN 1738			
☐ Sonia	1938-1949	750.00	850.00
HN 1739			
☐ Paisley Shawl (1st version)	1935-1949	400.00	450.00
HN 1740			
☐ Gladys	1935-1949	550.00	600.00
HN 1741			
☐ Gladys	1935-1938	575.00	625.00
HN 1742			
☐ Sir Walter Raleigh	1935-1949	700.00	800.00
HN 1743			
☐ Mirabel	1935-1949	750.00	850.00
HN 1744			
☐ Mirabel	1935-1949	750.00	850.00
HN 1745			
☐ The Rustic Swain	1935-1949	1750.00	2250.00
HN 1746			
☐ The Rustic Swain	1935-1949	1850.00	2350.00

	Date	Price Range	
HN 1747			
☐ Afternoon Tea...................	1935-	**325.00**	
HN 1748			
☐ Afternoon Tea...................	1935-1949	**450.00**	**550.00**
HN 1749			
☐ Pierrette (3rd version).............	1936-1949	**1000.00**	**1100.00**
HN 1750			
☐ Folly.........................	1936-1949	**1100.00**	**1250.00**
HN 1751			
☐ Sir Walter Raleigh	1936-1949	**1000.00**	**1100.00**
HN 1752			
☐ Regency	1936-1949	**600.00**	**700.00**
HN 1753			
☐ Eleanore	1936-1949	**700.00**	**850.00**
HN 1754			
☐ Eleanore	1936-1949	**700.00**	**850.00**
HN 1755			
☐ The Court Shoemaker	1936-1949	**1500.00**	**1700.00**
HN 1756			
☐ Lizana	1936-1949	**650.00**	**750.00**
HN 1757			
☐ Romany Sue	1936-1949	**650.00**	**750.00**
HN 1758			
☐ Romany Sue	1936-1949	**650.00**	**750.00**
HN 1759			
☐ The Orange Lady	1936-1975	**225.00**	**275.00**
HN 1760			
☐ 4 o'Clock	1936-1949	**475.00**	**575.00**
HN 1761			
☐ Lizana	1936-1938	**650.00**	**750.00**
HN 1762			
☐ The Bride (1st version)	1936-1949	**700.00**	**800.00**
HN 1763			
☐ Windflower (1st version)	1936-1949	**350.00**	**400.00**
HN 1764			
☐ Windflower (1st version)	1936-1949	**425.00**	**475.00**
HN 1765			
☐ Chloe.........................	1936-1950	**275.00**	**325.00**
HN 1766			
☐ Nana	1936-1949	**275.00**	**325.00**
HN 1767			
☐ Nana	1936-1949	**275.00**	**325.00**
HN 1768			
☐ Ivy...........................	1936-1949	**50.00**	**75.00**
HN 1769			
☐ Ivy...........................	1936-1938	**350.00**	**400.00**
HN 1770			
☐ Maureen	1936-1959	**350.00**	**400.00**
HN 1771			
☐ Maureen	1936-1949	**675.00**	**750.00**

	Date	Price Range	
HN 1772			
☐ Delight........................	1936-1967	**200.00**	**250.00**
HN 1773			
☐ Delight........................	1936-1949	**425.00**	**475.00**
HN 1774			
☐ Spring (2nd version) (Limited Edition, Figurines)......................	1933-	**2500.00**	**3000.00**
HN 1775			
☐ Salome (Limited Editon, Figurines)...	1933-	**4500.00**	**5000.00**
HN 1776			
☐ West Wind (Limited Edition, Figurines).	1933-	**4500.00**	**5000.00**
HN 1777			
☐ Spirit of the Wind (Limited Edition, Miscellaneous)	1933-	**3500.00**	**4000.00**
HN 1778			
☐ Beethoven (Limited Edition, Figurines).	1933-	**6000.00**	**6500.00**
HN 1779			
☐ BIRD MODEL (Macaw by R. Garbe)			
HN 1780			
☐ Lady of the Snows (withdrawn date not available)	1933-	**3500.00**	**4000.00**
HN 1781 · HN 1786 WALL MASKS			
HN 1787 · HN 1790 NO DETAILS AVAILABLE			
HN 1791			
☐ Old Balloon Seller and Bulldog......	1932-1938	**1250.00**	**1500.00**
HN 1792			
☐ Henry VIII (2nd version) (Limited Edition, Figurines).	1933-	**1750.00**	**2000.00**
HN 1793			
☐ This Little Pig	1936-	**75.00**	
HN 1794			
☐ This Little Pig	1936-1949	**300.00**	**350.00**
HN 1795			
☐ M'Lady's Maid	1936-1949	**1150.00**	**1300.00**
HN 1796			
☐ Hazel	1936-1949	**350.00**	**400.00**
HN 1797			
☐ Hazel	1936-1949	**300.00**	**350.00**
HN 1798			
☐ Lily.............................	1936-1949	**100.00**	**135.00**
HN 1799			
☐ Lily.............................	1936-1949	**100.00**	**135.00**
HN 1800			
☐ St. George (1st version)	1934-1950	**3000.00**	**3500.00**
HN 1801			
☐ An Old King....................	1937-1954	**950.00**	**1150.00**
HN 1802			
☐ Estelle	1937-1949	**700.00**	**800.00**

	Date	Price Range	
HN 1803			
□ Aileen	1937-1949	700.00	800.00
HN 1804			
□ Granny.........................	1937-1949	850.00	950.00
HN 1805			
□ To Bed	1937-1959	150.00	200.00
HN 1806			
□ To Bed	1937-1949	150.00	200.00
HN 1807			
□ Spring Flowers	1937-1959	325.00	375.00
HN 1808			
□ Cissie	1937-1951	225.00	275.00
HN 1809			
□ Cissie	1937-	100.00	
HN 1810			
□ Bo-Peep (2nd version)	1937-1949	250.00	300.00
HN 1811			
□ Bo-Peep (2nd version)	1937-	100.00	
HN 1812			
□ Forget-me-not	1937-1949	550.00	650.00
HN 1813			
□ Forget-me-not	1937-1949	550.00	650.00
HN 1814			
□ The Squire	1937-1949	2100.00	2600.00
HN 1815			
□ The Huntsman (2nd version)	1937-1949	2300.00	2500.00
HN 1816 - HN 1817 WALL MASKS			
HN 1818			
□ Miranda.........................	1937-1949	750.00	850.00
HN 1819			
□ Miranda.........................	1937-1949	750.00	850.00
HN 1820			
□ Reflections	1937-1938	1000.00	1100.00
HN 1821			
□ Reflections	1937-1938	1000.00	1100.00
HN 1822			
□ M'Lady's Maid	1937-1949	1150.00	1300.00
HN 1823 - HN 1824 WALL MASKS			
HN 1825			
□ Spirit of the Wind	1937-1949	3500.00	4000.00
HN 1826			
□ West Wind......................	1937-1949	4500.00	5000.00
HN 1827			
□ Spring (2nd version)	1937-1949	2500.00	3000.00
HN 1828			
□ Salome	1937-1949	4500.00	5000.00
HN 1829			
□ BIRD MODEL (Macaw)			
HN 1830			
□ Lady of the Snows	1937-1949	3500.00	4000.00

	Date	Price Range	
HN 1831			
☐ The Cloud	1937-1949	4000.00	4500.00
HN 1832			
☐ Granny.........................	1937-1949	850.00	950.00
HN 1833			
☐ Top o' the Hill	1937-1971	175.00	225.00
HN 1834			
☐ Top o' the Hill	1937-	170.00	
HN 1835			
☐ Verena........................	1938-1949	750.00	850.00
HN 1836			
☐ Vanessa	1938-1949	600.00	700.00
HN 1837			
☐ Mariquita......................	1938-1949	1400.00	1750.00
HN 1838			
☐ Vanessa	1938-1949	600.00	700.00
HN 1839			
☐ Christine (1st version)	1938-1949	650.00	750.00
HN 1840			
☐ Christine (1st version)	1938-1949	650.00	750.00
HN 1841			
☐ The Bride (1st version)	1938-1949	800.00	900.00
HN 1842			
☐ Babie.........................	1938-1949	150.00	200.00
HN 1843			
☐ Biddy Penny Farthing	1938-	175.00	
HN 1844			
☐ Odds and Ends	1938-1949	800.00	900.00
HN 1845			
☐ Modena	1938-1949	750.00	850.00
HN 1846			
☐ Modena	1938-1949	750.00	850.00
HN 1847			
☐ Reflections	1938-1949	1000.00	1100.00
HN 1848			
☐ Reflections	1938-1949	1000.00	1100.00
HN 1849			
☐ Top o' the Hill	1938-1975	225.00	275.00
HN 1850			
☐ Antoinette (1st version)	1938-1949	800.00	900.00
HN 1851			
☐ Antoinette (1st version)	1938-1949	800.00	900.00
HN 1852			
☐ The Mirror	1938-1949	800.00	1000.00
HN 1853			
☐ The Mirror	1938-1949	800.00	1000.00
HN 1854			
☐ Verena........................	1938-1949	750.00	850.00
HN 1855			
☐ Memories	1938-1949	450.00	500.00

	Date	Price Range	
HN 1856			
☐ Memories	1938-1949	450.00	500.00
HN 1857			
☐ Memories	1938-1949	450.00	500.00
HN 1858			
☐ Dawn	1938-1949	1350.00	1500.00
HN 1859			
☐ Tildy..........................	1938-1949	800.00	900.00
HN 1860			
☐ Millicent	1938-1949	1050.00	1150.00
HN 1861			
☐ Kate Hardcastle	1938-1949	600.00	700.00
HN 1862			
☐ Jasmine.......................	1938-1949	625.00	675.00
HN 1863			
☐ Jasmine.......................	1938-1949	625.00	675.00
HN 1864			
☐ Sweet and Fair	1938-1949	650.00	700.00
HN 1865			
☐ Sweet and Fair	1938-1949	650.00	700.00
HN 1866			
☐ Wedding Morn	1938-1949	1200.00	1300.00
HN 1867			
☐ Wedding Morn	1938-1949	1200.00	1300.00
HN 1868			
☐ Serena	1938-1949	1100.00	1200.00
HN 1869			
☐ Dryad of the Pines	1938-1949	2750.00	3000.00
HN 1870			
☐ Little Lady Make Believe	1938-1949	500.00	550.00
HN 1871			
☐ Annabella	1938-1949	450.00	525.00
HN 1872			
☐ Annabella	1938-1949	450.00	525.00
HN 1873			
☐ Granny's Heritage	1938-1949	450.00	500.00
HN 1874			
☐ Granny's Heritage	1938-1949	450.00	500.00
HN 1875			
☐ Annabella	1938-1949	450.00	525.00
HN 1876			
☐ Jasmine.......................	1938-1949	650.00	700.00
HN 1877			
☐ Jean..........................	1938-1949	475.00	525.00
HN 1878			
☐ Jean..........................	1938-1949	375.00	450.00
HN 1879			
☐ Bon Jour	1938-1949	650.00	750.00
HN 1880			
☐ The Lambeth Walk	1938-1949	1300.00	1400.00

	Date	Price Range	
HN 1881			
☐ The Lambeth Walk	1938-1949	**1300.00**	**1400.00**
HN 1882			
☐ Nell Gwynn	1938-1949	**600.00**	**700.00**
HN 1883			
☐ Prudence.......................	1938-1949	**750.00**	**800.00**
HN 1884			
☐ Prudence.......................	1938-1949	**750.00**	**800.00**
HN 1885			
☐ Nadine........................	1938-1949	**650.00**	**750.00**
HN 1886			
☐ Nadine........................	1938-1949	**650.00**	**750.00**
HN 1887			
☐ Nell Gwynn	1938-1949	**600.00**	**700.00**
HN 1888			
☐ Bon Jour	1938-1949	**600.00**	**700.00**
HN 1889			
☐ Goody Two Shoes	1938-1949	**250.00**	**300.00**
HN 1890			
☐ Lambing Time...................	1938-1980	**150.00**	**200.00**
HN 1891			
☐ Pecksniff (2nd version)	1938-1952	**400.00**	**450.00**
HN 1892			
☐ Uriah Heep (2nd version)	1938-1952	**275.00**	**325.00**
HN 1893			
☐ Fat Boy (2nd version)	1938-1952	**325.00**	**375.00**
HN 1894			
☐ Mr. Pickwick (2nd version)	1938-1952	**400.00**	**450.00**
HN 1895			
☐ Mr. Micawber (2nd version)	1938-1952	**400.00**	**450.00**
HN 1896			
☐ Sairey Gamp (2nd version)	1938-1952	**325.00**	**375.00**
HN 1897			
☐ Miss Fortune....................	1938-1949	**400.00**	**450.00**
HN 1898			
☐ Miss Fortune....................	1938-1949	**400.00**	**450.00**
HN 1899			
☐ Midsummer Noon.................	1939-1949	**550.00**	**600.00**
HN 1900			
☐ Midsummer Noon.................	1939-1949	**550.00**	**600.00**
HN 1901			
☐ Penelope.......................	1939-1975	**350.00**	**400.00**
HN 1902			
☐ Penelope.......................	1939-1949	**550.00**	**600.00**
HN 1903			
☐ Rhythm	1939-1949	**1000.00**	**1100.00**
HN 1904			
☐ Rhythm	1939-1949	**1000.00**	**1100.00**
HN 1905			
☐ Goody Two Shoes	1939-1949	**225.00**	**275.00**

HN 1906	Date	Price Range	
☐ Lydia	1939-1949	300.00	350.00
HN 1907			
☐ Lydia	1939-1949	300.00	350.00
HN 1908			
☐ Lydia	1939-	125.00	
HN 1909			
☐ Honey	1939-1949	350.00	400.00
HN 1910			
☐ Honey	1939-1949	375.00	450.00
HN 1911			
☐ Autumn Breezes	1939-1976	200.00	250.00
HN 1912			
☐ Old Balloon Seller and Bulldog	1939-1949	1350.00	1500.00
HN 1913			
☐ Autumn Breezes	1939-1971	250.00	300.00
HN 1914			
☐ Paisley Shawl (2nd version)	1939-1949	300.00	350.00
HN 1915			
☐ Veronica (2nd version)	1939-1949	400.00	450.00
HN 1916			
☐ Janet (2nd version)	1939-1949	350.00	400.00
HN 1917			
☐ Meryll	1939-1949	1200.00	1350.00
HN 1918			
☐ Sweet Suzy	1939-1949	650.00	750.00
HN 1919			
☐ Kate Hardcastle	1939-1949	800.00	900.00
HN 1920			
☐ Windflower (2nd version)	1939-1949	500.00	550.00
HN 1921			
☐ Roseanna	1940-1949	400.00	450.00
HN 1922			
☐ Spring Morning	1940-1973	225.00	275.00
HN 1923			
☐ Spring Morning	1940-1949	300.00	350.00
HN 1924			
☐ Fiona (1st version)	1940-1949	550.00	650.00
HN 1925			
☐ Fiona (1st version)	1940-1949	550.00	650.00
HN 1926			
☐ Roseanna	1940-1959	300.00	350.00
HN 1927			
☐ The Awakening	1940-1949	2050.00	2200.00
HN 1928			
☐ Marguerite	1940-1959	325.00	375.00
HN 1929			
☐ Marguerite	1940-1949	500.00	600.00
HN 1930			
☐ Marguerite	1940-1949	550.00	650.00

	Date	Price Range	
HN 1931			
☐ Meriel.........................	1940-1949	850.00	950.00
HN 1932			
☐ Meriel.........................	1940-1949	850.00	950.00
HN 1933			
☐ Fiona (1st version)	1940-1949	650.00	750.00
HN 1934			
☐ Autumn Breeezes	1940-	170.00	
HN 1935			
☐ Sweeting	1940-1973	200.00	250.00
HN 1936			
☐ Miss Muffet	1940-1967	150.00	200.00
HN 1937			
☐ Miss Muffet	1940-1952	300.00	350.00
HN 1938			
☐ Sweeting	1940-1949	325.00	375.00
HN 1939			
☐ Windflower (2nd version)	1940-1949	500.00	550.00
HN 1940			
☐ Toinette.......................	1940-1949	1450.00	1750.00
HN 1941			
☐ Peggy.........................	1940-1949	150.00	200.00
HN 1942			
☐ Pyjams........................	1940-1949	325.00	375.00
HN 1943			
☐ Veronica	1940-1949	400.00	450.00
HN 1944			
☐ Daydreams	1940-1949	350.00	400.00
HN 1945			
☐ Spring Flowers	1940-1949	500.00	550.00
HN 1946			
☐ Marguerite	1940-1949	400.00	500.00
HN 1947			
☐ June..........................	1940-1949	450.00	500.00
HN 1948			
☐ Lady Charmain	1940-1973	250.00	300.00
HN 1949			
☐ Lady Charmain	1940-1975	250.00	300.00
HN 1950			
☐ Claribel	1940-1949	350.00	400.00
HN 1951			
☐ Claribel	1940-1949	325.00	375.00
HN 1952			
☐ Irene..........................	1940-1950	550.00	600.00
HN 1953			
☐ Orange Lady	1940-1975	200.00	250.00
HN 1954			
☐ The Balloon Man	1940-	185.00	
HN 1955			
☐ Lavinia........................	1940-1979	100.00	150.00

HN 1956	Date	Price Range	
☐ Chloe.........................	1940-1949	425.00	475.00
HN 1957			
☐ The New Bonnet.................	1940-1949	500.00	550.00
HN 1958			
☐ Lady April	1940-1959	300.00	350.00
HN 1959			
☐ The Choice	1941-1949	850.00	950.00
HN 1960			
☐ The Choice	1941-1949	850.00	950.00
HN 1961			
☐ Daisy	1941-1949	275.00	325.00
HN 1962			
☐ Genevieve	1941-1975	200.00	250.00
HN 1963			
☐ Honey	1941-1949	400.00	450.00
HN 1964			
☐ Janet (2nd version)	1941-1949	350.00	400.00
HN 1965			
☐ Lady April	1941-1949	500.00	600.00
HN 1966			
☐ Orange Vendor	1941-1949	700.00	800.00
HN 1967			
☐ Lady Betty	1941-1951	325.00	375.00
HN 1968			
☐ Madonna of the Square	1941-1949	850.00	950.00
HN 1969			
☐ Madonna of the Square	1941-1949	850.00	950.00
HN 1970			
☐ Milady	1941-1949	900.00	950.00
HN 1971			
☐ Springtime	1941-1949	900.00	950.00
HN 1972			
☐ Regency Beau...................	1941-1949	850.00	950.00
HN 1973			
☐ The Corinthian	1941-1949	950.00	1050.00
HN 1974			
☐ Forty Winks....................	1945-1973	250.00	300.00
HN 1975			
☐ The Shepherd (4th version)	1945-1975	150.00	200.00
HN 1976			
☐ Easter Day.....................	1945-1951	425.00	475.00
HN 1977			
☐ Her Ladyship	1945-1959	325.00	375.00
HN 1978			
☐ Bedtime.......................	1945-	55.00	
HN 1979			
☐ Gollywog......................	1945-1959	300.00	350.00

	Date	Price Range	
HN 1980			
☐ Gwynneth	1945-1952	**300.00**	**350.00**
HN 1981			
☐ The Ermine Coat..................	1945-1967	**300.00**	**350.00**
HN 1982			
☐ Sabbath Morn	1945-1959	**300.00**	**350.00**
HN 1983			
☐ Rosebud (2nd version)	1945-1952	**450.00**	**500.00**
HN 1984			
☐ The Patchwork Quilt	1945-1959	**450.00**	**500.00**
HN 1985			
☐ Darling (2nd version)	1946-	**55.00**	
HN 1986			
☐ Diana	1946-1975	**125.00**	**175.00**
HN 1987			
☐ Paisley Shawl (1st version)	1946-1959	**250.00**	**300.00**
HN 1988			
☐ Paisley Shawl (2nd version)	1946-1975	**225.00**	**275.00**
HN 1989			
☐ Margaret	1947-1959	**350.00**	**400.00**
HN 1990			
☐ Mary Jane	1947-1959	**375.00**	**425.00**
HN 1991			
☐ Market Day (Country Lass)	1947-1955	**275.00**	**325.00**
HN 1991			
☐ Country Lass	1975-1981	**125.00**	**175.00**
HN 1992			
☐ Christmas Morn	1947-	**155.00**	
HN 1993			
☐ Griselda.......................	1947-1953	**500.00**	**600.00**
HN 1994			
☐ Karen	1947-1955	**350.00**	**400.00**
HN 1995			
☐ Olivia	1947-1951	**425.00**	**475.00**
HN 1996			
☐ Prue	1947-1955	**325.00**	**375.00**
HN 1997			
☐ Belle o' the Ball..................	1947-1979	**275.00**	**325.00**
HN 1998			
☐ Collinette	1947-1949	**450.00**	**500.00**
HN 1999			
☐ Collinette	1947-1949	**425.00**	**475.00**
HN 2000			
☐ Jacqueline	1947-1951	**400.00**	**450.00**
HN 2001			
☐ Jacqueline	1947-1951	**425.00**	**475.00**
HN 2002			
☐ Bess..........................	1947-1969	**275.00**	**325.00**
HN 2003			
☐ Bess..........................	1947-1950	**400.00**	**500.00**

	Date	Price	Range
HN 2004			
☐ A'Courting......................	1947-1953	650.00	750.00
HN 2005			
☐ Henrietta Maria	1948-1953	600.00	700.00
HN 2006			
☐ The Lady Anne Nevill	1948-1953	800.00	900.00
HN 2007			
☐ Mrs. Fitzherbert	1948-1953	700.00	800.00
HN 2008			
☐ Philippa of Hainault..............	1948-1953	650.00	725.00
HN 2009			
☐ Eleanor of Provence..............	1948-1953	600.00	700.00
HN 2010			
☐ The Young Miss Nightingale........	1948-1953	700.00	800.00
HN 2011			
☐ Matilda	1948-1953	600.00	700.00
HN 2012			
☐ Margaret of Anjou	1948-1953	700.00	800.00
HN 2013			
☐ Angelina	1948-1951	700.00	800.00
HN 2014			
☐ Jane...........................	1948-1951	600.00	700.00
HN 2015			
☐ Sir Walter Raleigh	1948-1955	750.00	800.00
HN 2016			
☐ A Jester (1st version)	1949-	200.00	
HN 2017			
☐ Silks and Ribbons	1949-	150.00	
HN 2018			
☐ Parson's Daughter	1949-1953	350.00	400.00
HN 2019			
☐ Minuet.........................	1949-1971	300.00	350.00
HN 2020			
☐ Deidre	1949-1955	350.00	400.00
HN 2021			
☐ Blithe Morning	1949-1971	250.00	300.00
HN 2022			
☐ Janice	1949-1955	450.00	500.00
HN 2023			
☐ Joan...........................	1949-1959	350.00	400.00
HN 2024			
☐ Darby..........................	1949-1959	350.00	400.00
HN 2025			
☐ Gossips........................	1949-1967	350.00	400.00
HN 2026			
☐ Suzette	1949-1959	325.00	375.00
HN 2027			
☐ June...........................	1949-1952	325.00	375.00
HN 2028			
☐ Kate Hardcastle	1949-1952	650.00	750.00

	Date	Price Range	
HN 2029			
☐ Windflower (1st version)	1949-1952	400.00	450.00
HN 2030			
☐ Memories	1949-1959	400.00	450.00
HN 2031			
☐ Granny's Heritage	1949-1969	400.00	450.00
HN 2032			
☐ Jean.........................	1949-1959	325.00	375.00
HN 2033			
☐ Midsummer Noon................	1949-1955	475.00	525.00
HN 2034			
☐ Madonna of the Square	1949-1951	800.00	900.00
HN 2035			
☐ Pearly Boy (2nd version)	1949-1959	225.00	250.00
HN 2036			
☐ Pearly Girl (2nd version)...........	1949-1959	225.00	250.00
HN 2037			
☐ Goody Two Shoes	1949-	100.00	
HN 2038			
☐ Peggy........................	1949-1979	75.00	125.00
HN 2039			
☐ Easter Day....................	1949-1969	275.00	325.00
HN 2040			
☐ Gollywog.....................	1949-1959	225.00	275.00
HN 2041			
☐ The Broken Lance	1949-1975	500.00	600.00
HN 2042			
☐ Owd Willum...................	1949-1973	275.00	325.00
HN 2043			
☐ The Poacher	1949-1959	325.00	375.00
HN 2044			
☐ Mary Mary	1949-1973	125.00	175.00
HN 2045			
☐ She Loves Me Not	1949-1962	150.00	200.00
HN 2046			
☐ He Loves Me	1949-1962	175.00	225.00
HN 2047			
☐ Once Upon a Time	1949-1955	200.00	250.00
HN 2048			
☐ Mary Had a Little Lamb	1949-	100.00	
HN 2049			
☐ Curly Locks...................	1949-1953	250.00	300.00
HN 2050			
☐ Wee Willie Winkie	1949-1953	225.00	250.00
HN 2051			
☐ St. George (2nd version)...........	1950-	475.00	
HN 2052			
☐ Grandma	1950-1959	325.00	400.00
HN 2053			
☐ The Gaffer....................	1950-1959	350.00	400.00

	Date	Price Range	
HN 2054			
☐ Falstaff (2nd version)	1950-	**150.00**	
HN 2055			
☐ The Leisure Hour	1950-1965	**500.00**	**600.00**
HN 2056			
☐ Susan	1950-1959	**275.00**	**350.00**
HN 2057			
☐ The Jersey Milkmaid	1950-1959	**325.00**	**375.00**
HN 2057			
☐ The Milkmaid	1975-1981	**135.00**	**185.00**
HN 2058			
☐ Hermione	1950-1952	**600.00**	**700.00**
HN 2059			
☐ The Bedtime Story	1950-	**215.00**	
HN 2060			
☐ Jack..........................	1950-1971	**125.00**	**175.00**
HN 2061			
☐ Jill	1950-1971	**150.00**	**200.00**
HN 2062			
☐ Little Boy Blue	1950-1973	**150.00**	**200.00**
HN 2063			
☐ Little Jack Horner...............	1950-1953	**225.00**	**275.00**
HN 2064			
☐ My Pretty Maid	1950-1954	**250.00**	**300.00**
HN 2065			
☐ Blithe Morning	1950-1973	**225.00**	**250.00**
HN 2066			
☐ Minuet.......................	1950-1955	**250.00**	**300.00**
HN 2067			
☐ St. George (1st version)	1950-1976	**3750.00**	**4500.00**
HN 2068			
☐ Calumet......................	1950-1953	**625.00**	**725.00**
HN 2069			
☐ Farmer's Wife	1951-1955	**500.00**	**600.00**
HN 2070			
☐ Bridget.......................	1951-1973	**300.00**	**350.00**
HN 2071			
☐ Bernice	1951-1953	**600.00**	**700.00**
HN 2072			
☐ The Rocking Horse...............	1951-1953	**1450.00**	**1750.00**
HN 2073			
☐ Vivienne......................	1951-1967	**300.00**	**350.00**
HN 2074			
☐ Marianne.....................	1951-1953	**475.00**	**550.00**
HN 2075			
☐ French Peasant	1951-1955	**600.00**	**700.00**
HN 2076			
☐ Promenade	1951-1953	**1150.00**	**1350.00**
HN 2077			
☐ Rowena	1951-1955	**550.00**	**650.00**

	Date	Price Range	
HN 2078			
☐ Elfreda.........................	1951-1955	600.00	700.00
HN 2079			
☐ Damaris.......................	1951-1952	800.00	950.00
HN 2080			
☐ Jack Point (Prestige Series)	1952-	1500.00	
HN 2081			
☐ Princess Badoura (Prestige Series) ..	1952-	14000.00	15000.00
HN 2082			
☐ The Moor (Prestige Series)	1952-	1450.00	
HN 2083 NO DETAILS AVAILABLE			
HN 2084			
☐ King Charles I (Prestige Series)	1952-	1500.00	
HN 2085			
☐ Spring (3rd version)	1952-1959	450.00	500.00
HN 2086			
☐ Summer (2nd version)	1952-1959	450.00	500.00
HN 2087			
☐ Autumn (2nd version)	1952-1959	450.00	500.00
HN 2088			
☐ Winter (2nd version)	1952-1959	450.00	500.00
HN 2089			
☐ Judith	1952-1959	300.00	350.00
HN 2090			
☐ Midinette (2nd version)	1952-1965	250.00	300.00
HN 2091			
☐ Rosemary	1952-1959	450.00	500.00
HN 2092			
☐ Sweet Maid (2nd version)..........	1952-1955	450.00	500.00
HN 2093			
☐ Georgiana	1952-1955	600.00	700.00
HN 2094			
☐ Uncle Ned	1952-1965	400.00	450.00
HN 2095			
☐ Ibrahim	1952-1955	800.00	900.00
HN 2096			
☐ The Fat Boy (3rd version)	1952-1967	300.00	350.00
HN 2097			
☐ Mr. Micawber (3rd version)	1952-1967	325.00	375.00
HN 2098			
☐ Pecksniff (3rd version)	1952-1967	300.00	350.00
HN 2099			
☐ Mr. Pickwick (3rd version)	1952-1967	325.00	375.00
HN 2100			
☐ Saiey Gamp (3rd version)..........	1952-1967	275.00	325.00
HN 2101			
☐ Uriah Heep (3rd version)	1952-1967	300.00	350.00
HN 2102			
☐ Pied Piper	1953-1976	250.00	300.00

	Date	Price Range	
HN 2103			
☐ Mask Seller	1953-	**175.00**	
HN 2104			
☐ Abdullah	1953-1962	**700.00**	**800.00**
HN 2105			
☐ Bluebeard (2nd version)	1953-	**375.00**	
HN 2106			
☐ Linda	1953-1976	**120.00**	**150.00**
HN 2107			
☐ Valerie	1953-	**100.00**	
HN 2108			
☐ Baby Bunting	1953-1959	**225.00**	**275.00**
HN 2109			
☐ Wendy	1953-	**75.00**	
HN 2110			
☐ Christmas Time	1953-1967	**350.00**	**400.00**
HN 2111			
☐ Betsy	1953-1959	**350.00**	**400.00**
HN 2112			
☐ Carolyn	1953-1965	**350.00**	**400.00**
HN 2113			
☐ Maytime	1953-1967	**325.00**	**375.00**
HN 2114			
☐ Sleepyhead	1953-1955	**800.00**	**900.00**
HN 2115			
☐ Coppelia	1953-1959	**525.00**	**600.00**
HN 2116			
☐ Ballerina	1953-1973	**300.00**	**350.00**
HN 2117			
☐ The Skater	1953-1971	**350.00**	**400.00**
HN 2118			
☐ Good King Wenceslas	1953-1976	**275.00**	**350.00**
HN 2119			
☐ Town Crier	1953-1976	**250.00**	**300.00**
HN 2120			
☐ Dinky Do	1983-	**65.00**	
HN 2121			
☐ Babie	1983-	**75.00**	
HN 2122			
☐ Yeoman of the Guard	1954-1959	**650.00**	**750.00**
HN 2123			
☐ Rose	1983-	**65.00**	
HN 2124 · HN 2127 NOT ISSUED			
HN 2128			
☐ River Boy	1962-1975	**150.00**	**200.00**
HN 2129 · HN 2131 NOT ISSUED			
HN 2132			
☐ The Suitor	1962-1971	**400.00**	**475.00**
HN 2133			
☐ Faraway	1958-1962	**350.00**	**400.00**

	Date	Price Range	
HN 2134			
☐ An Old King	1954-	475.00	
HN 2135			
☐ Gay Morning	1954-1967	300.00	350.00
HN 2136			
☐ Delphine	1954-1967	275.00	325.00
HN 2137			
☐.Lilac Time	1954-1969	250.00	300.00
HN 2138			
☐ La Sylphide	1956-1965	425.00	475.00
HN 2139			
☐ Giselle	1954-1969	350.00	400.00
HN 2140			
☐ Giselle, Forest Glade	1954-1965	375.00	475.00
HN 2141			
☐ Choir Boy	1954-1975	75.00	125.00
HN 2142			
☐ Rag Doll	1954-	75.00	
HN 2143			
☐ Friar Tuck	1954-1965	400.00	450.00
HN 2144			
☐ The Jovial Monk	1954-1967	200.00	250.00
HN 2145			
☐ Wardrobe Mistress	1954-1967	475.00	525.00
HN 2146			
☐ The Tinsmith	1962-1967	450.00	500.00
HN 2147			
☐ Autumn Breezes	1955-1971	325.00	375.00
HN 2148			
☐ The Bridesmaid (2nd version)	1955-1959	175.00	225.00
HN 2149			
☐ Love Letter	1958-1976	250.00	300.00
HN 2150			
☐ Willy Won't He	1955-1959	300.00	325.00
HN 2151			
☐ Mother's Help	1962-1969	175.00	225.00
HN 2152			
☐ Adrienne	1964-1976	175.00	225.00
HN 2153			
☐ The One That Got Away	1955-1959	225.00	275.00
HN 2154			
☐ A Child from Williamsburg	1964-	115.00	
HN 2155 NOT ISSUED			
HN 2156			
☐ The Polka	1955-1969	250.00	300.00
HN 2157			
☐ A Gypsy Dance (1st version)	1955-1957	400.00	450.00
HN 2158			
☐ Alice	1960-1980	85.00	115.00

	Date	Price Range	
HN 2159			
☐ Fortune Teller	1955-1967	**425.00**	**475.00**
HN 2160			
☐ The Apple Maid.	1957-1962	**400.00**	**450.00**
HN 2161			
☐ The Hornpipe	1955-1962	**750.00**	**850.00**
HN 2162			
☐ The Foaming Quart	1955-	**165.00**	
HN 2163			
☐ In the Stocks (2nd version)	1955-1959	**650.00**	**700.00**
HN 2164 NOT ISSUED			
HN 2165			
☐ Janice	1955-1965	**450.00**	**500.00**
HN 2166			
☐ The Bride (2nd version)	1956-1976	**225.00**	**275.00**
HN 2167			
☐ Home Again	1956-	**125.00**	
HN 2168			
☐ Esmeralda.	1956-1959	**350.00**	**400.00**
HN 2169			
☐ Dimity	1956-1959	**300.00**	**350.00**
HN 2170			
☐ Invitation.	1956-1975	**100.00**	**150.00**
HN 2171			
☐ The Fiddler	1956-1962	**850.00**	**1000.00**
HN 2172			
☐ Jolly Sailor	1956-1965	**600.00**	**700.00**
HN 2173			
☐ The Organ Grinder	1956-1965	**650.00**	**700.00**
HN 2174			
☐ The Tailer	1956-1959	**650.00**	**750.00**
HN 2175			
☐ The Beggar (2nd version)	1956-1962	**550.00**	**625.00**
HN 2176 NOT ISSUED			
HN 2177			
☐ My Teddy.	1962-1967	**250.00**	**300.00**
HN 2178			
☐ Enchantment	1957-1982	**155.00**	
HN 2179			
☐ Noelle	1957-1967	**350.00**	**400.00**
HN 2180 NOT ISSUED			
HN 2181			
☐ Summer's Day	1957-1962	**375.00**	**450.00**
HN 2182 NOT ISSUED			
HN 2183			
☐ Boy from Williamsburg	1969-	**115.00**	
HN 2184			
☐ Sunday Morning	1963-1969	**265.00**	**325.00**
HN 2185			
☐ Columbine (2nd version)	1957-1969	**225.00**	**275.00**

	Date	Price Range	
HN 2186			
☐ Harlequin	1957-1969	**225.00**	**275.00**
HN 2187 - HN 2190 NOT ISSUED			
HN 2191			
☐ Sea Sprite (2nd version)	1958-1962	**475.00**	**525.00**
HN 2192			
☐ Wood Nymph	1958-1962	**300.00**	**350.00**
HN 2193			
☐ Fair Lady	1963-	**155.00**	
HN 2194 - HN 2195 NOT ISSUED			
HN 2196			
☐ The Bridesmaid (3rd version)........	1960-1976	**100.00**	**125.00**
HN 2197 - HN 2201 NOT ISSUED			
HN 2202			
☐ Melody.........................	1957-1962	**300.00**	**350.00**
HN 2203			
☐ Teenager......................	1957-1962	**275.00**	**325.00**
HN 2204			
☐ Long John Silver.................	1957-1965	**350.00**	**400.00**
HN 2205			
☐ Master Sweep...................	1957-1962	**600.00**	**700.00**
HN 2206			
☐ Sunday Best	1979-	**295.00**	
HN 2207			
☐ Stayed at Home	1958-1969	**150.00**	**200.00**
HN 2208			
☐ Silversmith of Williamsburg	1960-	**200.00**	
HN 2209			
☐ Hostess of Williamsburg...........	1960-	**200.00**	
HN 2210			
☐ Debutante	1963-1967	**375.00**	**425.00**
HN 2211			
☐ Fair Maiden....................	1967-	**195.00**	
HN 2212			
☐ Rendezvous	1962-1971	**350.00**	**400.00**
HN 2213			
☐ Contemplation, white	1983-	**75.00**	
HN 2214			
☐ Bunny	1960-1975	**150.00**	**200.00**
HN 2215			
☐ Sweet April	1965-1967	**325.00**	**400.00**
HN 2216			
☐ Pirouette	1959-1967	**225.00**	**275.00**
HN 2217			
☐ Old King Cole	1963-1967	**750.00**	**850.00**
HN 2218			
☐ Cookie	1958-1975	**150.00**	**200.00**
HN 2219 NOT ISSUED			
HN 2220			
☐ Winsome.......................	1960-	**155.00**	

	Date	Price Range	
HN 2221			
☐ Nanny	1958-	**175.00**	
HN 2222			
☐ Camellia	1960-1971	**250.00**	**300.00**
HN 2223			
☐ Schoolmarm	1958-1980	**150.00**	**200.00**
HN 2224 NOT ISSUED			
HN 2225			
☐ Make Believe	1962-	**100.00**	
HN 2226			
☐ The Cellist	1960-1967	**475.00**	**525.00**
HN 2227			
☐ Gentleman from Williamsburg	1960-	**200.00**	
HN 2228			
☐ Lady from Williamsburg	1960-	**200.00**	
HN 2229			
☐ Southern Belle	1958-	**185.00**	
HN 2230			
☐ A Gypsy Dance (2nd version)........	1959-1971	**250.00**	**300.00**
HN 2231			
☐ Sweet Sixteen...................	1958-1965	**275.00**	**325.00**
HN 2232 NOT ISSUED			
HN 2233			
☐ Royal Governor's Cook	1960-	**200.00**	
HN 2234			
☐ Michelle........................	1967-	**155.00**	
HN 2235			
☐ Dancing Years	1965-1971	**375.00**	**425.00**
HN 2236			
☐ Affection	1962-	**100.00**	
HN 2237			
☐ Celeste	1959-1971	**250.00**	**300.00**
HN 2238			
☐ My Pet	1962-1975	**100.00**	**150.00**
HN 2239			
☐ Wigmaker of Williamsburg	1960-	**200.00**	
HN 2240			
☐ Blacksmith of Williamsburg	1960-	**200.00**	
HN 2241			
☐ Contemplation, black	1983-	**75.00**	
HN 2242			
☐ First Steps	1959-1965	**500.00**	**550.00**
HN 2243			
☐ Treasure Island..................	1962-1975	**150.00**	**200.00**
HN 2244			
☐ Newsboy	1959-1965	**600.00**	**700.00**
HN 2245			
☐ The Basket Weaver	1959-1962	**500.00**	**600.00**
HN 2246			
☐ Cradle Song	1959-1962	**400.00**	**450.00**

	Date	Price Range	
HN 2247			
☐ Omar Khayyam (2nd version)	1965-	**165.00**	
HN 2248			
☐ Tall Story........................	1968-1975	**200.00**	**250.00**
HN 2249			
☐ The Favourite	1960-	**165.00**	
HN 2250			
☐ The Toymaker...................	1959-1973	**425.00**	**475.00**
HN 2251			
☐ Masquerade (2nd version)	1960-1965	**350.00**	**400.00**
HN 2252 NOT ISSUED			
HN 2253			
☐ The Puppetmaker.................	1962-1973	**425.00**	**475.00**
HN 2254			
☐ Shore Leave	1965-1979	**200.00**	**250.00**
HN 2255			
☐ Teatime.........................	1972-	**165.00**	
HN 2256			
☐ Twilight	1971-1976	**200.00**	**250.00**
HN 2257			
☐ Sea Harvest	1969-1976	**150.00**	**200.00**
HN 2258			
☐ A Good Catch	1966-	**165.00**	
HN 2259			
☐ Masquerade (2nd version)	1960-1965	**325.00**	**375.00**
HN 2260			
☐ The Captain (2nd version)	1965-1982	**250.00**	
HN 2261			
☐ Marriage of Art and Industry (Limited Edition, Figurines)	1958-	**7000.00**	**8000.00**
HN 2262			
☐ Lights Out	1965-1969	**225.00**	**275.00**
HN 2263			
☐ Seashore.......................	1961-1965	**250.00**	**300.00**
HN 2264			
☐ Elegance	1961-	**155.00**	
HN 2265			
☐ Sara	1980-	**215.00**	
HN 2266			
☐ Ballad Seller	1968-1973	**300.00**	**350.00**
HN 2267			
☐ Rhapsody	1961-1973	**200.00**	**250.00**
HN 2268			
☐ Daphne	1963-1975	**175.00**	**225.00**
HN 2269			
☐ Leading Lady	1965-1976	**200.00**	**250.00**
HN 2270			
☐ Pillow Fight.....................	1965-1969	**200.00**	**250.00**
HN 2271			
☐ Melanie	1965-1980	**150.00**	**200.00**

	Date	Price Range	
HN 2272			
☐ Repose	1972-1979	150.00	200.00
HN 2273			
☐ Denise	1964-1971	275.00	325.00
HN 2274			
☐ Golden Days	1964-1973	125.00	175.00
HN 2275			
☐ Sandra	1969-	155.00	
HN 2276			
☐ Heart to Heart..................	1961-1971	400.00	500.00
HN 2277 - HN 2278 NOT ISSUED			
HN 2279			
☐ The Clockmaker	1961-1975	300.00	350.00
HN 2280			
☐ The Mayor	1963-1971	450.00	500.00
HN 2281			
☐ The Professor	1965-1980	150.00	200.00
HN 2282			
☐ The Coachman	1963-1971	475.00	550.00
HN 2283			
☐ Dreamweaver	1972-1976	250.00	300.00
HN 2284			
☐ The Craftsman	1961-1965	475.00	525.00
HN 2285 - HN 2286 NOT ISSUED			
HN 2287			
☐ Symphony.....................	1961-1965	350.00	425.00
HN 2288 - HN 2303 NOT ISSUED			
HN 2304			
☐ Adrienne	1964-	155.00	
HN 2305			
☐ Dulcie	1981-	185.00	
HN 2306			
☐ Reverie	1964-1981	250.00	300.00
HN 2307			
☐ Coralie.......................	1964-	155.00	
HN 2308			
☐ Picnic........................	1965-	100.00	
HN 2309			
☐ Buttercup	1964-	145.00	
HN 2310			
☐ Lisa	1969-	170.00	
HN 2311			
☐ Lorna........................	1965-	125.00	
HN 2312			
☐ Soiree	1967-	170.00	
HN 2313 NOT ISSUED			
HN 2314			
☐ Old Mother Hubbard	1964-1975	300.00	350.00
HN 2315			
☐ Last Waltz.....................	1967-	185.00	

	Date	Price Range	
HN 2316 NOT ISSUED			
HN 2317			
☐ The Lobster Man.................	1964-	165.00	
HN 2318			
☐ Grace..........................	1966-1980	125.00	175.00
HN 2319			
☐ The Bachelor...................	1964-1975	250.00	300.00
HN 2320			
☐ Tuppence a Bag	1968-	165.00	
HN 2321			
☐ Family Album	1966-1973	350.00	400.00
HN 2322			
☐ The Cup of Tea	1964-	150.00	
HN 2323 NOT ISSUED			
HN 2324			
☐ Matador and Bull (Prestige Series) ...	1964-	10500.00	
HN 2325			
☐ The Master	1967-	165.00	
HN 2326			
☐ Antoinette (2nd version)...........	1967-1979	150.00	175.00
HN 2327			
☐ Katrina........................	1965-1969	275.00	325.00
HN 2328			
☐ Queen of Sheba	1982-	1250.00	
HN 2329			
☐ Lynne..........................	1971-	170.00	
HN 2330			
☐ Meditation.....................	1971-	250.00	
HN 2331			
☐ Cello (Limited Edition, Lady Musicians)	1970-	750.00	800.00
HN 2332 NOT ISSUED			
HN 2333			
☐ Jacqueline	1983-	145.00	
HN 2334			
☐ Fragrance	1966-	170.00	
HN 2335			
☐ Hilary.........................	1967-1980	150.00	200.00
HN 2336			
☐ Alison	1966-	155.00	
HN 2337			
☐ Loretta........................	1966-1980	100.00	150.00
HN 2338			
☐ Penny.........................	1968-	65.00	
HN 2339			
☐ My Love	1969-	185.00	
HN 2340			
☐ Belle (2nd version)	1968-	65.00	
HN 2341			
☐ Cherie	1966-	100.00	

	Date	Price Range	
HN 2342 NOT ISSUED			
HN 2343			
☐ Premiere	1969-1979	175.00	225.00
HN 2344 NOT ISSUED			
HN 2345			
☐ Clarissa (2nd version)	1968-1981	150.00	200.00
HN 2345			
☐ Clarissa (2nd version)	1968-1981	150.00	200.00
HN 2346			
☐ Kathy (Kate Greenaway)	1981-	100.00	
HN 2347			
☐ Nina	1969-1976	125.00	175.00
HN 2348			
☐ Geraldine	1972-1976	125.00	175.00
HN 2349			
☐ Flora	1966-1973	175.00	225.00
HN 2350 · HN 2351 NOT ISSUED			
HN 2352			
☐ A Stitch In Time	1966-1980	150.00	200.00
HN 2353 · HN 2355 NOT ISSUED			
HN 2356			
☐ Ascot	1968-	185.00	
HN 2357 · HN 2358 NOT ISSUED			
HN 2359			
☐ The Detective	1977-	165.00	
HN 2360 NOT ISSUED			
HN 2361			
☐ The Laird	1969-	175.00	
HN 2362			
☐ The Wayfarer	1970-1976	200.00	250.00
HN 2363 · HN 2367 NOT ISSUED			
HN 2368			
☐ Fleur	1968-	185.00	
HN 2369 · HN 2372 NOT ISSUED			
HN 2373			
☐ Joan	1982-	95.00	
HN 2374 · NOT ISSUED			
HN 2375			
☐ The Viking	1973-1976	250.00	300.00
HN 2376			
☐ Indian Brave (Limited Edition, Figurines.	1967-	4000.00	5000.00
HN 2377			
☐ Georgina (Kate Greenaway)	1981-	100.00	
HN 2378			
☐ Simone	1971-1981	135.00	185.00
HN 2379			
☐ Ninette	1971-	185.00	
HN 2380			
☐ Sweet Dreams	1971-	150.00	

	Date	Price Range	
HN 2381			
☐ Kirsty	1971-	185.00	
HN 2382			
☐ Secret Thoughts	1971-	215.00	
HN 2383			
☐ Breton Dancer (Limited Edition, Dancers of the World)	1981-	850.00	
HN 2384			
☐ West Indian Dancer (Limited Edition, Dancers of the World)	1981-	850.00	
HN 2385			
☐ Debbie	1969-	100.00	
HN 2386			
☐ Prince Phillip (Limited Edition, Figurines.	1981-	750.00	
HN 2387			
☐ Helen of Troy (Limited Edition, Femme Fatale Series)	1981-	1250.00	
HN 2388			
☐ Karen	1982-	185.00	
HN 2389			
☐ Angela	1982-	95.00	
HN 2390 - NOT ISSUED			
HN 2391			
☐ TZ 'U-HSI Empress Dowager	1983-		
HN 2392			
☐ Jennifer	1982-	155.00	
HN 2393			
☐ Rosalind	1970-1975	150.00	200.00
HN 2394			
☐ Lisa	1983-	125.00	
HN 2395 - NOT ISSUED			
HN 2396			
☐ Wistful........................	1979-	325.00	
HN 2397			
☐ Margaret	1982-	95.00	
HN 2398			
☐ Alexandra	1970-1976	200.00	250.00
HN 2399			
☐ Buttercup	1983-	145.00	
HN 2400			
☐ Debbie	1983-	75.00	
HN 2401 - 2409 NOT ISSUED			
HN 2410			
☐ Breton Dancer	1981-	850.00	
HN 2411 - 2416 NOT ISSUED			
HN 2417			
☐ The Boatman	1971-	165.00	

	Date	Price Range	
HN 2418 - HN 2420 NOT ISSUED			
HN 2421			
☐ Charlotte	1972-	**185.00**	
HN 2422			
☐ Francine	1972-1980	**75.00**	**125.00**
HN 2423 - NOT ISSUED			
HN 2424			
☐ Penny.	1983-	**65.00**	
HN 2425 - NOT ISSUED			
HN 2426			
☐ Tranquility, (Image Series) (black) . . .	1980-	**75.00**	
HN 2427			
☐ Virginals (Limited Edition, Lady Musi-cians)	1971-	**750.00**	**800.00**
HN 2428			
☐ The Palio (Limited Edition, Miscellan-eous)	1971-	**N/A**	
HN 2429			
☐ Elyse	1972-	**185.00**	
HN 2430			
☐ Romance.	1972-1980	**125.00**	**175.00**
HN 2431			
☐ Lute (Limited Edition, Lady Musi-cians)	1972-	**750.00**	**800.00**
HN 2432			
☐ Violin (Limited Edition, Lady Musi-cians)	1972-	**750.00**	**800.00**
HN 2433			
☐ Peace (Image Series)	1980-	**50.00**	
HN 2434			
☐ Fair Maiden.	1983-	**95.00**	
HN 2435 NOT ISSUED			
HN 2436			
☐ Scottish Highland Dancer (Limited Edition, Dancers of the World)	1978-	**600.00**	**650.00**
HN 2437 — HN 2438 NOT ISSUED			
HN 2439			
☐ Phillippine Dancer (Limited Edition, Dancers of the World)	1978-	**550.00**	**650.00**
HN 2440 — HN 2441 NOT ISSUED			
HN 2442			
☐ Sailor's Holiday	1972-1979	**200.00**	**250.00**
HN 2443			
☐ The Judge	1972-	**175.00**	

	Date	Price Range	
HN 2444			
☐ Bon Appetit.....................	1972-1976	**225.00**	**275.00**
HN 2445			
☐ Parisian.......................	1972-1975	**225.00**	**275.00**
HN 2446			
☐ Thanksgiving	1972-1976	**200.00**	**250.00**
HN 2447 — HN 2454 NOT ISSUED			
HN 2455			
☐ The Seafarer	1972-1976	**225.00**	**275.00**
HN 2456 — HN 2460 NOT ISSUED			
HN 2461			
☐ Janine	1971-	**170.00**	
HN 2462 NOT ISSUED			
HN 2463			
☐ Olga...........................	1972-1975	**200.00**	**250.00**
HN 2464 — HN 2466 NOT ISSUED			
HN 2467			
☐ Melissa	1981-	**170.00**	
HN 2468 NOT ISSUED			
HN 2469			
☐ Tranquility (Image Series)	1980-	**75.00**	
HN 2470			
☐ Peace (Image Series)	1980-	**50.00**	
HN 2471			
☐ Victoria	1973-	**170.00**	
HN 2472 NOT ISSUED			
HN 2473			
☐ At Ease	1973-1979	**200.00**	**250.00**
HN 2474 NOT ISSUED			
HN 2475			
☐ Vanity	1973-	**100.00**	
HN 2476 — HN 2481 NOT ISSUED			
HN 2482			
☐ Harp (Limited Edition, Lady Musicians)	1973-	**750.00**	**800.00**
HN 2483			
☐ Flute (Limited Edition, Lady Musicians)	1973-	**750.00**	**800.00**
HN 2484			
☐ Past Glory......................	1973-1979	**200.00**	**250.00**
HN 2485			
☐ Lunchtime......................	1973-1980	**150.00**	**200.00**
HN 2486 NOT ISSUED			
HN 2487			
☐ Beachcomber	1973-1976	**200.00**	**250.00**
HN 2488 — HN 2491 NOT ISSUED			
HN 2492			
☐ The Huntsman (3rd version)	1974-1979	**175.00**	**225.00**
HN 2493 NOT ISSUED			

	Date	Price Range	
HN 2494			
☐ Old Meg...................	1974-1976	225.00	275.00
HN 2495 — HN 2498 NOT ISSUED			
HN 2499			
☐ Helmsman................	1974-	200.00	
HN 2500 — HN 2670 ANIMAL MODELS			
HN 2502			
☐ Queen Elizabeth II (Limited Edition, now sold out)	1973-	2000.00	2500.00
HN 2503 — HN 2519 ANIMAL MODELS			
HN 2520			
☐ The Farmers Boy	1938-1960	1000.00	1250.00
HN 2521 — HN 2541 ANIMAL MODELS			
HN 2542			
☐ Boudoir (Haute Ensemble)	1974-1979	325.00	375.00
HN 2543			
☐ Eliza (Haute Ensemble)	1974-1979	225.00	275.00
HN 2544			
☐ A la Mode (Haute Ensemble)	1974-1979	225.00	275.00
HN 2545			
☐ Carmen (Haute Ensemble) (2nd version)	1974-1979	250.00	300.00
HN 2546			
☐ Buddies...................	1973-1976	200.00	250.00
HN 2547 — HN 2553 BIRD MODELS			
HN 2554			
☐ Masque	1973-1982	170.00	
HN 2555 — HN 2670 ANIMAL MODELS			
HN 2671			
☐ Good Morning..............	1974-1976	200.00	250.00
HN 2672 — HN 2676 NOT ISSUED			
HN 2677			
☐ Taking Things Easy	1975-	200.00	
HN 2678 NOT ISSUED			
HN 2679			
☐ Drummer Boy	1976-1981	325.00	375.00
HN 2680 — HN 2682 NOT ISSUED			
HN 2683			
☐ Stop Press.................	1977-1980	200.00	250.00
HN 2684 — HN 2693 NOT ISSUED			
HN 2694			
☐ Fiona (2nd version)...........	1974-1980	175.00	175.00
HN 2695 — HN 2698 NOT ISSUED			
HN 2699			
☐ Cymbals (Limited Editions, Lady Musicians)	1974-	650.00	700.00
HN 2700			
☐ Chitarrone (Limited Editions, Lady Musicians)	1974-	650.00	700.00

HN 2701 — HN 2703 NOT ISSUED	Date	Price Range	
HN 2704			
☐ Pensive Moments	1974-1981	150.00	200.00
HN 2705			
☐ Julia	1975-	155.00	
HN 2706 — HN 2708 NOT ISSUED			
HN 2709			
☐ Regal Lady	1975-	170.00	
HN 2710 — HN 2711 NOT ISSUED			
HN 2712			
☐ Mantilla	1974-1979	300.00	350.00
HN 2713			
☐ Tenderness (White)	1983-	75.00	
HN 2714			
☐ Tenderness (Black)	1983-	75.00	
HN 2715			
☐ Patricia	1982-	95.00	
HN 2716			
☐ Cavalier (2nd version)	1976-1982	200.00	
HN 2717			
☐ Private, 2nd South Carolina Regiment 1781, (Limited Edition, Soldiers)	1975-	750.00	
HN 2718			
☐ Lady Pamela	1974-1980	150.00	200.00
HN 2719			
☐ Laurianne	1974-1979	150.00	200.00
HN 2720			
☐ Family (Image Series) (White)	1980-	95.00	
HN 2721			
☐ Family (Image Series) (Black)	1980-	95.00	
HN 2722			
☐ Veneta	1974-1980	150.00	200.00
HN 2723			
☐ Grand Manner	1975-1981	225.00	275.00
HN 2724			
☐ Clarinda	1975-1980	175.00	225.00
HN 2725			
☐ Santa Claus	1982-	195.00	
HN 2726			
☐ The Centurion	1982-	150.00	
HN 2727 NOT ISSUED			
HN 2728			
☐ Rest Awhile	1981-	200.00	
HN 2729			
☐ Song of the Sea	1983-	150.00	
HN 2730 NOT ISSUED			
HN 2731			
☐ Thanks Doc	1975-	200.00	
HN 2732			
☐ Thank You	1983-	145.00	

	Date	Price Range
HN 2733		
☐ Officer of the Line	1983-	**195.00**
HN 2734		
☐ Sweet Seventeen	1975-	**185.00**
HN 2735		
☐ Young Love	1975-	**695.00**
HN 2736		
☐ Tracy	1983-	**95.00**
HN 2737		
☐ Harlequin.......................	1982-	**750.00**
HN 2738		
☐ Columbine......................	1982-	
HN 2739 — HN 2751 NOT ISSUED		
HN 2752		
☐ Major, 3rd New Jersey Regiment,		
1776 (Limited Edition, Soldiers)	1975-	**750.00**
HN 2753 NOT ISSUED		
HN 2754		
☐ Private, 3rd North Carolina Regiment,		
1778 (Limited Edition, Soldiers)	1976-	**750.00**
HN 2755		
☐ Captain, 2nd New York Regiment,		
1775 (Limited Editon, Soldiers)	1976-	**750.00**
HN 2756 — HN 2758 NOT ISSUED		
HN 2759		
☐ Private, Rhode Island Regiment, 1781		
(Limited Edition, Soldiers)	1977-	**750.00**
HN 2760		
☐ Private, Massachusetts Regiment,		
1778 (Limited Edition, Soldiers)	1977-	**750.00**
HN 2761		
☐ Private, Delaware Regiment, 1776		
(Limited Edition, Soldiers)	1977-	**750.00**
HN 2762		
☐ Lovers (Image Series) (White)	1979-	**95.00**
HN 2763		
☐ Lovers (Image Series) (Black)	1979-	**95.00**
HN 2764 NOT ISSUED		
HN 2765		
☐ Punch & Judy Man	1981-	**250.00**
HN 2766 — HN 2769 NOT ISSUED		
HN 2770		
☐ New Companions.................	1982-	**185.00**
HN 2771 — HN 2778 NOT ISSUED		
HN 2779		
☐ Private, 1st Georgia Regiment, 1777		
(Limited Edition, Soldiers)	1975-	**750.00**
HN 2780		
☐ Corporal, 1st New Hampshire Regiment 1778 (Limited Edition, Soldiers).	1975-	**750.00**
HN 2781 — HN 2787 NOT ISSUED		

	Date	Price Range	
HN 2788			
☐ Marjorie.........................	1980-	**185.00**	
HN 2789			
☐ Kate............................	1978-	**155.00**	
HN 2790 NOT ISSUED			
HN 2791			
☐ Elaine	1980-	**185.00**	
HN 2792			
☐ Christine (2nd version)............	1978-	**250.00**	
HN 2793			
☐ Clare	1980-	**250.00**	
HN 2794 NOT ISSUED			
HN 2795			
☐ French Horn (Limited Editions, Lady Musicians)	1976-	**650.00**	**700.00**
HN 2796			
☐ Hurdy Gurdy (Limited Editions, Lady Musicians)	1975-	**650.00**	**750.00**
HN 2797			
☐ Viola d'Amore (Limited Editions, Lady Musicians)	1976-	**650.00**	**700.00**
HN 2798			
☐ Dulcimer (Limited Edition, Lady Musicians).........................	1975-	**650.00**	**700.00**
HN 2799			
☐ Ruth (Kate Greenaway)	1976-1982	**100.00**	
HN 2800			
☐ Carrie (Kate Greenaway)	1976-1981	**75.00**	**100.00**
HN 2801			
☐ Lori (Kate Greenaway)	1976-	**100.00**	
HN 2802			
☐ Anna (Kate Greenaway)	1976-	**100.00**	
HN 2803			
☐ First Dance	1977-	**170.00**	
HN 2804 NOT ISSUED			
HN 2805			
☐ Rebecca	1980-	**325.00**	
HN 2806			
☐ Jane............................	1983-	**135.00**	
HN 2807			
☐ Stephanie	1977-	**170.00**	
HN 2808			
☐ Balinese Dancer	1982-	**950.00**	
HN 2809			
☐ North American Indian Dancer	1982-	**950.00**	
HN 2810			
☐ Solitude.........................	1977-	**215.00**	
HN 2811			
☐ Stephanie	1983-	**170.00**	
HN 2812 — HN 2813 NOT ISSUED			

	Date	Price Range	
HN 2814			
☐ Eventide	1977-	**165.00**	
HN 2815			
☐ Sergeant, 6th Maryland Regiment			
1777 (Limited Edition, Soldiers)	1976-	**750.00**	
HN 2816			
☐ Votes for Women	1978-1981	**200.00**	**250.00**
HN 2817 NOT ISSUED			
HN 2818			
☐ Balloon Girl	1982-	**125.00**	
HN 2819 — HN 2823 NOT ISSUED			
HN 2824			
☐ Harmony	1978-	**170.00**	
HN 2825			
☐ Lady and the Unicorn	1982-	**2500.00**	
HN 2826			
☐ Leda and the Swan	1983-	**2500.00**	
HN 2827 — HN 2829 NOT ISSUED			
HN 2830			
☐ Indian Temple Dancer (Limited Edi-			
tion, Dancers of the World)	1977-	**800.00**	**850.00**
HN 2831			
☐ Spanish Flamenco Dancer (Limited			
Edition, Dancers of the World)	1977-	**800.00**	**850.00**
HN 2832			
☐ Fair Lady	1977-	**155.00**	
HN 2833			
☐ Sophie (Kate Greenaway)	1977-	**100.00**	
HN 2834			
☐ Emma (Kate Greenaway)	1977-1982	**75.00**	**100.00**
HN 2835			
☐ Fair Lady	1977-	**155.00**	
HN 2836			
☐ Polish Dancer (Limited Edition, Danc-			
ers of the World)	1980-	**750.00**	
HN 2837			
☐ Awakening (Image Series) (Black) . . .	1980-	**50.00**	
HN 2838			
☐ Sympathy (Image Series) (Black)	1980-	**75.00**	
HN 2839			
☐ Nicola	1978-	**250.00**	
HN 2840			
☐ Chinese Dancer (Limited Edition,			
Dancers of the World)	1980-	**750.00**	
HN 2841			
☐ Mother & Daughter (Image Series) . . .	1980-	**95.00**	
HN 2842			
☐ Innocence	1979-	**155.00**	

	Date	Price Range	
HN 2843			
☐ Mother & Daughter (Image Series) ...	1980-	95.00	
HN 2844			
☐ Sergeant, Virginia 1st Regiment Continental Light Dragoons, 1777 (Limited Edition, Soldiers)	1978-	1750.00	
HN 2845			
☐ Private, Connecticut Regiment, 1777 (Limited Edition, Soldiers)	1978-	750.00	
HN 2846			
☐ Private, Pennsylvania Rifle Battalion 1776, (Limited Edition, Soldiers)	1978-	750.00	
HN 2847 — HN 2850 NOT ISSUED			
HN 2851			
☐ Christmas Parcels	1978-1982	200.00	
HN 2852 — HN 2854 NOT ISSUED			
HN 2855			
☐ Embroidering	1980-	225.00	
HN 2856			
☐ St. George (3rd version) (Prestige Series)	1978-	6500.00	
HN 2857 NOT ISSUED			
HN 2858			
☐ The Doctor	1979-	225.00	
HN 2859 — HN 2860 NOT ISSUED			
HN 2861			
☐ George Washington at Prayer (Limited Edition, Soldiers)	1977-	1800.00	2000.00
HN 2862			
☐ First Waltz.....................	1979-	250.00	
HN 2863			
☐ Lucy (Kate Greenaway)	1980-	100.00	
HN 2864			
☐ Tom (Kate Greenaway)............	1978-1981	85.00	110.00
HN 2865			
☐ Tess (Kate Greenaway)	1978-	100.00	
HN 2866			
☐ Mexican Dancer (Limited Edition, Dancers of the World)	1979-	550.00	
HN 2868			
☐ Kurdish Dancer (Limited Edition, Dancers of the World)	1979-	550.00	
HN 2868			
☐ Cleopatra and Slave (Limited Edition, Femmes Fatales Series)	1979-	900.00	1000.00
HN 2869			
☐ Louise (Kate Greenaway)...........	1980-	100.00	
HN 2870			
☐ Beth (Kate Greenaway)	1980-	100.00	

	Date	Price Range
HN 2871		
☐ Beat You To It	1980-	**350.00**
HN 2872		
☐ The Young Master	1980-	**325.00**
HN 2873		
☐ Bride (4th version)	1980-	**170.00**
HN 2874		
☐ Bridesmaid (4th version)	1980-	**100.00**
HN 2875		
☐ Awakening (Image Series)	1980-	**50.00**
HN 2876		
☐ Sympathy (Image Series)	1980-	**75.00**
HN 2877		
☐ The Wizard	1979-	**215.00**
HN 2878		
☐ Her Majesty Queen Elizabeth II	1983-	
HN 2879 — HN 2881 NOT ISSUED		
HN 2882		
☐ Queen Mother (Limited Edition, Figurines)	1980-	**1250.00**
HN 2883		
☐ H.R.H. THE Prince of Wales.	1982-	**750.00**
HN 2884 NOT ISSUED		
HN 2885		
☐ Lady Diana Spencer	1982-	**750.00**
HN 2886 — HN 2887 NOT ISSUED		
HN 2888		
☐ His Holiness Pope John Paul II.	1982-	**150.00**
HN 2889		
☐ Captain Cook	1980-	**365.00**
HN 2890		
☐ The Clown	1979-	**295.00**
HN 2891 NOT ISSUED		
HN 2892		
☐ The Chief	1979-	**200.00**
HN 2893 — HN 2897 NOT ISSUED		
HN 2898		
☐ Ko-Ko (2nd version)	1980-	**750.00**
HN 2899		
☐ Yum-Yum (2nd version)	1980-	**750.00**
HN 2900		
☐ Ruth the Pirate Maid	1981-	**750.00**
HN 2901		
☐ The Pirate King	1981-	**750.00**
HN 2902		
☐ Elsie Maynard	1982-	**750.00**
HN 2903		
☐ Colonel Fairfax	1982-	**750.00**
HN 2904 — HN 2905 NOT ISSUED		

	Date	Price Range
HN 2906		
☐ Paula	1980-	**185.00**
HN 2907		
☐ The Piper	1980-	**250.00**
HN 2908		
☐ Ajax (Limited Edition, Ships		
Figurehead)	1980-	**750.00**
HN 2909		
☐ Benmore (Limited Edition, Ships		
Figurehead)	1980-	**750.00**
HN 2910		
☐ Lalla Rookh (Limited Edition, Ships		
Figurehead)	1981-	**750.00**
HN 2911		
☐ Gandolf (J.R.R. Tolkien Series)	1980-	**50.00**
HN 2912		
☐ Frado (J.R.R. Tolkien Series)	1980-	**35.00**
HN 2913		
☐ Gollum (J.R.R. Tolkien Series)	1980-	**35.00**
HN 2914		
☐ Bilbo (J.R.R. Tolkien Series)	1980-	**35.00**
HN 2915		
☐ Galadrial (J.R.R. Tolkien Series)	1981-	**45.00**
HN 2916		
☐ Aragorn (J.R.R. Tolkien Series)	1980-	**45.00**
HN 2917		
☐ Legolas (J.R.R. Tolkien Series)	1981-	**45.00**
HN 2918		
☐ Boromir (J.R.R. Tolkien Series)	1981-	**50.00**
HN 2919		
☐ Rachel	1981-	**185.00**
HN 2920		
☐ Yearning (White)	1983-	**75.00**
HN 2921		
☐ Yearning (Black)	1983-	**75.00**
HN 2922		
☐ Gimli (J.R.R. Tolkien Series)	1981-	**45.00**
HN 2923		
☐ Barliman Butterbur	1982-	**45.00**
HN 2924		
☐ Tom Bombadil	1982-	**50.00**
HN 2925		
☐ Samwise	1982-	**35.00**
HN 2926		
☐ Tom Sawyer	1982-	**50.00**
HN 2927		
☐ Huckleberry Finn	1982-	**50.00**
HN 2928		
☐ Nelson (Limited Edition, Ships		
Figureheads)	1981-	**750.00**

	Date	Price Range
HN 2929 — HN 2939 NOT ISSUED		
HN 2940		
☐ All Aboard	1982-	**175.00**
HN 2941		
☐ Tom Brown	1983-	**50.00**
HN 2942 NOT ISSUED		
HN 2943		
☐ The China Repairer	1983-	**185.00**
HN 2944 — HN 2945 NOT ISSUED		
HN 2946		
☐ Elizabeth	1982-	**225.00**
HN 2947 — HN 2951 NOT ISSUED		
HN 2952		
☐ Susan	1982-	**175.00**
HN 2953 NOT ISSUED		
HN 2954		
☐ Samantha	1982-	**95.00**
HN 2955		
☐ Nancy	1982-	**95.00**
HN 2956		
☐ Heather	1982-	**95.00**
HN 2957		
☐ Edith	1982-	**100.00**
HN 2958		
☐ Amy	1982-	**100.00**
HN 2959		
☐ Save Some For Me	1983-	**75.00**
HN 2960		
☐ Laura	1983-	**145.00**
HN 2961		
☐ Carol	1982-	**95.00**
HN 2962		
☐ Barbara	1982-	**95.00**
HN 2963		
☐ It Won't Hurt	1982-	**75.00**
HN 2964		
☐ Dressing Up	1982-	**75.00**
HN 2965		
☐ Pollyanna	1982-	**50.00**
HN 2966		
☐ And So To Bed	1983-	**75.00**
HN 2967		
☐ Please Keep Still	1983-	**75.00**
HN 2968 — HN 2969 NOT ISSUED		
HN 2970		
☐ And One For You	1982-	**75.00**
HN 2971		
☐ As Good As New	1982-	**75.00**
HN 2972		
☐ Little Lord Fauntleroy	1982-	**50.00**

		Date	Price Range
HN 2973 NOT ISSUED			
HN 2974			
☐ Carolyn		1983-	**155.00**
HN 2975			
☐ Heidi		1983-	**50.00**
HN 2976 — HN 2988 NOT ISSUED			
HN 2989			
☐ The Genie		1983-	**95.00**
HN 2990 — HN 3012 NOT ISSUED			
HN 3013			
☐ James		1983-	**100.00**
HN 3014			
☐ Nell		1983-	**100.00**

"M" NUMERICAL LISTINGS OF MINATURE FANCY & CHARACTER FIGURINES

	Date	Price Range	
M 1			
☐ Victorian Lady	1932-1945	**300.00**	**325.00**
M 2			
☐ Victorian Lady	1932-1945	**300.00**	**325.00**
M 3			
☐ Paisley Shawl	1932-1938	**275.00**	**325.00**
M 4			
☐ Paisley Shawl	1932-1945	**300.00**	**350.00**
M 5			
☐ Sweet Anne	1932-1945	**300.00**	**375.00**
M 6			
☐ Sweet Anne	1932-1945	**300.00**	**375.00**
M 7			
☐ Patricia	1932-1945	**300.00**	**350.00**
M 8			
☐ Patricia	1932-1938	**300.00**	**350.00**
M 9			
☐ Chloe	1932-1945	**275.00**	**325.00**
M 10			
☐ Chloe	1932-1945	**275.00**	**325.00**
M 11			
☐ Bridesmaid	1932-1938	**325.00**	**375.00**
M 12			
☐ Bridesmaid	1932-1945	**275.00**	**325.00**
M 13			
☐ Priscilla	1932-1938	**400.00**	**450.00**
M 14			
☐ Priscilla	1932-1945	**275.00**	**325.00**
M 15			
☐ Pantalettes	1932-1945	**250.00**	**300.00**
M 16			
☐ Panalettes	1932-1945	**250.00**	**300.00**

M 17	Date	Price Range	
☐ Shepherd......................	1932-1938	550.00	700.00
M 18			
☐ Shepherdess...................	1932-1938	600.00	700.00
M 19			
☐ Shepherd......................	1932-1938	550.00	700.00
M 20			
☐ Shepherdess...................	1932-1938	600.00	700.00
M 21			
☐ Polly Peachum	1932-1945	325.00	375.00
M 22			
☐ Polly Peachum	1932-1938	325.00	375.00
M 23			
☐ Polly Peachum	1932-1938	325.00	375.00
M 24			
☐ Priscilla......................	1932-1945	300.00	350.00
M 25			
☐ Victorian Lady	1932-1945	300.00	325.00
M 26			
☐ Paisley Shawl	1932-1945	275.00	325.00
M 27			
☐ Sweet Anne....................	1932-1945	300.00	375.00
M 28			
☐ Patricia	1932-1945	325.00	375.00
M 29			
☐ Chloe.........................	1932-1945	275.00	325.00
M 30			
☐ Bridesmaid	1932-1945	275.00	325.00
M 31			
☐ Pantalettes	1932-1945	250.00	300.00
M 32			
☐ Rosamund.....................	1932-1945	250.00	300.00
M 33			
☐ Rosamund.....................	1932-1945	325.00	375.00
M 34			
☐ Denise	1933-1945	350.00	400.00
M 35			
☐ Denise	1933-1945	350.00	400.00
M 36			
☐ Norma	1933-1945	375.00	425.00
M 37			
☐ Norma	1933-1945	375.00	425.00
M 38			
☐ Robin........................	1933-1945	275.00	325.00
M 39			
☐ Robin........................	1933-1945	275.00	325.00
M 40			
☐ Erminie	1933-1945	375.00	425.00
M 41			
☐ Mr. Pickwick	1932-	29.95	

M 42	Date	Price Range	
☐ Mr. Micawber	1932-	**29.95**	
M 43			
☐ Mr. Pecksniff.	1932-1983	**29.95**	
M 44			
☐ Fat Boy	1932-	**29.95**	
M 45			
☐ Uriah Heep	1932-	**29.95**	
M 46			
☐ Sairey Gamp	1932-	**29.95**	
M 47			
☐ Tony Weller	1932-	**29.95**	
M 48			
☐ Sam Weller	1932-	**29.95**	
M 49			
☐ Fagin	1932-	**29.95**	
M 50			
☐ Stiggins	1932-	**29.95**	
M 51			
☐ Little Nell	1932-	**29.95**	
M 52			
☐ Alfred Jingle	1932-	**29.95**	
M 53			
☐ Buz Fuz	1932-	**29.95**	
M 54			
☐ Bill Sykes	1932-	**29.95**	
M 55			
☐ Artful Dodger	1932-	**29.95**	
M 56			
☐ Tiny Tim.	1932-	**29.95**	
M 57 — M 62 DICKENS NAPKIN RINGS			
M 63 NOT ISSUED			
M 64			
☐ Veronica	1934-1949	**325.00**	**375.00**
M 65			
☐ June	1935-1949	**325.00**	**375.00**
M 66			
☐ Monica	1935-1949	**275.00**	**325.00**
M 67			
☐ Dainty May	1935-1949	**325.00**	**375.00**
M 68			
☐ Mirabel	1936-1949	**300.00**	**350.00**
M 69			
☐ Janet	1936-1949	**300.00**	**350.00**
M 70			
☐ Veronica	1936-1949	**325.00**	**375.00**
M 71			
☐ June	1936-1949	**325.00**	**375.00**
M 72			
☐ Monica	1936-1949	**300.00**	**350.00**

	Date	Price Range	
M 73			
☐ Dainty May	1936-1949	**325.00**	**375.00**
M 74			
☐ Mirabel	1936-1949	**300.00**	**350.00**
M 75			
☐ Janet	1936-1949	**300.00**	**350.00**
M 76			
☐ Bumble	1939-1982	**29.95**	
M 77			
☐ Captain Cuttle	1939-1983	**29.95**	
M 78			
☐ Windflower	1939-1949	**400.00**	**450.00**
M 79			
☐ Windflower	1939-1949	**500.00**	**550.00**
M 80			
☐ Goody Two Shoes	1939-1949	**400.00**	**450.00**
M 81			
☐ Goody Two Shoes	1939-1949	**350.00**	**400.00**
M 82			
☐ Bo-Peep	1939-1949	**425.00**	**475.00**
M 83			
☐ Bo-Peep	1939-1949	**400.00**	**450.00**
M 84			
☐ Maureen	1939-1949	**350.00**	**400.00**
M 85			
☐ Maureen	1939-1949	**350.00**	**400.00**
M 86			
☐ Mrs. Bardell.....................	1949-1983	**29.95**	
M 87			
☐ Scrooge........................	1949-1983	**29.95**	
M 88			
☐ David Copperfield	1949-	**29.95**	
M 89			
☐ Oliver Twist.....................	1949-	**29.95**	
M 90			
☐ Dick Swiveller	1949-	**29.95**	
M 91			
☐ Trotty Veck	1949-1983	**29.95**	

"HN" NUMERICAL LISTINGS OF ANIMALS & BIRD MODELS

HN 100
☐ Fox in red frock coat

HN 101
☐ Hare in red coat

HN 102
☐ Hare in white coat

HN 103
☐ Double Penguins

HN 104
☐ Single Penguin

HN 105
☐ Collie (sable)

HN 106
☐ Collie (white & sable)

HN 107
☐ Hare, crouching

HN 108
☐ Rabbit
HN 109
☐ Cat (white)
HN 110
☐ Titanian bowl, jade
HN 111
☐ Cockerel on stand
HN 112
☐ Alsatain (pale grey)
HN 113
☐ Penguin
HN 114
☐ Drake (malachite head)
HN 115
☐ Drake (blue head)
HN 116
☐ Drake (bright colours overall)
HN 117
☐ Two Foxes
HN 118
☐ Monkey
HN 119
☐ Polar Bear, sitting on green cube
HN 120
☐ Cat (white)
HN 121
☐ Polar Bear, sitting
HN 122
☐ Two Turtle Doves
HN 123
☐ Pelican
HN 124
☐ Cockerel, sitting
HN 125
☐ Guinea Fowl
HN 126
☐ Hare, crouching
HN 127
☐ Pekinese
HN 128
☐ Puppy
HN 129
☐ Bulldog, sitting
HN 130
☐ Fox
HN 131
☐ Kingfisher on rock
HN 132
☐ Drake on rock

HN 133
☐ Double Penguins
HN 134
☐ Single Penguin
HN 135
☐ Raven on rock
HN 136
☐ Robin on rock
HN 137
☐ Blue Tit on rock
HN 138
☐ Squirrel
HN 139
☐ Falcon on rock
HN 140
☐ Ape
HN 141
☐ Rhinoceros
HN 142
☐ Hare, crouching
HN 143
☐ Chaffinch on its back
HN 144
☐ Wren
HN 145
☐ Small yellow bird on rock,
beak open
HN 145A
☐ Small yellow bird on rock,
beak closed
HN 146
☐ 'Old Bill' Bulldog with helmet
and haversack
HN 147
☐ Fox on rock
HN 148
☐ Two Drakes
HN 149
☐ Swallow on rock
HN 150
☐ Duck
HN 151
☐ Rabbit
HN 152
☐ Kingfisher on rock
HN 153
☐ 'Old Bill' Bulldog with tammy
and haversack
HN 154
☐ Character Cat

HN 155
☐ Owl
HN 156
☐ Monkey, listening
HN 157
☐ Cockerel
HN 158
☐ Toucan
HN 159
☐ Toucan
HN 160
☐ Owl and Young
HN 161
☐ Four Thrush Chicks
HN 162
☐ Butterfly (blue and gold)
HN 163
☐ Budgerigar
HN 164
☐ Cockerel, crowing
HN 165
☐ Kingfisher
HN 166
☐ Foxhound, seated
HN 167
☐ Tern Duck
HN 168
☐ Tern Drake
HN 169
☐ Owl
HN 170
☐ Brown Bear, Titanian ware
HN 171
☐ Four Baby Birds
HN 172
☐ Buffalo
HN 173
☐ 'Wise Old Owl' in red cloak and
Ermine collar
HN 175
☐ Great Crested Grebe
HN 176
☐ Bloodhound
HN 177
☐ Powder Bowl with small ape
figure seated on lid
HN 178
☐ Cockerel, crouching
HN 179
☐ Two Foxes

HN 180
☐ Cockerel, crouching
HN 181
☐ Elephant
HN 182
☐ Character Monkey, green jacket
HN 183
☐ Character Monkey, blue jacket
HN 184
☐ Cockerel, crowing
HN 185
☐ Parrot on rock
HN 186
☐ Elephant
HN 187
☐ Character Owl (check shawl,
ermine collar)
HN 188
☐ Duckling (yellow and brown)
HN 189
☐ Duckling (black and yellow)
HN 190
☐ Duckling (green and blue)
HN 191
☐ Parrot, baby (blue and purple)
HN 192
☐ Parrot, baby (red and orange)
HN 193
☐ Tortoise
HN 194
☐ Terrier Puppy
HN 195
☐ Tern Duck
HN 196
☐ Toucan
HN 197
☐ Bird on rock
HN 198
☐ Penguin and Young
HN 199
☐ Budgerigar on stand (green and
yellow)
HN 200
☐ Parrot, baby (decorated in enamel
flowers)
HN 201
☐ Tabby cat and mouse
HN 202
☐ Black cat and mouse

HN 203
☐ Tortoiseshell cat on pillar
HN 204
☐ Tortoiseshell Cat
HN 205
☐ Two Ducklings (black and white)
HN 206
☐ Two Ducklings (brown and white)
HN 207
☐ Character Mouse
HN 208
☐ Character Toucan
HN 209
☐ Two Rabbits
HN 210
☐ Black and White Cat
HN 211
☐ Black-headed Gull
HN 212
☐ Black-headed Gull
HN 213
☐ Two Pigs
HN 214
☐ Bird and four Chicks (black, pink and brown)
HN 215
☐ Bird and four Chicks (grey, blue and lemon)
HN 216
☐ Bird and four Chicks (green, blue and lemon)
HN 217
☐ Two Rabbits (brown patches on faces)
HN 218
☐ Two Rabbits (brown and black patches on faces)
HN 219
☐ Two Rabbits (brown, black, and yellow patches on faces)
HN 220
☐ Bird on rock
HN 221
☐ Cat (black and white)
HN 222
☐ Owl in boat
HN 223
☐ Lion, sitting
HN 224
☐ Kingfisher on rock

HN 225
☐ Tiger, lying
HN 226
☐ Character Mouse (blue coat)
HN 227
☐ Tabby Cat, asleep
HN 228
☐ Character Mouse (yellow coat)
HN 229
☐ Teal Duck
HN 231
☐ Foxhound
HN 232
☐ Puppy with bone
HN 233
☐ Kitten
HN 234
☐ Two Cats
HN 235
☐ Duckling
HN 236
☐ Two Baby Birds
HN 237
☐ Character Mouse with basket of babies
HN 238
☐ Two Pigs
HN 239
☐ Two Ducks
HN 240
☐ Bird on Rock
HN 241
☐ Eagle (brown and gold)
HN 242
☐ Eagle (lighter color, white head and neck)
HN 243
☐ Piggy Bowl
HN 244
☐ Cat and Mouse (cat black and white)
HN 245
☐ Cat and Mouse (cat all black)
HN 246
☐ Character Pig
HN 247
☐ Guinea Fowl
HN 248
☐ Drake, large size

HN 249
☐ Mallard Drake, large size
HN 250
☐ Heron
HN 251
☐ Heron
HN 252
☐ Drake, large size
HN 253
☐ Small Ape, sitting
HN 254
☐ Two small Apes
HN 256 — HN 266
☐ Miniature Character Penguins and Puffins
HN 267
☐ Cockerel, sitting
HN 268
☐ Kingfisher
HN 269
☐ Blue Bird on Rock
HN 270
☐ Brown Bear, sitting up
HN 271
☐ Duck
HN 272
☐ Bird with three Chicks
HN 273
☐ Rabbit
HN 274
☐ Green Bird
HN 275
☐ Two Orange Birds
HN 276
☐ Rabbit
HN 277
☐ Wren
HN 278
☐ Two Green Birds
HN 279
☐ Green Bird on Rock
HN 280
☐ Three Chicks
HN 281
☐ Yellow Bird on Rock
HN 282
☐ Blue Bird
HN 283 — HN 293
☐ Miniature Character Penguins and Puffins

HN 294
☐ Toucan, large size (black and white, red beak)
HN 295
☐ Toucan, large size (black and green, brown beak)
HN 295A
☐ Toucan, large size (black and green, brown beak)
HN 296
☐ Penguin
HN 297
☐ Penguin and Young
HN 298
☐ Duck, sitting
HN 299
☐ Drake, lying
HN 800
☐ Pig, asleep
HN 801
☐ Pig asleep, larger version
HN 802
☐ Two Pigs
HN 803
☐ Rabbit
HN 804
☐ Miniature Pup, playing (pale orange)
HN 805
☐ Miniature Pup, playing (malachite and purple
HN 806
☐ Miniature Drake (white)
HN 807
☐ Miniature Drake (malachite and purple)
HN 808 — HN 812
☐ Miniature Character Pups
HN 813
☐ Miniature White Bird
HN 814
☐ Miniature Character Pup
HN 815
☐ Miniature Character Pup
HN 818
☐ Character Cat 'Lucky' (black and white)
HN 819
☐ Miniature Cat 'Lucky' (white)
HN 820 — HN 825
☐ Miniature Kittens

HN 826
☐ Character Pup
HN 827
☐ Character Cat (tortoiseshell)
HN 828
☐ Character Cat (tabby)
HN 829
☐ Character Cat (black and white)
HN 830
☐ NO RECORD
HN 831
☐ Beagle Puppy
HN 832
☐ Pekinese Puppy (sitting)
HN 833
☐ Pekinese Puppy, standing
HN 834
☐ Pekinese Puppy on Stand (black and brown)
HN 835
☐ Pekinesed Puppy on stand (lighter brown)
HN 836
☐ Pekinese Puppy on stand (light color)
HN 837
☐ Chow on stand (brown)
HN 838
☐ Chow on stand (lighter brown)
HN 839
☐ Chow on stand (white and grey)
HN 840 — HN 845
☐ Character Ducks
HN 846
☐ Toucan
HN 847
☐ Yellow Bird
HN 849
☐ Duck and Ladybird
HN 850
☐ Duck, standing on rocks
HN 851
☐ Bird on Tree Stump
HN 852
☐ Penguin, standing on rocks
HN 853
☐ Small Mallard Drake on rocks
HN 854
☐ Budgerigar

HN 855
☐ Small Bird on Tree Stump
HN 856
☐ Penguin on rocks
HN 858
☐ Kingfisher on rock
HN 859
☐ Tortoise on rocks
HN 860
☐ Small Bird on Tree Stump
HN 861
☐ Polar Bear
HN 862A
☐ Kingfisher on stand, with Primroses
HN 862B
☐ Kingfisher on stand, with Kingcups
HN 863
☐ Ducks, quacking
HN 864
☐ Ducks, quacking
HN 865
☐ Ducks, quacking
HN 866
☐ Fox, sitting
HN 867 — HN 874
HN 875
☐ Kingfisher on Tree Stump
HN 876
☐ Tiger On Rock
HN 877
☐ Baby Parrot
HN 878
☐ Cockerel (white)
HN 879
☐ Cockerel (blue and green)
HN 880
☐ Cockerel (brown and orange)
HN 881
☐ Bulldog, sitting
HN 882
☐ Penguin, large size
HN 883
☐ Two Monkeys
HN 884
☐ Cockatoo (blue and orange)
HN 885
☐ Cockatoo (pink, purple and orange)

HN 886
☐ Cockatoo (red, blue and orange)
HN 888
☐ Cockatoo (pale blue and yellow)
HN 889
☐ Dog, seated Greyhound
(black and white)
HN 890
☐ Dog, seated Greyhound
(brown)
HN 891
☐ Elephant, large size (silver grey)
HN 892
☐ Character Pigs, in Clown costume
HN 893
☐ Character Pigs, in Clown costume
HN 894
☐ Character Pigs, in Clown costume
HN 895
☐ Character Pigs, in Clown costume
HN 896
☐ Character Pigs, in Clown costume
HN 897
☐ Character Pigs, in Clown costume
HN 898
☐ Alsatian's Head
HN 899
☐ Alsatian, sitting
HN 900
☐ Fox Terrier (white and brown)
HN 901
☐ Fox Terrier (white and black)
HN 902
☐ Character Pigs
HN 903
☐ Character Pigs
HN 904
☐ Terrier Puppy
HN 905
☐ Small Frog
HN 906
☐ Spaniel Puppy (black and white)
HN 907
☐ Spaniel Puppy (brown and white)
HN 908
☐ Spaniel Puppy's Head
HN 909
☐ Fox Terrier, standing
HN 910
☐ Fox Terrier, sitting

HN 911
☐ Tiger, lying
HN 912
☐ Tiger, sitting
HN 913 — HN 918
☐ Toucan Head on round bowl-like
Bodies
HN 919
☐ Leopard, sitting
HN 920
☐ Two Foxes (brown)
HN 921
☐ Alsatian, sitting, large size
HN 922
☐ Character Hare
HN 923
☐ Fox Terrier, standing
HN 924
☐ Fox Terrier, sitting, large size
HN 925
☐ Two Foxes (grey and brown)
HN 926
☐ Two Foxes (miniature model)
HN 927
☐ Two Pekinese Dogs
HN 928
☐ Large Toucan Bowl
HN 929
☐ Miniature Terrier Pup, sitting
HN 930
☐ Miniature Alsatian, sitting
HN 931
☐ Miniature Terrier Pup
HN 932
☐ Miniature Scotch Terrier
HN 933
☐ Miniature Scotch Terrier
HN 934
☐ Miniature Scotch Terrier
HN 935
☐ Pip, Squeak and Wilfred Ash Tray
HN 936
☐ Teal, swimming
HN 937
☐ Alsatian on stand
HN 938
☐ Alsatian on stand, sitting
HN 939
☐ Large and small Brown Bears

HN 940
☐ Large and small Brown Bears, (light brown)
HN 941
☐ Elephant, large size (black)
HN 942
☐ Terrier
HN 943
☐ Terrier
HN 944
☐ Fox Terrier
HN 945
☐ Fox Terrier
HN 946
☐ Penguin Chick
HN 947
☐ Penguin Chick
HN 948
☐ Bulldog, large size (brown)
HN 949
☐ Baby Elephants
HN 950
☐ Baby Elephant
HN 951
☐ Baby Elephant
HN 952
☐ Baby Elephant
HN 953
☐ Terrier Pup (brown and black)
HN 954
☐ Terrier Pup (darker brown and black)
HN 955
☐ Brown Bear, Standing
HN 956
☐ Mallard Drake, large size
HN 957
☐ Spaniel (liver and white)
HN 958
☐ Spaniel (black and white)
HN 960
☐ Character Ape with book, eyes open
HN 961
☐ Character Ape with book, eyes closed
HN 962
☐ Terrier's Head
HN 963
☐ Fox, sitting

HN 964
☐ Scotch Terrier, large size (black)
HN 965
☐ Scotch Terrier, large size (brown)
HN 966
☐ Elephant, large size (brown and grey)
HN 967
☐ Tabby Cat
HN 968
☐ Pig, black and white
HN 969
☐ Two Rabbits
HN 970
☐ Dachshund
HN 971
☐ 'Lucky' Cat Ash tray
HN 972
☐ Character Ape in Dunce's cap, reading book
HN 973
☐ Character Duck (orange)
HN 974
☐ Character Duck (lemon yellow)
HN 975
☐ Collie (silver grey)
HN 976
☐ Collie (brown)
HN 977
☐ Duck
HN 978
☐ Fox, lying
HN 979
☐ Hare, lying
HN 980
☐ Scotch Terrier (black)
HN 981
☐ Scotch Terrier (light grey and brown)
HN 982
☐ Sealyham Terrier (black patches on face)
HN 983
☐ Sealyham Terrier (brown patches on face)
HN 984
☐ Hare, lying (white)
HN 985
☐ Hare, lying (grey)

HN 986
☐ Alsatian sitting on lid of Lustre Bowl
HN 987
☐ Bulldog sitting on lid of Lustre Bowl
HN 988
☐ Airedale Terrier (brown)
HN 989
☐ Sealyham Terrier (grey)
HN 990
☐ Tiger, crouching
HN 991
☐ Tiger, crouching (smaller model)
HN 992
☐ Sealyham Terrier (black)
HN 993
☐ Cat asleep on cushion
HN 994
☐ Fox on pedestal
HN 995
☐ Pekinese (brown)
HN 996
☐ Airedale Terrier (black, blue & brown)
HN 997
☐ Terrier, seated (black and brown)
HN 998
☐ Penguin and Baby
HN 999
☐ Persian Cat (black and white)
HN 1000
☐ Cocker Spaniel, large size (black)
HN 1001
☐ Cocker Spaniel and Pheasant, large size
HN 1002
☐ Cocker Spaniel (liver and white)
HN 1003
☐ Pekinese (dark colouring)
HN 1004
☐ Blue Tit on Bough with Blossom
HN 1005
☐ Thrush on Bough with Blossom
HN 1007
☐ Ch. 'Charley Startler' Rough haired Terrier, large size
HN 1008
☐ Ch. 'Albourne Arthur' Scottish Terrier, large size

HN 1009
☐ Hare and Two Leverets
HN 1010
☐ Ch. Biddie of Ifield 'Pekinese', large size
HN 1011
☐ Ch. Biddie of Ifield 'Pekinese', medium size
HN 1012
☐ Ch. Biddie of Ifield 'Pekinese', small size
HN 1013
☐ Ch. 'Charley Hunter' Fox Terrier, medium size
HN 1014
☐ Ch. 'Charley Hunter' Fox Terrier, small size
HN 1015
☐ Ch. 'Albourne Arthur' Scottish Terrier, medium size
HN 1016
☐ Ch. 'Albourne Arthur' Scottish Terrier, small size
HN 1017
☐ Scottish Terrier, sitting (black)
HN 1018
☐ Scottish Terrier, sitting (black)
HN 1019
☐ Scottish Terrier, sitting (black)
HN 1020
☐ Ch. 'Lucky Star of Ware' Cocker Spaniel, medium size
HN 1021
☐ Ch. 'Lucky Star of Ware' Cocker Spaniel, small size
HN 1022
☐ Ch. 'Cotsfold Topsail' Airedale Terrier, large size
HN 1023
☐ Ch. 'Cotsfold Topsail' Airedale Terrier, medium size
HN 1024
☐ Ch. 'Cotsfold Topsail' Airedale Terrier, small size
HN 1025
☐ Ch. 'Tring Rattler' Foxhound, large size
HN 1026
☐ Ch. 'Tring Rattler' Foxhound, medium size

HN 1027
- [ ] Ch. 'Tring Rattler' Foxhound, small size

HN 1028
- [ ] Cocker Spaniel and Pheasant, medium size

HN 1029
- [ ] Cocker Spaniel and Pheasant, small size

HN 1030
- [ ] Ch. 'Scotia Stylist' Sealyham, large size

HN 1031
- [ ] Ch. 'Scotia Stylist' Sealyham, medium size

HN 1032
- [ ] Ch. 'Scotia Stylist' Sealyham, small size

HN 1033
- [ ] Ch. 'Charming Eyes' Cairn, large size

HN 1034
- [ ] Ch. 'Charming Eyes' Cairn, medium size

HN 1035
- [ ] Ch. 'Charming Eyes' Cairn, small size

HN 1036
- [ ] Cocker Spaniel, medium size, (liver and white

HN 1037
- [ ] Cocker Spaniel, small size, (liver and white)

HN 1038
- [ ] Scottish Terrier, begging

HN 1039
- [ ] Pekinese, sitting, large size

HN 1040
- [ ] Pekinese, sitting, small size

HN 1041
- [ ] Sealyham, lying, large size

HN 1042
- [ ] Bulldog, large size, (brindle)

HN 1043
- [ ] Bulldog, medium size, (brindle)

HN 1044
- [ ] Bulldog, small size, (brindle)

HN 1045
- [ ] Bulldog, large size, (brown and white)

HN 1046
- [ ] Bulldog, medium size (brown and white)

HN 1047
- [ ] Bulldog, small size (brown and white)

HN 1048
- [ ] West Highland White Terrier, large size

HN 1049
- [ ] Ch. 'Maesydd Mustard' English Setter, large size

HN 1050
- [ ] Ch. 'Maesydd Mustard' English Setter, medium size

HN 1051
- [ ] Ch. 'Maesydd Mustard' English Setter, small size

HN 1052
- [ ] Sealyham, lying, medium size

HN 1053
- [ ] Sealyham, lying, small size

HN 1054
- [ ] Irish Setter, large size

HN 1055
- [ ] Irish Setter, medium size

HN 1056
- [ ] Irish Setter, small size

HN 1057
- [ ] Ch. 'Ashstead Applause' Collie, large size

HN 1058
- [ ] Ch. 'Ashstead Applause' Collie, medium size

HN 1059
- [ ] Ch. 'Ashstead Applause' Collie, small size

HN 1062
- [ ] Cocker Spaniel and Pheasant, (black and white) small size

HN 1063
- [ ] Cocker Spaniel and Hare, medium size (liver and white)

HN 1064
- [ ] Cocker Spaniel and Hare, small size (liver and white)

HN 1065
- [ ] Greyhound, large size (brown)

HN 1066
- [ ] Greyhound, medium size (brown)

HN 1067
☐ Greyhound, small size (brown)
HN 1068
☐ Smooth-haired Fox Terrier, large size
HN 1069
☐ Smooth-haired Fox Terrier, medium size
HN 1070
☐ Smooth-haired Fox Terrier, small size
HN 1071
☐ Hare, lying
HN 1072
☐ Bulldog, large size (white)
HN 1073
☐ Bulldog, medium size (white)
HN 1074
☐ Bulldog, small size (white)
HN 1075
☐ Greyhound, large size (black and white)
HN 1076
☐ Greyhound, medium size (black and white)
HN 1077
☐ Greyhound, small size (black and white)
HN 1078
☐ Cocker Spaniel, small size (black and white)
HN 1079
☐ Gordon Setter, large size
HN 1080
☐ Gordon Setter, medium size
HN 1081
☐ Gordon Setter, small size
HN 1082
☐ Tiger, stalking, large size
HN 1083
☐ Tiger, stalking, medium size
HN 1084
☐ Tiger, stalking, small size
HN 1085
☐ Lion, large size
HN 1086
☐ Lion, medium size
HN 1087 — HN 1093 A
☐ Ash Tray

HN 1094
☐ Leopard
HN 1095 - 1095 A
☐ Ash Tray
HN 1096
☐ Character Fox with stolen Goose (green cloak and hat)
HN 1097
☐ Character Dog, running with ball
HN 1098
☐ Character Dog
HN 1099
☐ Character Dog, yawning
HN 1100
☐ Character Dog
HN 1101
☐ Character Dog, lying
HN 1102
☐ Character Fox with stolen Goose (red cloak and hat)
HN 1103
☐ Character Dog, with ball
HN 1104
☐ Cairn, large size (black)
HN 1105
☐ Cairn, medium size (black)
HN 1106
☐ Cairn, small size (black)
HN 1107
☐ Cairn, large size (black), (earthenware)
HN 1108
☐ Cocker Spaniel, large size (black and white)
HN 1109
☐ Cocker Spaniel, medium size (black and white)
HN 1111
☐ Ch. 'Goworth Victor' Dalmatian, large size
HN 1112
☐ Lion, large size
HN 1113
☐ Ch. 'Goworth Victor' Dalmatian, medium size
HN 1114
☐ Ch. 'Goworth Victor' Dalmatian, small size

HN 1115
☐ Ch. 'Benign of Picardy' Alsatian, large size
HN 1116
☐ Ch. 'Benign of Picardy' Alsatian, medium size
HN 1117
☐ Ch. 'Benign of Picardy' Alsatian, small size
HN 1118
☐ Tiger on Rock, large size (earthenware)
HN 1119
☐ Lion on Rock, large size (earthenware)
HN 1120
☐ Fighting Elephant, large size (earthenware)
HN 1121
☐ Elephant, large size
HN 1122
☐ Elephant, large size
HN 1123
☐ Elephant, medium size
HN 1124
☐ Elephant, large size
HN 1125
☐ Lion on Alabaster Base
HN 1126
☐ Tiger on Alabaster Base
HN 1127
☐ Ch. 'Shrewd Saint' Dachshund, large size
HN 1128
☐ Ch. 'Shrewd Saint' Dachshund, medium size
HN 1129
☐ Ch. 'Shrewd Saint' Dachshund, small size
HN 1130
☐ Fox, large size
HN 1131
☐ Staffordshire Bull Terrier, large size
HN 1132
☐ Staffordshire Bull Terrier, medium size
HN 1133
☐ Staffordshire Bull Terrier, small size

HN 1134
☐ Cocker Spaniel, large size (liver and white)
HN 1135
☐ Cocker Spaniel, medium size (liver and white)
HN 1136
☐ Cocker Spaniel, small size (liver and white)
HN 1137
☐ Cocker Spaniel and Pheasant, large size (black and white)
HN 1138
☐ Cocker Spaniel and Pheasant, medium size (black and white)
HN 1139
☐ Dachshund, large size
HN 1140
☐ Dachshund, medium size
HN 1141
☐ Dachshund, small size
HN 1142
☐ Ch. 'Bokus Brock' Bull Terrier, large size
HN 1143
☐ Ch. 'Bokus Brock' Bull Terrier, medium size
HN 1144
☐ Ch. 'Bokus Brock' Bull Terrier, small size
HN 1145
☐ Moufflon, standing (green matte)
HN 1146
☐ Calf, sleeping (green matte).
HN 1147
☐ Calf, standing (green matte).
HN 1148
☐ Buffalo (green matte)
HN 1149
☐ Donkey, small size (green matte)
HN 1150
☐ Young Doe (green matte)
HN 1151
☐ Swiss Goat (green matte)
HN 1152
☐ Horse (green matte)
HN 1153
☐ Moufflon, lying (green matte)

HN 1154
☐ Jumping Goat (green matte)
HN 1155
☐ Donkey, large size, (green matte)
HN 1156
☐ Suspicious Doe (green matte)
HN 1157
☐ Antelope (green matte)
HN 1158
☐ Character Dog with plate
HN 1159
☐ Character Dog with bone
HN 1160
☐ Moufflon, standing (cream matte)
HN 1161
☐ Calf, sleeping (cream matte)
HN 1162
☐ Calf, standing (cream matte)
HN 1163
☐ Buffalo (cream matte)
HN 1164
☐ Donkey, small size (cream matte)
HN 1165
☐ Young Doe (cream matte)
HN 1166
☐ Swiss Goat (cream matte)
HN 1167
☐ Horse (cream matte)
HN 1168
☐ Moufflon, lying (cream matte)
HN 1169
☐ Jumping Goat (cream matte)
HN 1170
☐ Donkey, large size (cream matte)
HN 1171
☐ Suspicious Dog (cream matte)
HN 1172
☐ Antelope (cream matte)
HN 1173
☐ Calf, sleeping (natural colours)
HN 1174
☐ Calf, standing (natural colours)
HN 1175
☐ Buffalo (natural colours)
HN 1176
☐ Donkey, small size (natural colours)
HN 1177
☐ Young Doe (natural colours)

HN 1178
☐ Swiss Goat (natural colours)
HN 1179
☐ Moufflon, standing (natural colours)
HN 1180
☐ Horse (natural colours)
HN 1181
☐ Moufflon, lying (natural colours)
HN 1182
☐ Jumping Goat (natural colours)
HN 1183
☐ Donkey, large size (natural colours)
HN 1184
☐ Suspicious Doe (natural colours)
HN 1185
☐ Antelope (natural colours)
HN 1186
☐ Cocker Spaniel, large size (golden brown)
HN 1187
☐ Cocker Spaniel, medium size (golden brown)
HN 1188
☐ Cocker Spaniel, small size (golden brown)
HN 1189
☐ King Penguin
HN 1190
☐ Penguin
HN 1191
☐ Mallard
HN 1192
☐ Duck
HN 1193
☐ Tern
HN 1194
☐ Tern
HN 1195
☐ Seagull
HN 1196
☐ Seagull
HN 1197
☐ Gannet
HN 1198
☐ Drake
HN 1199
☐ Penguin

HN 2500
- [ ] Cerval

HN 2501
- [ ] Lynx

HN 2502
- [ ] Deer (green)

HN 2503
- [ ] Deer (white)

HN 2504
- [ ] Lamb (green)

HN 2505
- [ ] Lamb (white)

HN 2506
- [ ] Asiatic Elephant

HN 2507
- [ ] Zebra

HN 2508
- [ ] Character Dog

HN 2509
- [ ] Sealyham

HN 2510
- [ ] Character Dog

HN 2511
- [ ] Character Dog

HN 2512
- [ ] Ch. 'Chosen Dan of Notts' smooth-haired Terrier, large size

HN 2513
- [ ] Ch. 'Chosen Dan of Notts' smooth-haired Terrier medium size

HN 2514
- [ ] Ch. 'Chosen Dan of Notts' smoothhaired Terrier, small size

HN 2515
- [ ] Ch. 'Dry Toast' Springer Spaniel, large size

HN 2516
- [ ] Ch. 'Dry Toast' Springer Spaniel, medium size

HN 2517
- [ ] Ch. 'Dry Toast' Springer Spaniel, small size

HN 2518
- [ ] 'Pride of the Shires', mare and foal (brown)

HN 2519
- [ ] 'The Gude Grey Mare', with foal, large size

HN 2520
- [ ] The Farmer's Boy on dappled Shire

HN 2521
- [ ] 'The Dapple Grey' (girl on Shire Pony)

HN 2522
- [ ] 'The Chestnut Mare' with foal, large size

HN 2523
- [ ] 'Pride of the Shires' mare and foal (dapple grey)

HN 2524
- [ ] American Foxhound, large size

HN 2525
- [ ] American Foxhound, medium size

HN 2526
- [ ] American Foxhound, small size

HN 2527
- [ ] Fox (sitting)

HN 2528
- [ ] 'Pride of the Shires' replacing 2518

HN 2529
- [ ] English Setter and Pheasant

HN 2530
- [ ] 'Merely a Minor' large size (brown)

HN 2531
- [ ] 'Merely a Minor' large size (grey)

HN 2532
- [ ] 'The Gude Grey Mare' with foal, medium size

HN 2533
- [ ] 'The Chestnut Mare' with foal, small size

HN 2534
- [ ] 'Pride of the Shires' mare and foal, small size (brown)

HN 2535
- [ ] Tiger on Rock

HN 2536
☐ 'Pride of the Shires' mare
   and foal, small size (grey)
HN 2537
☐ 'Merely a Minor', medium
   size (brown)
HN 2538
☐ 'Merely a Minor', medium
   size (grey)
HN 2539
☐ Persian Cat (white)
HN 2540
☐ Kingfisher
HN 2541
☐ Kingfisher
HN 2542
☐ Baltimore Oriole
HN 2543
☐ Blue Bird
HN 2544
☐ Mallard
HN 2545
☐ Pheasant
HN 2546
☐ Yellow Throated Warbler
HN 2547
☐ Budgerigars (pair)
HN 2548
☐ Golden Crested Wren
HN 2549
☐ Robin
HN 2550
☐ Chaffinch
HN 2551
☐ Bullfinch
HN 2552
☐ Young Thrushes (pair)
HN 2553
☐ Young Robins (group)
HN 2554
☐ Cardinal Bird
HN 2555
☐ Drake Mallard
HN 2556
☐ Mallard
HN 2557
☐ Welsh Corgi, large size
HN 2558
☐ Welsh Corgi, medium size

HN 2559
☐ Welsh Corgi, small size
HN 2560
☐ Great Dane, large size
HN 2561
☐ Great Dane, medium size
HN 2562
☐ Great Dane, small size
HN 2563
☐ 'Pride of the Shires' (no foal)
   large size (brown)
HN 2564
☐ 'Pride of the Shires' (no foal)
   medium size (brown)
HN 2564
☐ 'Pride of the Shires' (no foal)
   medium size (brown)
HN 2565
☐ 'The Chestnut Mare' (no foal)
   large size
HN 2566
☐ 'The Chestnut Mare' (no foal)
   small size
HN 2567
☐ 'Merely a Minor' small size (grey)
HN 2568
☐ 'The Gude Grey Mare' (no foal)
   large size
HN 2569
☐ 'The Gude Grey Mare' (no foal)
   medium size
HN 2570
☐ 'The Gude Grey Mare' (no foal)
   small size
HN 2571
☐ 'Merely a Minor' small size,
   (brown)
HN 2572
☐ Drake Mallard small size
HN 2573
☐ Kingfisher, small size
HN 2574
☐ Seagull, small size
HN 2575
☐ Swan
HN 2576
☐ Pheasant, small size
HN 2577
☐ Peacock

HN 2578
☐ Horse without Boy (dapple grey)
HN 2579
☐ Kitten lying on Back (brown)
HN 2580
☐ Kitten, sitting licking hind paw (brown)
HN 2581
☐ Kitten, sleeping (brown)
HN 2582
☐ Kitten, sitting on haunches (tan)
HN 2583
☐ Kitten, sitting licking front paw (tan)
HN 2584
☐ Kitten, sitting, surprised (tan)
HN 2585
☐ Puppy in basket, lying (cocker)
HN 2586
☐ Puppy in basket (cocker)
HN 2587
☐ Puppy in basket (terrier)
HN 2588
☐ Puppies in basket, three (Terriers)
HN 2589
☐ Puppy, begging (Cairn)
HN 2590
☐ Cocker Spaniels, sleeping (pair)
HN 2591
☐ Drake Mallard
HN 2592
☐ Hare
HN 2593
☐ Hare
HN 2594
☐ Hare, lying, small size
HN 2595
☐ Lambs
HN 2596
☐ Lambs
HN 2597
☐ Lambs
HN 2598
☐ Lambs
HN 2599
☐ English Setter and Pheasant
HN 2600
☐ Cocker Spaniel and Pheasant, small size

HN 2601
☐ American Great Dane, large size
HN 2602
☐ American Great Dane, medium size
HN 2603
☐ American Great Dane, small size
HN 2604
☐ Peacock Butterfly
HN 2605
☐ Camberwell Beauty Butterfly
HN 2606
☐ Swallowtail Butterfly
HN 2607
☐ Red Admiral Butterfly
HN 2608
☐ Copper Butterfly
HN 2609
☐ Tortoiseshell Butterfly
HN 2610
☐ Hen Pheasant
HN 2611
☐ Chaffinch
HN 2612
☐ Baltimore Oriole
HN 2613
☐ Golden Crested Wren
HN 2614
☐ Blue Bird
HN 2615
☐ Cardinal Bird
HN 2616
☐ Bullfinch
HN 2617
☐ Robin
HN 2618
☐ Yellow Throated Warbler
HN 2619
☐ Grouse
HN 2620
☐ English Setter, large size (liver and white)
HN 2621
☐ English Setter, medium size (liver and white)
HN 2622
☐ English Setter, small size (liver and white)

HN 2523
☐ Horse without boy (brown)
HN 2624
☐ Pointer
HN 2625
☐ Poodle, large size
HN 2626
☐ Poodle, medium size
HN 2627
☐ Poodle, small size
HN 2628
☐ Chow, large size
HN 2629
☐ Chow, medium size
HN 2630
☐ Chow, small size
HN 2631
☐ French Poodle
HN 2632
☐ Cock Pheasant
HN 2633
☐ Penguin, large size
HN 2634
☐ Pheasant, large size
HN 2635
☐ Mallard, large size
HN 2636
☐ Indian Rummer Drake
HN 2637
☐ Polar Bear
HN 2638
☐ Leopard on Rock
HN 2639
☐ Tiger on Rock
HN 2640
☐ Fighter Elephant
HN 2641
☐ Lion on Rock
HN 2642
☐ Squirrel
HN 2643
☐ Ch. 'Warlord of Mazelaine', Boxer
HN 2644
☐ Elephant
HN 2645
☐ Dobermann Pinscher
HN 2646
☐ Tiger
HN 2647
☐ Drake

HN 2648
☐ Character Piglets
HN 2649
☐ Character Piglets
HN 2650
☐ Character Piglets
HN 2651
☐ Character Piglets
HN 2652
☐ Character Piglets
HN 2653
☐ Character Piglets
HN 2654
☐ Character Dog with slipper
HN 2655
☐ Siamese Cat, sitting (Chatcull Range)
HN 2656
☐ Pine Martin (Chatcull Range)
HN 2657
☐ Langur Monkey (Chatcull Range)
HN 2658
☐ White-tailed Deer (Chatcull Range)
HN 2659
☐ Brown Bear (Chatcull Range)
HN 2660
☐ Siamese Cat, standing (Chatcull Range)
HN 2661
☐ Mountain Sheep (Chatcull Range)
HN 2662
☐ Siamese Cat, lying (Chatcull Range)
HN 2663
☐ River Hog (Chatcull Range)
HN 2664
☐ Nyala Antelope (Chatcull Range)
HN 2665
☐ Llama (Chatcull Range)
HN 2666
☐ Badger (Chatcull Range)
HN 2667
☐ Ch. 'Bumblikite of Mansergh' Black Labrador (Chatcull Range)
HN 2668
☐ Puffins (Jefferson Sculptures)
HN 2669
☐ Snowy Owl (Jefferson Sculptures)

HN 2670
□ Snowy Owl (Jefferson Sculptures)
HN 3500
□ Black Throat Loon (Jefferson Sculptures)
HN 3501
□ White Winged Crossbills (Jefferson Sculptures)
HN 3502
□ King Eider (Jefferson Sculptures)
HN 3503
□ Roseate Terns (Jefferson Sculptures)
HN 3404
□ Golden-Crowned Kinglet (Jefferson Sculptures)
HN 3505
□ Winter Wren (Jefferson Sculptures)
HN 3506
□ Colorado Chipmunks (Jefferson Sculptures)
HN 3507
□ Harbor Seals (Jefferson Sculptures)
HN 3508
□ Snowshoe Hares (Jefferson Sculptures)

HN 3509
□ Downy Woodpecker (Jefferson Sculptures)
HN 3510
□ Fledgling Bluebird (Jefferson Sculptures)
HN 3511
□ Chipping Sparrow (Jefferson Sculptures)
HN 3522
□ The Leap
HN 3523
□ Capricorn
HN 3524
□ The Gift of Life
HN 3525
□ Courtship
HN 3526
□ Shadowplay
HN 3527
□ Going Home
HN 6406
□ Bulldog, Union Jack, large
HN 6407
□ Bulldog, Union Jack, small
HN 6448
□ Huntsman Fox (Jefferson Sculptures)

"K" NUMERICAL LISTINGS OF MINATURE ANIMALS & BIRD MODELS

K 1
☐ Bulldog
K 2
☐ Bull Pup
K 3
☐ Sealyham
K 4
☐ Sealyham
K 5
☐ Airedale
K 6
☐ Pekinese
K 7
☐ Foxhound
K 8
☐ Terrier
K 9
☐ Cocker Spaniel
K 10
☐ Scottish Terrier
K 11
☐ Cairn
K 12
☐ Cat
K 13
☐ Alsatian
K 14
☐ Bull Terrier
K 15
☐ Chow Chow
K 16
☐ Welsh Corgi
K 17
☐ Dachshund
K 18
☐ Scottish Terrier
K 30
☐ Blue Bird
K 31
☐ Bull Finch

K 32
☐ Budgerigar
K 33
☐ Golden Crested Wren
K 34
☐ Magpie
K 35
☐ Jay
K 36
☐ Goldfinch
K 37
☐ Hare, lying
K 38
☐ Hare, sitting, ears down
K 39
☐ Hare, sitting, ears up
K 19
☐ St. Bernard
K 20
☐ Penguins
K 21
☐ Penguin
K 22
☐ Penguins
K 23
☐ Penguin
K 24
☐ Penguin
K 25
☐ Penguins
K 26
☐ Mallard
K 27
☐ Yellow-Throated Warbler
K 28
☐ Cardinal Bird
K 29
☐ Baltimore Oriole

ANIMAL AND BIRD MODELS

The following alphabetical listings include all the Royal Doulton Animal and Bird figures in the HN and K series (the HN being full-sized figures and the K miniatures). Keep in mind when using these listings that titles were often similar or identical on a number of different figures, which can be distinguished by further description (as given) or by the difference in serial numbers. Similarity in figures is not necessarily an indication of similarity in value, as the experienced collector is well aware.

		Price Range	
☐ Airedale	K 5	75.00	100.00
☐ Airedale, 'Cotsford Topsail' large	HN 1022	350.00	400.00
☐ Airedale, 'Cotsford Topsail' medium	HN 1023	75.00	95.00
☐ Airedale, 'Cotsford Topsail' small	HN 1024	125.00	150.00
☐ Airedale Terrier	HN 988	175.00	215.00
☐ Alsatian	K 13	35.00	45.00
☐ Alsatian, pale grey	HN 112	200.00	300.00
☐ Alsatian, Head	HN 898	150.00	175.00
☐ Alsatian, sitting, large	HN 921	200.00	300.00
☐ Alsatian, 'Benign of Picardy' large	HN 1115	300.00	350.00
☐ Alsatian, 'Benign of Picardy' medium	HN 1116	75.00	95.00
☐ Alsatian, 'Benign of Picardy' small	HN 1117	75.00	125.00
☐ American Foxhound, large	HN 2524	225.00	350.00
☐ American Foxhound, medium	HN 2525	125.00	175.00
☐ American Foxhound, small	HN 2526	100.00	125.00
☐ American Great Dane, large	HN 2601	275.00	350.00
☐ American Great Dane, medium	HN 2602	140.00	175.00
☐ American Great Dane, small	HN 2603	100.00	175.00
☐ Baltimore Oriole	HN 2542	225.00	275.00
☐ Beagle, puppy	HN 831	150.00	175.00
☐ Black Labrador, 'Bumblikite of Mansergh'	HN 2667	85.00	95.00
☐ Bloodhound	HN 176	250.00	300.00
☐ Boxer, 'Warlord of Mazelaine'	HN 2643	75.00	100.00
☐ Brown Bear, Titanian ware	HN 170	250.00	300.00
☐ Budgerigars, pair	HN 2547	125.00	150.00
☐ Bulldog, pup	K 2	35.00	45.00
☐ Bulldog	K 1	35.00	45.00
☐ Bulldog, brown, large	HN 948	250.00	350.00
☐ Bulldog, sitting on lid of Lustre Bowl	HN 987	200.00	225.00
☐ Bulldog, sitting	HN 129	200.00	225.00
☐ Bulldog, sitting	HN 881	150.00	165.00
☐ Bulldog, Brindle, large	HN 1042	300.00	400.00
☐ Bulldog, Brindle, medium	HN 1043	150.00	200.00
☐ Bulldog, Brindle, small	HN 1044	125.00	150.00
☐ Bulldog, brown and white, large	HN 1045	300.00	400.00
☐ Bulldog, brown and white, medium	HN 1046	150.00	200.00
☐ Bulldog, brown and white, small	HN 1047	60.00	65.00

Bulldog, Brindle, HN1042, discontinued 1960, **300.00 — 400.00**

		Price Range	
☐ **Bulldog,** 'Old Bill' with helmet and haversack	HN 146	250.00	300.00
☐ **Bulldog,** 'Old Bill' with tammy and haversack	HN 153	250.00	300.00
☐ **Bulldog,** Union Jack, large	HN 6406	375.00	400.00
☐ **Bulldog,** Union Jack, medium	—	175.00	200.00
☐ **Bulldog,** Union Jack, small	HN 6407	135.00	160.00
☐ **Bulldog,** white, large	HN 1072	300.00	400.00
☐ **Bulldog,** white, medium	HN 1073	150.00	250.00
☐ **Bulldog,** white, small	HN 1074	60.00	65.00
☐ **Bull Terrier**	K 14	100.00	150.00
☐ **Bull Terrier,** 'Bokus Brock', large	HN 1142	500.00	600.00
☐ **Bull Terrier,** 'Bokus Brock', medium	HN 1143	350.00	400.00
☐ **Bull Terrier,** 'Bokus Brock', small	HN 1144	100.00	200.00
☐ **Bull Terrier,** Staffordshire, white, large	HN 1131	500.00	600.00
☐ **Bull Terrier,** Staffordshire, white, medium	HN 1132	300.00	400.00
☐ **Bull Terrier,** Staffordshire, white, small	HN 1133	100.00	200.00
☐ **Cairn**	K 11	35.00	45.00
☐ **Cairn,** black, large	HN 1104	275.00	300.00

			Price Range	
☐ **Cairn,** black, medium	HN 1105	150.00	200.00
☐ **Cairn,** black, small	HN 1106	75.00	100.00
☐ **Cairn,** black, large, earthenware	HN 1107	200.00	300.00
☐ **Cairn,** 'Charming Eyes' large	HN 1033	300.00	350.00
☐ **Cairn,** 'Charming Eyes' medium	HN 1034	150.00	175.00
☐ **Cairn,** 'Charming Eyes' small..........	HN 1035	60.00	65.00
☐ **Cat**	K 12	35.00	45.00
☐ **Cat,** Persian, black and white	HN 999	45.00	60.00
☐ **Cat,** Persian, white	HN 2539	125.00	150.00
☐ **Cat,** Siamese, standing	HN 2660	55.00	70.00
☐ **Cat,** Siamese, sitting	HN 2665	55.00	70.00
☐ **Cat,** Siamese, lying	HN 2662	55.00	70.00
☐ **Cat,** Tortoiseshell	HN 204	225.00	250.00
☐ **Cat,** two	HN 234	250.00	300.00
☐ **Character Dog**	HN 1100	125.00	175.00
☐ **Character Dog,** lying	HN 1101	100.00	145.00
☐ **Character Dog,** on back	HN 1098	100.00	125.00
☐ **Character Dog,** running with ball.......	HN 1097	20.00	35.00
☐ **Character Dog,** with ball..............	HN 1103	25.00	30.00
☐ **Character Dog,** with bone.............	HN 1159	20.00	35.00
☐ **Character Dog,** with plate	HN 1158	20.00	35.00
☐ **Character Dog,** with slipper	HN 2654	20.00	35.00
☐ **Character Dog,** yawning	HN 1099	20.00	35.00
☐ **Chestnut Mare with Foal,** large	HN 2522	300.00	350.00
☐ **Chow Chow**	K 15	35.00	45.00
☐ **Chow,** large	HN 2628	400.00	500.00
☐ **Chow,** medium......................	HN 2629	200.00	300.00
☐ **Chow,** small.......................	HN 2630	100.00	200.00
☐ **Chow,** on stand, brown	HN 837	100.00	200.00
☐ **Chow,** on stand, lighter brown	HN 838	100.00	200.00
☐ **Chow,** on stand, white and grey	HN 839	100.00	200.00
☐ **Cock Pheasant**	HN 2632	425.00	495.00
☐ **Cocker Spaniel**	K 9	35.00	45.00
☐ **Cocker Spaniel,** black................	HN 1000	200.00	225.00
☐ **Cocker Spaniel,** black and white, large..	HN 1108	150.00	250.00
☐ **Cocker Spaniel,** black and white, medium	HN 1109	75.00	95.00
☐ **Cocker Spaniel,** black and white, small .	HN 1078	80.00	125.00
☐ **Cocker Spaniel,** Golden brown, large ...	HN 1186	225.00	300.00
☐ **Cocker Spaniel,** Golden brown, medium	HN 1187	85.00	100.00
☐ **Cocker Spaniel,** Golden brown, small ...	HN 1188	65.00	95.00
☐ **Cocker Spaniel,** liver and white, large ...	HN 1002	200.00	250.00
☐ **Cocker Spaniel,** liver and white, large ...	HN 1134	250.00	275.00
☐ **Cocker Spaniel,** liver and white, medium	HN 1135	95.00	110.00
☐ **Cocker Spaniel,** liver and white, small ..	HN 1136	75.00	95.00
☐ **Cocker Spaniel,** 'Lucky Star of Ware' medium.	HN 1020	85.00	100.00
☐ **Cocker Spaniel,** 'Lucky Star of Ware' small............................	HN 1021	65.00	85.00

Cocker And Pheasant, HN1001, discontinued 1969, **225.00 — 275.00**

		Price Range	
☐ **Cocker Spaniels,** sleeping	HN 2590	45.00	55.00
☐ **Cocker Spaniel and Hare,** liver and white, medium	HN 1063	100.00	200.00
☐ **Cocker Spaniel and Hare,** liver and white, small	HN 1064	100.00	150.00
☐ **Cocker Spaniel and Pheasant,** large	HN 1001	225.00	275.00
☐ **Cocker Spaniel and Pheasant,** large	HN 1137	250.00	300.00
☐ **Cocker Spaniel and Pheasant,** medium .	HN 1028	110.00	135.00
☐ **Cocker Spaniel and Pheasant,** medium .	HN 1138	95.00	110.00
☐ **Cocker Spaniel and Pheasant,** small . . .	HN 1029	125.00	150.00
☐ **Cocker Spaniel and Pheasant,** small . . .	HN 1062	100.00	125.00
☐ **Cocker Spaniel and Pheasant,** small . . .	HN 2600	100.00	125.00
☐ **Cockerel,** sitting	HN 124	125.00	150.00
☐ **Collie,** Ashstead Applause, large	HN 1057	250.00	350.00
☐ **Collie,** Ashstead Applause, medium	HN 1058	85.00	95.00
☐ **Collie,** Ashstead Applause, small	HN 1059	100.00	125.00
☐ **Collie,** brown	HN 976	225.00	275.00
☐ **Collie,** silver grey	HN 975	250.00	300.00
☐ **Collie,** sable	HN 105	200.00	300.00
☐ **Collie,** sable and white	HN 106	250.00	300.00

		Price Range	
☐ **Dachshund**	K 17	35.00	45.00
☐ **Dachshund,** red, large	HN 1139	250.00	300.00
☐ **Dachshund,** red, medium	HN 1140	150.00	200.00
☐ **Dachshund,** red, small	HN 1141	75.00	100.00
☐ **Dachshund,** 'Shrewd Saint', large	HN 1127	200.00	275.00
☐ **Dachshund,** 'Shrewd Saint', medium	HN 1128	75.00	95.00
☐ **Dachshund,** 'Shrewd Saint', small	HN 1129	110.00	135.00
☐ **Dalmatian,** 'Goworth Victor', large	HN 1111	275.00	350.00
☐ **Dalmatian,** 'Goworth Victor', medium	HN 1113	85.00	95.00
☐ **Dalmatian,** 'Goworth Victor', small	HN 1114	95.00	125.00
☐ **Doberman Pinscher**	HN 2645	85.00	95.00
☐ **Drake,** Mallard, large	HN 956	175.00	200.00
☐ **Drake,** Mallard on rocks, small	HN 853	75.00	95.00
☐ **Drake,** Miniature, malachite and purple	HN 807	45.00	65.00
☐ **Drake,** Miniature, white	HN 806	75.00	95.00
☐ **Elephant**	HN 2644	80.00	95.00
☐ **Elephant,** fighting	HN 2640	1200.00	1350.00
☐ **English Setter,** liver and white, large	HN 2620	350.00	450.00
☐ **English Setter,** liver and white, medium	HN 2621	150.00	250.00
☐ **English Setter,** liver and white, small	HN 2622	100.00	175.00
☐ **English Setter,** 'Maesydd Mustard' large	HN 1049	300.00	350.00
☐ **English Setter,** 'Maesydd Mustard' medium	HN 1050	80.00	95.00
☐ **English Setter,** 'Maesydd Mustard' small	HN 1051	90.00	110.00
☐ **English Setter and Pheasant**	HN 2529	375.00	400.00
☐ **Fox,** on rock	HN 147	125.00	150.00
☐ **Fox,** Red Frock Coat	HN 100	350.00	400.00
☐ **Fox,** sitting	HN 2634	550.00	650.00

Fox-Hound, K7, discontinued 1977, **35.00 — 45.00**

☐ **Foxhound**	K 7	20.00	35.00
☐ **Foxhound**	HN 231	275.00	325.00
☐ **Foxhound,** seated	HN 166	200.00	225.00
☐ **Foxhound,** 'Tring Rattler' large	HN 1025	300.00	350.00
☐ **Foxhound,** 'Tring Rattler' medium	HN 1026	200.00	250.00

		Price Range	
☐ Foxhound, 'Tring Rattler' small	HN 1027	175.00	195.00
☐ Fox Terrier	HN 942	100.00	200.00
☐ Fox Terrier	HN 943	100.00	200.00
☐ Fox Terrier	HN 944	100.00	200.00
☐ Fox Terrier	HN 945	185.00	225.00
☐ Fox Terrier, 'Crackley Hunter' medium ..	HN 1013	150.00	200.00
☐ Fox Terrier, 'Crackley Hunter' small	HN 1014	60.00	65.00
☐ Fox Terrier, smooth-haired, large	HN 1068	350.00	450.00
☐ Fox Terrier, smooth-haired, medium	HN 1069	200.00	250.00
☐ Fox Terrier, smooth-haired, small	HN 1070	150.00	200.00
☐ Fox Terrier, standing	HN 909	100.00	200.00
☐ Fox Terrier, sitting	HN 910	100.00	200.00
☐ Fox Terrier, standing	HN 923	150.00	250.00
☐ Fox Terrier, sitting, large	HN 924	200.00	275.00
☐ French Poodle, medium	HN 2631	85.00	95.00
☐ Gordon Setter, large	HN 1079	325.00	400.00
☐ Gordon Setter, medium	HN 1080	175.00	200.00
☐ Gordon Setter, small................	HN 1081	100.00	150.00
☐ Great Dane, large	HN 2560	300.00	400.00
☐ Great Dane, medium.................	HN 2561	175.00	200.00
☐ Great Dane, small	HN 2562	100.00	175.00
☐ Greyhound, brown, large	HN 1065	300.00	400.00
☐ Greyhound, brown, medium	HN 1066	150.00	275.00
☐ Greyhound, brown, small	HN 1067	150.00	200.00
☐ Greyhound, black and white, large	HN 1075	300.00	400.00
☐ Greyhound, black and white, medium...	HN 1076	150.00	275.00
☐ Greyhound, black and white, small	HN 1077	150.00	200.00
☐ Greyhound, black and white, seated	HN 889	200.00	300.00
☐ Greyhound, brown, seated	HN 890	200.00	300.00
☐ Gude Grey Mare, no foal, medium	HN 2569	250.00	300.00
☐ Gude Grey Mare, with foal, medium	HN 2532	250.00	300.00
☐ Hare, lying	K 37	35.00	50.00
☐ Hare, lying, small	HN 2594	35.00	45.00
☐ Hare, sitting, ears down	K 38	40.00	55.00
☐ Hare, sitting, ears up	K 39	35.00	40.00
☐ Huntsman Fox.....................	HN 6448	40.00	50.00
☐ Irish Setter, large..................	HN 1054	300.00	400.00
☐ Irish Setter, medium	HN 1055	85.00	100.00
☐ Irish Setter, small	HN 1056	90.00	125.00
☐ Kingfisher, small...................	HN 2573	75.00	100.00
☐ Kitten, lying on back, brown..........	HN 2579	35.00	45.00
☐ Kitten, sitting licking hind paw, brown ..	HN 2580	35.00	45.00
☐ Kitten, sleeping, brown..............	HN 2581	35.00	45.00
☐ Kitten, sitting on haunches, tan	HN 2582	35.00	45.00
☐ Kitten, sitting, licking front paw	HN 2583	35.00	45.00
☐ Kitten, sitting, surprised, tan	HN 2584	35.00	45.00
☐ Langur Monkey	HN 2657	150.00	175.00
☐ Leopard on Rock	HN 2638	1300.00	1500.00
☐ Lion on Rock	HN 2641	1300.00	1500.00

		Price Range	
☐ Mallard	HN 2556	200.00	225.00
☐ Mountain Sheep	HN 2661	150.00	200.00
☐ Nyala Antelope	HN 2664	250.00	300.00
☐ Owl, character, check shawl, ermine collar	HN 187	750.00	850.00
☐ Owl, 'Wise Old' in red cloak and ermine collar	HN 173	400.00	500.00
☐ Parrot, on rock	HN 185	250.00	300.00
☐ Peacock	HN 2577	150.00	175.00
☐ Pekinese	K 6	35.00	45.00
☐ Pekinese, 'Biddee of Ifield', large	HN 1010	325.00	375.00
☐ Pekinese, 'Biddee of Ifield', medium	HN 1011	250.00	300.00
☐ Pekinese, 'Biddee of Ifield', small	HN 1012	60.00	65.00
☐ Pekinese, sitting, large	HN 1039	250.00	300.00
☐ Pekinese, sitting, small	HN 1040	125.00	150.00
☐ Pekinese Puppy, sitting	HN 832	125.00	175.00
☐ Pekinese Puppy, standing	HN 833	125.00	185.00
☐ Pekinese Puppy, on stand, black and brown	HN 834	150.00	195.00
☐ Pekinese Puppy, on stand, lighter brown	HN 835	150.00	195.00
☐ Pekinese Puppy, on stand, light color	HN 836	150.00	195.00
☐ Penquins	K 20	100.00	125.00
☐ Penquins	K 21	75.00	100.00
☐ Penquins	K 22	100.00	125.00
☐ Penquins	K 23	75.00	100.00
☐ Penquins	K 24	75.00	100.00
☐ Penquins	K 25	100.00	125.00
☐ Pheasant	HN 2545	235.00	275.00
☐ Pheasant, small	HN 2576	150.00	175.00
☐ Pig, asleep	HN 800	75.00	95.00
☐ Pig, asleep, large	HN 801	125.00	150.00
☐ Piglets, character	HN 2648	100.00	150.00
☐ Piglets, character	HN 2649	100.00	150.00
☐ Piglets, character	HN 2650	100.00	150.00
☐ Piglets, character	HN 2651	100.00	150.00
☐ Piglets, character	HN 2652	100.00	150.00
☐ Piglets, character	HN 2653	100.00	150.00
☐ Pointer	HN 2624	250.00	300.00
☐ Polar Bear, sitting on green cube	HN 119	175.00	250.00
☐ Poodle, large	HN 2625	400.00	500.00
☐ Poodle, medium	HN 2626	200.00	300.00
☐ Poodle, small	HN 2627	100.00	200.00
☐ 'Pride of Shires', mare and foal, grey, small	HN 2536	200.00	250.00
☐ 'Pride of Shires', mare, no foal, brown, medium	HN 2564	185.00	225.00
☐ Puppies in Basket, three, terriers	HN 2588	45.00	55.00
☐ Puppy	HN 128	135.00	185.00
☐ Puppy, begging, Cairn	HN 2589	45.00	55.00

		Price	Range
☐ **Puppy,** in basket, Cocker	HN 2586	45.00	55.00
☐ **Puppy,** in basket, lying, Cocker	HN 2585	45.00	55.00
☐ **Puppy,** in basket, Terrier	HN 2587	45.00	55.00
☐ **Rhinoceros**	HN 141	200.00	300.00
☐ **River Hog**	HN 2663	175.00	225.00
☐ **Sealyham**	K 3	35.00	45.00
☐ **Sealyham**	K 4	75.00	100.00
☐ **Sealyham**	HN 2508	125.00	150.00
☐ **Sealyham,** character dog	HN 2509	125.00	150.00
☐ **Sealyham,** running	HN 2510	110.00	135.00
☐ **Sealyham,** barking	HN 2511	125.00	175.00
☐ **Sealyham,** lying, large	HN 1041	275.00	300.00
☐ **Sealyham,** lying, medium	HN 1052	200.00	250.00
☐ **Sealyham,** lying, small	HN 1053	150.00	200.00

Sealyham, HN1030, large, discontinued 1957, **500.00 — 600.00**

☐ **Sealyham,** 'Scotia Stylist', large	HN 1030	500.00	600.00
☐ **Sealyham,** 'Scotia Stylist', medium	HN 1031	175.00	225.00
☐ **Sealyham,** 'Scotia Stylist', small	HN 1032	125.00	150.00
☐ **Sealyham,** Terrier, black patches on face	HN 982	150.00	175.00
☐ **Sealyham,** Terrier, brown patches on face	HN 983	150.00	175.00
☐ **Scottish Terrier**	K 10	35.00	45.00
☐ **Scottish Terrier**	K 18	35.00	45.00

		Price Range	
☐ **Scottish Terrier,** large	HN 1008	300.00	400.00
☐ **Scottish Terrier,** 'Albourne Arthur' medium	HN 1015	150.00	200.00
☐ **Scottish Terrier,** 'Albourne Arthur' small	HN 1016	65.00	95.00
☐ **Scottish Terrier,** sitting, black	HN 1017	300.00	400.00
☐ **Scottish Terrier,** sitting, black	HN 1018	200.00	250.00
☐ **Scottish Terrier,** sitting, black	HN 1019	100.00	125.00
☐ **Scottish Terrier,** begging	HN 1038	300.00	350.00
☐ **Scottish Terrier,** light grey and brown . . .	HN 981	225.00	250.00
☐ **Springer Spaniel,** 'Dry Toast', large	HN 2515	225.00	275.00
☐ **Springer Spaniel,** 'Dry Toast', medium . .	HN 2516	150.00	175.00
☐ **Springer Spaniel,** 'Dry Toast', small	HN 2517	50.00	60.00
☐ **St. Bernard**	K 19	35.00	45.00
☐ **Staffordshire Bull Terrier,** medium	HN 1132	175.00	225.00
☐ **Teal Duck**	HN 229	150.00	185.00
☐ **Terrier**	K 8	35.00	45.00
☐ **Terrier,** seated, black and brown	HN 997	175.00	225.00
☐ **Terrier's Head**	HN 962	150.00	175.00
☐ **Terrier,** 'Crackley Startler', rough-haired, large	HN 1007	300.00	400.00
☐ **Terrier,** 'Chosen Dan of Notts', smooth-haired, large	HN 2512	400.00	500.00
☐ **Terrier,** 'Chosen Dan of Notts', smooth-haired, medium	HN 2513	200.00	300.00
☐ **Terrier,** 'Chosen Dan of Notts', smooth-haired, small	HN 2514	175.00	200.00
☐ **Tiger**	HN 2646	750.00	850.00
☐ **Tiger,** lying	HN 911	375.00	425.00
☐ **Tiger,** sitting	HN 912	375.00	425.00
☐ **Tiger on Rock**	HN 2639	1350.00	1500.00
☐ **Welsh Corgi**	K 16	35.00	45.00
☐ **Welsh Corgi,** large	HN 2557	300.00	350.00
☐ **Welsh Corgi,** medium	HN 2558	200.00	250.00
☐ **Welsh Corgi,** small	HN 2559	45.00	60.00
☐ **West Highland White Terrier,** large	HN 1048	500.00	600.00
☐ **Yellow Bird on Rock,** beak closed	HN 145A	100.00	125.00
☐ **Yellow Bird on Rock,** beak open	HN 145	100.00	125.00

CHATCULL RANGE OF ANIMALS

This is a series bearing standard HN prefix numbers, which originated in 1940. The designer of these appealing portrayals was Joseph Ledger, whose estate was known as "Chatcull Hall" — thus the title for the series. These were not limited editions but the majority are now out of production and they are becoming harder to find. The collector interested in adding them to his cabinet might be well advised to do his shopping early, as prices are likely to rise more sharply across-the-board on Chatculls when the entire series is out of production.

		Price Range	
☐ **Badger**	HN 2666	225.00	250.00
☐ **Black Labrador** 'Bumblikite of Mansergh'	HN 2667	85.00	95.00
☐ **Brown Bear**	HN 2659	250.00	300.00
☐ **Langur Monkey**	HN 2657	250.00	300.00
☐ **Llama**	HN 2665	175.00	225.00
☐ **Mountain Sheep**	HN 2661	150.00	200.00
☐ **Nyala Antelope**	HN 2664	250.00	300.00
☐ **Pine Martin**	HN 2656	225.00	250.00
☐ **River Hog**	HN 2663	175.00	225.00
☐ **Siamese Cat,** lying	HN 2662	55.00	70.00
☐ **Siamese Cat,** sitting	HN 2655	55.00	70.00
☐ **Siamese Cat,** standing	HN 2660	55.00	70.00
☐ **White-tailed Deer**	HN 2658	250.00	300.00

JEFFERSON SCULPTURES

The following wildlife sculptures were created by Robert Jefferson. Beautiful renditions of nature, most were produced in limited edition, however, a few models were unlimited. First limited edition was released in 1974.

		Date	Price
☐ **Black-Throated Loon** Limited edition of 150	HN 3500	1974	2350.00
☐ **Chipping Sparrow** Limited edition of 200	HN 3511	1976	950.00
☐ **Colorado Chipmunks** Limited edition of 75	HN 3506	1974	7500.00
☐ **Downy Woodpecker** Edition unlimited	HN 3509	1975	525.00
☐ **Fledgling Bluebird** Limited edition of 250	HN 3510	1976	600.00
☐ **Golden-Crowned Kinglet** Edition unlimited	HN 3504	1974	525.00
☐ **Harbor Seals** Limited edition of 75	HN 3507	1975	1600.00
☐ **Huntsman Fox** Edition unlimited	HN 6448	—	50.00
☐ **King Eider** Limited edition of 150	HN 3502	1974	1800.00
☐ **Puffins** Limited edition of 250	HN 2668	1974	1600.00
☐ **Roseate Terns** Limited edition of 150	HN 3503	1974	2500.00
☐ **Snowshoe Hares** Limited edition of 75	HN 3508	1975	2750.00
☐ **Snowy Owl,** Female, Limited edition of 150	HN 2670	1974	2150.00
☐ **Snowy Owl,** Male Limited edition of 150	HN 2669	1974	1750.00
☐ **White-Winged Cross Bills** Limited edition of 250	HN 3501	1974	1450.00
☐ **Winter Wren** Edition unlimited	HN 3505	1974	375.00

FIGURINES

(see separate sections for images, limited edition and prestige figurines)
The following ALPHABETICAL listing gives series numbers, dates, descriptions, and current retail selling prices for figures in the HN series. Descriptions indicate the color schemes found on the majority of specimens on each model. Color variations do exist on many models. While some collectors take a special interest in "off-color" models, the market on them is not widespread enough to establish firm values.

	Date	Price Range	
ABDULLAH			
HN 1410			
☐ Dark skinned figure seated on blue cushions, green turban, height 5¾", designer L. Harradine	1930-1938	950.00	1150.00
HN 2104			
☐ Dark skinned figure seated on black base which has blue rug with red, green, black squares, large cushion of yellow and green grey trousers, black coat, orange shirt, red waistband, orange and red turban with green feather, height 6", designer L. Harradine.	1953-1962	700.00	800.00
A'COURTING			
HN 2004			
☐ Boy and girl figure on light green base, boy's costume is shaded blues, jacket dark blue with gold buttons, hat black, girl's costume is red dress with white collar, white apron in hand, white head cap with blue ribbon, height 7¼", designer L. Harradine. . .	1947-1953	650.00	750.00
ADRIENNE			
HN 2152			
☐ Gown of purple with yellow scarf, height 7½", designer M. Davies.	1964-1976	175.00	225.00
HN 2304			
☐ Gown of blue with very light green scarf, height 7½", designer M. Davies	1964-	155.00	

	Date	Price Range

AFTERNOON CALL, The
(sometimes referred to as Lady
With Ermine Muff)

HN 82
☐ Lady seated on beige coloured couch,
cream coloured gown with green
designs, coat of blue with white fur
trim and muff green hat with blue
feather, height 6¾", designer E. W.
Light............................ 1918-1938   2250.00 2500.00

AFTERNOON TEA
HN 1747
☐ Two ladies seated on light coloured
sofa, one gown is pink, bonnet of
green with blue ribbons, the other
gown is white skirt with blue and yellow flower design, jacket is light blue,
bonnet is white with red ribbons,
height 5¾", designer P. Railston..... 1935-1982   325.00

HN 1748
☐ Green dress, height 5¼", designer
P. Railston. 1935-1949   450.00   550.00

AILEEN
HN 1645
☐ Seated figure in green dress, shawl is
light blue with red flowers and blue
flowers, white necklace, red shoes,
height 6", designer L. Harradine. 1934-1938   750.00   850.00

HN 1664
☐ Pink skirt, height 6", designer L. Har-
radine. 1934-1938   850.00   950.00

HN 1803
☐ Cream dress, with blue shawl, height
6", designer L. Harradine........... 1937-1949   700.00   800.00

A LA MODE
HN 2544
☐ Tall figure with red hair and green
dress with a darker green design,
height 12½", designer E. J. Griffiths . 1974-1979   225.00   275.00

	Date	Price Range	

ALL ABOARD
HN 2940
☐ Depicts an old sea captain, standing on a grey base alongside is a clock and a sign telling departure time of deep sea trips. Mans outfit is a shade of blue turtle neck sweater over beige trousers, black boots, height 9¼", designer R. Tabbenor   1982-   **175.00**

ALCHEMIST, The
HN 1259
☐ Mottled robe, red hat, height 11½", designer L. Harradine.   1927-1938   **1550.00 1750.00**

HN 1282
☐ Dark brown robe with multicoloured sleeves and red scarf, dark brown hat, holding small object in one hand, height 11¼", designer L. Harradine. .   1928-1938   **1550.00 1750.00**

ALEXANDRA
HN 2398
☐ Green dress with white flowers and flowing yellow cape, height 7¾", designer M. Davies.   1970-1976   **200.00   250.00**

ALFRED JINGLE
HN 541
This was discontinued in 1932 renumbered in 1932 and still produced.
☐ A character from Dickens "Pickwick Papers," height 3¾", designer L. Harradine.   1922-1932   **45.00   60.00**
☐ **M-52** Renumbered as a miniature, height 3¾", designer L. Harradine. . .   1932-   **29.95**

ALICE
HN 2158
☐ Blue dress, white ribbon in blonde hair, open book on lap, height 5", designer M. Davies.   1960-1980   **85.00   115.00**

ALISON
HN 2336
☐ White skirt with small red and green design, blue overdress, height 7½", designer M. Davies.   1966-   **155.00**

	Date	Price Range	

ALL-A-BLOOMING

HN 1457
☐ Blue dress, height 6½", designer
L. Harradine. 1931-Unknown   900.00   1000.00

HN 1466
☐ Lady seated on brown wicker stand, yellow/green basket of flowers beside her, skirt red, apron white, shawl dark blue with shades of yellow and green, hat is shades of blue with green feathers, height 6½", designer L. Harradine.   1931-1938   1000.00   1100.00

AMY

HN 2958
☐ One of the charming Kate Greenaway figures. Young figure in very pale blue dress with darker blue ruffles on bottom dark blue ribbon at waist. Dark hair with white cap. Figure is holding a doll in red dress, yellow hair, height 6", designer P. Parsons.   1982-   100.00

ANGELA

HN 1204
☐ Figure on light coloured pedestal, costume of shaded reds and blue, red shoes, holding large fan behind head of dark blue and red, height 7¼", designer L. Harradine.   1926-1938   675.00   850.00

HN 1303
☐ Blue fan and spotted costume, height 7¼", designer L. Harradine.   1928-1938   950.00   1100.00

ANGELINA

HN 2013
☐ Red dress trimmed in white, holding green hat with blue ribbon, height 6¾", designer L. Harradine.   1948-1951   700.00   800.00

ANNA (Kate Greenaway)

HN 2802
☐ Small girl, purple dress, white apron and bonnet, holding flower in one hand, on white base, height 5¾", designer M. Davies.   1976-1982   100.00

Annabella, HN1871, **450.00 — 525.00**

ANNABELLA	Date	Price Range	
HN 1871			
☐ Small figure in curtsey position, orange coloured skirt with green bodice, holding basket of flowers on arm, hat matches skirt, height 5¼", designer L. Harradine.	1938-1949	**450.00**	**525.00**
HN 1872			
☐ Green skirt and blue bodice, height 5¼", designer L. Harradine.	1938-1949	**450.00**	**525.00**
HN 1875			
☐ Red dress, height 4¾", designer L. Harradine.	1938-1949	**450.00**	**525.00**
ANNETTE			
HN 1471			
☐ Dutch figure in blue gown with white apron, white dutch cap carrying light coloured basket with red fruit, light wooden shoes, height 6¼", designer L. Harradine.	1931-1938	**375.00**	**425.00**

ANNETTE	Date	Price Range	

HN 1472

☐ Gown of green, apron shaded green, red and cream, red basket, height 6", designer L. Harradine. 1931-1949   425.00   475.00

HN 1550

☐ Green skirt, apron with light stripes, red blouse, height 6¼", designer L. Harradine. 1933-1949   450.00   500.00

ANTHEA

HN 1526

☐ Green dress with white designs, blue shawl with red flowers, green hat with red feather, carrying parasol, height 6½", designer L. Harradine. 1932-1938   550.00   650.00

HN 1527

☐ Gown of shaded blues and reds with cream, shawl white with red and black designs, blue hat with light feather, height 6½", designer L. Harradine. 1932-1949   600.00   700.00

HN 1669

☐ Skirt of cream, jacket red, shawl green, hat green, height 6½", designer L. Harradine. 1934-1938   600.00   700.00

ANTOINETTE

HN 1850

☐ Black base and pedestal, gown is red with green trim, hat green with black ribbons (1st version), height 8¼", designer L. Harradine. 1938-1949   800.00   900.00

HN 1851

☐ Base black, pedestal blue and cream, gown shaded blue and red with blue overdress, blue hat with green ribbons (1st version), height 8¼", designer L. Harradine. 1938-1949   800.00   900.00

HN 2326

☐ White gown with gold design and trim, gold shoe, seated figure (2nd version), height 6¼", designer M. Davies. 1967-1979   150.00   175.00

APPLE MAID, The

Date   Price Range

HN 2160
☐ Figure seated on brown wicker chair, black skirt, green blouse, white apron, white head covering, brown basket with apples, height 6½ ", designer L. Harradine.   1957-1962   400.00   450.00

ARAB/MOOR

HN   33
☐ Green costume, blue cloak, height 15¾ ", designer C. J. Noke.   1913-1938   1600.00   1800.00

HN 343
☐ Striped yellow and purple costume, height 16½ ", designer C. J. Noke. . . .   1919-1938   1750.00   2000.00

HN 378
☐ Costume of patchwork colours of green, brown, yellow hooded cloak of dark blue, multicoloured base, height 16½ ", designer C. J. Noke.   1920-1930   1500.00   1750.00

ARTFUL DODGER, The

HN 546
☐ A character from Dickens "Oliver Twist," height 3¾ ", designer L. Harradine.   1922-   45.00   60.00
☐ **M-55** Renumbered as a miniature, height 4¼ ", designer L. Harradine. . .   1932-   29.95

ASCOT

HN 2356
☐ Seated lady on brown chair, green dress, green hat with blue trim, yellow boa, light blue parasol, height 5¾ ", designer M. Davies.   1968-   185.00

AT EASE

HN 2473
☐ Lady seated on green and brown chaise lounge, dark hair, pale green gown trimmed in brown, height 6", designer M. Davies.   1973-1979   200.00   250.00

At Ease, HN2473, **200.00 — 250.00**

AUTUMN	Date	Price Range	
HN 314			
☐ Blue/grey base, pink gown, autumn coloured flowers in arm (1st version), height 7¼ ", designer unknown.	1918-1938	**1200.00**	**1400.00**
HN 474			
☐ Patterned robe (1st version), height 7½ ", designer unknown.	1921-1938	**1300.00**	**1400.00**
HN 2087			
☐ Green/yellow base, gown of red, blue/white apron, small white cap with blue ribbons, brown broom (2nd version), height 7¼ ", designer M. Davies	1952-1959	**450.00**	**500.00**

AUTUMN BREEZES

HN 1911			
☐ Pink and pale blue skirt, green bodice and hat, white muff. Earlier mold has two feet, height 7½ ", designer L. Harradine.	1939-1976	**200.00**	**250.00**

AUTUMN BREEZES (cont.)	Date	Price Range	

HN 1913
☐ Green skirt, dark blue bodice, blue hat with black apron, white muff, height 7½", designer L. Harradine. . . 1939-1971 250.00 300.00

HN 1934
☐ Red skirt and bodice, white hat, height 7½", designer L. Harradine. . . 1940- 170.00

HN 2147
☐ White skirt, black bodice, white hat and muff, height 7½", designer L. Harradine. 1955-1971 325.00 375.00

AWAKENING, The

HN 1927
☐ Nude figure on light coloured base with a full length of light material draped down front, height unknown, designer L. Harradine. 1940-1949 2050.00 2200.00

BABA

HN 1230
☐ Small seated figure with striped yellow and purple trousers and cone shaped hat, height 3¼", designer L. Harradine. 1927-1938 550.00 650.00

HN 1243
☐ Trousers of orange, height 3¼", designer L. Harradine. 1927-1927 550.00 650.00

HN 1244
☐ Trousers of yellow and green stripes, height 3¼", designer L. Harradine. . . 1927-1938 550.00 650.00

HN 1245
☐ White trousers with blue/black markings, height 3¼", designer L. Harradine. 1927-1938 550.00 650.00

HN 1246
☐ Trousers of green, height 3¼", designer L. Harradine. 1927-1938 550.00 650.00

HN 1247
☐ Trousers of white with black spots, height 3¼", designer L. Harradine. . . 1928-1938 550.00 650.00

HN 1248
☐ Green striped trousers, white striped sleeves, red waistband, white cone shaped hat, height 3¼", designer L. Harradine. 1927-1938 550.00 650.00

Babette, HN1423, 500.00 — 600.00

BABETTE	Date	Price Range	
HN 1423			
☐ Small figure in bathing costume on base, with open parasol, blue and white costume, height 5″, designer L. Harradine.	1930-1938	**500.00**	**600.00**
HN 1424			
☐ Costume yellow and red stripes, height 5″, designer L. Harradine.	1930-1938	**550.00**	**650.00**
BABIE			
HN 1679			
☐ Small figure in gown of green and cream, blue bonnet with red feather, carrying red parasol, height 4¾″, designer L. Harradine.	1935-	**75.00**	
HN 1842			
☐ Pink dress, green hat and umbrella, height 4¾″, designer L. Harradine.	1938-1949	**150.00**	**200.00**

	Date	Price Range
BABIE (cont.)		

HN 2121
☐ Dress is shades of pinks decorated with white summer flowers. Bonnet is pink with gold ribbon, gold parasol, height 4¾", designer L. Harradine. . .   1983-   75.00

BABY

HN 12
☐ Small child figure on light coloured base, wrapped entirely in blue/grey robe, height unknown, designer C. J. Noke.   1913-1938   2050.00 2200.00

BABY BUNTING

HN 2108
☐ White child figure with brown covering arms and head, head cover has ears, height 5¼", designer M. Davies.   1953-1959   225.00   275.00

BACHELOR, The

HN 2319
☐ Character figure seated in dark brown chair with foot stool, brown trousers, black vest, white shirt, brown tie, blue socks, brown shoes, darning blue sock, height 7", designer M. Nicoll . . .   1964-1975   250.00   300.00

BALLAD SELLER

HN 2266
☐ Skirt and bonnet of pink, bodice white with gold, holding white sheet with printing in one hand, rolled white sheet in other, height 7½", designer M. Davies.   1968-1973   300.00   350.00

BALLERINA

HN 2116
☐ White dress with shades of blue and red, red ribbon at waist, red ballet shoes on dark base, blue ribbon and flower trim on gown, height 7¼", designer M. Davies.   1953-1973   300.00   350.00

Balloon Girl, HN2818, **125.00**

	Date	Price Range
BALLOON GIRL		
HN 2818		
☐ Seated blonde girl dressed in grey skirt, yellow blouse, red scarf tied around neck, green shawl with red fringe, hat is black with beige ribbon, colorful balloons in her hand, height 6½ ", designer W. K. Harper.	1982-	**125.00**
BALLOON MAN, The		
HN 1954		
☐ Character figure seated on brown box, green trousers, black shoes, black coat, brown vest, white shirt, brown hat, holding multicolour balloons, with red knapsack with white dots beside box, height 7¼ ", designer L. Harradine.	1940-	**175.00**

	Date	Price Range	

BALLOON SELLER, The

HN 479

☐ Blue dress, white spots, height 9",
designer L. Harradine. 1921-1938   **2250.00 2500.00**

HN 486

☐ Blue dress, no hat, height 9", de-
signer L. Harradine. 1921-1938   **1500.00 1700.00**

HN 548

☐ Black shawl, blue dress, height 9",
designer L. Harradine. 1922-1938   **800.00 900.00**

HN 583

☐ White skirt with small green design,
green shawl with red fringe, red
blouse, black hat with green feather,
baby in orange and red, balloons multicoloured, height 9", designer L. Har-
radine. 1923-1949   **500.00 600.00**

HN 697

☐ Striped red shawl, blue dress, height
9", designer L. Harradine. 1925-1938   **800.00 900.00**

BARBARA

HN 1421

☐ Brown base, gown of cream with red
and blue flower design, shawl is blue/
red with black designs, bonnet blue/
red, holding small envelope in one
hand and small round red/yellow
purse, height 7¾", designer L. Har-
radine. 1930-1938   **750.00 850.00**

HN 1432

☐ Black base, gown of shaded blue, red,
green, shawl multicoloured, bonnet
light multicoloured, also small purse,
height 7¾", designer L. Harradine. . . 1930-1938   **775.00 875.00**

HN 1461

☐ Green dress, height 7¾", designer
L. Harradine. 1931-1938   **750.00 800.00**

BATHER, The

HN 597

☐ Mottled grey robe, blue base (1st version), height 7¾", designer L. Harra-
dine. 1924-1938   **900.00 1000.00**

BATHER, The (cont.)	Date	Price Range	

HN 687
- ☐ Royal blue base, also royal blue lining of purple robe which has blue designs, nude white figure with greenish shoes (1st version), height 7¾", designer L. Harradine. . . . . 1924-1949 — **675.00 775.00**

HN 773
- ☐ Pink robe, blue and black markings (2nd version), height 7½", designer L. Harradine. . . . . 1925-1938 — **900.00 1100.00**

HN 774
- ☐ Nude white figure on black base with purple robe which has red lining, black spots (2nd version), height 7¾", designer L. Harradine. . . . . 1925-1938 — **900.00 1100.00**

HN 781
- ☐ Blue and green robe (1st version), height 7¾", designer L. Harradine. . . 1926-1938 — **800.00 900.00**

HN 782
- ☐ Mottled purple robe, black lining (1st version), height 7¾", designer L. Harradine. . . . . 1926-1938 — **800.00 900.00**

HN 1227
- ☐ Flowered pink robe (2nd version), height 7½", designer L. Harradine. . . 1927-1938 — **900.00 1000.00**

HN 1238
- ☐ Brown base, white nude figure, black robe with gold design, lining of robe is red (1st version), height 7¾", designer L. Harradine. . . . . 1927-1938 — **900.00 1000.00**

HN 1708
- ☐ Light green base, figure has black bathing suit, black shoes, robe of red with black and green shadings, blue lining (1st version), height 7¾", designer L. Harradine. . . . . 1935-1938 — **1250.00 1450.00**

BASKET WEAVER, The
HN 2245
- ☐ Seated figure in gown of light green with white trim, with light coloured basket on lap and at side, height 5¾", designer M. Nicoll. . . . . 1959-1962 — **500.00 600.00**

	Date	Price Range

BEACHCOMBER
HN 2487
☐ Light coloured base, barefooted character figure, grey pants, lavender shirt, green scarf, grey hat, holding shell, matt finish, height 6¼", designer M. Nicoll.   1973-1976   200.00   250.00

BEAT YOU TO IT
HN 2871
☐ Blue base, light tan wicker chair, brown dog in chair with blue cushions, girl's gown is white with shaded red and yellow sleeves, tiny flower design at hem line, height 6½", designer M. Davies.   1980-   350.00

BEDTIME
HN 1978
☐ Small girl in white nightgown on black base, height 5¾", designer L. Harradine.   1945-   55.00

BEDTIME STORY, The
HN 2059
☐ Three figures, lady's gown is red, girl's gown is white skirt with blue design, blue bodice, boy's tan trousers, blue jacket, height 4¾", designer L. Harradine.   1950-   215.00

BEGGAR, The
HN 526
☐ A character from "The Beggar's Opera," with blue trousers, red sash and dark grey cloak (1st version), height 6½", designer L. Harradine. . .   1921-1949   600.00   700.00
HN 591
☐ Different glaze finish (1st version), height 6¾", designer L. Harradine. . .   1924-1949   650.00   750.00
HN 2175
☐ Taller version but with brown trousers, red sash and darker grey cloak (2nd version), height 6¾", designer L. Harradine.   1956-1962   550.00   625.00

	Date	Price Range	
BELLE, The			

HN 754

☐ 18th century style gown of multicolours, trimmed in green, blue bonnet with red ribbons, red shoes, on green/black base, height 6½", designer L. Harradine. 1925-1938 **1150.00 1250.00**

HN 776

☐ No colour detail available, height 6½", designer L. Harradine. 1925-1938 **1250.00 1350.00**

BELLE

HN 2340

☐ Small female figure in green tiered dress, trimmed in white (2nd version), height 4½", designer M. Davies. 1968- **65.00**

BELLE O' THE BALL

HN 1997

☐ Shaded yellow, red, blue gown with red overdress, small light coloured hat, holding masking in one hand, seated on couch of brown and light yellow with shaded blue/red, pillow multicoloured 1947-1979 **275.00 325.00**

BERNICE

HN 2071

☐ Dress is shaded colours of red with red cloak, black hat with blue feather, height 7¾", designer M. Davies. 1951-1953 **600.00 700.00**

BESS

HN 2002

☐ White dress with coloured flowers, red cloak, height 7¼", designer L. Harradine. 1947-1969 **275.00 325.00**

HN 2003

☐ Pink dress with blue cloak with red lining, height 7¼", designer L. Harradine. 1947-1950 **400.00 500.00**

BETH (Kate Greenaway)

HN 2870

☐ Small figure on white base, light lavender dress and white apron with green trim, holding single flower, white bonnet with green ribbon, height 5¾", designer M. Davies. 1980- **100.00**

BETSY	Date	Price Range	
HN 2111			
☐ Gown of shaded blues and reds, white apron with blue flower design trimmed in green, white cap, height 7″, designer L. Harradine.	1953-1959	350.00	400.00

BETTY

	Date	Price Range	
HN 402			
☐ Full pink gown with black collar, tall hat of black with gold feather and trim (1st version), height unknown, designer L. Harradine.	1920-1938	2000.00	2250.00
HN 403			
☐ Green skirt, blue, yellow and white border (1st version), height unknown, designer L. Harradine.	1920-1938	2000.00	2250.00
HN 435			
☐ Blue skirt with yellow spots (1st version), height unknown, designer L. Harradine.	1921-1938	2000.00	2250.00
HN 438			
☐ Green skirt (1st version), height unknown, designer L. Harradine.	1921-1938	2000.00	2250.00
HN 477			
☐ Spotted green skirt (1st version), height unknown, designer L. Harradine.	1921-1938	2500.00	3000.00
HN 478			
☐ White spotted skirt (1st version), height unknown, designer L. Harradine.	1921-1938	2500.00	3000.00
HN 1404			
☐ Small girl with white dog at feet, gown of white with shaded reds trimmed in blue, with tiny blue figure on dress (2nd version), height 4½″, designer L. Harradine.	1930-1938	500.00	600.00
HN 1405			
☐ Green dress (2nd version), height 4½″, designer L. Harradine.	1930-1938	500.00	600.00
HN 1435			
☐ Mottled multicoloured dress (2nd version), height 4½″, designer L. Harradine.	1930-1938	500.00	600.00
HN 1436			
☐ Patterned green dress (2nd version), height 4½″, designer L. Harradine. . .	1930-1938	500.00	600.00

BIDDY	Date	Price Range	
HN 1445			
☐ Green tiered gown with blue shawl, blue bonnet, holding a green parasol, height 5½", designer L. Harradine. . .	1931-1938	300.00	350.00
HN 1500			
☐ Yellow dress, height 5½", designer L. Harradine.	1932-1938	300.00	350.00
HN 1513			
☐ Shaded gown of red with blue shawl, blue bonnet, holding shaded blue and yellow parasol, height 5½", designer L. Harradine.	1932-1951	200.00	250.00

BIDDY PENNY FARTHING

HN 1843
☐ Older lady figure in very light blue skirt, lavender bodice with gold design, dark grey shawl with lavender fringe, holding balloon and basket of flowers, height 9", designer L. Harradine. 1938- 175.00

BILL SYKES

HN 537
☐ A character from Dicken's "Oliver Twist," height 3¾", designer L. Harradine. 1922- 45.00 60.00
☐ **M-54** Made as a miniature, height 4¼", designer L. Harradine. 1932- 29.95

BLACKSMITH OF WILLIAMSBURG

HN 2240
☐ Blue trousers, black boots with light top, brown apron and cap, white shirt, grey anvil also on white base, height 6¾", designer M. Davies. 1960- 200.00

BLITHE MORNING

HN 2021
☐ Pink skirt with blue bodice, red shawl, green hat, height 7¼", designer L. Harradine. 1949-1971 250.00 300.00
HN 2065
☐ Red dress, green and yellow shawl, pale coloured hat, height 7¼", designer L. Harradine. 1950-1973 225.00 250.00

	Date	Price Range

BLIGHTY

HN 323

☐ Mottled green/brown costume of British soldier, on same coloured base, height 11¼″, designer E. W. Light. . . .   1918-1938   **1250.00   1500.00**

BLOSSOM

HN 1667

☐ Seated lady in light green gown with multicoloured shawl, small girl standing in between knees of lady, in gown of shaded blue, white collar, basket of multicoloured flowers at lady's side. height 6¾″, designer L. Harradine. . .   1934-1949   **700.00   800.00**

Bluebeard, HN2105, **365.00**

	Date	Price Range
BLUE BEARD		

HN 75
☐ Costume of white with blue trim, cloak blue with yellow lining (1st version), height unknown, designer E. W. Light. 1917-1938 **2550.00 3000.00**

HN 410
☐ Blue costume (1st version), height unknown, designer E. W. Light. 1920-1938 **3000.00 3500.00**

HN 1528
☐ Red costume with multicoloured robe and turban (2nd version), height 11½ ″, designer L. Harradine. 1932-1949 **1000.00 1100.00**

HN 2105
☐ Yellow, green and orange costume with dark blue robe (2nd version), height 11 ″, designer L. Harradine. . . . 1953- **375.00**

BLUE BIRD

HN 1280
☐ Small kneeling white figure on red and cream coloured base, holding dark coloured bird on one hand, height 4¾ ″, designer L. Harradine. . . 1928-1938 **650.00 750.00**

BOATMAN, The

HN 2417
☐ Character figure seated on grey chest, white life preserver at side, black boots, green trousers, yellow slicker, yellow hat, painting on white preserver, height 6½ ″, designer M. Nicoll. 1971- **165.00**

BON APPETIT

HN 2444
☐ Character figure on green/yellow base which has small bonfire and tan wicker basket on it, costume of brown with long blue coat, blue hat, yellow shirt, brown tie, frying fish in black skillet, matt finish, height 6 ″, designer M. Nicoll. 1972-1976 **225.00 275.00**

	Date	Price Range	
BON JOUR			

HN 1879

☐ Green tiered gown with white trim, red shawl with black designs, red bonnet with dark ribbons, height 6¾", designer L. Harradine. . . . .

HN 1888

☐ Red gown trimmed in white, shawl red with darker design, black bonnet with green ribbons, height 6¾", designer L. Harradine. . . . .

BONNIE LASSIE

HN 1626

☐ Seated figure in cream coloured gown, red shawl with black stripes, hat to match, black shoes, light coloured basket of flowers at feet, also light coloured pail with flowers, height 5¼", designer L. Harradine. . .

BO-PEEP

HN 777

☐ Gown of purple with green design, black hat with red ribbon, black staff, black base with small lamb (1st version), height 6¾", designer L. Harradine. . . . .

HN 1202

☐ Skirt is purple with green, pink and black trim (1st version), height 6¾", designer L. Harradine. . . . .

HN 1327

☐ Flowered multicoloured costume (1st version), height 6¾", designer L. Harradine. . . . .

HN 1328

☐ Skirt is cream coloured with black and blue small squares, overlay is red with black designs, bodice is dark with green squares, bonnet light with dark ribbon, staff is brown, base black with small lamb (1st version), height 6¾", designer L. Harradine. . .

Entry	Date	Price Range	
HN 1879	1938-1949	650.00	750.00
HN 1888	1938-1949	600.00	700.00
HN 1626	1934-1953	275.00	325.00
HN 777	1926-1938	1250.00	1350.00
HN 1202	1926-1938	1050.00	1200.00
HN 1327	1929-1938	1050.00	1200.00
HN 1328	1929-1938	1050.00	1200.00

	Date	Price Range	
BO-PEEP (cont.)			
HN 1810			
☐ Skirt is white with blue and red, overlay is blue, bonnet is blue with red ribbon, holding staff in both hands (2nd version), height 5″, designer L. Harradine.	1937-1949	250.00	300.00
HN 1811			
☐ Skirt is light red, overlay is darker red, bonnet is green with green ribbons, staff light green (2nd version), height 5″, designer L. Harradine.	1937-	100.00	
☐ **M-82** Made as a miniature, gown of red, height 4″, designer L. Harradine.	1939-1949	425.00	475.00
☐ **M-83** Gown of blue, height 4″, designer L. Harradine.	1939-1949	400.00	450.00
BOUDOIR			
HN 2542			
☐ Tall figure in greyest blue with white design gown, height 12¼″, designer E. J. Griffiths.	1974-1979	325.00	375.00
BOUQUET, The			
HN 406			
☐ No record of colouring, height 9″, designer G. Lambert.	1920-1938	1500.00	1700.00
HN 414			
☐ Shawl of pink and yellow, height 9″, designer G. Lambert.	1920-1938	1550.00	1700.00
Hn 422			
☐ Skirt of yellow and pink stripes, height 9″, designer G. Lambert.	1920-1938	1550.00	1700.00
HN 428			
☐ Gown is shades of blue, shawl striped, height 9″, designer G. Lambert.	1921-1938	1550.00	1700.00
HN 429			
☐ Multicoloured gown, with green designed shawl, coloured flowers, height 9″, designer G. Lambert.	1921-1938	1550.00	1700.00
HN 567			
☐ Shaded design pink dress with white shawl with designs of red and green, coloured flowers, height 9″, designer G. Lambert.	1923-1938	1550.00	1700.00
HN 794			
☐ Shawl blue with red and green spots, height 9″, designer G. Lambert.	1926-1938	1550.00	1700.00

	Date	Price Range

BOY FROM WILLIAMSBURG
HN 2183
☐ Dark blue trousers and coat with gold trim, red long vest, white cravat, black hat, holding brown and white object, brown stamp behind figure, height 5½", designer M. Davies.   1969-   **115.00**

BOY ON A CROCODILE
HN 373
☐ Small white figure seated on dark coloured crocodile, height 5", designer C. J. Noke.   1920-1938   **4000.00 4500.00**

BOY ON PIG
HN 1369
☐ Small white figure seated on multicolored pig, height 4", designer C. J. Noke.   1930-1938   **900.00 1000.00**

BOY WITH TURBAN
HN 586
☐ Small seated Arab figure with blue and green costume, height 3¾", designer L. Harradine.   1923-1938   **550.00 650.00**
HN 587
☐ Green trousers and red shirt, height 3¾", designer L. Harradine.   1923-1938   **550.00 650.00**
HN 661
☐ Blue costume, height 3¾", designer L. Harradine.   1924-1938   **500.00 600.00**
HN 662
☐ Costume of black and white checks, height 3¾", designer L. Harradine. . .   1924-1938   **500.00 600.00**
HN 1210
☐ Turban of black and red, white pants with large red dots, height 3¾", designer L. Harradine.   1926-1938   **500.00 600.00**
HN 1212
☐ Trousers of blue and green, turban and shirt multicoloured, height 3¾", designer L. Harradine.   1926-1938   **550.00 650.00**
HN 1213
☐ White costume with black squares, height 3¾", designer L. Harradine. . .   1926-1938   **500.00 600.00**

BOY WITH TURBAN (cont.)	Date	Price Range
HN 1214		
☐ White costume with black and green markings, height 3¾", designer L. Harradine.	1926-1938	500.00 650.00
HN 1225		
☐ Yellow trousers and blue spots, height 3¾", designer L. Harradine. . .	1927-1938	500.00 650.00

BRIDE

	Date	Price Range
HN 1588		
☐ White bridal gown and veil, holding lilies in arm (1st version), height 8¾", designer L. Harradine.	1933-1938	750.00 850.00
HN 1600		
☐ Flowers are roses (1st version), height 8¾", designer L. Harradine.	1933-1949	650.00 750.00
HN 1762		
☐ Cream dress (1st version), height 8¾", designer L. Harradine.	1936-1949	700.00 800.00
HN 1841		
☐ Blue dress (1st version), height 9½", designer L. Harradine.	1938-1949	800.00 900.00
HN 2166		
☐ Full bridal gown, holding flower bouquet in hand (2nd version), height 8", designer M. Davies.	1956-1976	225.00 275.00
HN 2873		
☐ Empire style gown of white trimmed in gold, holding single flower (4th version), height 8", designer M. Davies. .	1980-	170.00

BRIDESMAID, The LITTLE

	Date	Price Range
HN 1433		
☐ Multicoloured tiered gown, holding bouquet with green ribbon, flowered band in hair (1st version), height 5¼", designer L. Harradine.	1930-1951	175.00 225.00
HN 1434		
☐ Gown of shaded green and yellow, band in hair is blue (1st version), height 5", designer L. Harradine.	1930-1949	225.00 275.00
HN 1530		
☐ Yellow and green dress, height 5", designer L. Harradine.	1932-1938	200.00 250.00
☐ **M 11** Made as a miniature, pink and lilac dress, height 3¾", designer L. Harradine.	1932-1938	325.00 375.00

	Date	Price Range	
BRIDESMAID, The LITTLE (cont.)			
☐ **M 12** Multicoloured gown, height 3¾″, designer L. Harradine.	1932-1945	**275.00**	**325.00**
☐ **M 30** Red and lavender gown, height 3¾″, designer L. Harradine.	1932-1945	**275.00**	**325.00**
HN 2148			
☐ Full gown of cream colour with blue sash, holding flowers in right arm (2nd version), height 5½″, designer M. Davies.	1955-1959	**175.00**	**225.00**
HN 2196			
☐ Full skirted gown of light blue colour with raised design of white, small red ribbons on white collar, small brimmed head piece, holding small flowers in hand (3rd version), height 5¼″, designer M. Davies.	1960-1976	**100.00**	**125.00**
HN 2874			
☐ White gown trimmed in gold, cap of white trimmed in gold, holding very small bouquet in hand (4th version), height 5¼″, designer M. Davies.	1980-	**100.00**	
BRIDGET			
HN 2070			
☐ Older lady, green dress with yellow design, orange coloured shawl and hand bag, black hat with red ribbon, height 8¾″, designer M. Davies.	1951-1973	**300.00**	**350.00**
BROKEN LANCE, The			
HN 2041			
☐ Green base with design, horse is white with blue cloth cover that has darker blue and yellow designs, red lining, suit of armor is grey, red and dark blue headdress, red and gold shield, brown and light red lance, height 8¾″, designer M. Davies.	1949-1975	**500.00**	**600.00**
BUDDIES			
HN 2546			
☐ Black and green base, seated boy in brown shorts, blue shirt, dog brown and black, matt finish, height 6″, designer E. J. Griffiths.	1973-1976	**200.00**	**250.00**

Broken Lance HN2041, **500.00 — 600.00**

	Date	Price Range

BUMBLE
Issued only as a miniature

☐ **M 76** Red vest, black pants, green cape with yellow trim, black tri-cornered hat with yellow trim, black stand, height 4″, designer L. Harradine. 1939-1982   **29.95**

BUNNY
HN 2214

☐ Small girl, green and pink gown, holding bunny, height 5″, designer M. Davies. 1960-1975   **150.00   200.00**

BUTTERCUP
HN 2309

☐ Gown of shaded yellow, green bodice, hand on green hat, height 7″, designer M. Davies. 1964-   **145.00**

	Date	Price Range	
BUTTERCUP (cont.)			

HN 2399

□ Gown and hat scarlet, sleeves of gown lemon yellow, lemon bow on dress, height 7½", designer M. Davies   1983-   **145.00**

BUTTERFLY

HN 719

□ Butterfly costumed figure on black pedestal type base, wings are multicoloured, dress pink and black, height 6½", designer L. Harradine. . .   1925-1938   **700.00   800.00**

HN 720

□ Red wings, dress white with black checks, height 6½", designer L. Harradine.   1925-1938   **700.00   800.00**

HN 730

□ Yellow dress, blue/black wings, height 6½", designer L. Harradine. . .   1925-1938   **800.00   900.00**

HN 1203

□ Gold wings, height 6½", designer L. Harradine.   1926-1938   **900.00   1000.00**

HN 1456

□ Wings in shades of lavender and pink, dress shades of green, height 6½", designer L. Harradine.   1931-1938   **800.00   900.00**

BUZ FUZ

HN 538

□ A character from Dicken's "Pickwick Papers," height 3¾", designer L. Harradine.   1922-   **45.00   60.00**

□ **M 53** Renumbered as a miniature, height 4", designer L. Harradine. . . .   1932-   **29.95**

'CALLED LOVE, A LITTLE BOY . . .'

HN 1545

□ Small naked child crouching on base, holding red and blue bucket, height 3½", designer unknown.   1933-1949   **325.00   375.00**

CALUMET

HN 1428

□ Base is multicoloured striped blanket, Indian costume is light brown, robe is stripes of green, yellow, red and tan, bowl on base is light coloured with red and green stripe, height 6", designer C. J. Noke.   1930-1949   **1050.00   1150.00**

CALUMET (cont.)	Date	Price Range	
HN 1689			
☐ Base is green blanket with patch of blue, red and green, Indian costume is darker brown, robe is green with yellow, bowl is blue, height 6½ ", designer C. J. Noke.	1935-1949	875.00	975.00
HN 2068			
☐ HN 1689 with minor glaze differences, height 6¼", designer C. J. Noke.	1950-1953	625.00	725.00
CAMELLIA			
HN 2222			
☐ Pink gown with very light blue scarf and bow in hair, height 7¾", designer M. Davies.	1960-1971	250.00	300.00
CAMILLA			
HN 1710			
☐ 18th century style gown of red and white with red lines, dark hair with green bow, on light coloured base, height 7", designer L. Harradine.	1935-1949	700.00	800.00
HN 1711			
☐ Light hair, gown is light red with darker red design, overdress is green with white designs, height 7", designer L. Harradine.	1935-1949	700.00	800.00
CAMILLE			
HN 1586			
☐ 18th century style gown of very light red with overdress of darker red, black hat with light red trim, holding mirror, height 6½", designer L. Harradine.	1933-1949	650.00	700.00
HN 1648			
☐ Gown of very light red with overdress of cream skirt with red flower design, green bodice with red bows, green hat with red trim, height 6½", designer L. Harradine.	1934-1949	600.00	675.00
HN 1736			
☐ Red and white costume, height 6½", designer L. Harradine.	1935-1949	700.00	800.00

	Date	Price Range	

CAPTAIN

HN 778

☐ Black pedestal style base, red long coat with gold trim, white trousers and long vest with gold buttons, black boots, black hat with white and gold trim, white cravat, black strap holding sword (1st version), height 7″, designer L. Harradine. 1926-1938   1250.00 1400.00

HN 2260

☐ White trousers, white stockings, black shoes with gold trim, black coat with trim and white and gold, black hat with trim of white and gold, hand on map lies on brown stand, book and paper on bottom of stand (2nd version), height 9½ ″, designer M. Nicoll.   1965-1982   250.00

CAPTAIN COOK

HN 2889

☐ Navy uniform of white trousers, black coat with yellow trim and white buttons, seated on stool on base of light brown, maps in drawer on base, map on lap, black bag leaning against yellow pedestal, height 8″, designer W. K. Harper.   1980-   365.00

CAPTAIN CUTTLE

Issued only as a miniature

☐ **M 77** Yellow vest, light yellow pants, red tie, black coat, light brown hat with black band, black stand, height 4″, designer L. Harradine.   1939-   29.95

CAPTAIN MAC HEATH

HN 464

☐ A character of "The Beggar's Opera," red coated figure on black material, height 7″, designer L. Harradine.   1921-1949   750.00   850.00

HN 590

☐ Yellow cravat only difference, height 7″, designer L. Harradine.   1924-1949   750.00   850.00

HN 1256

☐ Earthenware, height 7″, designer L. Harradine.   1927-1949   700.00   800.00

	Date	Price Range	

CARMEN

HN 1267

☐ Dark haired figure with red dress, red and black shawl, red shoes, on light coloured base, holding tambourine (1st version), height 7″, designer L. Harradine. 1928-1938   750.00   850.00

HN 1300

☐ Gown in shades of blue and yellow, green shoes, green base (1st version), height 7″, designer L. Harradine. 1928-1938   800.00   900.00

HN 2545

☐ Tall figure with black hair, gown shades of blue and black, light blue bodice (2nd version), height 11½″, designer E. J. Griffiths 1974-1979   250.00   300.00

CARNIVAL

HN 1260

☐ Half nude figure with pink tights on black base, height 8¼″, designer L. Harradine. 1927-1938   1500.00   1650.00

HN 1278

☐ Half nude figure with blue tights, waist band of black and gold, holding long cloth behind head which is yellow and purple, on black base, height 8½″, designer L. Harradine. 1928-1938   1400.00   1550.00

CAROLYN

HN 2112

☐ White gown with coloured flowers, green cummerbund and gloves of green, holding black hat and white handkerchief, height 7″, designer L. Harradine. 1953-1959   350.00   400.00

HN 2974

☐ Gown two colors green, frilled white cuffs and white trim. Low neckline accented by yellow rose, (2nd version), height 5½″, designer A. Hughes. 1983-   155.00

CARPET SELLER, The

HN 1464

☐ Blue robed figure with black and multicolored rug on black base, hand open, height 9″, designer L. Harradine. 1931-1969   400.00   450.00

	Date	Price Range	

CARPET SELLER, The (cont.)

HN 1464A

☐ Same figure with same coloring except hand closed, height 9¼", designer L. Harradine. . . . . 1931-? 375.00 425.00

Carpet Vendor, HN76, **3000.00 — 3500.00**

CARPET VENDOR, The

HN 38

☐ Kneeling figure on green base, holding one end of unrolled blue striped carpet, costume of blue trousers, yellow and red shirt trimmed in white, turban of dark blue and red (1st version), height unknown, designer C. J. Noke. 1914-1938 2750.00 3000.00

HN 38A

☐ Persian style carpet (1st version), height unknown, designer C. J. Noke. 1914-1938 2750.00 3000.00

	Date	Price Range
CARPET VENDOR, The (cont.)		

HN   76
☐ Kneeling figure on blue and black checked cushion, costume of blue with orange trim, turban green, rug in front of figure is also orange (2nd version), height 5½", designer C. J. Noke. 1917-1938   3000.00 3500.00

HN 348
☐ Blue/green costume with chequered base (1st version), height unknown, designer C. J. Noke. 1919-1938   1750.00 2000.00

HN 350
☐ Blue costume and green/brown floral carpet (1st version), height 5½", designer C. J. Noke. 1919-1938   3000.00 3500.00

CARRIE (Kate Greenaway)

HN 2800
☐ Small girl with blue coat, white hat with blue/red ribbons, holding single flower in one hand, on white base, height 6", designer M. Davies. 1976-1981   75.00   100.00

CASSIM

HN 1231
☐ Small seated Arab figure, with blue trousers, multicoloured vest and blue cone shaped hat (1st version), height 3", designer L. Harradine. 1927-1938   550.00   600.00

HN 1232
☐ White and orange striped trousers, dark coloured vest with red hat (1st version), height 3", designer L. Harradine. 1927-1938   550.00   600.00

HN 1311
☐ HN 1231 mounted on lidded pink bowl (2nd version), height 3¾", designer L. Harradine. 1929-1938   700.00   800.00

HN 1312
☐ Mounted on blue bowl (2nd version), height 3¾", designer L. Harradine. . . 1929-1938   700.00   800.00

	Date	Price Range

CAVALIER

HN 369

☐ Light coloured base, blue trousers, white stockings, black shoes with blue bows, dark blue coat, light green waistcoat with white collar, hat, dark with yellow feather (1st version), height unknown, designer unknown. . 1920-1938   2100.00 2400.00

HN 2716

☐ Black trousers, boots, vest and hat, white shirt, dark cape with red lining (2nd version), height 9¾", designer E. J. Griffiths. 1976-1982   200.00

CELESTE

HN 2237

☐ Gown of shaded greens with dark ribbon at waist, also sleeves and at shoulder, height 6¾", designer M. Davies . . . 1959-1971   250.00   300.00

CELIA

HN 1726

☐ Tall figure with pale pink night gown, height 11½", designer L. Harradine. . 1935-1949   750.00   850.00

HN 1727

☐ Pale green night gown, height 11½", designer L. Harradine. 1935-1949   750.00   850.00

CELLIST, The

HN 2226

☐ Black suit, white shirt, black bow tie, playing brown cello seated on brown stool, blue and purple books under cello, height 8", designer M. Davies. . 1960-1967   475.00   525.00

CENTURION, The

HN 2726

☐ Depicts a warrior perhaps from the old Roman Empire in his armor, sword in hand and shield of light and dark brown standing at his feet. Figure is on a grey base, height 9½", designer W. K. Harper. 1982-   250.00

The Cellist, HN2226, **475.00 — 525.00**

	Date	Price Range	

CERISE

HN 1607
☐ Small figure in light red figured gown
with darker sash, holding fruit basket,
height 5¼", designer L. Harradine. .. 1933-1949 **300.00 375.00**

CHARLOTTE

HN 2421
☐ Purple gown with gold design at hem
line, holding small light tan dog,
seated on yellow chair, height 6½",
designer J. Bromley. 1972- **185.00**

CHARMIAN

HN 1568
☐ White gown with shaded red overdress, holding small dark fan, height
6½", designer L. Harradine. 1933-1938 **500.00 600.00**

	Date	Price Range	

CHARMIAN (cont.)

HN 1569
☐ Gown of shaded green with overdress of shaded reds and blues, height 6½", designer L. Harradine.   1933-1938   **500.00   600.00**

HN 1651
☐ Red bodice, green skirt, height 6½", designer L. Harradine.   1934-1938   **700.00   800.00**

CHARLEY'S AUNT

HN 35
☐ Black and white gowned figure on base which has the inscription 'W. S. Penley as Charley's Aunt' (1st version), height 7", designer A. Toft.   1914-1938   **700.00   800.00**

HN 640
☐ Green dress, mauve spotted (1st version), height 7", designer A. Toft.   1924-1938   **900.00   1000.00**

HN 1411
☐ Seated figure with dark dress and white lace shawl (2nd version), height 8", designer H. Fenton.   1930-1938   **1375.00   1425.00**

HN 1554
☐ Purple dress (2nd version), height 8", designer H. Fenton.   1933-1938   **1200.00   1350.00**

HN 1703
☐ Not mounted on base, dress is shades of lilac and white with dark ribbons on bonnet (3rd version), height 6", designer A. Toft.   1935-1938   **800.00   900.00**

CHELSEA PAIR (Female)

HN 577
☐ 18th century styled figure seated on three on green base, gown white with blue flower design, red bonnet with blue ribbons, height 6", designer L. Harradine.   1923-1938   **700.00   800.00**

HN 578
☐ Blouse is red, height 6", designer L. Harradine.   1923-1938   **700.00   800.00**

CHELSEA PAIR (Male)

HN 579
☐ 18th centur style figure seated on tree, reddish-brown coat, black trousers, black hat, base is green, height 6", designer L. Harradine.   1923-1938   **725.00   800.00**

	Date	Price Range
CHELSES PAIR (Male) (cont.)		

HN 580
☐ Blue flowers instead of white, height 6″, designer L. Harradine.   1923-1938   **725.00   800.00**

CHELSEA PENSIONER

HN 689
☐ Red coated seated figure with black trousers, hat, cane and pipe on brown base, height 5¾″, designer L. Harradine.   1924-1938   **1250.00 1400.00**

CHERIE

HN 2341
☐ Small figure wearing blue gown with white cuffs holding yellow gloves in hands, blue hat with light blue feather and yellow ribbon bow, height 5½″, designer M. Davies.   1966-   **100.00**

CHIEF, The

HN 2892
☐ Seated figure on green/brown base, costume of light brown with blue trim on front, green cloth with design of red, blue and orange on lap, feathered headdress of blue/black/white feathers, band of blue with yellow design, mocassins of white tops with brown and blue design, brown peace pipe in hands, height 7″, designer W. K. Harper.   1979-   **200.00**

CHILD FROM WILLIAMSBURG

HN 2154
☐ Small girl figure in blue gown, holding flower, height 5¾″, designer M. Davies   1964-   **115.00**

CHILD AND CRAB

HN 32
☐ Crab is green and brown, child wears pale blue robe, height 5¼″, designer C. J. Noke.   1913-1938   **1600.00 1800.00**

	Date	Price Range	

CHILD'S GRACE, A

HN 62
☐ HN 62A except there is additional black patterning over the green coat, height 6¾", designer L. Perugini..... 1916-1938 — 1400.00 1600.00

HN 62A
☐ Small girl figure with hands clasped on pedestal which contains printed poem, green dress with orange underlay, height 6¾", designer L. Perugini. 1916-1938 — 1500.00 1700.00

HN 510
☐ Chequered dress, green base, height 6¾", designer L. Perugini. .... 1921-1938 — 1650.00 1800.00

CHILD STUDY

HN 603A
☐ White child's nude figure on rock with base which has flowers, figure seated, height 4¾", designer L. Harradine. .. 1924-1938 — 275.00 325.00

HN 603B
☐ Flowers are kingcups round base, height 4¾", designer L. Harradine. .. 1924-1938 — 300.00 350.00

HN 604A
☐ HN 604B except flowers round base are primroses, height 5¾", designer L. Harradine.................... 1924-1938 — 300.00 350.00

HN 604B
☐ White nude lady figure kneeling on pedestal which is on a base with flowers, height 5¾", designer L. Harradine. .... 1924-1938 — 300.00 350.00

HN 605A
☐ Standing white nude child's figure on pedestal and base covered with flowers, height 5¾", designer L. Harradine. .... 1924-1938 — 300.00 350.00

HN 605B
☐ Different flowers, height 5¾", designer L. Harradine. .... 1924-1938 — 300.00 350.00

HN 606A
☐ White nude child's figure standing on rock bending over to look at flowers on base, height 5", designer L. Harradine. .... 1924-1938 — 300.00 350.00

HN 606B
☐ Flowers are kingcups on base, height 5", designer L. Harradine. .... 1924-1938 — 300.00 350.00

CHILD STUDY (cont.)	Date	Price Range	

HN 1441
☐ Seated white nude child's figure with blonde hair, rock is multicoloured, with applied flowers on base, height 5″, designer L. Harradine. 1931-1938 **350.00 400.00**

HN 1442
☐ Standing white nude child's figure with blonde hair, rock is multicoloured, with applied flowers on base, height 6¼″, designer L. Harradine. . . 1931-1938 **350.00 400.00**

HN 1443
☐ Figure 1540, with applied flowers on base, height 5″, designer L. Harradine. 1931-1938 **350.00 400.00**

The China Repairer, HN2943, **185.00**

	Date	Price Range

CHINA REPAIRER, The
HN 2943
☐ Man seated at his work bench working on a broken horse. Grey hair, blue shirt, white apron, height 6¾", designer R. Tabbenor.   1983-   185.00

CHLOE
HN 1470
☐ Red and cream tiered gown, blue bonnet with ribbons, height 5¾", designer L. Harradine.   1931-1949   300.00   350.00
☐ **M 29** Made as a miniature, height 3", designer L. Harradine.   1932-1945   275.00   325.00
HN 1476
☐ Blue gown with pink bonnet with ribbons, height 5¾", designer L. Harradine.   1931-1938   300.00   350.00
HN 1479
☐ Gown in shades of blue with bonnet and ribbons in shaded reds, height 5¾", designer L. Harradine.   1931-1949   275.00   325.00
HN 1498
☐ Yellow green, height 5¾", designer L. Harradine.   1932-1938   350.00   400.00
HN 1765
☐ Gown blue with blue ribbon on bonnet, height 6", designer L. Harradine.   1936-1950   275.00   325.00
☐ **M 10** Made as a miniature, height 3", designer L. Harradine.   1932-1945   275.00   325.00
HN 1956
☐ HN 1470 except red skirt and green ribbon, height 6", designer L. Harradine.   1940-1949   425.00   475.00
☐ **M 9** Made as a miniature, height 3", designer L. Harradine.   1932-1945   275.00   325.00

CHOICE, The
HN 1959
☐ Red gowned lady trying on bonnet, with box at foot, height 7", designer L. Harradine.   1941-1949   850.00   950.00
HN 1960
☐ Gown is shaded reds and blues, height 7", designer L. Harradine.   1941-1949   850.00   950.00

	Date	Price Range	

CHOIR BOY
HN 2141
☐ Choir robe of red and white, height 4⅞″, designer M. Davies. 1954-1975   75.00   125.00

CHORUS GIRL
HN 1401
☐ Costume of red, yellow and black, figure on pedestal, height and designer unknown. 1930-1938   1650.00   1800.00

CHRISTINE
HN 1839
☐ Lilac tiered dress with blue shawl, bonnet trimmed with flowers (1st version), height 7¾″, designer L. Harradine. 1938-1949   650.00   750.00
HN 1840
☐ Dress of shaded reds with blue figured shawl (1st version), height 7¾″, designer L. Harradine. 1938-1949   650.00   750.00
HN 2792
☐ Gown of very light cream with shades of very light red and yellow, with multicoloured flowers over skirt, no bonnet on this figure (2nd version), height 7⅞″, designer M. Davies. 1978-   250.00

CHRISTMAS MORN
HN 1992
☐ Red coat with jacket trimmed in white fur, with muff, height 7¼″, designer M. Davies. 1947-   155.00

CHRISTMAS PARCELS
HN 2851
☐ Dark green cloak with yellow trim, figure holding one Christmas parcel of purple and red, many parcels around foot, also small basket, also green Christmas tree, height 8⅝″, designer W. K. Harper. 1978-1982   200.00

CHRISTMAS TIME
HN 2110
☐ Red cloak trimmed with white around bottom, holding small parcels in hand, black bonnet, height 6⅞″, designer M. Davies. 1953-1967   350.00   400.00

	Date	Price Range	

CICELY

HN 1516

☐ Light blue skirt with darker blue jacket figure seated on small couch, height 5½ ", designer L. Harradine. ... 1932-1949 1100.00 1200.00

CIRCE

HN 1249

☐ White nude figure of woman on base, with multicoloured robe hanging from one arm, height 7½ ", designer L. Harradine. 1927-1938 1200.00 1400.00

HN 1250

☐ Robe is of orange and black, height 7½ ", designer L. Harradine. 1927-1938 1200.00 1400.00

HN 1254

☐ Robe of orange and red, height 7½ ", designer L. Harradine. 1927-1938 1200.00 1400.00

HN 1255

☐ Blue robe, height 7½ ", designer L. Harradine. 1927-1938 1200.00 1400.00

CISSIE

HN 1808

☐ Small figure with green dress, holding basket of flowers on arm, height 5", designer L. Harradine. 1937-1951 225.00 275.00

HN 1809

☐ Dress of shaded reds with blue bonnet and green ribbons, height 5", designer L. Harradine. 1937- 100.00

CLARE

HN 2793

☐ Shaded blue gown with multicoloured flower design, yellow shawl and bonnet with red ribbon, height 7½ ", designer M. Davies. 1980- 250.00

CLARIBEL

HN 1950

☐ Small figure with blue skirt and shaded reds, white cap with green ribbon, height 4¾ ", designer L. Harradine. 1940-1949 350.00 400.00

HN 1951

☐ Dress of red and shaded blue, blue ribbon on cap, height 4¾ ", designer L. Harradine. 1940-1949 325.00 375.00

	Date	Price Range	
CLARINDA			

HN 2724

□ Blue/green gown with light blue designs, darker blue/green overdress, figure on green base with blue and white bird on green pedestal at side, height 8½ ", designer W. K. Harper. . . — 1975-1980 — **175.00** — **225.00**

CLARISSA

HN 1525

□ Green gown with red shawl, holding open parasol (1st version), height 10", designer L. Harradine. . . . . — 1932-1938 — **625.00** — **700.00**

HN 1687

□ Gown of pale blue and green shawl (1st version), height 10", designer L. Harradine. — 1935-1949 — **675.00** — **750.00**

HN 2345

□ Gown of green with white sleeves, figure holding basket with two hands (2nd version), height 8", designer M. Davies. . . . . — 1968-1981 — **150.00** — **200.00**

CLEMENCY

HN 1633

□ White, two tiered dress with flower design, blue jacket, green bonnet with red ribbons, height 7", designer L. Harradine. — 1934-1938 — **650.00** — **750.00**

HN 1634

□ White dress trimmed in red, multicoloured jacket, height 7", designer L. Harradine. — 1934-1949 — **650.00** — **750.00**

HN 1643

□ White gown trimmed in green, red jacket, height 7", designer L. Harradine. . . . . — 1934-1938 — **650.00** — **750.00**

CLOCKMAKER, The

HN 2279

□ Character figure in green coat, green shirt, ligher green apron, blue shirt, brown tie, black shoes, looking a clock piece, clock is brown and green setting on dark stand, height 7¼ ", designer M. Nicoll. . . . . — 1961-1975 — **300.00** — **350.00**

	Date	Price Range	
CLOTHILDE			

HN 1598
☐ Pale pink gown with red robe, height 7¼″, designer L. Harradine.   1933-1949   **600.00   700.00**

HN 1599
☐ Pale blue gown with multi-flowered top and sleeves with blue robe with red lining, height 7¼″, designer L. Harradine.   1933-1949   **600.00   700.00**

CLOUD, The

HN 1831
☐ Flowing white robed figure with long golden hair, height 23″, designer R. Garbe.   1937-1949   **4000.00   4500.00**

The Coachman, HN2282, **475.00 — 550.00**

	Date	Price Range
CLOWN, The		
HN 2890		
☐ Clown on brown and yellow base, blue trousers, gold coat, spotted yellow tie, dark hat with flower, grey bucket also on base, height 8¾", designer W. K. Harper............	1979-	295.00
COACHMAN, The		
HN 2282		
☐ Character figure seated in brown chair, long purple coat, green coat and trousers, purple coat has blue lining, black tall hat with green trim, holding tankard of blue, height 7", designer M. Nicoll................	1963-1971	475.00 550.00
COBBLER, The		
HN 542		
☐ Costumed in shades of green, round turban, seated on brown base (1st version), height 7½", designer C. J. Noke...........................	1922-1939	1100.00 1200.00
HN 543		
☐ Specially fired (1st version), height 7½", designer C. J. Noke..........	1922-1938	1200.00 1300.00
HN 681		
☐ Larger figure on black base, with green costume, red shirt and cone shaped turban (2nd version), height 8½", designer C. J. Noke..........	1924-1938	600.00 700.00
HN 682		
☐ Red shirt with green robe (1st version), height 7½", designer C. J. Noke...........................	1924-1938	700.00 800.00
HN 1251		
☐ Black trousers and red shirt, height 8½", designer C. J. Noke..........	1927-1938	600.00 700.00
HN 1283		
☐ Green costume with yellow and red shirt (2nd version), height 8½", designer C. J. Noke................	1928-1949	600.00 700.00
HN 1705		
☐ Multicoloured costume with blue shirt on coloured base (3rd version), height 8", designer C. J. Noke.......	1935-1949	550.00 600.00

	Date	Price Range	
COBBLER, The (cont.)			
HN 1706			
☐ Brown costume with green striped shirt (3rd version), height 8″, designer C. J. Noke.	1935-1969	275.00	325.00
COLLINETTE			
HN 1998			
☐ White gown with long blue cloak, height 7¼″, designer L. Harradine.	1947-1969	450.00	500.00
HN 1999			
☐ Cloak is red, height 7¼″, designer L. Harradine.	1947-1949	425.00	475.00
COLUMBINE			
HN 1296			
☐ A tutu style costume on figure seated on cream colored pedestal, costume shades of red and blue, striped (1st version), height 6″, designer L. Harradine.	1928-1938	700.00	800.00
HN 1297			
☐ Costume not striped, base white (1st version), height 6″, designer L. Harradine.	1928-1938	700.00	800.00
HN 1439			
☐ Costume multicoloured floral design, base light green (1st version), height 6″, designer L. Harradine.	1930-1938	700.00	800.00
HN 2185			
☐ Standing figure on white base, dress light pink with blue design, small crown on head, holding tambourine (2nd version), height 7″, designer M. Davies.	1957-1969	225.00	275.00
COMING OF SPRING, The			
HN 1722			
☐ Pink costume on barefoot figure on flower ringed base, holding light coloured robe above head, height 12½″, designer L. Harradine.	1935-1949	1250.00	1400.00
HN 1723			
☐ Light green costume, height 12½″, designer L. Harradine.	1935-1949	1250.00	1400.00

CONSTANCE	Date	Price Range

HN 1510
☐ Four tiered gown of purple and yellow, holding small purse, height unknown, designer L. Harradine.   1932-1938   1500.00 1700.00

HN 1511
☐ Pale pink gown, holding red handbag, height unknown, designer L. Harradine.   1932-1938   1500.00 1700.00

CONTENTMENT

HN 395
☐ Woman seated in chair with small child in arms, yellow skirt with pink stripes, blue patterned blouse, height 7¼", designer L. Harradine.   1920-1938   1850.00 2000.00

HN 396
☐ Chair is yellow and pink striped, height 7¼", designer L. Harradine. . .   1920-1938   1850.00 2000.00

HN 421
☐ Gown of light blue patterned with darker blue, blouse light yellow with coloured circle pattern, height 7¼", designer L. Harradine.   1920-1938   1500.00 1700.00

HN 468
☐ Green spotted dress, height 7¼", designer L. Harradine.   1921-1938   1750.00 2000.00

HN 572
☐ Spotted cream skirt with spotted pink blouse, height 7¼", designer L. Harradine.   1923-1938   1750.00 2000.00

HN 685
☐ Black and white floral dress, height 7¼", designer L. Harradine.   1923-1938   1900.00 2000.00

HN 686
☐ Black and white striped chair, height 7¼", designer L. Harradine.   1924-1938   1900.00 2000.00

HN 1323
☐ Shades of blue and red skirt, with red blouse, blue chair, height 7¼", designer L. Harradine.   1929-1938   1550.00 1700.00

COOKIE

HN 2218
☐ Small figure, red dress, white apron, holding a small object in each hand, height 4¾", designer M. Davies.   1958-1975   150.00 200.00

	Date	Price Range	

COPPELIA

HN 2115

☐ Ballet figure, costume of red, blue, white, standing on toes on base that has books on it, height 7¼ ″, designer M. Davies. 1953-1959 525.00 600.00

COQUETTE, The

HN 20

☐ Red haired, bare footed figure on base, green gown holding fan, height 9¼ ″, designer W. White. 1913-1938 2500.00 3000.00

HN 37

☐ Green costume with flower sprays, height 9¼ ″, designer W. White. 1914-1938 2500.00 3000.00

CORALIE

HN 2307

☐ Yellow gown with white with brown dots under gown and cuffs, height 7⅛ ″, designer M. Davies. 1964- 155.00

CORINTHIAN, The

HN 1973

☐ Male figure on base, cream trousers, blue coat, white vest with multicoloured design, black cloak with red lining, black hat, holding cane, height 7¾ ″, designer H. Fenton. 1941-1949 950.00 1050.00

COUNTRY LASS

HN 1991

☐ Figure on base, blue dress, white apron, white kerchief on head, goose in arm, basket on the other arm, brown shawl. Also see Market Day, height 7⅜ ″, designer L. Harradine. 1975-1981 125.00 175.00

COURTIER, The

HN 1338

☐ Male figure seated in chair on base, chair is red and gold, costume is red and white, base black, height 4½ ″, designer L. Harradine. 1929-1938 1200.00 1350.00

	Date	Price Range	

COURT SHOEMAKER, The

HN 1755

☐ Two figures, 18th century style, costume of man is red, woman's gown is shaded blue, trying on red shoes, height 6¾", designer L. Harradine. ... 1936-1949   1500.00 1700.00

COVENT GARDEN

HN 1339

☐ Figure wearing green dress with shaded red and blue apron, green hat, holding basket on head and carrying basket in other hand, height 9", designer L. Harradine. 1929-1938   1000.00 1200.00

CRADLE SONG

HN 2246

☐ Seated lady rocking cradle, green dress, dark hair, baby in brown cradle, height 5½", designer M. Davies. 1959-1962   400.00   450.00

CRAFTSMAN, The

HN 2284

☐ Character figure on one knee, in blue shirt, tan apron, black shoes, white stockings, tools in pocket, working on brown and cream coloured chair, height 6", designer M. Nicoll. 1961-1965   475.00   525.00

CRINOLINE, The

HN   8

☐ Figure is wearing a wide hooped gown of shaded blue, flowers at neck and in hand, height 6¼", designer G. Lambert. 1913-1938   1300.00 1450.00

HN   9

☐ Pale green skirt with flower sprays, height 6¼", designer G. Lambert. ... 1913-1938   1300.00 1450.00

HN   9A

☐ No flower sprays on skirt, height 6¼", designer G. Lambert. 1913-1938   1300.00 1450.00

HN   21

☐ Yellow skirt with rosebuds, height 6¼", designer G. Lambert. 1913-1938   1300.00 1450.00

HN   21A

☐ No rosebuds on skirt, height 6¼", designer G. Lambert. 1913-1938   1250.00 1400.00

CRINOLINE, The (cont.)	Date	Price Range	

HN 413
☐ Skirt cream with trimming of blue, ribbons on flowers also blue, height 6¼ ", designer G. Lambert. 1920-1938 **1700.00 1950.00**

HN 566
☐ Skirt of cream with green spots, green blouse, height 6¼ ", designer G. Lambert. 1923-1938 **1250.00 1400.00**

HN 628
☐ Bodice of yellow and blue checks, height 6¼ ", designer G. Lambert. . . . 1924-1938 **1350.00 1500.00**

CRINOLINE LADY (Miniature)

HN 650
☐ Small 18th century style figure with wide hooped gown, white with red rosebuds trim, light green overlay, green bodice, height 3", designer unknown. 1924-1938 **550.00 650.00**

HN 651
☐ Gown is white with orange trim and green design, black bodice, height 3", designer unknown. 1924-1938 **550.00 650.00**

HN 652
☐ Purple dress, height 3", designer unknown 1924-1938 **550.00 650.00**

HN 653
☐ Grey and white striped dress, height 3", designer unknown. 1924-1938 **550.00 650.00**

HN 654
☐ Orange and green mottled dress, height 3", designer unknown. 1924-1938 **550.00 650.00**

HN 655
☐ Blue dress, height 3", designer unknown. 1924-1938 **550.00 650.00**

CROUCHING NUDE

HN 457
☐ Crouching white figure on green base, height 5½ ", designer unknown. 1921-1938 **1100.00 1300.00**

CUP OF TEA, The

HN 2322
☐ Older lady figure seated in chair, feet on stool holding cup and saucer, black dress, grey sweater, height 7½ ", designer M. Nicoll. 1964- **150.00**

	Date	Price Range	

CURLY LOCKS
HN 2049
☐ Small female figure seated on base, red dress with blue designs, golden curly locks, height 4½ ", designer M. Davies.   1949-1953   250.00   300.00

CURLY KNOB
HN 1627
☐ Seated figure on box style base holding baby in arms, costume blue with red and blue striped shawl, basket of flowers in front of figure, height 6¼ ", designer L. Harradine.   1934-1938   525.00   575.00

CURTSEY, The
HN 57
☐ Figure making curtsey, orange lustre dress, height 11", designer E. W. Light.   1916-1938   1500.00   1750.00
HN 57B
☐ Lilac dress, height 11", designer E. W. Light.   1916-1938   1500.00   1750.00
HN 66A
☐ Lilac dress, this could possibly be renumbered version of 57B, height 11", designer E. W. Light.   1916-1938   1550.00   1700.00
HN 327
☐ Dress of dark blue, height 11", designer E. W. Light.   1918-1938   1550.00   1700.00
HN 334
☐ Lilac dress with brown patterning and green trim, height 11", designer E. W. Light.   1918-1938   1450.00   1600.00
HN 363
☐ Lilac and peach costume, height 11", designer E. W. Light.   1919-1938   1600.00   1700.00
HN 371
☐ Yellow dress, height 11", designer E. W. Light.   1920-1938   1650.00   1800.00
HN 518
☐ Lilac skirt with orange spots, height 11", designer E. W. Light.   1921-1938   1650.00   1800.00
HN 547
☐ Blue bodice, green and yellow skirt, height 11", designer E. W. Light.   1922-1938   1450.00   1600.00
HN 629
☐ Green dress with black trimmings, height 11", designer E. W. Light.   1924-1938   1650.00   1800.00

CURTSEY, The (cont.)	Date	Price Range

HN 670
☐ Pink and yellow spotted dress, height 11″, designer E. W. Light............ 1924-1938   1450.00   1600.00

CYNTHIA

HN 1685
☐ Seated figure with gown of pink and blue, holding flowers, height 5¾″, designer L. Harradine............. 1935-1949   500.00   600.00

HN 1686
☐ Gown of red with multicoloured cloak, green ribbons on bonnet, height 5¾″, designer L. Harradine. .. 1935-1949   500.00   600.00

DAFFY DOWN DILLY

HN 1712
☐ Green gown with green bonnet, height 8″, designer L. Harradine. 1935-1975   275.00   325.00

HN 1713
☐ Gown of shaded blues with white apron, light coloured bonnet with red trim, holding flat baskets of flowers under each arm, height 8″, designer L. Harradine...................... 1935-1949   475.00   525.00

DAINTY MAY

HN 1639
☐ 18th century figure with ball gown of red and green, small green hat, holding small bouquet, height 6″, designer L. Harradine............. 1934-1949   400.00   450.00

HN 1656
☐ White gown with shaded blues and flowers, small blue hat, height 6″, designer L. Harradine............. 1934-1949   300.00   350.00

☐ **M 67** Made as a miniature, blue and white gown, dark hat, height 4″, designer L. Harradine............. 1935-1949   325.00   375.00

☐ **M 73** Red and green gown, green hat, height 4″, designer L. Harradine. 1935-1949   325.00   375.00

DAISY

HN 1575
☐ Small figure with blue gown, white flowers design, height 3½″, designer L. Harradine...................... 1933-1949   250.00   300.00

Daisy, HN1575, 250.00 — 300.00

DAISY (cont.)	Date	Price Range	
HN 1961			
☐ Pink dress, height 3½″, designer L. Harradine.	1941-1949	275.00	325.00

DAMARIS

	Date	Price Range	
HN 2079			
☐ Blue and white gown, long cloak of blues and reds trimmed with white fur, head piece of white and dark blue, height 7½″, designer M. Davies.	1951-1952	800.00	950.00

'DANCING EYES AND SUNNY HAIR'

	Date	Price Range	
HN 1543			
☐ Small dark haired white female seated on shaded blue rock, height 5″, designer unknown.	1933-1949	300.00	350.00

	Date	Price Range	

DANCING FIGURE
HN 311
☐ Pink flowing gown, holding tambourine in hand, height 17¾", designer unknown 1918-1938   3500.00   4000.00

DANCING YEARS
HN 2235
☐ Dancers costume of blue and pink, blue ribbon in hair, figure in deep curtsey position, height 7", designer M. Davies. 1965-1971   375.00   425.00

The Dandy, HN753, **1100.00 — 1250.00**

DANDY, The
HN 753
☐ 18th century style costume of male, white trousers, black boots, red coat, red and black hat, leaning against tree, height 6¾", designer L. Harradine. 1925-1938   1100.00   1250.00

	Date	Price Range	

DAPHNE

HN 2268
☐ Pink gowned figure on white base, height 8½ ″, designer M. Davies. 1963-1975 175.00 225.00

DARBY

HN 1427
☐ Grey haired male seated in high backed blue-green chair, black trousers, blue jacket, red patterned long coat, black shoes, white stockings, height 5½ ″, designer L. Harradine. . . 1930-1949 375.00 425.00

HN 2024
☐ Minor glaze differences, height 5½ ″, designer L. Harradine. 1949-1959 350.00 400.00

DARLING

HN   1
☐ Blonde haired figure in white nightshirt, on white base (1st version), height 7½ ″, designer C. Vyse. 1913-1928 1000.00 1150.00

HN 1319
☐ Black base (1st version), height 7½ ″, designer C. Vyse. 1929-1959 150.00 200.00

HN 1371
☐ Green nightshirt (1st version), height 7½ ″, designer C. Vyse. 1930-1938 275.00 325.00

HN 1372
☐ Pink nightshirt (2nd version), height 7½ ″, designer C. Vyse. 1930-1938 275.00 325.00

HN 1985
☐ Small figure in white nightshirt on black base (2nd version), height 5¼ ″, designer C. Vyse. 1946- 55.00

DAVID COPPERFIELD
Issued only as a miniature.

☐ **M 88** White collar, yellow vest, tan pants, brown hat in hand, black jacket and black stand, height 4¼ ″, designer L. Harradine. 1949- 29.95

	Date	Price Range	

DAWN
HN 1858
☐ White nude figure on blue base, holding blue coloured material down front. Earlier version of this figure had a headdress making it 10¼ " in height without figure is approximately 9¾ ", designer L. Harradine.   1938-1949   1350.00   1500.00
☐ With headdress 1000.00   1250.00

DAYDREAMS
HN 1731
☐ Figure seated on bench, gown cream coloured with red bodice with blue trim, light red bonnet, holding small bouquet, height 5½ ", designer L. Harradine.   1935-   155.00
HN 1732
☐ Pale blue dress with pink trim, height 5½ ", designer L. Harradine.   1935-1949   300.00   350.00
HN 1944
☐ Red dress with white trim, figure holding larger bouquet, height 5½ ", designer L. Harradine.   1940-1949   350.00   400.00

DEBBIE
HN 2385
☐ Small figure in dark blue over gown, white with green design under gown, height 5¾ ", designer M. Davies.   1969-   100.00
HN 2400
☐ Gown is soft yellow with an overdress of pale rose w/frilled sleeves of half length. Hair blonde, height 6", designer M. Davies.   1983-   75.00

DEBUTANTE
HN 2210
☐ Bowing figure in blue dress with high blue headdress, height 5", designer M. Davies.   1963-1967   375.00   425.00

DEIDRE
HN 2020
☐ Blue and red gown with blue bonnet with red lining, height 7", designer L. Harradine.   1949-1955   350.00   400.00

	Date	Price Range	
DELICIA			

HN 1662
☐ Pink, shaded blue and white gown, small ribbon tied hat has small bouquet on wrist, height 5¾", designer L. Harradine. 1934-1938 550.00 650.00

HN 1663
☐ Flowered purple, green and yellow skirt, height 5¾", designer L. Harradine. 1934-1938 550.00 650.00

HN 1681
☐ Green and purple dress, height 5¾", designer L. Harradine. 1935-1938 600.00 700.00

DELIGHT

HN 1772
☐ Red gowned figure on black base, small white cap, trimmed with blue ribbons, height 6¾", designer L. Harradine. 1936-1967 200.00 250.00

HN 1773
☐ Blue gown with red bow, height 6¾", designer L. Harradine. 1936-1949 425.00 475.00

DELPHINE

HN 2136
☐ Light lavender gown with blue coat that has cream lining, fur stole, bonnet with flower trim, height 7¼", designer M. Davies. 1954-1967 275.00 325.00

DENISE

HN 2273
☐ Red gown with white trim, bonnet with blue ribbons, height 7¼", designer M. Davies. 1964-1971 275.00 325.00
☐ **M 34** Made as a miniature, pale green dress, rose overskirt, blue bodice and cap, height 4½", designer unknown. . 1933-1945 350.00 400.00
☐ **M 35** No colour detail available, height 4½", designer unknown. 1933-1945 350.00 400.00

DERRICK

HN 1398
☐ Dutch boy on light coloured base, blue trousers, white and light blue shirt, yellow buttons, red hat, height 8", designer L. Harradine. 1930-1938 600.00 700.00

	Date	Price Range	

DESPAIR

HN 596

☐ Small figure all wrapped in cobalt blue cape, features are light blue, height 4½", designer unknown. 1924-1938 **1400.00 1650.00**

DETECTIVE, The

HN 2359

☐ Green/black base, character figure in long brown coat with cape, double billed brown cap, white shirt, black tie, brown trousers, black shoes, holding magnifying glass and white object, height 9¼", designer E. J. Griffiths. 1977- **165.00**

DIANA

HN 1716

☐ Small figure in blue skirt, pink blouse, holding small bouquet, height 5¾", designer L. Harradine. 1935-1949 **300.00 375.00**

HN 1717

☐ Green and white dress, white gloves, dark ribbons, height 5¾", designer L. Harradine. 1935-1949 **300.00 375.00**

HN 1986

☐ Shaded red dress, red bonnet, height 5¾", designer L. Harradine. 1946-1975 **125.00 175.00**

DICK SWIVELLER

Issued only as a miniature.

☐ **M 90** Brown hat, yellow vest and pants, coat, cane and stand are dark brown, height 4¼", designer unknown 1949- **29.95**

DIGGER (New Zealand)

HN 321

☐ Green mottled figure of soldier, same coloured base, height 11¼", designer E. W. Light. 1918-1938 **1250.00 1500.00**

DIGGER (Australian)

HN 322

☐ Brown soldier figure on same coloured base, height 11¼", designer E. W. Light. 1918-1938 **1250.00 1500.00**

HN 353

☐ This figure painted naturalistically, height 11¾", designer E. W. Light. . . . 1919-1938 **1350.00 1600.00**

	Date	Price Range
DILIGENT SCHOLAR, The **HN 26** ☐ Seated figure on green base, green trousers, light shirt, multicoloured coat, holding slate, height 7″, designer W. White.	1913-1938	**1750.00 2000.00**
DIMITY **HN 2169** ☐ Two tiered gown of white with lavender and green flowers, green bodice, lavender sleeves, height 5¾″, designer L. Harradine.	1956-1959	**300.00 350.00**
DINKY DOO **HN 1678** ☐ Small figure in gown of shaded blues, white cap, height 4¾″, designer L. Harradine.	1934-	**65.00**
HN 2120 ☐ Figure is in curtsey position. Gown is red bodice with shades of pink in her skirt. (2nd Version), height 4¾″, designer L. Harradine.	1983-	**65.00**
DOCTOR, The **HN 2858** ☐ Black coat, blue trouser and vest, seated in chair with doctor's bag at side, height 7½″, designer W. K. Harper.	1979-	**225.00**
DOLLY **HN 355** ☐ Figure in shaded blue and white gown, holding doll, height 7¼″, designer C. J. Noke.	1919-1938	**1250.00 1500.00**
DOLLY VARDON **HN 1514** ☐ Gown of white with flower figures, cloak red patterned with light lining, white muff, green basket at feet, height 8½″, designer L. Harradine. . .	1932-1938	**700.00 800.00**
HN 1515 ☐ White and shaded blue gown, cloak multicoloured with light green lining, brown basket at feet, height 8½″, designer L. Harradine.	1932-1949	**800.00 900.00**

	Date	Price Range

DORCAS
HN 1490
□ Light coloured gown with darker over blouse, Dutch style bonnet with dark ribbons, holding bowl of flowers, height 7″, designer L. Harradine. 1932-1938   450.00   500.00

HN 1491
□ Shaded green gown with darker blouse, height 7″, designer L. Harradine. 1932-1938   450.00   500.00

HN 1558
□ Shaded red gown with designed red over blouse, height 7″, designer L. Harradine. 1933-1952   350.00   400.00

DOREEN
HN 1363
□ Figure in curtsey position wearing pink gown, height 5¼″, designer L. Harradine. 1929-1938   900.00   1000.00

HN 1389
□ Green gown trimmed in white, dark haired figure, height 5¼″, designer L. Harradine. 1930-1938   700.00   800.00

HN 1390
□ Shaded blue gown with white trim, light haired, height 5¼″, designer L. Harradine. 1929-1938   700.00   800.00

DORIS KEENE as Cavallini
HN 90
□ Black hair, black full gown with silver jewelery (1st version), height 11″, designer C. J. Noke. 1918-1936   2000.00   2250.00

HN 96
□ Black gown, white fur coat and muff, small hat (2nd version), height 10½″, designer C. J. Noke. 1918-1932   2250.00   2500.00

HN 345
□ Dark fur collar, striped muff (2nd version), height 10½″, designer C. J. Noke. 1919-1949,   2750.00   3000.00

HN 467
□ Gold jewelry (1st version), height 11″, designer C. J. Noke. 1921-1936   2000.00   2200.00

	Date	Price Range	
'DO YOU WONDER . . .'			
HN 1544			
☐ Small blonde figure wearing blue sun suit on light base, height 5″, designer unknown.	1933-1949	300.00	350.00
DOUBLE JESTER			
HN 365			
☐ Jester costume of multicolour, standing on base which holds pole which has on top a bust which faces first front and then reverse, height unknown, designer C. J. Noke.	1920-1938	2750.00	3250.00
DREAMLAND			
HN 1473			
☐ Figure lying on multicoloured sofa, costume of several colors, throw on back of couch is also multicoloured, height 4¾″, designer L. Harradine. . .	1931-1938	1850.00	2000.00
HN 1481			
☐ Darker sofa, yellow and red costume, height 4¾″, designer L. Harradine. . .	1931-1938	1350.00	1500.00
DREAMWEAVER			
HN 2283			
☐ Bearded figure seated on base which contains small animals playing pipes, green trousers, dark blue shirt, wearing sandals, this figure has matt finish, height 8¾″, designer M. Nicoll. . .	1972-1976	250.00	300.00
DRUMMER BOY			
HN 2679			
☐ Brown base, soldier uniform of blue trousers, red and white jacket, black tall hat with white and gold trim, grey knapsack, black boots, sitting on drum of red, white and blue, height 8½″, designer M. Nicoll.	1976-1981	325.00	375.00
DRYAD OF THE PINES			
HN 1869			
☐ White nude figure with flowing gold hair, standing on gold coloured rock on base, height 23″, designer R. Garbe. .	1938-1949	2750.00	3000.00

	Date	Price Range

DULCIE

HN 2305
☐ Full white skirt, bodice of white with designs of red, yellow and white, trimmed in blue, overshirt of royal blue, height 7¼ ", designer M. Davies.   1981-   185.00

DULCINEA

HN 1343
☐ Figure seated on multicoloured chaise lounge, costume of red and black, black Spanish style hat, height 5¼ ", designer L. Harradine.   1929-1938   900.00   1050.00

HN 1419
☐ Red and pink dress with green shoes, height 5¼ ", designer L. Harradine. . .   1930-1938   1000.00   1150.00

DUNCE

HN 6
☐ Cloaked figure on base wearing dunce cap, height 10½ ", designer C. J. Noke.   1913-1938   2750.00   3000.00

HN 310
☐ Black and white patterned costume, green base, height 10½ ", designer C. J. Noke.   1918-1938   2750.00   3000.00

HN 357
☐ Grey costume with black pattern, height 10½ ", designer C. J. Noke. . . .   1919-1938   2750.00   3000.00

EASTER DAY

HN 1976
☐ Full skirted pale lavender flowered gown, dark bodice, height 7½ ", designer M. Davies.   1945-1951   425.00   475.00

HN 2039
☐ Light coloured gown with multicoloured flowers around bottom, black bonnet with blue ribbons and green lining, height 7½ ", designer M. Davies.   1949-1969   275.00   325.00

	Date	Price Range	

EDITH
HN 2957
☐ One of the charming Kate Greenaway collection. Small figure with green dress, white underskirt, white apron held up containing red flowers. Blonde hair, white bonnet, height 5¾", designer P. Parsons. 1982-   100.00

ELAINE
HN 2791
☐ Blue ball gown, holding fan, height 7½", designer M. Davies. 1980-   185.00

ELEANORE
HN 1753
☐ Figure leaning against post, green and pink skirt with blue bodice, wearing small bonnet on side of head, height 7", designer L. Harradine. 1936-1949   700.00   850.00
HN 1754
☐ Gown of white with blue and red flowers, shaded red bodice, blue bonnet with blue ribbons, height 7", designer L. Harradine. 1936-1949   700.00   850.00

ELEANOR OF PROVENCE
HN 2009
☐ Queen figure, gown of dark blue and red, red cloak, and white covering on head, height 9½", designer M. Davies . 1948-1953   600.00   700.00

ELEGANCE
HN 2264
☐ Gown of shaded greens trimmed in white and green, green cloak, blue ribbon in hair, height 7½", designer M. Davies. 1961-   155.00

ELFREDA
HN 2078
☐ Ball gown of patterned red and blue, carrying fan of white, feathers trimmed in black, height 7¼", designer L. Harradine. 1951-1955   600.00   700.00

	Date	Price Range

ELIZA

HN 2543

☐ Tall figure (11¾"), brown costume, black flat hat, carrying basket of flowers on arm, holding bouquet in hand, designer E. J. Griffiths.   1974-1979   225.00   275.00

ELIZABETH

HN 2946

☐ A regal lady in her gown of shaded green with gold ruffle showing layers of white skirt underneath. Gold shawl adorns her shoulders. Carrying a very light green parasol. Red hair underneath a bonnet of yellow, height 8", designer B. Franks.   1982-   225.00

ELIZABETH FRY

HN   2

☐ Shaded light blue costume, head covering in same color, on light green base, height 17", designer C. Vyse. . .   1913-1938   4000.00   4500.00

HN   2A

☐ Blue base, height 17", designer C. Vyse.   1913-1938   4000.00   4500.00

ELLEN TERRY as Queen Catherine

HN   379

☐ Gown of shaded blues trimmed in black, white and green on black base, head gear of blue, yellow and white, height 12½ ", designer C. J. Noke. . . .   1920-1949   2750.00   3000.00

ELSIE MAYNARD

HN   639

☐ Multicoloured costume, white stockings, black shoes on black base, holding tambourine in hand above head, height 7", designer C. J. Noke. .   1924-1949   800.00   900.00

ELYSE

HN 2429

☐ Seated figure, blue gown, flowers in hair, holding white hat with red ribbons, height 6¾ ", designer M. Davies   1972-   185.00

	Date	Price Range	

EMBROIDERING
HN 2855
☐ Older figure seated in chair, blue gown, green apron, with embroidery on lap, sewing basket at side, height 7¼ ", designer W. K. Harper. 1980-   **225.00**

EMIR
HN 1604
☐ Cream coloured robe with red-green patterned scarf, height 7½ ", designer C. J. Noke. 1933-1949   **900.00   1000.00**
HN 1605
☐ Cream coloured robe with shades of yellow, multicoloured striped scarf, height 7½ ", designer C. J. Noke. 1933-1949   **900.00   1000.00**

EMMA (Kate Greenaway)
HN 2834
☐ Small figure, red dress, white apron trimmed with red flowers, holding green flowers in hands on white base, height 5¾ ", designer M. Davies. 1977-1981   **75.00   100.00**

ENCHANTMENT
HN 2178
☐ Shaded blue gown with white and yellow sleeves, gown has dark blue designs, height 7¾ ", designer M. Davies . 1957-1982   **125.00   175.00**

ERMINE COAT, The
HN 1981
☐ Red gown with white fur coat and muff, red stole with light blue and green designs, height 6¾ ", designer L. Harradine. 1945-1967   **300.00   350.00**

ERMINIE
Issued only as a miniature.

☐ **M 40** Pink skirt with white cape, pink shoes on white stand, height 4", designer unknown. 1933-1945   **375.00   425.00**

ESMERALDA
HN 2168
☐ Cream coloured gown with blue design, red shawl, dark blue parasol, holding small bird on hand, height 5¼ ", designer M. Davies. 1956-1959   **350.00   400.00**

	Date	Price Range

ESTELLE

HN 1566
☐ Light cloured gown with shaded blues, blue bonnet, blue muff, blue shoes, height 8″, designer L. Harradine.   1933-1938   800.00   900.00

HN 1802
☐ Pink dress, height 8″, designer L. Harradine.   1937-1949   700.00   800.00

EUGENE

HN 1520
☐ Seated figure in gown of shaded greens and pink, holding fan, height 5¾″, designer L. Harradine.   1932-1938   650.00   750.00

HN 1521
☐ Gown of shaded reds and white, height 5¾″, designer L. Harradine. . .   1932-1938   650.00   750.00

EUROPA AND THE BULL

HN   95
☐ Lady seated on bull, naturalistically painted, height 9¾″, designer H. Tittensor.   1918-1938   3000.00   3500.00

EVELYN

HN 1622
☐ Cream coloured gown with red bodice, red bonnet with shaded blue feathers, holding parasol across lap, height 6″, designer L. Harradine.   1934-1949   700.00   850.00

HN 1637
☐ Blue bodice, green hat, red parasol, height 6″, designer L. Harradine.   1934-1938   850.00   950.00

EVENTIDE

HN 2814
☐ Seated old lady figure in blue dress with white apron, patchwork quilt on lap, height 7¾″, designer W. K. Harper.   1977-   165.00

FAGIN

HN   534
☐ A character from Dicken's "Oliver Twist," height 4″, designer L. Harradine.   1922-   45.00   60.00

☐ **M 49** Renumbered as a miniature, height 4″, designer L. Harradine.   1932-   29.95

FAIR LADY	Date	Price Range

HN 2193
☐ Green gown, yellow sleeves, bonnet hanging on arm, height 7¾", designer M. Davies. 1963-   155.00

HN 2832
☐ Red gown, green sleeves, dark hair, height 7¾", designer M. Davies. 1977-   155.00

HN 2835
☐ Orange gown with multicoloured designs on white sleeves, height 7¾", designer M. Davies. 1977-   155.00

FAIR MAIDEN

HN 2211
☐ Small figure, green dress, yellow sleeves, bonnet handing on right wrist, height 5¼", designer M. Davies 1967-   100.00

HN 2434
☐ Gown of scarlet with green puffed sleeves and a multi-layered petticoat. Green hat trimmed in gold, gold coif in her dark brown hair, height 5¼", designer M. Davies. 1983-   95.00

FAIRY

HN 1324
☐ Nude white child figure seated on pedestal style base with multicoloured wings, height unknown, designer L. Harradine 1929-1938   850.00   950.00

HN 1374
☐ Nude white figure seated on toad stool, which is on green base surrounded by yellow flowers, height 4", designer L. Harradine. 1930-1938   850.00   950.00

HN 1375
☐ Fairy type figure lying on base covered with flowers, height 3", designer L. Harradine. 1930-1938   750.00   850.00

HN 1376
☐ No mushroom, height 2½", designer L. Harradine. 1930-1938   650.00   750.00

HN 1378
☐ Small white kneeling figure on green base with orange flowers, height 2½", designer L. Harradine. 1930-1938   550.00   650.00

FAIRY (cont.)	Date	Price Range	

HN 1379
☐ Small white kneeling figure on green base, has blue and white flowers around figure, height 2½", designer L. Harradine. 1930-1938 **550.00 650.00**

HN 1380
☐ Dark mottled mushroom, height 4", designer L. Harradine. 1930-1938 **850.00 950.00**

HN 1393
☐ Small white figure seated on green base covered with yellow flowers and green leaves, height 2½", designer L. Harradine. 1930-1938 **650.00 750.00**

HN 1394
☐ Yellow flowers, height 2½", designer L. Harradine. 1930-1938 **550.00 650.00**

HN 1395
☐ Blue flowers, height 3", designer L. Harradine. 1930-1938 **750.00 850.00**

HN 1396
☐ Small white kneeling figure on green base with blue and white flowers on base and on arm, height 2½", designer L. Harradine. 1930-1938 **550.00 650.00**

HN 1532
☐ Nude white figure seated on toad stool, which is on green base surrounded by multicoloured flowers, height 4", designer L. Harradine. 1932-1938 **550.00 650.00**

HN 1533
☐ Multicoloured flowers, height 3", designer L. Harradine. 1932-1938 **550.00 650.00**

HN 1534
☐ Large yellow flowers, height 2½", designer L. Harradine. 1932-1938 **550.00 650.00**

HN 1535
☐ Yellow and blue flowers, height 2½", designer L. Harradine. 1932-1938 **550.00 650.00**

HN 1536
☐ Light green base, height 2½", designer L. Harradine 1932-1938 **550.00 650.00**

FALSTAFF	Date	Price Range	
HN 571			
☐ Rotund figure in shades of brown costume on base, base has wicker stand covered with green and black striped cover, dark hat with orange feather (1st version), height 7″, designer C. J. Noke.	1923-1938	700.00	800.00
HN 575			
☐ Brown coat, yellow spotted cloth over base (1st version), height 7″, designer C. J. Noke.	1923-1938	700.00	800.00
HN 608			
☐ Red coat with red cloth over base (1st version), height 7″, designer C. J. Noke.	1924-1938	700.00	800.00
HN 609			
☐ Green coat with green cloth over base (1st version), height 7″, designer C. J. Noke.	1924-1938	700.00	800.00
HN 618			
☐ Black color, spotted lilac cloth on green base (2nd version), height 7″, designer C. J. Noke.	1924-1938	700.00	800.00
HN 619			
☐ Brown coat with green collar, yellow cloth over base (1st version), height 7″, designer C. J. Noke.	1924-1938	700.00	800.00
HN 638			
☐ Red coat, spotted cream cloth over base (1st version), height 7″, designer C. J. Noke.	1924-1938	700.00	800.00
HN 1216			
☐ With multicoloured costume (1st version), height 7″, designer C. J. Noke. .	1926-1949	700.00	800.00
HN 1606			
☐ Red costume, brown boots, black hat with red feathers, green cloth with red design on base (1st version), height 7″, designer C. J. Noke.	1933-1949	700.00	800.00
HN 2054			
☐ Red jacket, brown boots, gloves and collar, no hat, cream coloured cloth on orange coloured base (2nd version), height 7″, designer C. J. Noke. .	1950-	150.00	

	Date	Price Range	

FAMILY ALBUM

HN 2321

☐ Older lady seated in chair with album in lap, blue skirt, lavender blouse and cap, blue and black striped shawl, height 6¼ ", designer M. Nicoll. 1966-1973 350.00 400.00

FARAWAY

HN 2133

☐ Girl figure lying on tummy on pillow, reading book, white dress, blue bodice and shoes, height 2½ ", designer M. Davies. 1958-1962 350.00 400.00

FARMER'S BOY, The

HN 2520

☐ Farmer figure seated on large horse, mounted on base, height 8¾ ", designer W. M. Chance. 1938-1960 1000.00 1250.00

FARMER'S WIFE

HN 2069

☐ Green skirt, red blouse with green collar, white bonnet, skirt has chicken feed in it, base has two chickens on it, height 9 ", designer L. Harradine. . . 1951-1955 500.00 600.00

FAT BOY, The

HN 530

☐ A character from Dicken's "Pickwick" Papers" (1st version), height 3½ ", designer L. Harradine. 1922- 45.00 60.00

☐ **M 44** Renumbered as a miniature, height 4¼ ", designer L. Harradine. . . 1932- 29.95

HN 555

☐ Larger version of character, white trousers, blue coat with white buttons, white neck scarf and cloth over hand, on same base (2nd version), height 7 ", designer L. Harradine. 1923-1952 400.00 500.00

HN 1893

☐ Very minor colour changes (2nd version), height 7 ", designer L. Harradine. 1938-1952 325.00 375.00

Fat Boy, HN555, **400.00 — 500.00**

FAT BOY, The (cont.)	Date	Price Range

HN 2096

☐ White trousers, blue coat, yellow and black dotted scarf, white cloth with red trim on arm, on dark green base (3rd version), height 7¼", designer L. Harradine 1952-1967 **300.00 350.00**

FAVORITE, The

HN 2249

☐ Older lady figure with cream pitcher and saucer in hands, blue gown with white apron, brown cat at feet, height 7¼", designer M. Nicoll 1960- **165.00**

	Date	Price Range	
FIDDLER, The			

HN 2171

☐ 18th century figure, dancing and playing fiddle on brown base, light yellow trouser, jacket has yellow and green stripes, black hat with feather, height 8¾ ", designer M. Nicoll. 1956-1962 850.00 1000.00

FIONA

HN 1924

☐ Shaded red gown with purple jacket trimmed in black and white, black small bonnet, seated on green couch with multicoloured design (1st version), height 5¾", designer L. Harradine. 1940-1949 550.00 650.00

HN 1925

☐ Green skirt (1st version), height 5¾ ", designer L. Harradine. 1940-1949 550.00 650.00

HN 1933

☐ Multicoloured gown, red hat, couch shaded blues (1st version), height 5¾ ", designer L. Harradine. 1940-1949 650.00 750.00

HN 2694

☐ Standing figure with blue/red skirt, white bodice and sleeves with small lavender designs (2nd version), height 7½ ", designer M. Davies. 1974-1980 175.00 225.00

FISHERWOMAN

HN 80

☐ Three figures on brown base, first figure with green shawl, height unknown, designer unknown 1917-1938 3000.00 3500.00

HN 349

☐ Central figure has yellow shawl, height unknown, designer unknown. . 1919-1968 2750.00 3000.00

HN 359

☐ Central figure has red with black stripes in shawl, height unknown, designer unknown. 1919-1938 3000.00 3500.00

HN 631

☐ Central figure has green shawl, height unknown, designer unknown. . 1924-1938 3000.00 3500.00

	Date	Price Range

FIRST DANCE

HN 2803

☐ White gown with flower trim, green
bodice, holding multi-flowered fan,
height 7¼", designer M. Davies.   1977-   170.00

FIRST STEPS

HN 2242

☐ Blue gown with beige sleeves and
white collar, figure holding hands of
small figure, wearing blue trousers
with beige skirt, height 6¾", designer
M. Davies.   1959-1965   500.00   550.00

FIRST WALTZ

HN 2862

☐ Ball gown of red with blue and green
designs, light blue sleeves, holding
large white feather fan, height 7½",
designer M. Davies.   1979-   250.00

Fleur, HN2368, **185.00**

	Date	Price Range

MRS. FITZHERBERT
HN 2007
☐ Yellow and white gown, blue and white bonnet, holding blue and white fan, height 9″, designer M. Davies.... — 1948-1953 — 700.00 800.00

FLEUR
HN 2368
☐ Green gown with gold design at hemline, darker green jacket with gold dots, holding single flower in upraised hand, light green drape from top of bodice back, height 7½″, designer J. Bromley. .... — 1968- — 185.00

FLEURETTE
HN 1587
☐ White gown with red designs, red overlay, holding fan, height 6½″, designer L. Harradine. .... — 1933-1949 — 625.00 700.00

FLORA
HN 2349
☐ Older lady figure in dark brown dress with white apron, flowers in pot on stool, also under stool, height 7¾″, designer M. Nicoll. .... — 1966-1973 — 175.00 225.00

FLOUNCED SKIRT, The
HN 57A
☐ Many tiered orange lustre dress, figure wearing jewelry, height 9¾″, designer E. W. Light. .... — 1916-1938 — 1650.00 1800.00
HN 66
☐ Lilac dress, height 9¾″, designer E. W. Light. .... — 1916-1938 — 1650.00 1800.00
HN 77
☐ Lemon yellow dress with black trimmings, height 9¾″, designer E. W. Light. .... — 1917-1938 — 1650.00 1800.00
HN 78
☐ Flowered yellow lustre dress, height 9¾″, designer E. W. Light.......... — 1917-1938 — 1650.00 1800.00
HN 333
☐ Mottled brown tone dress, height 9¾″, designer E. W. Light.......... — 1918-1938 — 1550.00 1700.00

	Date	Price Range
FLOWER SELLER, The		

HN 789

☐ Yellow dress with green designs, red blouse, green shawl, green feathers on black hat, holding wrapped baby in one arm and a basket of flowers on other arm, height 8¾″, designer L. Harradine. 1926-1938   600.00   700.00

FLOWER SELLER'S CHILDREN, The

HN 525

☐ Boy and girl seated on stone bench with basket of flowers, green costume on boy, blue costume on girl, height 8¼″, designer L. Harradine. . . 1921-1949   650.00   750.00

HN 551

☐ Costume of boy blue, girl's chequered orange and yellow, height 8¼″, designer L. Harradine. 1922-1949   450.00   500.00

HN 1206

☐ Costume of girl multicoloured, boy's in shaded blues, cloth of dark blue, most flowers dark blue, height 8¼″, designer L. Harradine. 1926-1949   450.00   500.00

HN 1342

☐ Boy's costume shades of blue and red, girl's red with black design, robe shades of red and blue, height 8¼″, designer L. Harradine. 1929-   395.00

HN 1406

☐ Girl's costume is yellow, dark blue cloth over basket, height 8¼″, designer L. Harradine. 1930-1938   550.00   600.00

FOAMING QUART, The

HN 2162

☐ Rotund figure seated in dark grey and white chair, purple trousers, tunic purple/red with yellow collar, gloves and long boots of greyish green, purple hat with beige trim, blue/grey beard and hair, tankard very little blue, height 5¾″, designer M. Davies. 1955-   165.00

	Date	Price Range	
FOLLY			

HN 1335

☐ Short red costume, green collar, dark blue sash, light green dunce type hat, holding several small round objects of red, yellow and white, height 9″, designer L. Harradine.   1929-1938   **1600.00   1750.00**

HN 1750

☐ Earthenware, with brown hat, white muff, dark dress, height 9½″, designer L. Harradine   1936-1949   **1100.00   1250.00**

FORGET-ME-NOT

HN 1812

☐ Red haired figure seated on bench style base, pink dress, green ribbons, holding small round purse, height 6″, designer L. Harradine.   1937-1949   **550.00   650.00**

HN 1813

☐ Red dress, dark blue bonnet with ribbons, height 6″, designer L. Harradine.   1937-1949   **550.00   650.00**

FORTUNE TELLER

HN 2159

☐ Gypsy figure seated on wicker stand, at small table with green and black cover, crystal ball and cards on table, red dress with green shawl, height 6½″, designer L. Harradine.   1955-1967   **425.00   475.00**

FORTY WINKS

HN 1974

☐ Elderly lady seated in tall backed chair of reds and yellow, dark skirt, white apron, red blouse, dark shawl, cat at feet, height 6¾″, designer H. Fenton.   1945-1973   **250.00   300.00**

FOUR O'CLOCK

HN 1760

☐ Gown of shaded blues with white trim, multicoloured bonnet, holding tea cup and saucer, height 6″, designer L. Harradine.   1936-1949   **475.00   575.00**

	Date	Price Range
FRAGRANCE		

FRAGRANCE

HN 2334
☐ Gown of blue with white circular designs and white trim, height 7⅜″, designer M. Davies.   1966-   170.00

FRANCINE

HN 2422
☐ Small dark haired figure with green dress and yellow sleeves, blue waist ribbon, holding brown bird on arm, height 5¼″, designer J. Bromley.   1972-1980   75.00   125.00

FRANGCON

HN 1720
☐ Multicoloured flowered gown with black hat and shoes, on light coloured base trimmed in black, height 7½″, designer L. Harradine.   1935-1949   650.00   750.00

HN 1721
☐ Green dress, green hat and shoes, base light coloured trimmed in brown, height 7½″, designer L. Harradine. . .   1935-1949   650.00   750.00

FRENCH PEASANT

HN 2075
☐ Light red skirt with red designs, shaded blues blouse, white headdress with red ribbons, on multicoloured base, height 9½″, designer L. Harradine.   1951-1955   600.00   700.00

FRIAR TUCK

HN 2143
☐ Brown monk's robe, holding sword and shield, on brown base, height 7½″, designer M. Davies.   1954-1965   400.00   450.00

FRUIT GATHERING

HN 449
☐ Blue striped blouse, blue skirt, figure holding basket, has dog on base with figure, height 7¾″, designer L. Harradine.   1921-1938   2750.00   3000.00

HN 476
☐ Green check blouse, blue check skirt, height 7¾″, designer L. Harradine. . .   1921-1938   2650.00   2800.00

FRUIT GATHERING (cont.)	Date	Price Range
HN 503		
☐ Brown and blue chequered dress, height 7¾", designer L. Harradine. ...	1921-1938	**2500.00 3000.00**
HN 561		
☐ Yellow designed skirt, green blouse, bonnet same as skirt, height 7¾", designer L. Harradine.	1923-1938	**2500.00 3000.00**
HN 562		
☐ Pink blouse with spotted skirt, height 7¾", designer L. Harradine.	1923-1938	**2500.00 3000.00**
HN 706		
☐ Purple blouse with yellow skirt, height 7¾", designer L. Harradine. ...	1925-1938	**2500.00 3000.00**
HN 707		
☐ Red blouse, spotted skirt, height 7¾", designer L. Harradine.	1925-1938	**3000.00 3500.00**

GAFFER, The

	Date	Price Range
HN 2053		
☐ Elderly male figure with white beard on base, green trousers, dark coat, red vest, brown hat, holding staff and red and white dotted kerchief, height 7¾", designer L. Harradine.	1950-1959	**350.00 400.00**

GAINESBOROUGH HAT, The

	Date	Price Range
HN 46		
☐ Lilac dress, wearing huge hat, black with white, height 8¾", designer H. Tittensor.	1915-1938	**1100.00 1200.00**
HN 46A		
☐ Black patterned collar was added to costume, height 8¾", designer H. Tittensor.	1915-1938	**1100.00 1200.00**
HN 47		
☐ Green dress, height 8¾", designer H. Tittensor.	1915-1938	**1100.00 1200.00**
HN 329		
☐ Patterned blue dress, height 8¾", designer H. Tittensor.	1918-1938	**1100.00 1200.00**
HN 352		
☐ Yellow dress and purple hat, height 8¾", designer H. Tittensor.	1919-1938	**1750.00 2000.00**
HN 383		
☐ Striped dress, height 8¾", designer H. Tittensor.	1920-1938	**1050.00 1200.00**

GAINESBOROUGH HAT, The (cont.)

	Date	Price Range

HN 453
☐ Red, blue and green costume, height 8¾", designer H. Tittensor. 1921-1938   1250.00   1400.00

HN 675
☐ Cream coloured gown with red and yellow design, black hat, height 8¾", designer H. Tittensor. 1924-1938   1350.00   1500.00

HN 705
☐ Shaded blue gown with red and yellow designs, height 8¾", designer H. Tittensor. 1925-1938   1100.00   1200.00

GAY MORNING

HN 2135
☐ Cream coloured skirt, with very light red bodice, large white sleeves trimmed in blue, blue and red scarf in hand, height 7", designer M. Davies. . 1954-1967   300.00   350.00

GEISHA, A

HN 354
☐ Japanese style figure, yellow kimono, pink cuffs, blue flowered waistband, holding fan (1st version), height 10¾", designer H. Tittensor. 1919-1938   2250.00   2500.00

HN 376
☐ Blue and yellow mottled kimono (1st version), height 10¾", designer H. Tittensor. 1920-1938   2300.00   2500.00

HN 387
☐ Blue kimono, yellow cuffs (1st version), height 10¾", designer H. Tittensor. 1920-1938   2250.00   2500.00

HN 634
☐ Black and white kimono (1st version), height 10¾", designer H. Tittensor. . . 1924-1938   2250.00   2500.00

HN 741
☐ Dark multicoloured kimono, black trim (1st version), height 10¾", designer H. Tittensor. 1925-1938   2250.00   2500.00

HN 779
☐ Red kimono with black spots (1st version), height 10¾", designer H. Tittensor. 1926-1938   2250.00   2500.00

GEISHA, A (cont.)	Date	Price Range

HN 1223
☐ Seated Japanese style figure playing instrument on base, red and black striped costume, flowers in hair (2nd version), height 6¾", designer C. J. Noke. 1927-1938 **900.00 1000.00**

HN 1234
☐ Multicoloured costume (2nd version), height 6¾", designer C. J. Noke. 1927-1938 **900.00 1000.00**

HN 1292
☐ Orange kimono, blue/green collar (2nd version), height 6¾", designer C. J. Noke. 1928-1938 **900.00 1000.00**

HN 1310
☐ Multicoloured spotted kimono (2nd version), height 6¾", designer C. J. Noke. 1929-1938 **800.00 900.00**

HN 1321
☐ HN 779 with green kimono (1st version), height 10¾", designer H. Tittensor. 1929-1938 **2250.00 2500.00**

HN 1322
☐ Pink kimono, with blue markings (1st version), height 10¾", designer H. Tittensor. 1929-1938 **2250.00 2500.00**

GENEVIEVE

HN 1962
☐ Full red gown with blue and pink ribbons, white muff, black ribbon on dark blue hat with green lining, height 7", designer L. Harradine. 1941-1975 **200.00 250.00**

GENIE, The

HN 2989
☐ Rising from a lamp this figure has a dark blue cloak around his bare torso. Head bald except for a black topknot. Arms are folded, height 9¾", designer R. Tabbenor. 1983- **95.00**

The Genie, HN2989, **95.00**

	Date	Price Range	
GENTLEMEN FROM WILLIAMSBURG			
HN 2227			
☐ Green costume, white stockings, black shoes, black hat, seated figure on wooden bench, height 6¼", designer M. Davies.	1960-	200.00	
GENTLEWOMAN, A			
HN 1632			
☐ Older woman in lavender gown holding green parasol and bonnet, height 7½", designer L. Harradine.	1934-1949	675.00	775.00
GEORGIANA			
HN 2093			
☐ 18th century ball gown in red, blue and pale yellow, headdress of red and blues, height 8¼", designer M. Davies	1952-1955	600.00	700.00

	Date	Price Range
GEORGINA (Kate Greenaway)		
HN 2377		
☐ White base, shaded yellow gown, red cloak, white bonnet with blue ribbons, holding hoop and stick, height 5¾", designer M. Davies.	1981-	100.00
GERALDINE		
HN 2348 '		
☐ Brown gown with white flowers on bottom edge, white collar, brown ribbon in hair, matte finish, height 7½", designer M. Davies.	1972-1976	125.00 175.00
GILLIAN		
HN 1670		
☐ Shaded red gown, green bonnet and ribbons, white shawl with multicoloured design, height 7¾", designer L. Harradine.	1934-1949	700.00 800.00
GIRL WITH YELLOW FROCK		
HN 588		
☐ Young girl in yellow frock on green base, height 6¼", designer unknown.	1923-1938	1350.00 1500.00
GISELLE		
HN 2139		
☐ Seated ballet dancer on wooden bench on shaded green base, light blue costume with white trim, blue headdress, height 6¼", designer M. Davies.	1954-1969	350.00 400.00
GISELLE, The FOREST GLADE		
HN 2140		
☐ Ballet figure standing on toes on base of shaded greens, white costume, holding blue cloth by one hand, height 7¼", designer M. Davies.	1954-1965	375.00 475.00
GLADYS		
HN 1740		
☐ Figure only of head, shoulders and arms leaning on green base, green gown, height 5", designer L. Harradine.	1935-1949	550.00 600.00

	Date	Price Range	
GLADYS (cont.)			
HN 1741			
☐ Pink dress, height 5″, designer L. Harradine.	1935-1938	575.00	625.00
GLORIA			
HN 1488			
☐ Gown and cloak of shaded blues, fur trimmed sleeves, blue hat with red feather, red purse, height 7″, designer L. Harradine.	1932-1938	900.00	1000.00
HN 1700			
☐ Skirt light green, blouse green with black designs, black jacket, cloak multicoloured, black hat, height 7″, designer L. Harradine.	1935-1938	1000.00	1100.00
GNOME, A			
HN 319			
☐ Seated elf type figure, with pale blue costume, height 6¼″, designer H. Tittensor.	1918-1938	1000.00	1200.00
HN 380			
☐ Purple costume, height 6¼″, designer H. Tittensor.	1920-1938	1000.00	1200.00
HN 381			
☐ Purple costume with green, face, hands and arms green, height 6¼″, designer H. Tittensor.	1920-1938	1000.00	1200.00
GOLDEN DAYS			
HN 2274			
☐ Small girl and dog on dark brown and green base, gown is shaded yellows with blue trim, dog is white and brown, height 4″, designer M. Davies.	1964-1973	125.00	175.00
GOLLYWOG			
HN 1979			
☐ Small boy figure in white coveralls with animal designs, on light coloured base, holding coloured doll, height 5¼″, designer L. Harradine. . .	1945-1959	300.00	350.00
HN 2040			
☐ Light blue coveralls, green hat, height 5¼″, designer L. Harradine.	1949-1959	225.00	275.00

	Date	Price Range

GOOD CATCH, A
HN 2258
☐ Man in dark brown suit, sitting on light coloured base with fish in hand, net and hamper on base, height 7", designer M. Nicoll. 1966- 165.00

Good King Wenceslas, HN2118, **275.00 — 325.00**

GOOD KING WENCESLAS
HN 2118
☐ Costume of shaded oranges, dark cloak, holding lantern in one hand, on light brown base, height 9", designer M. Davies. 1953-1976 275.00 325.00

GOOD MORNING
HN 2671
☐ Lady feeding birds, bird house on tree stump, gown white with flower design edge, light red blouse, matt finish, height 8", designer M. Nicoll. 1974-1976 200.00 250.00

GOODY TWO SHOES	Date	Price Range	

HN 1889
☐ Small figure in green dress with white trim, white cap, height 4¾", designer L. Harradine. 1938-1949   250.00   300.00

HN 1905
☐ Pink skirt with red overdress, height 4¾", designer L. Harradine. 1939-1949   225.00   275.00

HN 2037
☐ Red dress with white trim, red shoes, white cap, height 5¼", designer L. Harradine. 1949-   100.00

☐ **M 80** Made as a miniature, blue skirt, height 4", designer L. Harradine. 1939-1949   400.00   450.00

☐ **M 81** Cream coloured skirt with mottled overlay, height 4", designer L. Harradine. 1939-1949   350.00   400.00

GOOSEGIRL, The

HN 425
☐ Figure on dark base with goose, blue skirt, striped blue blouse, holding basket, height unknown, designer L. Harradine. 1921-1938   2750.00   3000.00

HN 436
☐ Green skirt with blue spots, with spotted blouse, height unknown, designer L. Harradine. 1921-1938   2500.00   3000.00

HN 437
☐ Chequered brown and blue dress, height unknown, designer L. Harradine 1921-1938   2500.00   3000.00

HN 448
☐ Blue striped blouse, blue hat, height unknown, designer L. Harradine. 1921-1938   2750.00   3000.00

HN 559
☐ Spotted pink dress, height unknown, designer L. Harradine. 1923-1938   2750.00   3000.00

HN 560
☐ Red striped skirt, red blouse, white apron, white with designed rings head kerchief, height unknown, designer L. Harradine. 1923-1938   2750.00   3000.00

	Date	Price Range	

GOSSIPS, The

HN 1426

☐ Two ladies seated on brown sofa, one costume of shaded blues, with blue ribbon on bonnet, other costume of white with shaded reds, dark hair with small hat, height 5¾", designer L. Harradine.   1930-1949   500.00   750.00

HN 1429

☐ Red sofa, one gown of red with bonnet, other is white with flower design, small red hat, height 5¾", designer L. Harradine.   1930-1949   525.00   575.00

HN 2025

☐ Minor glaze differences, height 5¾", designer L. Harradine.   1949-1967   350.00   400.00

GRACE

HN 2318

☐ Green skirt, dark green jacket with fur trim, small fur hat and muff, figure seems to be skating, height 7⅞", designer M. Nicoll.   1966-1980   125.00   175.00

GRANDMA

HN 2052

☐ White skirt, red jacket, shawl is multi-coloured, carrying basket on arm, walking stick in other hand. There are some known color variations of this number, height 6¾", designer L. Harradine.   1950-1959   325.00   400.00

GRANNY

HN 1804

☐ Seated figure on chair, grey dress, purple and brown chequered shawl, small tea table at side, height 7", designer L. Harradine.   1937-1949   850.00   950.00

HN 1832

☐ Yellow dress with green trim on edge, shawl of red and blue, height 7", designer L. Harradine.   1937-1949   850.00   950.00

	Date	Price Range	
GRANNY'S HERITAGE			

HN 1873
☐ Seated older lady with child in front, flower baskets on each side, red flowered shawl on granny, green dress on child, height 6¼", designer L. Harradine. 1938-1949 450.00 500.00

HN 1874
☐ Granny in blue shawl, green skirt, height 6¼", designer L. Harradine. . . 1938-1949 450.00 500.00

HN 2031
☐ Granny in green skirt with mottled blue shawl, child in shaded blue dress, height 6¼", designer L. Harradine. 1949-1969 400.00 450.00

GRANNY'S SHAWL

HN 1642
☐ White dress, blue cloak with red ribbons, bonnet with green ribbons, holding basket of flowers, height 6", designer L. Harradine. 1934-1949 400.00 500.00

HN 1647
☐ White dress, red cloak, bonnet with dark green ribbons, height 6", designer L. Harradine. 1934-1949 350.00 400.00

GRAND MANNER

HN 2723
☐ Gown of light yellow with shades of blue/red with white flower design, with hat to match, dark green ribbon on dress, height 7¾", designer W. K. Harper. 1975-1981 225.00 275.00

GRETA

HN 1485
☐ Small figure on base, gown white with blue tinge, red scarf, holding basket in front of her with both hands, height 5½", designer L. Harradine. 1931-1953 300.00 350.00

GRETCHEN

HN 1397
☐ Dutch girl on base, blue gown with white apron, white bonnet with green trim, holding jug, height 7¾", designer L. Harradine. 1930-1938 650.00 700.00

	Date	Price Range	

GRETCHEN (cont.)
HN 1562
☐ Dark hair, multicoloured skirt, red blouse, height 7¾", designer L. Harradine. 1933-1938   **700.00**   **800.00**

GRIEF
HN 595
☐ Small seated figure wrapped completely in blue robe, dark hair, has only toes peeking from robe, height 2", designer unknown. 1924-1938   **900.00**   **1000.00**

GRIZEL
HN 1629
☐ Pink tiered skirt with multicoloured blouse, green hat and green shoes, small bit of pantalettes showing, height 6¾", designer L. Harradine. . . 1934-1938   **550.00**   **650.00**

GRISELDA
HN 1993
☐ Cream coloured gown with lavender overlay, trimmed in white, green bonnet with red ribbons, height 5¾", designer L. Harradine. 1947-1953   **500.00**   **600.00**

GROSSMITH'S 'TSANG IHANG' PERFUME OF TIBET
HN 582
☐ Chinese lady on black base with printing, costume of yellow with red flowers, trimmed in blue, wearing white jewelry (See classification Tibetian Lady), height 11½", designer unknown   1923-Unknown   **650.00**   **700.00**

GUY FAWKES
HN 98
☐ Black costume covered with red cloak, black hat, carrying lantern, height 10½", designer C. J. Noke. . . . 1918-1949   **1300.00**   **1500.00**
HN 347
☐ Brown cloak, height 10½", designer C. J. Noke. 1919-1938   **1250.00**   **1400.00**
HN 445
☐ Green cloak, height 10½", designer C. J. Noke. 1921-1938   **1250.00**   **1400.00**

	Date	Price Range

GWENDOLEN

HN 1494
☐ Seated dark haired figure, tiered gown of green and pink, green shoes, holding small flower bouquet on lap, height 6″, designer L. Harradine. 1932-1938 775.00 850.00

HN 1503
☐ Gown of shaded yellows and orange, height 6″, designer L. Harradine. 1932-1949 700.00 800.00

HN 1570
☐ Pink gown, height 6″, designer L. Harradine. 1933-1949 675.00 750.00

GWYNNETH

HN 1980
☐ Red gown trimmed with white, small white head cap, height 7″, designer L. Harradine. 1945-1952 300.00 350.00

GYPSY DANCE, A

HN 2157
☐ Gown of white and shaded blues, bare footed, hand free not attached to dress (1st version), height 7″, designer M. Davies. 1955-1957 400.00 450.00

HN 2230
☐ Gown of white and shaded purples, hand is attached to gown (2nd version), height 7″, designer M. Davies. . 1959-1971 250.00 300.00

GYPSY WOMAN WITH CHILD

HN 1301
☐ Blue skirt, red blouse, green shawl, holding wrapped baby in one arm, red tied scarf in other hand, height unknown, designer unknown. 1928-1938 2250.00 2400.00

GYPSY GIRL WITH FLOWERS

HN 1302
☐ Striped green skirt, red blouse, holding flowers, height unknown, designer unknown. 1928-1938 2250.00 2400.00

'HAPPY JOY, BABY BOY'

HN 1541
☐ Small white figure standing on multi-coloured rock, holding small very light green coloured robe, height 6¼″, designer unknown. 1933-1949 300.00 350.00

	Date	Price Range

HARLEQUIN
HN 2186
☐ Trousers of light blue with darker blue design, jacket blue with darker blue and white checks, white stockings, hat of blue with white trim, on light coloured base, height 7¼", designer M. Davies.   1957-1969   **225.00   275.00**

HARLEQUINADE
HN 585
☐ Costume of black, yellow, green, purple checks, trimmed in white, black hat, black shoes, dark stockings, standing on pedestal style base, height 6½", designer L. Harradine. . .   1923-1938   **850.00   950.00**

HN 635
☐ Gold costume, height 6½", designer L. Harradine.   1924-1938   **1150.00   1300.00**

HN 711
☐ Black and white costume, height 6½", designer L. Harradine.   1925-1938   **850.00   950.00**

HN 780
☐ Pink dress with blue, black and orange markings, height 6½", designer L. Harradine.   1926-1938   **850.00   950.00**

HARLEQUINADE MASKED
HN 768
☐ Black, red, green, chequered costume, figure standing on black pedestal style base, height 6½", designer L. Harradine.   1925-1938   **1350.00   1450.00**

HN 769
☐ Blue, red and yellow chequered costume, height 6½", designer L. Harradine.   1925-1938   **1350.00   1450.00**

HN 1274
☐ Red and black chequered costume with red hat, height 6½", designer L. Harradine.   1928-1938   **1350.00   1450.00**

HN 1304
☐ Spotted black costume, height 6½", designer L. Harradine.   1928-1938   **1350.00   1450.00**

Harmony, HN2824, **170.00**

HARMONY	Date	Price Range	
HN 2824			
☐ Figure holding small white bird in hand, blue/grey gown, height 8", designer R. Jefferson.	1978-	**170.00**	
HAZEL			
HN 1796			
☐ Small figure in green tiered dress, green bonnet, holding small round purse, height 5¼", designer L. Harradine.	1936-1949	**350.00**	**400.00**
HN 1797			
☐ Dress of shaded reds, trimmed with small flower design, blue and red shawl, small blue purse, height 5¼", designer L. Harradine.	1936-1949	**300.00**	**350.00**

	Date	Price Range

HEART TO HEART
HN 2276
☐ Two figures each seated in yellow chairs, one dressed in lavender gown trimmed in white, the other in white with blue designs and blue shawl, the figures are facing each other, height 5½ ", designer M. Davies.   1961-1971   **400.00**   **500.00**

HELEN
HN 1508
☐ Green gown with red flower design trimmed in white, bonnet with red ribbons, black shoes on base, open parasol, height 8″, designer L. Harradine.   1932-1938   **750.00**   **900.00**
HN 1509
☐ White gown with red flower design, red shoes, height 8″, designer L. Harradine.   1932-1938   **750.00**   **900.00**
HN 1572
☐ Red gown, bonnet has shaded red and blue ribbons, height 8″, designer L. Harradine.   1933-1938   **650.00**   **800.00**

HELMSMAN
HN 2499
☐ Foul weather costume, black hat, figure standing on base before helm with hands on wheel, height 8½ ", designer M. Nicoll.   1974-   **200.00**

HE LOVES ME
HN 2046
☐ Blonde small girl figure standing on yellow rock, red and blue sun dress, holding single flower in hands, height 5½ ", designer L. Harradine.   1949-1962   **175.00**   **225.00**

HENRIETTA MARIA
HN 2005
☐ Gown of red and yellow with light designs of blue, holding small round fan of red and white, height 9½ ", designer M. Davies.   1948-1953   **600.00**   **700.00**

	Date	Price Range	

HENRY VIII

HN 370

☐ Robes of purple, brown, yellow, green, standing on base (1st version), height unknown, designer C. J. Noke.   1920-1938   **2350.00 2600.00**

HN 673

☐ Robes of brown and lilac (1st version), height unknown, designer C. J. Noke.   1924-1938   **2350.00 2600.00**

HENRY IRVING as CARDINAL WOLSEY

HN 344

☐ Figure with red costume and red hat on black base, height 13¼ ″, designer C. J. Noke.   1919-1949   **2000.00 2500.00**

HENRY LYTTON as JACK POINT

HN 610

☐ Figure in clown costume of blue with red and black stripes, green stockings and shoes, on black base, height 6½ ″, designer C. J. Noke.   1924-1949   **800.00 900.00**

'HERE A LITTLE CHILD I STAND'

HN 1546

☐ Small child standing on multicoloured rock, light blue gown, height 6¼ ″, designer unknown.   1933-1949   **325.00 375.00**

HER LADYSHIP

HN 1977

☐ Gown of light green with green flower design, paisley shawl, pale green bonnet with green ribbons, white fur muff, height 7¼ ″, designer L. Harradine.   1945-1959   **325.00 375.00**

HERMINIA

HN 1644

☐ Gown and shawl of white with red flower and green design, light green bonnet with green ribbons, small red purse, height 6½ ″, designer L. Harradine.   1934-1938   **850.00 950.00**

HN 1646

☐ Red dress, white stripes, height 6½ ″, designer L. Harradine.   1934-1938   **900.00 1000.00**

	Date	Price Range	

HERMINIA (cont.)

HN 1704

☐ Red gown, mottled green shawl and purse, green bonnet with red ribbons, height 6½ ", designer L. Harradine. . . 1935-1938 **850.00   950.00**

HERMIONE

HN 2058

☐ Cream and shaded blues color gown with red trim, large red hat with feathers and ribbons, black ribbon around neck, height 7½ ", designer M. Davies . 1950-1952 **600.00   700.00**

The Highwayman, HN527, **700.00 — 800.00**

HIGHWAYMAN, The

HN 527

☐ A character from "The Beggar's Opera," red coat with dark overcoat, black hat with red trim, black stockings and shoes, drawing pistol, figure on black base, height 6½ ", designer L. Harradine. 1921-1949 **700.00   800.00**

	Date	Price Range	

HN 592
☐ Different glaze finish, height 6½", designer L. Harradine. 1924-1949   **700.00   800.00**

HN 1257
☐ Earthenware, height 6½", designer L. Harradine. 1927-1949   **600.00   700.00**

HILARY

HN 2335
☐ Gown of blue with white designs, trimmed in white and blue, holding hat of yellow and white, height 7¼", designer unknown. 1967-1980   **150.00   200.00**

HINGED PARASOL, The

HN 1578
☐ Tiered gown of cream and reds with large blue dots, green hat, shoes and parasol, height 6½", designer L. Harradine. 1933-1949   **400.00   500.00**

HN 1579
☐ Gown of red and blues, red shoes, parasol and hat, height 6½", designer L. Harradine. 1933-1949   **400.00   500.00**

HIS HOLINESS POPE JOHN PAUL II

HN 2888
☐ Beautiful likeness of His Holiness inspired by his visit to the United Kingdom, height 10", designer E. J. Griffiths. 1982-   **150.00**

HOME AGAIN

HN 2167
☐ Small girl in red gown with white dog on light coloured base, green small hat, green shoes and ribbons, height 3½", designer M. Davies. 1956-   **125.00**

HONEY

HN 1909
☐ Pink dress with red jacket, blue shawl with white dots, blue bonnet with green ribbons, holding small round purse in one hand, small bouquet in other, height 7", designer L. Harradine. 1939-1949   **350.00   400.00**

HONEY (cont.)	Date	Price Range	

HN 1910

☐ Blue dress with darker blue jacket, white shawl with blue designs, bonnet has black ribbons, holding larger bouquet of flowers, height 7″, designer L. Harradine. 1939-1949   375.00   450.00

HN 1963

☐ Red, blue hat strings and shawl, height 7″, designer L. Harradine. 1941-1949   400.00   450.00

HORNPIPE, The

HN 2161

☐ Figure of sailor in dancing position on bae, striped trousers, blue and white jacket, white shirt, black hat, height 9¼″, designer M. Nicoll. 1955-1962   750.00   850.00

HOSTESS OF WILLIAMSBURG

HN 2209

☐ Pink gown with trim of white and blue ribbons, holding closed fan in hand, height 7¼″, designer M. Davies. 1960-   200.00

HUNTING SQUIRE

HN 1409

☐ Figure seated on blue and white horse mounted on black base, red jacket, white trousers, black boots, black hat, height 9¾″, designer unknown. 1930-1938   2000.00   2500.00

HUNTS LADY

HN 1201

☐ Riding costume of white trousers, blue/grey coat, brown boots and hat, white shirt, standing on brown base, height 8¼″, designer L. Harradine. . . 1926-1938   1100.00   1200.00

HUNTSMAN, The

HN 1226

☐ Riding costume of red jacket, white trousers, black boots and hat, holding riding crop, standing on brown base (1st version), height 8¾″, designer L. Harradine. 1927-1938   1350.00   1500.00

HUNTSMAN, The (cont.)

	Date	Price Range	

HN 1815

☐ Seated figure on brown horse mounted on black base, red jacket, white trousers, black boots and hat, blowing horn. This figure was made of earthenware (2nd version), height 9½", designer unknown. 1937-1949 2300.00 2500.00

HN 2492

☐ Seated figure on wooden bench with dog at side, yellow trousers, grey jacket, black riding cap, black boots with brow trim (3rd version), height 7½", designer M. Nicoll. 1974-1980 175.00 225.00

IBRAHIM

HN 2095

☐ Shaded light red robe with cream coloured scarf, height 7¾", designer C. J. Noke. 1952-1955 800.00 900.00

IONA

HN 1346

☐ Lady and German Shepherd dog on black base, costume of shaded blues trimmed in purple, red and green, tall hat of green with purple feather, height 7½", designer L. Harradine. . . 1929-1938 2500.00 3000.00

IN GRANDMA'S DAY

HN 339

☐ See classification "LILAC SHAWL, A", height 8¾", designer C. J. Noke. 1919-1938 1250.00 1500.00

HN 340

☐ See classification "LILAC SHAWL, A", height 8¾", designer C. J. Noke. 1919-1938 1250.00 1500.00

HN 362

☐ See classification "LILAC SHAWL, A", height 8¾", designer C. J. Noke. 1919-1938 1550.00 1700.00

HN 388

☐ See classification "LILAC SHAWL, A", height 8¾", designer C. J. Noke. 1920-1938 1650.00 1800.00

HN 442

☐ See classification "LILAC SHAWL, A", height 8¾", designer C. J. Noke. 1921-1938 1650.00 1800.00

In The Stocks, HN2163, **650.00 — 700.00**

IN THE STOCKS	Date	Price Range	
HN 1474			
☐ This figure also known as LOVE IN THE STOCKS and LOVE LOCKED IN — Small white angel in stocks, girl seated beside stocks in red dress, holding bonnet by ribbons (1st version), height 5¼", designer L. Harradine.	1931-1938	**1300.00**	**1500.00**
HN 1475			
☐ Gown is shaded greens with green slippers, blue ribbons (1st version), height 5¼", designer L. Harradine. ..	1931-1938	**1000.00**	**1250.00**
HN 2163			
☐ Character figure in stocks of brown on brown base, costume of red with black hat (2nd version), height 5", designer M. Nicoll.	1955-1959	**650.00**	**700.00**
INNOCENCE			
HN 2842			
☐ Dark haired figure in red gown with black ribbon straps, height 7½", designer E. J. Griffiths.	1979-	**155.00**	

INVITATION	Date	Price Range	

HN 2170

☐ Pink gown with shoulder trim of blue ribbon and white flowers, holding open fan of blue, red and white, height 5½ ", designer M. Davies. 1956-1975 100.00 159.00

IRENE

HN 1621

☐ Tiered gown of light yellow, with red bodice, light red bonnet with green ribbon, holding small flower, height varies from 6½ to 7", designer L. Harradine. 1934-1951 450.00 500.00

HN 1697

☐ Gown of shaded reds, green bonnet, yellow roses bouquet, height varies from 6½ to 7", designer L. Harradine. 1935-1949 500.00 575.00

HN 1952

☐ Gown in shades of red and blue, bonnet blue, flowers in bouquet light multicolour, height varies from 6½ to 7", designer L. Harradine. 1940-1950 550.00 600.00

IRISH COLLEEN

HN 766

☐ Figure standing on black base, short skirt of black and white stipes, red jacket, black vest, black tall hat with red flower trim, height 6½ ", designer L. Harradine. 1925-1938 1650.00 1800.00

HN 767

☐ Skirt of black, red, green stripes, black jacket, red vest, also red shoes, height 6½ ", designer L. Harradine. .. 1925-1938 1650.00 1800.00

IRISHMAN, An

HN 1307

☐ Figure standing on shaded blue base, coat of green, vest red, trousers brown striped, green hat, height 6¾ ", designer H. Fenton. 1928-1938 1150.00 1250.00

IVY

HN 1768

☐ Small figure in gown of shaded blues, red bonnet with white feather and green ribbon, holding small round purse, small bit of white pantalettes showing, height 4¾ ", designer L. Harradine. 1936-1979 50.00 75.00

	Date	Price Range	

IVY (cont.)

HN 1769
☐ Details of colour not recorded, made for a brief period, height 4¾", designer L. Harradine.   1938-   **350.00   400.00**

JACK

HN 2060
☐ Small boy figure on green/yellow base, holding pail, black trousers, blue coat, white shirt, red sash, black shoes, height 5½", designer L. Harradine.   1950-1971   **125.00   175.00**

JACK POINT

HN 85
☐ Jester type figure standing on green base, red chequered costume, holding small pouch, hand under chin, height 16¼", designer C. J. Noke. . . .   1918-1938   **2000.00   3200.00**

HN 91
☐ Green, black and purple chequered costume, very light coloured base, height 16¼", designer C. J. Noke. . . .   1918-1938   **2000.00   2250.00**

HN 99
☐ Heraldic tunic, height 16¼", designer C. J. Noke.   1918-1938   **2000.00   2250.00**

JACQUELINE

HN 2000
☐ Blue/grey gown with white apron, flower trimmed sleeves, height 7½", designer L. Harradine.   1947-1951   **400.00   450.00**

HN 2001
☐ Red gown with white apron, darker flowers on sleeves, height 7½", designer L. Harradine.   1947-1951   **425.00   475.00**

HN 2333
☐ Light grey gown with yellow band and flower at the waist, height 7½", designer M. Davies.   1983-   **145.00**

JAMES

HN 3013
☐ Young male figure in grey knee length breeches, wearing a white smock, black shoes. Wearing wide hat with black bow, reddish brown hair, holding a puppy, height 6", designer P. Parsons.   1983-   **100.00**

	Date	Price Range	

JANE

HN 2014

☐ Red skirt, red overlay with blue dots, trimmed in white, white cap with blue ribbons, holding water jug and glass in hands, height 6¼", designer L. Harradine...................... 1948-1951 **600.00 700.00**

JANE

HN 2806

☐ Pastel yellow gown, black ribbon at the waist, holding an umbrella reflecting many colors, blonde hair, height 8", designer M. Davies............. 1983- **135.00**

JANET

HN 1537

☐ Gown of red and white, bonnet white with green ribbons, carrying flat basket of flowers (1st version), height 6½", designer L. Harradine......... 1932- **125.00**

HN 1538

☐ Gown of shaded reds and blues, bonnet white with green ribbon (1st version), height 6½", designer L. Harradine......................... 1932-1949 **275.00 325.00**

HN 1652

☐ Pink skirt with floral pattern, red bodice (1st version), height 6½", designer L. Harradine.............. 1934-1949 **300.00 350.00**

HN 1737

☐ Gown of shaded greens, red shoe (1st version), height 6½", designer L. Harradine.......................... 1935-1949 **300.00 350.00**

HN 1916

☐ Smaller figure with red skirt, blue bodice, red shoe (2nd version), height 5¼", designer L. Harradine......... 1939-1949 **350.00 400.00**

HN 1964

☐ Pink dress (2nd version), height 5¼", designer L. Harradine.............. 1936-1949 **350.00 400.00**

☐ **M69** Made as a miniature, dress of shaded greens, height 4", designer L. Harradine..................... 1936-1949 **300.00 350.00**

☐ **M75** Dress of shaded reds and blues, height 4", designer L. Harradine..... 1936-1949 **300.00 350.00**

Janice, HN2165, 450.00 — 500.00

JANICE	Date	Price Range	
HN 2022			
☐ Regal gown of green and orange, small green headdress, jewels at neck, holding small book in hand, height 7¼", designer M. Davies.	1949-1955	**450.00**	**500.00**
HN 2165			
☐ Gown of very dark green and white, blonde hair, height 7¼", designer M. Davies.	1955-1965	**450.00**	**500.00**
JANINE			
HN 2461			
☐ Gown of green and white with green designs, height 7⅞", designer J. Bromley.	1971-	**170.00**	

	Date	Price Range	

JAPANESE FAN

HN 399

☐ Japanese lady seated, gown of purple with multicoloured jacket, holding round fan, also made as a lidded bowl, height 4¾", designer H. Tittensor.............................. 1920-1938 1450.00 1600.00

HN 405

☐ Pale yellow costume, height 4¾", designer H. Tittensor. 1920-1938 1250.00 1500.00

HN 439

☐ Blue costume, green spots, height 4¼", designer H. Tittensor 1921-1938 1500.00 1600.00

HN 440

☐ Yellow costume, orange spots, height 4¼", designer H. Tittensor. 1921-1938 1500.00 1600.00

JASMINE

HN 1862

☐ Green gown with multicoloured, flowered jacket, strand of long beads on front, head covering of same material as jacket, height 7½", designer L. Harradine..................... 1938-1949 625.00 675.00

HN 1863

☐ White gown with multicoloured, flowered jacket, beige with green border on jacket, light coloured beads, head covering is flowered to match jacket, height 7½", designer L. Harradine. .. 1938-1949 625.00 675.00

HN 1876

☐ With flowered blue coat with pink trim, height 7½", designer L. Harradine. 1938-1949 650.00 675.00

JEAN

HN 1877

☐ Shaded light red gown with blue cloak with ribbon of green, holding basket of flowers on one arm, height 7½", designer L. Harradine. 1938-1949 475.00 525.00

HN 1878

☐ Green dress with red shawl, height 7½", designer L. Harradine. 1938-1949 375.00 450.00

HN 2032

☐ Green dress with accents of darker green, red cloak with black ribbons, flowers yellow in basket, height 7½", designer L. Harradine. 1949-1959 325.00 375.00

	Date	Price Range

JENNIFER

HN 1484

☐ Gown of light yellow with yellow flower design, jacket of multi-yellow flowered, cloak of dark blue, bonnet green, height 6½", designer L. Harradine. 1931-1949 **500.00 550.00**

HN 2392

☐ Beautiful figure of young girl in blue gown with yellow sash, cream coloured sleeves, long blonde hair, height 7", designer M. Davies. 1982- **155.00**

JERSEY MILKMAID, The

HN 2057

☐ Green skirt, brown blouse, blue/white apron trimmed in brown, blue/white farm bonnet, carrying brown jug. In 1975 re-issued same number titled "THE MILKMAID," see proper classification, there are known color variations of this number dress and jug, height 6½", designer L. Harradine. . . 1950-1959 **275.00 325.00**

JESTER, A

HN 45

☐ Figure seated on light pedestal base, black and white chequered costume, holding one leg (1st version), height 10", designer C. J. Noke. 1915-1938 **1250.00 1500.00**

HN 45A

☐ Costume of green and white checks, legs crossed, one hand to face (2nd version), height 10", designer C. J. Noke. 1915-1938 **1250.00 1500.00**

HN 45B

☐ Brown and white chequered costume (2nd version), height 10", designer C. J. Noke. 1915-1938 **1250.00 1500.00**

HN 55

☐ Black and lilac costume (2nd version), height 10", designer C. J. Noke. 1916-1938 **1300.00 1500.00**

HN 71

☐ Costume of black and green, with black and green checks and orange balls (1st version), height 10", designer C. J. Noke. 1917-1938 **1250.00 1500.00**

JESTER, A (cont.)	Date	Price Range	
HN 71A			
☐ No colour details available (1st version), height 10″, designer C. J. Noke.	1917-1938	**1250.00**	**1500.00**
HN 308			
☐ A note below HN 308 in the figure design book says, 'same as 55' (2nd version), height 10″, designer C. J. Noke.	1918-1938	**1250.00**	**1500.00**
HN 320			
☐ HN 45, costume of green and black (1st version), height 10″, designer C. J. Noke.	1918-1938	**1250.00**	**1500.00**
HN 367			
☐ Costume of green and shaded reds, seated on black pedestal (1st version), height 10″, designer C. J. Noke.	1920-1938	**1400.00**	**1500.00**
HN 412			
☐ Green and red striped tights (1st version), height 10″, designer C. J. Noke.	1920-1938	**1350.00**	**1500.00**
HN 426			
☐ Costume of pink markings, black tights (1st version), height 10″, designer C. J. Noke.	1921-1938	**1250.00**	**1500.00**
HN 446			
☐ Green sleeves, blue pedestal (1st version), height 10″, designer C. J. Noke.	1921-1938	**1350.00**	**1500.00**
HN 552			
☐ Black and red costume (1st version), height 10″, designer C. J. Noke.	1922-1938	**1350.00**	**1500.00**
HN 616			
☐ Quartered heraldic tunic (1st version), height 10″, designer C. J. Noke.	1924-1938	**1350.00**	**1500.00**
HN 627			
☐ Brown chequered costume (1st version), height 10″, designer C. J. Noke.	1924-1938	**1350.00**	**1500.00**
HN 630			
☐ HN 45A, brown striped tights (2nd version), height 10″, designer C. J. Noke.	1924-1938	**1350.00**	**1500.00**
HN 1295			
☐ Costume of brown, brown and orange stripes and dark blue seated on black pedestal (1st version), height 10″, designer C. J. Noke.	1928-1949	**900.00**	**1000.00**
HN 1333			
☐ Blue tunic with yellow and black stripes (2nd version), height 10″, designer C. J. Noke.	1929-1949	**1350.00**	**1500.00**

	Date	Price Range	
JESTER, A (cont.)			
HN 1702			
☐ HN 2016, with minor variations (1st version), height 10″, designer C. J. Noke.	1935-1949	900.00	1000.00
HN 2016			
☐ Costume of shaded browns and blue-reds, one leg with darker stripes, costume trimmed in orange with orange balls, pedestal is grey with darker base (1st version), height 10″, designer C. J. Noke.	1949-	200.00	
JILL			
HN 2061			
☐ Small girl figure on yellow and green base, red dress with white apron, white bonnet with green ribbons, height 5½″, designer L. Harradine.	1950-1971	150.00	200.00
JOAN			
HN 1422			
☐ Older lady figure seated in blue and green back chair, blue dress, black shawl, holding red yarn in hands, small foot stool, height 5½″, designer L. Harradine.	1930-1949	450.00	550.00
HN 2023			
☐ Minor glaze differences, height 5¾″, designer L. Harradine.	1949-1959	350.00	400.00
JOHN PEEL			
HN 1408			
☐ Figure seated on brown horse mounted on black base, red coat, white trousers, black hat and boots, blowing horn. Later re-issued with the new title, THE HUNTSMAN, height 9¼″, designer unknown.	1930-1937	2750.00	3000.00
JOLLY SAILOR			
HN 2172			
☐ Seated character figure of sailor, black trousers, white and blue striped shirt, straw coloured hat, playing instrument, height 6½″, designer M. Nicoll.	1956-1965	600.00	700.00

	Date	Price Range
JOVIAL MONK, The		
HN 2144		
☐ Brown robe with rope style belt, carrying basket in one hand, height 7¾", designer M. Davies.	1954-1976	200.00 250.00
JUDGE, The		
HN 2443		
☐ Costume of red and white, seated in brown high back chair, white wig, black shoes, holding papers in hand, height 6½", designer M. Nicoll.	1972-	175.00
In 1976 this figure was changed from a matte to a glazed finish, height 6½", designer M. Nicoll.	Matte Finish	200.00 250.00
JUDGE AND JURY		
HN 1264		
☐ Judge figure in costume of red and white, little dog chained to chair, three small children in witness stand, another child outside of stand, all on black base, height 6", designer J. G. Hughes.	1927-1938	3000.00 3500.00
JUDITH		
HN 2089		
☐ Red dress with blue vest which has a darker blue design and blue trim on sleeves, blue shoe, height 6⅞", designer L. Harradine.	1952-1959	300.00 350.00
JULIA		
HN 2705		
☐ Brown gown with white trim, brown hat with yellow ribbons, carrying yellow parasol, height 7⅝", designer M. Davies.	1975-	155.00
JUNE		
HN 1690		
☐ Green and white gown, green bonnet with black ribbons, carrying flowers in one arm, holding parasol in other, height 7½", designer L. Harradine. . .	1935-1949	450.00 500.00

	Date	Price Range	

JUNE (cont.)

HN 1691
☐ Gown of cream with light shades of green and yellow, front panel has flower designs, red bonnet, parasol has green trim, shawl black, height 7½ ", designer L. Harradine.   1935-1949   **350.00**   **400.00**

HN 1947
☐ Gown of shaded reds and blues trimmed with white, bonnet same trimmed with blue ribbons, parasol dark, height 7½ ", designer L. Harradine.   1940-1949   **450.00**   **500.00**

HN 2027
☐ Minor glaze changes, height 7½ ", designer L. Harradine.   1949-1952   **325.00**   **375.00**

☐ **M-65** Made as a miniature figure, gown of shaded reds with dark trim, height 4 ", designer L. Harradine.   1935-1949   **325.00**   **375.00**

☐ **M-71** Gown of shaded blues with red trim, height 4 ", designer L. Harradine.   1936-1949   **325.00**   **375.00**

KAREN

HN 1994
☐ Figure in Edwardian riding costume of red and white, with green hat with feather, holding riding crop, on base of brown, height 8 ", designer L. Harradine.   1947-1955   **350.00**   **400.00**

HN 2388
☐ Gown is red with white bodice, black waistband, dark hair (2nd version), height 8 ", designer M. Davies.   1982-   **185.00**

KATE

HN 2789
☐ White gown with multicoloured flower design around bottom, white headband, height 7½ ", designer M. Davies .   1978-   **155.00**

KATE HARDCASTLE

HN 1718
☐ 18th century style gown of pink and green, pink bonnet with green ribbons, green gloves, leaning on light coloured pedestal on base, height 8 ", designer L. Harradine.   1935-1949   **600.00**   **650.00**

KATE HARDCASTLE (cont.)

	Date	Price Range	

HN 1719
☐ Gown of red and green, green bonnet with red ribbons, red gloves, leaning on dark pedestal with light base, height 8¼", designer L. Harradine. . . 1935-1949 650.00 700.00

HN 1734
☐ Gown of green and white with green designs, light yellow bonnet with green ribbons, green gloves, dark pedestal on light base, height 8¼", designer L. Harradine. 1935-1949 650.00 750.00

HN 1861
☐ Red gown with shaded blues and greens overlay, black bonnet with blue ribbons, red gloves, green coloured pedestal on light base, height 8¼", designer L. Harradine. 1938-1949 600.00 700.00

HN 1919
☐ Red overskirt, green dress, black base, height 8¼", designer L. Harradine. 1939-1949 800.00 900.00

HN 2028
☐ HN 1719, with minor glaze difference, height 8¼", designer L. Harradine. . . 1949-1952 650.00 750.00

KATHERINE

HN 61
☐ Full covering gown of green with white collar, green hat with white brim, height 5¾", designer C. J. Noke. 1916-1938 1500.00 1700.00

HN 74
☐ Pale blue dress with green spots, height 5¾", designer C. J. Noke. 1917-1938 1650.00 1800.00

HN 341
☐ Gown is red, height 5¾", designer C. J. Noke. 1919-1938 1250.00 1500.00

HN 471
☐ Spotted blouse and dress, height 5¾", designer C. J. Noke. 1921-1938 2000.00 2500.00

HN 615
☐ Pink skirt with green spots, height 5¾", designer C. J. Noke. 1924-1938 1650.00 1800.00

HN 793
☐ Lilac dress with green spots, height 5¾", designer C. J. Noke. 1926-1938 1650.00 1800.00

	Date	Price Range

KATHLEEN

HN 1252
☐ Skirt of shaded blues, red jacket, shawl is red and blue, black ribbon in hair, holding black bonnet in one hand, height 7½", designer L. Harradine.   1927-1938   800.00   850.00

HN 1253
☐ Skirt of red, jacket of shaded multicolours, shawl dark blue and black, height 7½", designer L. Harradine. . .   1927-1938   800.00   850.00

HN 1275
☐ HN 1252, Flowered black shawl, height 7½", designer L. Harradine. . .   1928-1938   800.00   850.00

HN 1279
☐ Skirt and jacket of mottled red, shawl solid red, height 7½", designer L. Harradine.   1928-1938   800.00   850.00

HN 1291
☐ Red shawl with mottled yellow dress, height 7½", designer L. Harradine. . .   1928-1938   850.00   950.00

HN 1357
☐ Pink, orange and yellow mottled skirt, height 7½", designer L. Harradine. . .   1929-1938   800.00   850.00

HN 1512
☐ Pale lilac dress, blue hat, height 7½", designer L. Harradine.   1932-1938   700.00   800.00

KATHY (Kate Greenaway)

HN 2346
☐ This figure is seated on green stool, wearing white gown with red sash, bonnet white with light blue ribbon, red shoes, holding small light blue flower in one hand, height 4¾", designer M. Davies.   1981-   100.00

KATRINA

HN 2327
☐ Red gown trimmed with white collar, high comb in hair, both hands on head, height 7½", designer M. Davies   1965-1969   275.00   325.00

KING CHARLES

HN 404
☐ Deep navy blue costume, deep navy blue cloak, navy blue with light blue feather hat, deep navy stockings, black shoes, black walking stick on pink base, height 16¾", designers C. J. Noke and H. Tittensor.   1920-1951   1750.00   2000.00

	Date	Price Range
KIRSTY		
HN 2381		
☐ Gown of yellow with shades of brown with design around rim of skirt, white trim on sleves and white collar with ribbon, height 7¾", designer M. Davies.	1971-	**185.00**
KITTY		
HN 1367		
☐ Lady seated with foot on foot-stool, gown of white with shaded yellows and darker thin stripes of blue, holding dark kitten in hands, has small white cap with red ribbon on head, height 4", designer unknown.	1930-1938	**1000.00 1100.00**
KO-KO		
HN 1266		
☐ Japanese figure with black and yellow costume, standing on green and yellow base, holding fan, height 5", designer L. Harradine.	1928-1949	**650.00 750.00**
HN 1286		
☐ Costume of red and blue standing on dark base, height 5", designer L. Harradine.	1938-1949	**650.00 750.00**
HN 2898		
☐ Japanese figure with black hair on light brown base, costume of orange, blue, green, black, red, holding scroll, with large ax-like weapon on stand (2nd version), height 11½", designer W. K. Harper.	1980-	**750.00**
LADY ANNE, The		
HN 83		
☐ Yellow gown with dark trim, one foot on stool, has high head covering of net and flowers, height unknown, designer E. W. Light.	1918-1938	**2750.00 3000.00**
HN 87		
☐ Green gown, red shoes, height unknown, designer E. W. Light	1918-1938	**2750.00 3000.00**
HN 93		
☐ Blue gown, height unknown, designer E. W. Light.	1918-1938	**2750.00 3000.00**

	Date	Price Range	

LADY ANNE NEVILL, The

HN 2006

☐ Gown of purple and white fur trim, gold belt and jewels, very high and wide head covering of white, height 9¾ ", designer M. Davies. 1948-1953   800.00   900.00

LADY APRIL

HN 1958

☐ Red gown, purple, blue and red cloak with green straps, red bonnet with red and black trim, holding small bouquet in one arm, green gloves, height 7", designer L. Harradine. 1940-1959   300.00   400.00

HN 1965

☐ Green dress, height 7", designer L. Harradine. 1941-1949   350.00   400.00

LADY BETTY

HN 1967

☐ Red gown with blue ruffle trim collar, bonnet very light blue with cream coloured feather and black ribbons, holding flower basket, height 6½ ", designer L. Harradine. 1941-1951   325.00   375.00

LADYBIRD

HN 1638

☐ Young girl in ballet costume of pink, standing on toes on light coloured base, spray of flowers in hair, height 7¾ ", designer L. Harradine. 1924-1949   900.00   1000.00

HN 1640

☐ Costume of light blue, also ballet shoes of blue, height 7¾ ", designer L. Harradine. 1934-1938   900.00   1000.00

LADY AND BLACKAMOOR

HN 374

☐ Large full skirted gown of blue and green patterns with blue bodice, holding fan in one hand, high hair style with small black figure behind her, with blue costume and yellow turban (1st version), height unknown, designer H. Tittensor. 1920-1938   2500.00   2700.00

LADY AND BLACKMOOR (cont.)	Date	Price Range	

HN 375
☐ Light coloured skirt with designs of flowers and leaves with purple trim, black bodice trimmed in pink (2nd version), height unknown, design H. Tittensor. 1920-1938   2500.00 2700.00

HN 377
☐ Pink and green dress (2nd version), height unknown, designer H. Tittensor. 1920-1938   2500.00 2700.00

HN 470
☐ Green and lilac dress (2nd version), height unknown, design H. Tittensor.   1921-1938   2500.00 2700.00

LADY CHARMIAN

HN 1948
☐ Green gown, mottled red shawl, green bonnet, holding single flower in one hand and basket of flowers with other, height 8″, designer L. Harradine. 1940-1973   250.00   300.00

HN 1949
☐ Red gown, green shawl, red bonnet with black ribbons, height 8″, designer L. Harradine. 1940-1975   250.00   300.00

LADY CLARE

HN 1465
☐ Red and blue tiered gown, with shawl of shaded blue and red, holding small purse and parasol, light bonnet with red ribbons, height 7¾″, designer L. Harradine. 1931-1938   650.00   750.00

LADY CLOWN

HN 717
☐ Costume of white with red and green stripes and black blocks, dunce style hat, red shoes, standing on one foot on black base, height 7½″, designer L. Harradine. 1925-1938   1300.00 1450.00

HN 718
☐ White costume, red stripes, black spots, height 7½″, designer L. Harradine. 1925-1938   1300.00 1450.00

HN 738
☐ Black and white trousers, red spots, height 7½″, designer L. Harradine. . . 1925-1938   1300.00 1450.00

	Date	Price Range

LADY CLOWN (cont.)

HN 770
☐ Costume painted with green masks and streamers, height 7½ ", designer L. Harradine. 1925-1938   1300.00 1450.00

HN 1263
☐ Particoloured trousers, one leg blue, the other one with red stripes, height 7½ ", designer L. Harradine. 1927-1938   1300.00 1450.00

LADY ERMINE

HN 54
☐ Gown of very light green, coat of blue with fur trim, muff of fur, green hat with yellow ribbon and feather, height 8½ ", designer C. J. Noke. 1916-1938   1250.00 1500.00

HN 332
☐ Red coat and hat, green and yellow patterned skirt, height 8½ ", designer C. J. Noke. 1918-1938   1450.00 1750.00

HN 671
☐ Green coat, yellow skirt, height 8½ ", designer C. J. Noke. 1924-1938   1650.00 1800.00

LADY FAYRE

HN 1265
☐ Gown of shaded blues and red, bodice darker blue with reds, blonde hair, red shoe, in curtsey position, height 5¾ ", designer L. Harradine. 1928-1938   550.00 650.00

HN 1557
☐ Gown of pink, height 5¾ ", designer L. Harradine. 1933-1938   750.00 850.00

LADY FROM WILLIAMSBURG

HN 2228
☐ Figure seated on bench, gown of green with yellow ribbon trim, small white covering on head, holding bonnet in hands, height 6", designer M. Davies. 1960-   200.00

LADY JESTER

HN 1221
☐ Costume of chequered pink and black skirt, standing on light coloured pedestal style base (1st version), height 7", designer L. Harradine. 1927-1938   1350.00 1500.00

Lady Jester, HN1284, **750.00 — 850.00**

LADY JESTER (cont.)	Date	Price Range	
HN 1222			
☐ Costume of chequered black and white, also shoes (1st version), height 7″, designer L. Harradine.	1927-1938	1350.00	1500.00
HN 1284			
☐ Seated figure with legs crossed, costume of red tights, dark blue vest with chequered red and black sleeves, holding jester doll with costume of black and white (2nd version), height 4¼″, designer L. Harradine.	1928-1938	750.00	850.00
HN 1285			
☐ Costume of blue with red stripes on tights, red vest with very light red sleeves, holds jester doll in costume of white, black and blue (2nd version), height 4¼″, designer L. Harradine. . .	1928-1938	750.00	850.00
HN 1332			
☐ Costume red, blue and black scalloped pattern on skirt (1st version), height 7″, designer L. Harradine.	1929-1938	1250.00	1300.00

	Date	Price Range	
LADY OF THE ELIZABETHAN PERIOD			

HN   40
☐ Very full gown of brown and patterned orange, high wide white collar, head-dress dark and has a long hanging cloth (1st version), height 9½ ", designer E. W. Light.   1914-1938   **1750.00 2000.00**

HN   40A
☐ No pattern on dress (1st version), height 9½ ", designer E. W. Light.   1914-1938   **1750.00 2000.00**

HN   73
☐ Costume of dark blue-green (1st version), height 9½ ", designer E. W. Light.   1917-1938   **1800.00 2000.00**

HN 309
☐ Costume of green patterned, with white patterned and raised green dots, gown trimmed in blue, head-dress dark (2nd version), height 9½ ", designer E. W. Light.   1918-1938   **1750.00 2000.00**

HN 411
☐ Costume of purple patterned with mottled colours in sleeves and under-skirt, wide white collar (1st version), height 9½ ", designer E. W. Light.   1920-1938   **2000.00 2250.00**

LADY OF THE FAN

HN   48
☐ Lilac dress, black shoe, feather in hair, holding fan, figure in bowing position, height 9½ ", designer E. W. Light.   1916-1938   **1650.00 1800.00**

HN   52
☐ Gown of shaded yellows, height 9½ ", designer E. W. Light.   1916-1938   **1650.00 1800.00**

HN   53
☐ Dark blue dress, height 9½ ", designer E. W. Light.   1916-1938   **1650.00 1800.00**

HN   53A
☐ Green/blue dress, height 9½ ", designer E. W. Light.   1916-1938   **1650.00 1800.00**

HN 335
☐ Blue dress with brown patterning, height 9½ ", designer E. W. Light.   1919-1938   **1650.00 1800.00**

HN 509
☐ Green lilac and blue spotted dress, height 9½ ", designer E. W. Light.   1921-1938   **1650.00 1800.00**

LADY OF THE GEORGIAN PERIOD	Date	Price Range

HN 41
☐ Very full gown of red and white which has shaded blue and dark bows, has large turban style headdress of white trimmed with dark blue ribbons, height 10¼", designer E. W. Light.... 1914-1938   **2000.00 2300.00**

HN 331
☐ Gown of patterned brown and patterned yellow, headdress of dark brown with red ribbons, height 10¼", designer E. W. Light. 1918-1938   **1650.00 1800.00**

HN 444
☐ Green-blue spotted dress, height 10¼", designer E. W. Light.......... 1921-1938   **2100.00 2300.00**

HN 690
☐ Color design not available, height 10¼", designer E. W. Light.......... 1925-1938   **2150.00 2300.00**

HN 702
☐ Striped pink skirt, green overdress, height 10¼", designer E. W. Light.... 1925-1938   **2150.00 2300.00**

LADY OF THE SNOWS

HN 1780
☐ No further information available, height unknown, designer R. Garbe. . 1933-   **3500.00 4000.00**

HN 1830
☐ Tinted model, height unknown, designer R. Garbe. 1937-1949   **3500.00 4000.00**

LADY OF THE TIME OF HENRY VI

HN 43
☐ Gown of yellows with overdress of green trimmed in fur, head covering also green, height 9¼", designer E. W. Light. 1914-1938   **2750.00 3250.00**

LADY PAMELA

HN 2718
☐ Gown of lavender with ligher lavender overlay, bonnet dark lavender with still darker ribbon trim, holding mirror, height 8", designer D. V. Tootle... 1974-1980   **150.00   200.00**

LADY WITH ROSE

HN 48A
☐ Gown of white with dark ribbon style trim on ruffles and orange lining, black waistband, holding red rose, height 9½", designer E. W. Light..... 1916-1938   **1650.00 1800.00**

	Date	Price Range

LADY WITH ROSE (cont.)

HN 52A
☐ Yellow dress, height 9½", designer
E. W. Light. 1916-1938 **1650.00 1800.00**

HN 68
☐ Green and yellow dress, height 9½",
designer E. W. Light. 1916-1938 **1650.00 1800.00**

HN 304
☐ Grey-lilac dress with brown pattern-
ing, height 9½", designer E. W. Light. 1918-1938 **1650.00 1800.00**

HN 336
☐ Multicoloured dress with brown pat-
terning, height 9½", designer E. W.
Light. 1919-1938 **1700.00 1800.00**

HN 515
☐ Striped lilac and green dress, height
9½", designer E. W. Light. 1921-1938 **1700.00 1800.00**

HN 517
☐ Lilac dress with orange spots, height
9½", designer E. W. Light. 1921-1938 **1650.00 1800.00**

HN 584
☐ Green and pink dress, height 9½",
designer E. W. Light. 1923-1938 **1650.00 1800.00**

HN 624
☐ Green-blue skirt, pink and black cuffs,
height 9½", designer E. W. Light. 1924-1938 **1650.00 1800.00**

LADY WITHOUT BOUQUET

HN 393
☐ Gown of light red with blue and white
ring designs, bodice blue with gold
trim, large stole of blue with purple
lining with blue and white ring design,
height 9", designer G. Lambert. 1920-1938 **2000.00 2500.00**

HN 394
☐ Blue and yellow costume, height 9",
designer G. Lambert. 1920-1938 **2000.00 2500.00**

LADY WITH SHAWL

HN 447
☐ Figure on mottled blue base, gown of
white and blue stripes, waistband
darker blue with white round designs,
shawl of white with blue and gold ring
designs, height 13¼", designer L. Har-
radine. 1921-1938 **3250.00 3500.00**

HN 458
☐ Multicoloured shawl, pink dress,
height 13¼", designer L. Harradine. . 1921-1938 **3000.00 3500.00**

LADY WITH SHAWL (cont.)	Date	Price Range	
HN 626			
☐ Yellow shawl with pink spots, white dress with green spots, height 13¼ ", designer L. Harradine.	1924-1938	3000.00	3500.00
HN 678			
☐ Black and white shawl, yellow and white dress, height 13¼ ", designer L. Harradine.	1924-1938	3250.00	3500.00
HN 679			
☐ Black, yellow and blue shawl, black and white dress, height 13¼ ", designer L. Harradine.	1924-1938	3250.00	3500.00

LAIRD, The

HN 2361
☐ Character figure in Scottish costume, green and black striped skirt, dark green and beige jacket, brown tam, shoes brown and green stockings, holding staff, greenish tan shawl over shoulder, height 8⅛ ", designer M. Nicoll. 1969- 175.00

LAMBETH WALK, The

HN 1880
☐ Blue dress, height 10", designer L. Harradine. 1938-1949 1300.00 1400.00

HN 1881
☐ Shaded red dress with red flower design on bottom, large blue hat with red trim, red shoe, light coloured base, height 10", designer L. Harradine. 1938-1949 1300.00 1400.00

LAMBING TIME

HN 1890
☐ Character figure on brown base, brown trousers with long yellow/ brown coat, brown hat and small scarf, holding a lamp under each arm, height 8½ ", designer L. Harradine. . . 1938-1980 150.00 200.00

LAND OF NOD, The

HN 56
☐ HN 56A, ivory nightshirt, height 9¾ ", designer H. Tittensor. 1916-1938 1750.00 2000.00

LAND OF NOD, The (cont.)	Date	Price Range	

HN 56A
☐ Small figure in very light blue nightshirt, holding candle with brown and
white owl on light base with printing,
height 9¾", designer H. Tittensor.... 1916-1938 **2000.00 2300.00**

HN 56B
☐ Pale grey nightshirt and red candle-
stick, height 9¾", designer H. Titten-
sor.............................. 1916-1938 **1750.00 2000.00**

LAST WALTZ

HN 2315
☐ Gown of white with gold designs,
overlay of dark yellow trimmed in
green, holding dance program book
and pencil, height 8", designer
M. Davies. 1967- **185.00**

LA SYLPHIDE

HN 2138
☐ Gown of white with light blue trim,
ribbon around head, hands crossed,
light blue ballet slippers on green and
yellow base, height 7¼", designer
M. Davies. 1956-1965 **425.00 475.00**

LAURA

HN 2960
☐ Seated figure with gown of blue and
white decorated on the bodice and
overskirt with orange flowers, blonde
hair, height 7¼", designer P. Par-
sons. 1983- **145.00**

LAURIANNE

HN 2719
☐ Seated lady with blue/white gown,
dark blue overdress, with book on lap,
height 6½", designer D. V. Tootle. ... 1974-1979 **150.00 200.00**

LAVENDER WOMAN, The

HN 22
☐ Light blue dress and shawl, holding
wrapped infant in one arm and brown
basket with flowers in other arm, on
light blue base, height 8¼", designer
P. Stabler. 1913-1938 **1750.00 2000.00**

	Date	Price Range
LAVENDER WOMAN, The (cont.)		
HN 23		
☐ Green dress, height 8¼", designer P. Stabler.	1913-1938	**1750.00 2000.00**
HN 23A		
☐ Blue and green dress, height 8¼", designer P. Stabler.	1913-1938	**1750.00 2000.00**
HN 342		
☐ Patterned dress and lilac shawl, height 8¼", designer P. Stabler.	1919-1938	**1750.00 2000.00**
HN 569		
☐ Gown of blue with large red spots, shawl red with shaded blue stripes, on brown base, height 8¼", designer P. Stabler.	1924-1938	**1150.00 1300.00**
HN 744		
☐ Spotted dress and striped shawl, height 8¼", designer P. Stabler.	1925-1938	**1750.00 2000.00**
LAVINIA		
HN 1955		
☐ Small figure with red gown trimmed with white, white ruffled cap with blue ribbon trim, carrying basket on arm and small object in other hand, height 5", designer L. Harradine.	1940-1978	**100.00 150.00**
LEADING LADY		
HN 2269		
☐ Pale yellow gown with lavender overdress, red bow on bodice, yellow ribbon in hair, lavender shoe, holding brown and white object in uplifted hand, height 7¾", designer M. Davies	1965-1976	**200.00 250.00**
LEISURE HOUR, The		
HN 2055		
☐ Lady seated in very high backed brown chair on brown base, gown of pale orange with overdress of patterned green and white with red trim, holding large red backed open book on lap, height 6¾", designer M. Davies	1950-1965	**500.00 600.00**

	Date	Price Range

LIDO LADY

HN 1220

☐ Pajama clad figure seated on pedestal style base of light colour, holding very small brown dog, costume light blue with designs of red and darker blue at edges, height 6¾", designer L. Harradine.   1927-1938   **1000.00   1100.00**

HN 1229

☐ Flowered pink costume, height 6¾", designer L. Harradine.   1927-1938   **1100.00   1200.00**

LIGHTS OUT

HN 2262

☐ Small figure of boy in pajama costume, blue trousers, top of white with gold dots, pillow white with red stripes on white base, height 5", designer M. Davies.   1965-1969   **225.00   275.00**

LILAC SHAWL, A

HN   44

☐ Cream coloured tiered gown with dark ribbon trim, lilac shawl with red rose figure design, light coloured bonnet with yellow ribbons, height 8¾", designer C. J. Noke.   1915-1938   **1250.00   1500.00**

HN   44A

☐ Roses on shawl replaced by printed pattern, height 8¾", designer C. J. Noke.   1915-1938   **1250.00   1500.00**

HN   339

☐ This figure is now called IN GRANDMA'S DAY. Gown of yellow with brown trim, shawl dark patterned brown, dark bonnet with red rose trim and with blue ribbon with darker dots and fringe, height 8¾", designer C. J. Noke.   1919-1938   **1250.00   1500.00**

HN   340

☐ Yellow and lilac costume, height 8¾", designer C. J. Noke.   1919-1938   **1250.00   1500.00**

HN   362

☐ Green, red, yellow striped skirt, height 8¾", designer C. J. Noke.   1919-1938   **1550.00   1700.00**

HN   388

☐ Patterned blue costume, height 8¾", designer C. J. Noke.   1920-1938   **1650.00   1800.00**

	Date	Price Range	

LILAC SHAWL, A (cont.)

HN 442
☐ White spotted skirt, green shawl, height 8¾″, designer C. J. Noke. 1921-1938 1650.00 1800.00

HN 612
☐ This figure is now called THE POKE BONNET. Gown of dark yellow with dark blue circle design, blue and green patterned shawl, dark blue bonnet with red flower trim, ribbons of red with blue and white stripes and small dark dots, height 8¾″, designer C. J. Noke. 1924-1938 1350.00 1500.00

HN 765
☐ Mottled dark green, blue and purple skirt, height 8¾″, designer C. J. Noke. 1925-1938 1500.00 1600.00

LILAC TIME

HN 2137
☐ Red costume with hat which has lilac trim, figure holding bouquet of lilacs in arm, height 7½″, designer M. Davies 1954-1969 250.00 300.00

LILY

HN 1798
☐ Small figure with shaded red gown, white shawl with red and blue designs, cream coloured bonnet with blue ribbons, small bit of pantalettes showing, height 5″, designer L. Harradine. 1936-1949 100.00 135.00

HN 1799
☐ Blue shawl, with green dress, height 5″, designer L. Harradine. 1936-1949 100.00 135.00

LINDA

HN 2106
☐ Small figure seated on white bench, red cloak, light coloured hat with blue ribbon trim, light coloured basket on bench also, height 4¾″, designer L. Harradine. 1953-1976 120.00 150.00

LISA

HN 2310
☐ Skirt of dark blue with large white trim at bottom, bodice and sleeves of white with small dark blue dots, matte-finish, height 7½″, designer M. Davies 1969- 170.00

LISA (cont.)

	Date	Price Range

HN 2394
☐ Gown of pink and blue, lilac slippers, dark hair (2nd version), height 7½", designer M. Davies. 1983- 125.00

LISETTE

HN 1523
☐ Small figure with cream coloured tiered skirt, red bodice, holding open fan, red ribbon in hair, height 5¼", designer L. Harradine. 1932-1938 900.00 1000.00

HN 1524
☐ Gown of reds and blues with blue bows as trim, height 5¼", designer L. Harradine. 1932-1938 900.00 1000.00

HN 1684
☐ Pink dress with green trim, height 5¼", designer L. Harradine. 1935-1938 900.00 1000.00

LITTLE BOY BLUE

HN 2062
☐ Small boy figure on yellow and green base, light blue trousers, darker long coat with white collar and red bow, black shoes, with horn strapped over shoulder, height 5½", designer L. Harradine. 1950-1973 150.00 200.00

'LITTLE CHILD SO RARE AND SWEET'

HN 1540
☐ Small white nude blonde haired figure on multicoloured rock, figure is bending as if looking for something, height 5", designer unknown. 1933-1949 425.00 475.00

HN 1542
☐ Small white nude figure seated on shaded blue rock, figure has dark hair, height 5", designer unknown. . . . 1933-1949 375.00 425.00

LITTLE JACK HORNER

HN 2063
☐ Small figure seated on bench style base of shaded blue and yellows, red jacket with black buttons, holding pie on lap, has plum in hand at mouth, height 4½", designer L. Harradine. . . 1950-1953 225.00 275.00

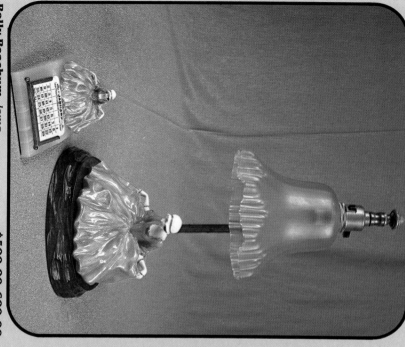

Polly Peachum, *lamp*. **$500.00-600.00**
Polly Peachum, *calendar*. **$400.00-500.00**

The Judge, *lamp*. **$500.00-600.00**

Mermaid, HN97. . . . . $650.00-700.00

One Of The Forty, HN677. . . . . $1100.00-1200.00

Puff And Powder, HN433 . . . . $2000.00-2200.00

The Squire, HN1814 . . . . $2100.00-2600.00

Wandering Minsteral, HN1224. . . $1350.00-1500.00

Sunshine Girl HN1344. . . . . $1400.00-1500.00

Toinette, HN1940. . . . . $1450.00-1750.00

Sleepyhead, HN2114. . . . . $800.00-900.00

Toothless Granny, *has a different hairline.* **$900.00-1000.00**

Winston Churchill, D6170. . . . . **$8500.00-10000**

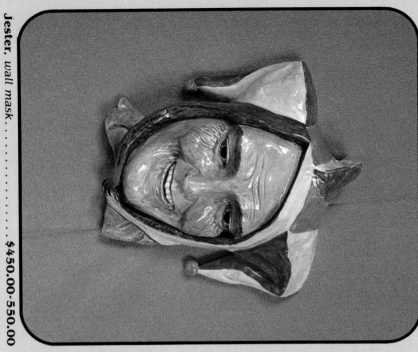

Jester, *wall mask*. $450.00-550.00

Gladys, HN1741, *bust*. $550.00-600.00

Leaping Salmon, 666 Rouge Flambé............$1000.00-1100.00

Tibetian Lady, HN582.................$650.00-700.00

	Date	Price Range	
LITTLE LADY MAKE BELIEVE			
HN 1870			
☐ Small figure seated on light coloured bench style base, blue dress, red cloak with blue, green bonnet with blue ribbons, holding small parasol in both hands, height 6″, designer L. Harradine.	1938-1949	500.00	550.00
LITTLE LAND, The			
HN 63			
☐ Costume of green and yellow, height 7½″, designer H. Tittensor.	1916-1938	2000.00	2500.00
HN 67			
☐ Light coloured grey gown with trim of black and small round raised white dots, seated on green base which contains little fairies and elfs, height 7½″, designer H. Tittensor.	1916-1938	1750.00	2000.00
LITTLE MISTRESS, The			
HN 1449			
☐ Gown of light green, shawl of shaded blue with trim of green and red stripes and darker blue fringe, red bonnet with red ribbons, carrying basket, height 6″, designer L. Harradine.	1931-1949	500.00	550.00
LITTLE MOTHER, The			
HN 389			
☐ Figure in pink coloured nightdress, standing on brown pillow, holding small black animal, fair hair (1st version), height unknown, designer H. Tittensor.	1920-1938	2500.00	2700.00
HN 390			
☐ Dark hair (1st version), height unknown, designer H. Tittensor.	1920-1938	2500.00	2700.00
HN 469			
☐ Cream coloured nightdress, brown hair (1st version), height unknown, designer H. Tittensor.	1921-1938	1750.00	2000.00

	Date	Price Range	
LITTLE MOTHER, The (cont.)			

HN 1418

☐ Young girl and small boy seated on light coloured block, girl's costume of mottled dark blue, red and light blues, shawl multicoloured, boy's costume striped red and blue, girl holding bouquet of flowers and large brown basket with flowers in front of figures (2nd version), height unknown, designer H. Tittensor. 1930-1938 1100.00 1200.00

HN 1641

☐ Green shawl, pale skirt and basket is of a lighter colour (2nd version), height unknown, designer H. Tittensor. 1934-1949 900.00 1000.00

LITTLE NELL

HN 540

☐ A character from Dicken's "The Old Curiosity Shop," height 4″, designer L. Harradine. 1922- 45.00 60.00

☐ **M 51** Renumbered as a miniature, height 4¼″, designer L. Harradine. . . 1932- 29.95

LIZANA

HN 1756

☐ Shaded red gown, shawl of multicoloured flowers, second shawl which is very long and of patterned greens, Spanish comb in hair, height 8½″, designer L. Harradine. 1936-1949 650.00 750.00

HN 1761

☐ Green dress, leopard-skin cloak, height 8½″, designer L. Harradine. . . 1936-1938 650.00 750.00

LOBSTER MAN, The

HN 2317

☐ Character figure seated on green base, with brown lobster basket, brown trousers, dark blue sweater, black cap, black boots with white tops, has lobster in hand, pipe in mouth, height 6⅞″, designer M. Nicoll. . 1964- 165.00

	Date	Price Range	

LONDON CRY, STRAWBERRIES

HN 749

☐ Lady and small girl figures on brown base, lady's skirt is red, white apron, red belt, white bonnet, girl's skirt is dark color, red blouse, white bonnet, each is carrying basket of light colour, with large basket on base at their feet, height 6¾", designer L. Harradine.   1925-1938   **900.00   1000.00**

HN 772

☐ Both gowns are multicoloured, baskets are of darker brown, base is of a lighter brown, height 6¾", designer L. Harradine.   1925-1938   **900.00   1000.00**

LONDON CRY, TURNIPS AND CARROTS

HN 752

☐ Lady and small boy figures on brown base, lady's skirt purple and red with lightly coloured apron, boy's brown trousers, jacket and hat, with light shirt, both are holding vegetables with basket on base, height 6¾", designer L. Harradine.   1925-1938   **900.00   1000.00**

HN 771

☐ Lady's dress of shaded blues and reds, boy's ligher brown suit and hat, basket on base is darker brown, base is light cream coloured, height 6¾", designer L. Harradine.   1925-1938   **900.00   1000.00**

LONG JOHN SILVER

HN 2204

☐ Pirate costume of black, gold and white, on base of red and green, parrot is green, red and light brown, height 9", designer M. Nicoll.   1957-1965   **350.00   400.00**

LORETTA

HN 2337

☐ Gown of purple with yellow shawl, green and white feathers in hair, height 7¾", designer M. Davies.   1966-1980   **100.00   150.00**

	Date	Price Range

LORI (Kate Greenaway)
HN 2801
☐ Small girl on white base, white gown with red sash and red flowers around bottom, large brim hat of white with red ribbon trim, holding single flower, height 5⅞", designer M. Davies.   1976-   **100.00**

LORNA
HN 2311
☐ Green gown trimmed in yellow, yellow stole, holding small blue/white fan, blue long gloves, height 8⅜", designer M. Davies.   1965-   **125.00**

LOUISE (Kate Greenaway)
HN 2869
☐ Small figure with brown gown with white crossed collar, black bonnet with yellow ribbon, single flower in both hands, height 6", designer M. Davies.   1979-   **100.00**

LOVE LETTER
HN 2149
☐ Two figures seated on couch with small red table at side, one gown is red and white with gold design, black shoes, small white head covering, other gown is shaded blues with black trim, pillow on couch light blue, one figure holding small white paper, height 5", designer M. Davies.   1958-1976   **250.00   300.00**

LUCY (Kate Greenaway)
HN 2863
☐ Small figure on white base, holding single flower in hands, skirt of light blue and white, vest of darker blue, blouse of white and blue, tall hat of blue with white and blue ribbon, height 6", designer M. Davies.   1980-   **100.00**

LUCY ANN
HN 1502
☐ Gown of shaded reds with blue ribbon, holding skirt up which is filled with flowers, height 5¼", designer L. Harradine.   1932-1951   **300.00   350.00**

	Date	Price Range	

LUCY ANN (cont.)
HN 1565
☐ Pale green dress, height 5¼", designer L. Harradine.   1933-1938   **325.00**   **375.00**

LUCY LOCKETT
HN 485
☐ Very wide skirted gown of green with red gloves and red small purse, long strand of dark beads, on black base, has hands crossed. A character from "The Beggar's Opera" (1st version), height 6", designer L. Harradine.   1921-1949   **800.00**   **900.00**

HN 524
☐ HN 695, mustard coloured dress, wine gloves and purse (2nd version), height 6", designer L. Harradine.   1921-1949   **850.00**   **950.00**

HN 695
☐ Orange gown with red gloves and purse, also beads, this figure has one hand in waist and one hand in front (2nd version), height 6", designer L. Harradine.   1925-1949   **650.00**   **750.00**

HN 696
☐ Powder blue costume (2nd version), height 6", designer L. Harradine.   1925-1949   **650.00**   **750.00**

LUNCHTIME
HN 2485
☐ Male figure seated on brown bench on light coloured base, one squirrel also on base and bench, green suit with light brown overcoat, hat and scarf same colour as suit, holding open paperbag, feeding one squirrel, height 8", designer M. Nicoll.   1973-1980   **150.00**   **200.00**

LYDIA
HN 1906
☐ Figure seated with flowers in back on each side, gown of orange/pink overdress, pale pink flowered underskirt, holding open book in one hand, height 4¼", designer L. Harradine. . .   1939-1949   **300.00**   **350.00**

HN 1907
☐ Gown of green, bonnet green with black ribbon, height 4¼", designer L. Harradine.   1939-1949   **300.00**   **350.00**

	Date	Price Range

LYDIA (cont.)
HN 1908
☐ Gown and bonnet of red, height 4⅛", designer L. Harradine.   1939-   **125.00**

LYNNE
HN 2329
☐ Yellow-green gown with white designs on bottom, yellow-green ribbon in hair, height 7", designer M. Davies.   1971-   **170.00**

MADONNA OF THE SQUARE
HN 10
☐ Lilac costume, height 7", designer P. Stabler.   1913-1938   **1450.00 1600.00**
HN 10A
☐ Seated lady, costume of blue which covers her entirely, only face and hand shows, infant in lap also wrapped in blue, small basket at feet with multi-coloured flowers, height 7", designer P. Stabler.   1913-1938   **1350.00 1500.00**
HN 11
☐ Grey costume, height 7", designer P. Stabler.   1913-1938   **1450.00 1700.00**
HN 14
☐ Renumbered version of HN 10A, height 7", designer P. Stabler.   1913-1938   **1450.00 1700.00**
HN 27
☐ Mottled green and blue costume, height 7", designer P. Stabler.   1913-1938   **1650.00 1800.00**
HN 326
☐ Grey/blue costume, earthenware, height 7", designer P. Stabler.   1918-1938   **1650.00 1800.00**
HN 573
☐ Orange skirt and cubist-style shawl, height 7", designer P. Stabler.   1913-1938   **1650.00 1800.00**
HN 576
☐ Green skirt and patterned black shawl, height 7", designer P. Stabler.   1923-1938   **1650.00 1800.00**
HN 594
☐ Green skirt and patterned brown shawl, height 7", designer P. Stabler.   1924-1938   **1650.00 1800.00**
HN 613
☐ Striped pink skirt and spotted orange shawl, height 7", designer P. Stabler.   1924-1938   **1650.00 1800.00**
HN 764
☐ Blue and purple striped shawl, yellow skirt, height 7", designer P. Stabler. . .   1925-1938   **1650.00 1800.00**

MADONNA OF THE SQUARE (cont.)	Date	Price Range	
HN 1968			
☐ Pale green costume, height 7″, designer P. Stabler.	1941-1949	850.00	950.00
HN 1969			
☐ Lilac costume, height 7″, designer P. Stabler.	1941-1949	850.00	950.00
HN 2034			
☐ Costume of shaded greens and blues, height 7″, designer P. Stabler.	1949-1951	800.00	900.00

MAISIE

	Date	Price Range	
HN 1618			
☐ Tiered skirt of pale green, blouse of shaded blue, red bonnet, pantalettes of white showing, on light coloured base, height 6¼″, designer L. Harradine.	1934-1949	475.00	525.00
HN 1619			
☐ Gown of shaded reds, dark hair, dark base, height 6¼″, designer L. Harradine.	1934-1949	475.00	525.00

MAKE BELIEVE

	Date	Price Range	
HN 2225			
☐ Small figure in very light blue gown, holding very large yellow hat with flower trim, green shoes on one side, red purse on other side, height 5¾″, designer M. Nicoll.	1962-	100.00	

MAM'SELLE

	Date	Price Range	
HN 658			
☐ Black and white costume with black triangular hat, black shoes, standing on black pedestal style base, height 7″, designer L. Harradine.	1924-1938	850.00	950.00
HN 659			
☐ Costume of dark blue and red, hat matches costume, height 7″, designer L. Harradine.	1924-1938	900.00	1000.00
HN 724			
☐ Red hat, yellow trimmed dress, height 7″, designer L. Harradine.	1925-1938	900.00	1000.00
HN 786			
☐ Costume skirt of red with black squares, top is black with gold stripe, height 7″, designer L. Harradine.	1926-1938	900.00	1000.00

Make Believe, HN2225, 100.00

MANDARIN, A	Date	Price Range	
HN 84			
☐ HN 318, mauve shirt, green cloak (1st version), height 10¼ ", designer C. J. Noke.	1918-1938	**2250.00**	**2500.00**
HN 316			
☐ Rotund Chinese figure, costume of black and gold, tunic of yellow with dragon of green and gold flower design (1st version), height 10¼ ", designer C. J. Noke.	1918-1938	**2250.00**	**2500.00**
HN 318			
☐ Rotund Chinese figure with costume of black with gold designs, tunic is gold with raised pattern design of dragon and other designs (1st version), height 10¼ ", designer C. J. Noke.	1918-1938	**2250.00**	**2500.00**

MARDARIN, A (cont.)	Date	Price Range	

HN 366

☐ This figure is a small seated Chinese male on a pedestal, costume of yellow and blue (2nd version), height 8¼", designer C. J. Noke. 1920-1938 **1400.00 1550.00**

HN 382

☐ Costume blue and yellow (1st version), height 10¼", designer C. J. Noke. 1920-1938 **2250.00 2500.00**

HN 450

☐ Costume of red with black designs in circle of deeper red trimmed in green, also has red and black design, cap is red, black and green (3rd version), height unknown, designer C. J. Noke. 1921-1938 **1500.00 1750.00**

HN 455

☐ Green costume (2nd version), height 8¼", designer C. J. Noke. 1921-1938 **1750.00 2000.00**

HN 460

☐ Blue costume (3rd version), height unknown, designer C. J. Noke. 1921-1938 **2250.00 2500.00**

HN 461

☐ Red costume (3rd version), height unknown, designer C. J. Noke. 1921-1938 **2250.00 2500.00**

HN 601

☐ Blue costume (3rd version), height unknown, designer C. J. Noke. 1924-1938 **2250.00 2500.00**

HN 611

☐ Yellow patterned tunic (3rd version), height 10¼", designer C. J. Noke. . . . 1924-1938 **2000.00 2500.00**

HN 641

☐ HN 366, onyx style colouring (2nd version), height 8¼", designer C. J. Noke. 1924-1938 **1100.00 1200.00**

HN 746

☐ Black costume with green dragons (1st version), height 10¼", designer C. J. Noke. 1925-1938 **2250.00 2500.00**

HN 787

☐ Pink and orange tunic decorated with black flowers (1st version), height 10¼", designer C. J. Noke. 1926-1938 **2250.00 2500.00**

HN 791

☐ Yellow tunic with green and red markings (1st version), height 10¼", designer C. J. Noke. 1926-1938 **2250.00 2500.00**

	Date	Price Range	

MAN IN TUDOR COSTUME
HN 563
☐ Costume of gold, green, purple on black base, height 3¾, designer unknown...................... 1923-1938 **1400.00 1750.00**

MANTILLA
HN 2712
☐ Tall figure in spanish style costume of red with black and red shawl which covers high comb in hair, height 11¾", designer E. J. Griffiths. 1974-1979 **300.00 350.00**

MARGARET
HN 1989
☐ Gown of green with overdress of mottled red, blue and yellow, green hat with red ribbon, height 7¼", designer L. Harradine.................... 1947-1959 **350.00 400.00**

MARGARET OF ANJOU
HN 2012
☐ Gown of mottled green and yellow trimmed in white with wide and high bluish white head covering, height 9¼", designer M. Davies. 1948-1953 **700.00 800.00**

MARGERY
HN 1413
☐ Gown of red and patterned black trimmed in white with various colors, green bonnet with black ribbons, height 10¾", designer L. Harradine. . 1930-1949 **400.00 450.00**

MARGOT
HN 1628
☐ Full skirted gown of shaded blues, large brim hat of light blue with red ribbons, carrying small basket of flowers, height 5¾", designer L. Harradine. 1934-1938 **700.00 800.00**
HN 1636
☐ Red bodice, pink and yellow skirt, height 5¾", designer L. Harradine. .. 1934-1938 **700.00 800.00**
HN 1653
☐ Skirt of white with blue flower design, red bodice, red hat, height 5¾", designer L. Harradine. 1934-1938 **700.00 800.00**

MARGUERITE	Date	Price Range

HN 1928
☐ HN 1946, pink dress, height 8″,
designer L. Harradine.   1940-1959   325.00   375.00
HN 1929
☐ Pink fading to yellow at bottom of
dress, height 8″, designer L. Harradine   1940-1949   500.00   600.00
HN 1930
☐ Blue dress with purple stripes, height
8″, designer L. Harradine.   1940-1949   550.00   650.00
HN 1946
☐ Red gown with white and green trim
on bodice, black bonnet with green
lining and green feather trim, holding
small bouquet of flowers to face,
height 8″, designer L. Harradine.   1940-1949   400.00   500.00

MARIANNE

HN 2074
☐ Red skirt with darker red jacket
trimmed in white, black hat trimmed
in white, holding riding crop, height
7¼″, designer L. Harradine.   1951-1953   475.00   550.00

MARIE

HN 401
☐ Skirt of white with purple designs
trimmed in gold, with overlay of pur-
ple and pink, bodice of pink trimmed
with white (1st version), height
unknown, designer L. Harradine.   1920-1938   2250.00   2500.00
HN 434
☐ Yellow skirt with orange stripes (1st
version), height unknown, designer
L. Harradine.   1921-1938   2250.00   2500.00
HN 502
☐ White dress, red and blue bodice (1st
version), height unknown, designer
L. Harradine.   1921-1938   2250.00   2500.00
HN 504
☐ Green and blue dress, red spots (1st
version), height unknown, designer
L. Harradine.   1921-1938   2250.00   2500.00
HN 505
☐ Spotted blue bodice, green and lilac
skirt (1st version), height unknown,
designer L. Harradine.   1921-1938   2250.00   2500.00

MARIE (cont.)	Date	Price Range	
HN 506			
☐ Blue and green striped bodice, spotted lilac skirt (1st version), height unknown, designer L. Harradine.	1921-1938	**2250.00**	**2500.00**
HN 1370			
☐ Small figure in full shaded purple gown (2nd version), height 4½", designer L. Harradine.	1930-	**65.00**	
HN 1388			
☐ Red and blue flowered dress (2nd version), height 4½", designer L. Harradine.	1930-1938	**250.00**	**300.00**
HN 1417			
☐ Orange dress (2nd version), height 4½", designer L. Harradine.	1930-1949	**250.00**	**300.00**
HN 1489			
☐ Shaded green dress (2nd version), height 4½", designer L. Harradine. . .	1932-1949	**250.00**	**300.00**
HN 1531			
☐ Yellow/green dress (2nd version), height 4½", designer L. Harradine. . .	1932-1938	**250.00**	**300.00**
HN 1635			
☐ Flowered pink skirt (2nd version), height 4½", designer L. Harradine. . .	1934-1949	**250.00**	**300.00**
HN 1655			
☐ Pink bodice, flower white shirt (2nd version), height 4½", designer L. Harradine.	1934-1938	**250.00**	**300.00**

MARIETTA

	Date	Price Range	
HN 1341			
☐ Stylish bat costume of black and red on red base, height 8", designer L. Harradine.	1929-1949	**700.00**	**800.00**
HN 1446			
☐ Costume of shaded blues and reds with cloak of green on green, height 8", designer L. Harradine.	1931-1949	**700.00**	**800.00**
HN 1699			
☐ Green costume with cloak of red with blue lining, height 8", designer L. Harradine.	1935-1949	**700.00**	**800.00**

MARIGOLD

	Date	Price Range	
HN 1447			
☐ Gown of shaded blues, green bonnet with green ribbons, height 6", designer L. Harradine.	1931-1949	**450.00**	**500.00**

MARIGOLD (cont.)	Date	Price Range	
HN 1451			
☐ Yellow dress, height 6″, designer L. Harradine.	1931-1938	450.00	500.00
HN 1555			
☐ Costume is red skirt with light blue jacket, blue bonnet with darker blue ribbons, height 6″, designer L. Harradine.	1931-1951	450.00	500.00

MARION
HN 1582
☐ Green bonnet, pink skirt, height 6½″, designer L. Harradine. 1933-1938   700.00   800.00

HN 1583
☐ Figure seated in cream coloured chair, blue skirt, darker blue blouse, multicoloured shawl, bonnet of shaded blues and red with red ribbons, height 6½″, designer L. Harradine. 1933-1938   700.00   800.00

MARIQUITA
HN 1837
☐ Skirt of red and shaded blues, bodice and sleeves red trimmed with white, hat of blue, holding open fan in one hand, height 8″, designer L. Harradine. 1938-1949   1400.00   1750.00

MARJORIE
HN 2788
☐ Figure in seating position, gown of white with blue trim, bodice of blue, height 5¼″, designer M. Davies. 1980-   185.00

MARKET DAY
HN 1991
☐ Skirt of blue, white apron, shawl of shaded blues and red, head covering white, goose under one arm and basket of flowers under other. Reissued as Country Lass, height 7¼″, designer L. Harradine. 1947-1955   275.00   325.00

MARY HAD A LITTLE LAMB

HN 2048

☐ Small figure in seated position in gown of shaded blue/red trimmed in white, blue ribbon in hair, small lamb on lap with blue ribbon, height 3⅝", designer M. Davies. . . . .

	Date	Price Range	
	1949-	100.00	

MARY JANE

HN 1990

☐ Light red dress with flower design, apron of shaded blue, small white cap with black ribbon, height 7½", designer L. Harradine. . . . .

	1947-1959	375.00	425.00

MARY MARY

HN 2044

☐ Small girl figure on yellow-green base, pink skirt, red blouse, blue sash, holds watering can, height 5", designer L. Harradine. . . . .

	1949-1973	125.00	175.00

MASK, The

HN 656

☐ Blue and purple costume, height 6¾", designer L. Harradine. . . . .

	1924-1938	850.00	950.00

HN 657

☐ Costume of white with black trim and black spots, on black base, holding mask, small black cap, height 6¾", designer L. Harradine. . . . .

	1924-1938	850.00	950.00

HN 729

☐ Costume of red with black squares and black collar, height 6¾", designer L. Harradine. . . . .

	1925-1938	850.00	950.00

HN 733

☐ Costume of white with black squares, height 6¾", designer L. Harradine. . .

	1925-1938	850.00	950.00

HN 785

☐ Blue costume, pink striped skirt, height 6¾", designer L. Harradine. . .

	1926-1938	850.00	950.00

HN 1271

☐ Black and red costume with spots of blue, green, yellow, height 6¾", designer L. Harradine. . . . .

	1928-1938	850.00	950.00

MASK SELLER	Date	Price Range	

MASK SELLER

HN 1361

☐ Character figure in black cloak, red hat with green feather, green stockings and shoes on grey/green base, holds masks of white on red carrier, holds flute in hands, height 8⅜", designer L. Harradine. 1929-1938 650.00 750.00

HN 2103

☐ Green cloak, black hat, brown stockings and shoes on brown base, masks of different colours, flute is larger, lantern panes are coloured, height 8⅜", designer L. Harradine. . . . 1953- 175.00

MASQUE

HN 2554

☐ Dark blue with black shadings, cloak covers figure, has mask on long handle. Note: Second figure has hand up to mask with dark blue cloak, discontinued this past year, height 8⅞", designer D. V. Tootle. 1973-1982 170.00

MASQUERADE

HN 599

☐ Male figure standing on brown base with brown bush, 18th century style costume of red coat, brown trousers, white stockings, brown shoes and hat (1st version), height 6¾", designer L. Harradine. 1924-1949 750.00 800.00

HN 600

☐ Female figure standing on brown base with bush, holding basket of fruit, costume 18th century style of white with red designs, white hair (1st version), height varies from 6" to 6¾", designer L. Harradine. 1924-1949 750.00 800.00

HN 636

☐ Male, gold costume (1st version), height 6¾", designer L. Harradine. . . 1924-1938 1000.00 1250.00

HN 637

☐ Female, everything gold (1st version), height varies from 6" to 6¾", designer L. Harradine. 1924-1938 1000.00 1250.00

	Date	Price Range	
MASQUERADE (cont.)			

HN 674
☐ Female, orange and yellow chequered dress (1st version), height varies from 6″ to 6¾″, designer L. Harradine.   1924-1938   700.00   800.00

HN 683
☐ Male, green coat (1st version), height 6¾″, designer L. Harradine.   1924-1938   700.00   800.00

HN 2251
☐ 18th century style figure on white base, costume of blue and white with green designs, tiny head cap of blue (2nd version), height 8½″, designer M. Davies.   1960-1965   350.00   400.00

HN 2259
☐ Dress is red with white that does not have gold design (2nd version), height 8½″, designer M. Davies.   1960-1965   325.00   375.00

MASTER, The

HN 2325
☐ Character figure seated on rock with dog and staff, brown trousers and shoes, green coat, light tan hat lying beside figure, height 5⅝″, designer M. Davies.   1967-   165.00

MASTER SWEEP

HN 2205
☐ Boy figure with black trousers, dark green coat, black hat and shoes, orange scarf, standing on dark base, has brown bag in one hand, chimney brush in other, height 8½″, designer M. Nicoll.   1957-1962   600.00   700.00

MATILDA

HN 2011
☐ Gown of purple and red, long cloak of red, gold rope belt, holding open book, dark braided hair, height 9¼″, designer M. Davies.   1948-1953   600.00   700.00

MAUREEN

HN 1770
☐ Light red gown, black gloves, black hat with white and black tip feathers, holding black riding crop, height 7½″, designer L. Harradine.   1936-1959   350.00   400.00

	Date	Price Range	
MAUREEN (cont.)			

HN 1771

☐ Dress of shaded blues, green bonnet with white feather, green gloves, holding brown riding crop, height 8″, designer L. Harradine. 1936-1959 **675.00 750.00**

☐ **M 84** Made as a miniature, gown of shaded oranges, height 4″, designer. L. Harradine. 1939-1949 **350.00 400.00**

☐ **M 85** Light blue skirt, red and blue jacket, height 4″, designer L. Harradine 1939-1949 **350.00 450.00**

The Mayor, HN2280, 450.00 — 550.00

MAYOR, The

HN 2280

☐ Costume of red and white, black hat with white trim, black shoes with buckle trim, gold chain around chest, height 8¼″, designer M. Nicoll. 1963-1971 **450.00 500.00**

	Date	Price Range	
MAYTIME **HN 2113** ☐ Gown of shaded reds, scarf of light blues and greens, bonnet with red ribbons, dark haired, height 6¾", designer L. Harradine.	1953-1967	**325.00**	**375.00**
MEDITATION **HN 2330** ☐ Lady seated at skirted writing table of white with shaded green which contains yellow candleholder, yellow ink bottle and open book, gown of brown with cream which contains orange designs, white hair, height 5¾", designer M. Davies.	1971-	**250.00**	
MELANIE **HN 2271** ☐ Gown of blue with yellow collar, hair tied with pink ribbon, holding small wrapped bouquet in hand, height 7⅞", designer M. Davies.	1965-1980	**150.00**	**200.00**
MELISSA **HN 2467** ☐ Undergown and cuffs of white, overdress is of shaded reds and purples, one hand raised to blonde hair, height 6¾", designer M. Davies.	1981-	**170.00**	
MELODY **HN 2202** ☐ Lady seated, gown of light orange skirt with green bodice trimmed in white, playing white instrument held on lap, height 6¼", designer M. Davies.	1957-1962	**300.00**	**350.00**
MEMORIES **HN 1855** ☐ Green bodice and hat, red skirt, height 6", designer L. Harradine.	1938-1949	**450.00**	**500.00**
HN 1856 ☐ Lady seated leaning against brown tree stump, gown of pale blue with darker blue designs, blue bodice trimmed in white, bonnet with black ribbons, holding green open book on knee, height 6", designer L. Harradine.	1938-1949	**450.00**	**500.00**

MEMORIES (cont.)	Date	Price Range	

HN 1857
☐ Red bodice with red and lilac skirt, height 6″, designer L. Harradine. 1938-1949   450.00   500.00

HN 2030
☐ Skirt of shaded reds, bodice green, bonnet with green ribbons, height 6″, designer L. Harradine. 1949-1959   400.00   450.00

MENDICANT, The

HN 1355
☐ Costume of shaded browns, black and green, turban of orange, green and browns, seated on base of reddish bricks with multicoloured cloth, holding tambourine, height 8¼″, designer L. Harradine. 1929-1938   350.00   400.00

HN 1365
☐ Minor glaze differences, height 8¼″, designer L. Harradine. 1929-1969   300.00   350.00

MEPHISTO

HN 722
☐ Black blouse, height 6½″, designer L. Harradine. 1925-1938   1350.00   1500.00

HN 723
☐ Masquerade type costume of red with black stripes on skirt, red jacket, cap is red with black lining, wide white collar, small triangular hat of red and black, on black pedestal style base, height 6½″, designer L. Harradine. . . 1925-1938   1500.00   1600.00

MEPHISTOPHELES AND MARGUERITE

HN 755
☐ Two-sided figure with black base, one side lady in orange dress, purple cloak, other side male figure in red outfit with red cloak, height 7¾″, designer C. J. Noke. 1925-1949   1350.00   1500.00

HN 775
☐ This is two figures on black base, the lady in costume of white with gold designs, cloak red with white lining, red shoe, reverse side is male figure in red with black stripes and cloak of red with black lining, height 7¾″, designer C. J. Noke. 1925-1949   1350.00   1500.00

	Date	Price Range	

MERIEL
HN 1931
☐ Gown of pink with wide white collar, bonnet with trim of black, seated on bench, height 7¼", designer L. Harradine. 1940-1949   850.00   950.00
HN 1932
☐ Gown of green, height 7¼", designer L. Harradine. 1940-1949   850.00   950.00

MERMAID, The
HN 97
☐ Mermaid seated on rock of brown and yellow, green/blue fish tail, upper torso white, red beads and red decoration in hair, height 7", designer H. Tittensor. 1918-1936   650.00   750.00
HN 300
☐ Red berries in hair, with darker base, height 7", designer H. Tittensor. 1918-1936   850.00 1000.00

MERYLL
HN 1917
☐ Red jacket and green skirt. This figure was renamed shortly after its introduction, height 6¾", designer L. Harradine. 1939-1940   1200.00 1350.00

MICHELLE
HN 2234
☐ Gown of green with white design on edge, undergown of light red, also sleeves of light red, height 6⅞", designer M. Davies. 1967-   155.00

MIDINETTE
HN 1289
☐ Short skirt of light red with flower design, mottled red jacket, red shoes on light base, carrying two hat boxes, one is white with yellow stripes and yellow and brown dots, the other is yellow, dark blue, black and white stripes (1st version), height 9", designer L. Harradine. 1928-1938   1500.00 1600.00

	Date	Price Range
MIDINETTE (cont.)		

HN 1306
☐ Skirt of green, jacket red, base is black, hat boxes are white with green and gold stripes, the other is white with red and green stripes (1st version), height 9″, designer L. Harradine.. — 1928-1938 — 1500.00 1600.00

HN 2090
☐ Skirt and jacket of light blue, hat with red feather, hat box white with blue design and red ribbon, this figure is not on a base, and the skirt is full length (2nd version), height 7¼″, designer L. Harradine. . . . . — 1952-1965 — 250.00 300.00

MIDSUMMER NOON

HN 1899
☐ Figure seated on bench, skirt is beige, bodice is red, bodice is white with very light blue, on bench is basket of flowers and shawl of light colour with green border, height 4½″, designer L. Harradine. . . . . — 1939-1949 — 550.00 600.00

HN 1900
☐ Blue dress, height 4½″, designer L. Harradine. — 1939-1949 — 550.00 600.00

HN 2033
☐ Only minor colour differences, height 4½″, designer L. Harradine. . . . . — 1949-1955 — 475.00 525.00

MILADY

HN 1970
☐ Gown of shaded reds with white collar, with black ribbon, black gloves, black hat with feather trim, holding riding crop, height 6½″, designer L. Harradine. . . . . — 1941-1949 — 900.00 950.00

MILKING TIME

HN   3
☐ Gown of light blue with white apron, standing on round base with goat of brown and white, figure holding jug on arm, height unknown, designer P. Stabler. . . . . — 1913-1938 — 3000.00 3500.00

HN 306
☐ Pale costume with black printed markings, height unknown, designer P. Stabler. — 1913-1938 — 2750.00 3000.00

	Date	Price Range	
MILKMAID, The			
HN 2057			
☐ Green skirt, brown blouse, blue/white apron trimmed in brown, white farm bonnet, carrying brown jug, height 6½ ", designer L. Harradine.	1975-1981	135.00	185.00
MILLICENT			
HN 1714			
☐ Gown of red and white with blue designs and stripes, red shawl, bonnet blue with green ribbons, holding small round purse, height 8", designer L. Harradine.	1935-1949	1050.00	1150.00
HN 1715			
☐ Flowered shawl and purple dress, height 8", designer L. Harradine.	1935-1949	1050.00	1150.00
HN 1860			
☐ No details of colour available, height 8", designer L. Harradine.	1938-1949	1050.00	1150.00
MINUET			
HN 2019			
☐ Gown of white with blue and gold designs, light blue shoe, height 7¼", designer M. Davies.	1949-1971	300.00	350.00
HN 2066			
☐ Gown of reds and blues, height 7¼", designer M. Davies.	1950-1955	250.00	300.00
MIRABEL			
HN 1743			
☐ Gown of cream and shaded blue, cloak also cream and blue with red edge trim, green hat, red open parasol, height 7¾", designer L. Harradine. . .	1935-1949	750.00	850.00
HN 1744			
☐ Gown of shaded reds with red flowers and cream coloured stripes, cloak red, bonnet light green, open parasol light colour, height 7¾", designer L. Harradine.	1935-1949	750.00	800.00
☐ **M 68** Introduced as a miniature, gown of shaded reds with green cloak, black bonnet, green parasol, height 4", designer L. Harradine.	1936-1949	300.00	350.00
☐ **M 74** Green dress, height 4", designer L. Harradine.	1936-1949	300.00	350.00

	Date	Price Range

MIRANDA

HN 1818

☐ Red skirt, with blue mottled bodice and overskirt, trimmed with green, small wrapped head covering of green with black ribbon, holding open fan in one hand, on black base, height 8½ ", designer L. Harradine.   1937-1949   750.00   850.00

HN 1819

☐ Green skirt, height 8½ ", designer L. Harradine.   1937-1949   750.00   850.00

MIRROR, The

HN 1852

☐ Slender figure in gown of shaded red and blues with white collar that has blue and red flowers, holding small mirror, height 7½ ", designer L. Harradine.   1938-1949   800.00   1000.00

HN 1853

☐ Blue costume, height 7½ ", designer L. Harradine.   1938-1949   800.00   1000.00

MISS DEMURE

HN 1402

☐ Pink gown with shawl of blue that has yellow and green stripe, bonnet of light green with darker green ribbons, open parasol of red with white fringe, height 7", designer L. Harradine.   1930-1975   225.00   275.00

HN 1440

☐ Gown of blue with darker blue shawl, blue bonnet with darker blue ribbons, open parasol red with reddish white trim, height 7", designer L. Harradine.   1930-1949   350.00   400.00

HN 1463

☐ Green dress, height 7", designer L. Harradine.   1931-1949   350.00   400.00

HN 1499

☐ Yellow bonnet, pink dress, height 7", designer L. Harradine.   1932-1938   400.00   450.00

HN 1560

☐ Gown of cream and shaded blues, shawl of shaded reds and blues, bonnet very light red with dark blue ribbons, open parasol multicoloured, height 7", designer L. Harradine.   1933-1949   350.00   400.00

MISS 1926	Date	Price Range

HN 1205

☐ Figure standing on brown pedestal style base, with dark fur coat with white fur trim, height 7¼", designer L. Harradine.   1926-1938   **2050.00 2200.00**

HN 1207

☐ Black fur collar, height 7¼", designer L. Harradine.   1926-1938   **2050.00 2200.00**

MISS FORTUNE

HN 1897

☐ Red skirt, shawl of white with blue and green designs, blue bonnet with red ribbons, on light coloured base which has basket of flowers and single flowers of yellow on it, height 5¾", designer L. Harradine.   1938-1949   **450.00   500.00**

HN 1898

☐ Green and yellow shawl, mauve dress, height 5¾", designer L. Harradine.   1938-1949   **450.00   500.00**

Miss Muffet, HN1937, 300.00 — 350.00

	Date	Price Range

MISS MUFFET
HN 1936
☐ Small figure in gown of white, red long coat with white fur trim, white fur muff, white open parasol, red cap with black ribbons, height 5½", designer L. Harradine. 1940-1967 **150.00 200.00**

HN 1937
☐ Very light red gown, green long coat with white fur trim, green cap with red ribbons, light coloured parasol, height 5½", designer L. Harradine. . . 1940-1952 **300.00 350.00**

MISS WINSOME
HN 1665
☐ Gown of shaded purple, shawl white with red flower design, green bonnet, small green round purse, height 6¾", designer L. Harradine. 1934-1949 **600.00 700.00**

HN 1666
☐ Green gown, shawl multicoloured, red bonnet with green ribbons, small red purse, height 6¾", designer L. Harradine. 1934-1938 **650.00 750.00**

M'LADY'S MAID
HN 1795
☐ Red gown with very small white apron, white trim on sleeves, small white cap with ribbon trim, gold coloured rope with key attached, carrying small tray with objects on it, height 9", designer L. Harradine. . . . 1936-1949 **1150.00 1300.00**

HN 1822
☐ Multicoloured dress, height 9", designer L. Harradine. 1937-1949 **1150.00 1300.00**

MODENA
HN 1845
☐ Blue dress, height 7¼", designer L. Harradine. 1938-1949 **750.00 850.00**

HN 1846
☐ Full red skirt with green bows, green bodice with red rose trim, shawl of white with green and red design, shawl covers comb in hair, red rose in hair, height 7¼", designer L. Harradine. 1938-1949 **750.00 850.00**

	Date	Price Range

MODERN PIPER, The
HN 756
☐ Costume of pink tights with diamond design of blue and gold jacket mottled red and blue, cloak of green and blue, pipe of gold on green/yellow base with four tiny figures, height 8½ ", designer L. Harradine.   1925-1938   1650.00 1800.00

MOIRA
HN 1347
☐ Figure of lady with dog on pedestal style base, woman's costume of blue, green, yellow, black, vest also multicoloured, hat is green and blue stripes, gloves green, dog dark brown with white, height 6½ ", designer L. Harradine.   1929-1938   2750.00 3000.00

MOLLY MALONE
HN 1455
☐ Skirt of dark colour with white apron with blue int, overdress is of red and darker blue, bodice is dark with multicoloured collar, kerchief on head is also multicoloured, the base contains figure, wheel barrow and basket of brown, height 7", designer L. Harradine.   1931-1938   1350.00 1500.00

MONICA
HN 1458
☐ Small seated figure, white gown with multicoloured flower designs, black bonnet with green ribbons, holds red basket of flowers, height 4", designer L. Harradine.   1931-1949   200.00   250.00
HN 1459
☐ Lilac dress, height 4", designer L. Harradine. 1931-Unknown   200.00   250.00
HN 1467
☐ Gown of white and shaded blues with a very faint flower design, bodice red, sleeves red and blue, red bonnet with blue ribbon, basket is light colour, flowers red, height 4", designer L. Harradine.   1931-   100.00
☐ **M 66** Introduced as a miniature, height 3", designer L. Harradine.   1935-1949   300.00   350.00

MONICA (cont.)	Date	Price Range	

☐ **M 72** Gown is white with large blue spots, bodice blue, bonnet pink with black ribbons, basket has yellow and red flowers, height 3″, designer L. Harradine.   1936-1949   **300.00   350.00**

MOOR, The
HN 1308
☐ Patterned blue costume with mottled red cloak, height 16½ ″, designer C. J. Noke.   1929-1938   **1500.00   1750.00**
HN 1366
☐ Red costume with multicoloured patterning, height 16½ ″, designer C. J. Noke.   1930-1949   **1500.00   1750.00**
HN 1425
☐ Dark multicoloured costume, height 16½ ″, designer C. J. Noke.   1930-1949   **1500.00   1750.00**
HN 1657
☐ Striped waistband, black cloak, height 16½ ″, designer C. J. Noke. . . .   1934-1949   **1500.00   1750.00**

MOORISH MINSTREL
HN   34
☐ Brown figure on pedestal of brown, costume is very dark blue, small hat and shoes brown, holding brown instrument, height 13½ ″, designer C. J. Noke.   1913-1938   **2000.00   2200.00**
HN   364
☐ Blue, green and orange striped costume, height 13½ ″, designer C. J. Noke.   1920-1938   **2750.00   3000.00**
HN   415
☐ Green and yellow striped costume, height 13½ ″, designer C. J. Noke. . . .   1920-1938   **2750.00   3000.00**
HN   797
☐ Purple costume, height 13½ ″, designer C. J. Noke.   1926-1949   **2150.00   2300.00**

MOORISH PIPER MINSTREL
HN   301
☐ Dark figure on dark brown base, purple costume with orange scarf around neck, dunce shaped orange/brown hat, light coloured pipe, height 13½ ″, designer C. J. Noke.   1918-1938   **2750.00   3000.00**

MORRISH PIPER MINSTREL (cont.)	Date	Price Range	
HN 328			
☐ Green and brown striped robe, height 13½ ", designer C. J. Noke.	1918-1938	2750.00	3000.00
HN 416			
☐ Green and yellow striped robe, height 13½ ", designer C. J. Noke.	1920-1938	2750.00	3000.00

MOTHERHOOD

HN 28			
☐ Grey costume, height unknown, designer P. Stabler.	1913-1938	1750.00	2000.00
HN 30			
☐ Figure seated on bench which is on base, gown of white with blue designs and dots, apron of white with designs of blue and blue trim, holding small nude child figure, height unknown, designer P. Stabler.	1913-1938	2250.00	2500.00
HN 303			
☐ White dress with black patterning, height unknown, designer P. Stabler. .	1918-1938	2250.00	2500.00

MOTHER'S HELP

HN 2151			
☐ Small figure in brown gown with white bib apron, white sleeves and collar, white head covering, height 5", designer M. Davies.	1962-1969	175.00	225.00

MR. MICAWBER

HN 532			
☐ Character from Dicken's "David Copperfield" (1st version), height 3½ ", designer L. Harradine.	1922-	45.00	60.00
☐ **M 42** Renumbered as a miniature, height 4", designer L. Harradine. . . .	1932-	29.95	
HN 557			
☐ Larger figure standing on brown base with green bush, black trousers, brown coat, yellow vest, white shirt with black bow tie (2nd version), height 7", designer L. Harradine. . . .	1923-1939	400.00	500.00
HN 1895			
☐ Very minor colour changes (2nd version), height 7", designer L. Harradine. .	1938-1952	400.00	450.00

	Date	Price Range	
MR. MICAWBER (cont.)			

HN 2097
☐ Figure standing on small black base, light brown trousers, black coat, brown and yellow vest, white shirt, red bow tie (3rd version), height 7½", designer L. Harradine. 1952-1967 **325.00 375.00**

MR. PICKWICK

HN 529
☐ Character from Dicken's "Pickwick Papers" (1st version), height 3¾", designer L. Harradine. 1922- **45.00 60.00**
☐ **M 41** Renumbered as a miniature, height 4", designer L. Harradine. 1932- **29.95**

HN 556
☐ Figure standing on brown base with bush, yellow trousers, blue coat, tan vest, white cravat, black hat in hand, black boots (2nd version), height 7", designer L. Harradine. 1923-1939 **400.00 500.00**

HN 1894
☐ Very minor colour changes (2nd version), height 7", designer L. Harradine. 1938-1942 **400.00 450.00**

HN 2099
☐ Figure on green base, light brown trousers, black coat, brown/orange vest, white cravat, brown hat, yellow spats (3rd version), height 7½", designer L. Harradine. 1952-1967 **325.00 375.00**

MRS. BARDELL
Issued only as a miniature

☐ **M 86** White dress, white hood with black trim, very light pink shawl, black stand, height 4¼", designer L. Harradine. 1949- **29.95**

MRS. FITZHERBERT

HN 2007
☐ Gown of white with blue bow trim, mottled yellow, blue and orange overdress, red bodice, head covering of white with blue ribbon trim, holding open fan of red and white, height 9", designer M. Davies. 1948-1953 **700.00 800.00**

	Date	Price Range

MY LOVE

HN 2339

☐ White gown with gold trim and gold design in part of gown, gold shoe, holding single red rose, dark hair, height 6¼", designer M. Davies. 1969-   185.00

MY PET

HN 2238

☐ Small figure seated on cushion, in skirt of blue and white, blouse with blue trim holding small brown dog in one arm and open book in other, brown shoes, height 3", designer M. Davies. 1962-1975   100.00   150.00

MY PRETTY MAID

HN 2064

☐ Small figure on yellow and green base, gown of shaded blues with white collar, waistband of darker blue with red trim, holding milking stool and bucket is on base, height 5½", designer L. Harradine. 1950-1954   250.00   300.00

MY TEDDY

HN 2177

☐ Small figure seated on white base, gown of shaded greens with white collar, holding brown teddy bear and small mirror, height 3¼", designer M. Davies. 1962-1967   250.00   300.00

NADINE

HN 1885

☐ Gown of light blue with green sash, shawl of multicolour, bonnet of green, blue shoe, height 7¾", designer L. Harradine. 1938-1949   650.00   750.00

HN 1886

☐ Gown of very light orange with shades of red with blue sash, shawl shaded reds with blue/green trim, bonnet blue, height 7¾", designer L. Harradine. ... 1938-1949   650.00   750.00

NANA	Date	Price Range	

HN 1766
☐ Small figure in light red and white gown, tiny hat on side of head is blue with red trim, open fan in hand, height 4¾", designer L. Harradine. . . . . 1936-1949 | **275.00** | **325.00**

HN 1767
☐ Gown of shaded blues and green, hat green with red trim, height 4¾", designer L. Harradine. . . . . 1936-1949 | **275.00** | **325.00**

NANNY

HN 2221
☐ Older figure seated in grey rocker with brown teddy bear on lap, gown of blue/green with white apron and headcap, toys on base, also basket, height 5⅝", designer M. Davies. . . . . . 1958- | **175.00**

NEGLIGEE

HN 1219
☐ Figure kneeling on brown and orange cushion base, short gown of shaded blues, blue ribbon in hair, height 5", designer L. Harradine. . . . . 1927-1938 | **1100.00** | **1200.00**

HN 1228
☐ Cushion is blac, red and blue, gown of shaded blues, red ribbon in hair, height 5", designer L. Harradine. . . . . 1927-1938 | **1100.00** | **1200.00**

HN 1272
☐ Mottled red and yellow negligee, height 5", designer L. Harradine. . . . . 1928-1938 | **1100.00** | **1200.00**

HN 1273
☐ White negligee, height 5", designer L. Harradine. 1928-1938 | **1100.00** | **1200.00**

HN 1454
☐ Cushion of red with multicoloured design, gown of shaded pink, pink ribbon in hair, height 5", designer L. Harradine. . . . . 1931-1938 | **1100.00** | **1200.00**

NELL

HN 3014
☐ Seated figure in white pinafore over a pink dress. Seated in blue cart, bright yellow wheels. Light brown hair, height 4", designer P. Parsons. . . . . 1983- | **100.00**

Nell, HN3014, 100.00

NELL GWYNN	Date	Price Range
HN 1882		
☐ Skirt of blue, overlay of red, bodice red, white shawl, apron white, sleeves white with blue trim, green bonnet with red feather and red ribbons, blue shoes, standing on base which is shaded blue, pedestal has white cloth with basket, height 6¾", designer L. Harradine.	1938-1949	600.00 700.00
HN 1887		
☐ Red skirt, green bodice and overlay, bonnet red with blue feather and ribbons, black shoes, base cream coloured, height 6¾", designer L. Harradine.	1938-1949	600.00 700.00

NEW BONNET, The   Date   Price Range

HN 1728

☐ Red full gown with very wide white collar, red shoes, small white cap on head, holding green bonnet with yellow roses trim and red ribbons, standing on base of light green, height 7″, designer L. Harradine.   1935-1949   **525.00**   **575.00**

HN 1957

☐ Gown of red with shaded blues at hemline, white collar, small cap is red and white, bonnet is green with black ribbon trim and red flower, blue shoes, black base, height 7″, designer L. Harradine.   1940-1949   **500.00**   **550.00**

New Companion, HN2770, **175.00**

	Date	Price Range

NEW COMPANIONS
HN 2770
☐ Grey and black skirt, white apron, blue shawl, black hat with pink ribbons, black and white puppy in beige basket, height 7¾", designer W. K. Harper.   1982-   185.00

NEWHAVEN FISHWIFE
HN 1480
☐ Skirt of red and white stripes, apron black and white stripes, blouse white with red and blue designs, brown cloak, head-covering white with design, carrying brown basket with strap around head, on base of light brown with another basket, height 7¾", designer H. Fenton.   1931-1938   1350.00 1500.00

News Boy, HN2244, **600.00 — 700.00**

NEWSBOY	**Date**	**Price Range**

HN 2244

☐ Boy figure on green base, brown trousers, black coat, green scarf, cap of black and green stripes, holding newspaper placard, also folded newspapers — Note: A limited edition of 250 was also produced for Stoke-on-Trent's local paper, The Evening Sentinel; figure had the word Sentinel printed on newsboy's placard, height 8½ ", designer M. Davies. 1959-1965 **600.00 700.00**

Nicola, HN2839, **250.00**

NICOLA

HN 2839

☐ Gown of shaded blues and reds with flower design of white, yellow and green, white trim, dark bow on hair curls, holding bird in hand, height 7⅛", designer M. Davies. 1978- **250.00**

	Date	Price Range	

NINA
HN 2347
☐ Blue gown with white design at hemline, white collar, with white ribbon in hair, this figure has a matt finish, height 7½", designer M. Davies. 1969-1976 **125.00 175.00**

NINETTE
HN 2379
☐ Gown of yellow with white trim and golden design, flower in hair, height 8", designer M. Davies. 1971- **185.00**

Noelle, HN2179, **350.00 — 400.00**

NOELLE
HN 2179
☐ Gown of white with black stripes, long jacket of red with hood trimmed in white fur, white muff, height 6¾", designer M. Davies. 1957-1967 **350.00 400.00**

NORMA

Issued only as a miniature

	Date	Price Range	
☐ **M 36** No colour details available, height 4½ ", designer unknown.	1933-1945	**375.00**	**425.00**
☐ **M 37** Red/blue print dress, blue sleeves, shawl green and blue, hat green and red, height 4½ ", designer unknown.	1933-1945	**375.00**	**425.00**

NUDE ON ROCK

HN 593

	Date	Price Range	
☐ White nude figure lying of blue/white rock, height unknown, designer unknown.	1924-1938	**950.00**	**1000.00**

Odds And Ends, HN1844, **800.00 — 900.00**

	Date	Price Range	

ODDS AND ENDS
HN 1844
☐ Skirt of green with black, red and yellow stripes, yellow bibbed apron, red blouse, green shawl, black hat with coloured feathers, holding potted plants in one arm, height 7¾", designer L. Harradine. 1938-1938 800.00 900.00

OFFICER OF THE LINE
HN 2733
☐ Depicts a soldier of the Napoleon era. High boots, light waistcoat and pants, coat red with matching sash, hair powdered white to grey, black tricorn hat, height 9", designer W. K. Harper. 1983- 195.00

OLD BALLOON SELLER
HN 1315
☐ Older figure seated holding many different coloured balloons, skirt of green, white apron, red blouse, green shawl with red fringe, hat multicoloured, basket at side, height 7", designer L. Harradine. 1929- 185.00

OLD BALLOON SELLER AND BULLDOG
HN 1791
☐ Same figure as Old Balloon Seller with the addition of bulldog, all mounted on mahogany stand, height 7", designer L. Harradine. 1932-1938 1250.00 1500.00
HN 1912
☐ No details available, height 7", designer L. Harradine. 1939-1949 1350.00 1500.00

OLD HUNTSMAN, The
HN 1403
☐ Not issued . . . .

OLD KING, An
HN 358
☐ HN 2134, green shirt, purple robe, height 9¾", designer C. J. Noke. 1919-1938 1150.00 1300.00
HN 623
☐ Grey, red and green robes, height 9¾", designer C. J. Noke. 1924-1938 1300.00 1500.00

	Date	Price Range	

OLD KING, AN (cont.)

HN 1801
☐ No detail available, height 9¾", designer C. J. Noke.   1937-1954   950.00   1150.00

HN 2134
☐ Figure seated in brown chair on brown base, green robe, with purple overrobe trimmed in a green design, red scarf, gold crown, holding sword, height 10¾", designer C. J. Noke. . . .   1954-   475.00

OLD KING COLE

HN 2217
☐ Figure seated in light coloured chair, costume of brown and beige with robe trimmed in white fur, crown of brown and gold, small stool at feet holding goblet, height 6¾", designer M. Davies.   1963-1967   750.00   850.00

OLD LAVENDER SELLER

HN 1492
☐ Older figure seated, very dark green gown with white apron, shawl of red and yellow stripes with green squares, basket on one arm and small basket at side, hat black with flowers, height 6", designer L. Harradine.   1932-1949   600.00   700.00

HN 1571
☐ Patterned orange cap, height 6", designer L. Harradine.   1933-1949   600.00   700.00

OLD MAN, An

HN 451
☐ A seated figure covered completely by robe of blue, green and browns, height unknown, designer unknown. .   1921-1938   2250.00   2500.00

OLD MEG

HN 2494
☐ Gown of blue/grey, white/blue apron, shawl of patterned purple, green hat with blue/white scarf, red shoes, base looks like stones with brown basket, height 8", designer M. Nicoll.   1974-1976   225.00   275.00

	Date	Price Range	

OLD MOTHER HUBBARD
HN 2314
☐ Gown of dark green with lighter green trim, apron is white with dark green dots, head cap is green, holds bone in hand for brown and white dog, height 8″, designer M. Nicoll.   1964-1975   300.00   350.00

OLGA
HN 2463
☐ Yellow underskirt with blue overgown, holds single red rose, yellow ribbon in light brown hair, height 8¼″, designer J. Bromley.   1972-1975   200.00   250.00

OLIVER TWIST
Issued only as a miniature

☐ **M 89** White shirt, red tie, black jacket, tan pants, black stand, height 4¼″, designer L. Harradine.   1949-   29.95

OLIVIA
HN 1995
☐ Light green gown with cape of red with blue trim, holding white lilies in one arm, height 7½″, designer L. Harradine.   1947-1951   425.00   475.00

OMAR KHAYYAM AND THE BELOVED
HN 407
☐ Colours were unrecorded, height 10″, designer C. J. Noke.   1920-1938   3500.00   4000.00
HN 419
☐ Two figures standing together, his costume of blue with darker blue robe with green dot trim, green/blue turban, her costume is gown of shaded blues with yellow dots, robe has orange designs and orange dots, head trim is of same colouring, she holds jug, height 10″, designer C. J. Noke.   1920-1938   3500.00   4000.00
HN 459
☐ Multicoloured costumes, height 10″, designer C. J. Noke.   1921-1938   3500.00   4000.00
HN 598
☐ Lady has striped pink cloak, striped blue dress, height 10″, designer C. J. Noke.   1924-1938   3500.00   4000.00

OMAR KHAYYAM	Date	Price Range	
HN 408			
☐ Seated figure with robes of blue and black with brown (1st version), height 6″, designer C. J. Noke.	1920-1938	**2250.00**	**3000.00**
HN 409			
☐ Black robe, yellow trousers (1st version), height 6″, designer C. J. Noke. .		**2250.00**	**3000.00**
HN 2247			
☐ Costume of brown with robe of orange/brown, turban of orange, holding grey jug and red open book (2nd version), height 6¼″, designer M. Nicoll.	1965-	**165.00**	

ONCE UPON A TIME

HN 2047
☐ Small figure of little girl seated on tan bench, on a yellow-green base, dress of red with white dots with blue trim, blue shoes, open book on bench, height 4¼″, designer L. Harradine. . . — 1949-1955 — **200.00** **250.00**

ONE OF THE FORTY

All of the "One of the Forty" models were designed by H. Tittensor, their height ranging from 2¾″ to 7″.

HN 417
☐ **HN 528,** green and blue robes (1st version), height 5″, designer H. Tittensor. — 1920-1938 — **1100.00** **1200.00**

HN 418
☐ HN 494, striped green robes (2nd version) . . . . — 1920-1938 — **1100.00** **1200.00**

HN 423
☐ These figures were very small and produced in a variety of colour finishes (3rd version) . . . . — 1921-1938 — **450.00** **500.00**

HN 427
☐ Costume of brown, turban of brown and green, holding bag of green in one arm (9th version) . . . . — 1921-1938 — **1100.00** **1200.00**

HN 480
☐ Trousers yellow with black stripes, robe of mottled dark green, high hat of blue, bag in arms of mottled green (10th version), height 7″. . . . . — 1921-1938 — **800.00** **900.00**

ONE OF THE FORTY (cont.)	Date	Price Range	

HN 481
☐ HN 491, dark spotted robes (11th version) 1921-1938 **1100.00 1200.00**

HN 482
☐ HN 492, spotted waistband (12th version) . . . . : 1921-1938 **1100.00 1200.00**

HN 483
☐ HN 491, brown hat, green striped robes (11th version) 1921-1938 **1100.00 1200.00**

HN 484
☐ HN 492, mottled green robes (12th version) 1921-1938 **1100.00 1200.00**

HN 490
☐ HN 528, blue and brown chequered coat (1st version), height 5″ 1921-1938 **1100.00 1200.00**

HN 491
☐ Blue costume with white robe, blue hat, white bag which he holds under one arm and holds closed with other hand (11th version) 1921-1938 **1100.00 1200.00**

HN 492
☐ White costume with yellow band and yellow turban, white bag which is in front of him he holds with one hand, bag is open (12th version) 1921-1938 **1100.00 1200.00**

HN 493
☐ HN 480, blue hat and waistband (10th version) 1921-1938 **1100.00 1200.00**

HN 494
☐ White costume with blue waistband and blue turban, holds white bag over shoulder with one hand, white bag at feet also (2nd version) 1921-1938 **1100.00 1200.00**

HN 495
☐ HN 528, blue hat and waistband (1st version), height 5″ 1921-1938 **1100.00 1200.00**

HN 496
☐ HN 665, yellow hat and vase (13th version) 1921-1938 **1100.00 1200.00**

HN 497
☐ HN 480, brown hat, chequered trousers (10th version) 1921-1938 **1100.00 1200.00**

HN 498
☐ HN 494, dark striped coat, pale striped trousers (2nd version) 1921-1938 **1100.00 1200.00**

HN 499
☐ HN 480, cream costume, green hat (10th version) 1921-1938 **1100.00 1200.00**

ONE OF THE FORTY (cont.)	Date	Price Range
HN 500		
☐ HN 665, chequered coat and red hat (13th version)	1921-1938	**1100.00 1200.00**
HN 501		
☐ HN 528, green striped coat (1st version), height 5″	1921-1938	**1100.00 1200.00**
HN 528		
☐ Costume of brown, robe is browns and purple, waistband is green with red and yellow dots, turban is green, red and yellow squares, one hand on open bag at feet, other hand holds necklace, second bag open in front of him (1st version)	1921-1938	**1100.00 1200.00**
HN 645		
☐ HN 492, blue, black and white robes (12th version)	1924-1938	**1100.00 1200.00**
HN 646		
☐ HN 491, blue-black and white robes (2nd version)	1924-1938	**1100.00 1200.00**
HN 647		
☐ HN 494, blue, black and white robes (2nd version)	1924-1938	**1100.00 1200.00**
HN 648		
☐ HN 528, blue, black and white robes (1st version).....................	1924-1938	**1100.00 1200.00**
HN 649		
☐ HN 665, blue, black and white robes (13th version)	1924-1938	**1100.00 1200.00**
HN 663		
☐ HN 492, chequered red robes (12th version)	1924-1938	**1100.00 1200.00**
HN 664		
☐ HN 480, patterned yellow robes (10th version)	1924-1938	**1100.00 1200.00**
HN 665		
☐ Robes of orange with red and black stripes and black and green dots, turban of same colour, holding black bag and green jug or bottle (13th version)........................	1924-1938	**1100.00 1200.00**
HN 666		
☐ HN 494, chequered yellow robes (2nd version)	1924-1938	**1100.00 1200.00**
HN 667		
☐ HN 491, chequered yellow robes (11th version)	1924-1938	**1100.00 1200.00**

ONE OF THE FORTY (cont.)

	Date	Price Range	

HN 677
☐ HN 528, orange, green and red striped coat (1st version) 1924-1938 **1100.00 1200.00**

HN 704
☐ HN 494, chequered red robe (2nd version) 1925-1938 **1100.00 1200.00**

HN 712
☐ HN 491, chequered red robes (11th version) 1925-1938 **1100.00 1200.00**

HN 713
☐ HN 492, chequered red robes (12th version) 1925-1938 **1100.00 1200.00**

HN 714
☐ HN 480, patterned red robes (10th version) 1925-1938 **1100.00 1200.00**

HN 1336
☐ HN 491, mottled red, orange and blue robes (11th version) 1929-1938 **1100.00 1200.00**

HN 1350
☐ HN 491, multicoloured robes (11th version) 1929-1949 **1100.00 1200.00**

HN 1351
☐ HN 528, no colour detail available (1st version) 1929-1949 **1100.00 1200.00**

HN 1352
☐ HN 528, multicoloured robes (1st version) 1929-1949 **1100.00 1200.00**

HN 1353
☐ HN 494, multicoloured robes (2nd version) 1929-1949 **1100.00 1200.00**

HN 1354
☐ HN 665, multicoloured robes (13th version) 1929-1949 **1100.00 1200.00**

ONE THAT GOT AWAY, The

HN 2153
☐ Fisherman's costume of brown coat, green trousers, brown hat, black boots, on base of yellow and green, fishing basket of brown also on base, height 6¼", designer M. Davies. 1955-1959 **225.00 275.00**

ORANGE LADY, The

HN 1759
☐ Older lady in gown of pink, with shawl of black and red, hat black with red trim, two brown baskets with oranges, height 8¾", designer L. Harradine. 1936-1975 **225.00 275.00**

	Date	Price Range	

ORANGE LADY, The (cont.)
HN 1953
☐ Light green gown, shawl of black and green, height 8¾", designer L. Harradine. 1940-1975 200.00 250.00

ORANGE SELLER, The
HN 1325
☐ Gown of shaded greens and blues, blouse and apron of shaded reds and blues, head-covering of green with red trim holding brown basket of oranges, height 7", designer L. Harradine. 1929-1949 900.00 1000.00

ORANGE VENDOR, AN
HN   72
☐ Costume of light green, robe and hood darker green, face and hands are lighter colour, smaller brown basket of oranges. This model was made in earthenware, height 6¼", designer C. J. Noke. 1941-1949 700.00 800.00
HN 508
☐ Purple coat, height 6¼", designer C. J. Noke. 1921-1938 1000.00 1100.00
HN 521
☐ Pale blue costume, black collar, purple hood, height 6¼", designer C. J. Noke. 1921-1938 1000.00 1100.00
HN 1966
☐ Dark seated male figure in costume of shaded reds and blues, robe of darker blues and red, hood of shaded blues and reds, large basket of oranges in front of figure, height 6¼", designer C. J. Noke. 1917-1938 950.00 1100.00

ORGAN GRINDER, The
HN 2173
☐ Yellow/brown trousers, green coat, blue/red scarf, brown hat, on brown base, brown organ grinder instrument, monkey in red coat with yellow trim, blue trousers, height 8¾", designer M. Nicoll. 1956-1965 650.00 700.00

	Date	Price Range	

OUT FOR A WALK
HN 86
☐ Pink and grey dress, height unknown, designer H. Tittensor.   1918-1936   **2250.00   2500.00**

HN 443
☐ Chequered skirt, green coat with white fur trim, white muff, green hat with feather trim, height unknown, designer H. Tittensor.   1921-1936   **2250.00   2500.00**

HN 748
☐ Dark multicoloured dress, white muff, height unknown, designer H. Tittensor.   1925-1936   **2350.00   2500.00**

OWD WILLUM
HN 2042
☐ Character figure seated on green/ grey stones, dark green trousers, brown leg coverings, green coat, brown hat with darker brown band, very light tan vest, red tie, large mug of white and blue in one hand, red bag with white dots also on base, height 6¾", designer L. Harradine.   1949-1959   **275.00   325.00**

PAISLEY SHAWL
HN 1392
☐ White gown with shaded green and yellow flower designs, shawl of red paisley design, bonnet light red with darker red lining with feather trim, carrying parasol (1st version), height 9", designer L. Harradine.   1930-1949   **300.00   350.00**

HN 1460
☐ Gown of light green, shawl darker green with pink trim, bonnet dark green with red feather and ribbon trim, parasol is light red (1st version), height 9", designer L. Harradine.   1931-1949   **400.00   450.00**

HN 1707
☐ HN 1392, purple shawl, green hat (1st version), height 9", designer L. Harradine.   1935-1949   **525.00   575.00**

HN 1739
☐ Gown of shaded greens, shawl red with paisley designs of darker greens and black, bonnet has green feather and ribbons as trim, parasol is dark blue (1st version), height 9", designer L. Harradine.   1935-1949   **400.00   450.00**

PAISLEY SHAWL (cont.)	Date	Price Range	

HN 1914

☐ Small figure, green gown, shawl of red paisley design, bonnet green with black trim and blue ribbons, white feather, parasol, white with black, green, red trim (2nd version), height 9", designer L. Harradine. 1939-1949 300.00 350.00

HN 1987

☐ Light cream coloured gown, shawl paisley design black on red, bonnet black with red lining, blue feather and ribbons, parasol also blue (1st version), height 8½", designer L. Harradine. 250.00 300.00

HN 1988

☐ HN 1914, cream and light red skirt, black bonnet (2nd version), height 6¼", designer L. Harradine. 1946-1975 225.00 275.00

☐ **M 3** Made as a miniature, gown of blue, shawl mottled blue, bonnet and parasol also light blue, height 4", designer L. Harradine. 1932-1938 275.00 325.00

☐ **M 4** Gown of green, shawl darker green, bonnet black with red feather and ribbons, height 4", designer L. Harradine. 1932-1945 300.00 350.00

☐ **M-26** Gown of cream and green, shawl of red, bonnet black and red, parasol red, height 4", designer L. Harradine. 1932-1945 275.00 325.00

PAMELA

HN 1468

☐ Dark blue tiered gown with red sash, holding long stemmed flowers in one arm, height 8", designer L. Harradine. 1931-1938 750.00 850.00

HN 1469

☐ Tiered gown of shaded cream, red and green with red sash, height 8", designer L. Harradine. 1931-1938 650.00 750.00

HN 1564

☐ Tiered gown of cream and red, sash of red and blue, height 8", designer L. Harradine. 1933-1938 650.00 750.00

	Date	Price Range	

PAN ON ROCK

HN 621

☐ White nude figure of Pan seated on dark brown base, height unknown, designer unknown.   1924-1938   **1100.00   1200.00**

HN 622

☐ Black base, height unknown, designer unknown.   1924-1938   **1100.00   1200.00**

PANTALETTES

HN 1362

☐ Skirt of green with reddish blue jacket, white pantalettes, light green bonnet with red trim and ribbons, black shoes, 7¾", designer L. Harradine.   1929-1938   **350.00   400.00**

HN 1412

☐ Skirt of pink, jacket of blue trimmed in yellow and green, light green bonnet with darker green trim and ribbons, white pantalettes, red and black shoes, height 7¾", designer L. Harradine.   1930-1949   **350.00   400.00**

HN 1507

☐ HN 1362, yellow dress, height 7¾", designer L. Harradine.   1932-1949   **450.00   500.00**

HN 1709

☐ Red gown, red bonnet with very light blue trim and ribbons, red shoes, white pantalettes, height 7¾", designer L. Harradine.   1935-1938   **500.00   600.00**

☐ **M 15** Made as a miniature, light blue skirt, darker blue bodice, red bonnet with blue trim, height 3¾", designer L. Harradine.   1932-1945   **250.00   300.00**

☐ **M 16** Light red skirt, darker red bodice, black bonnet with red trim, height 3¾", designer L. Harradine. . .   1932-1945   **250.00   350.00**

☐ **M 31** Green skirt with darker green bodice, light bonnet with red trim, height 3¾", designer L. Harradine. . .   1932-1945   **250.00   300.00**

PARISIAN

HN 2445

☐ Grey trousers, blue jacket, brown shoes, brown tam, holding newspaper in hand, with brown fox at feet, height 8", designer M. Nicoll.   1972-1975   **225.00   275.00**

PARSON'S DAUGHTER

	Date	Price Range	

HN 337
☐ HN 564, lilac dress with brown floral pattern, height 10″, designer H. Tittensor.   1919-1938   800.00   900.00

HN 338
☐ Patterned blue dress, red bonnet and shawl, height 10″, designer H. Tittensor.   1919-1938   800.00   900.00

HN 441
☐ Yellow dress with orange spots, height 10″, designer H. Tittensor.   1921-1938   850.00   950.00

HN 564
☐ This figure is 10″ in height, skirt of yellow with red, blue, green and black blocks, red shawl and bonnet with black ribbon trim, large yellow sleeves, designer H. Tittensor.   1923-1949   350.00   400.00

HN 790
☐ Patchwork skirt, dark multicoloured shawl, height 10″, designer H. Tittensor.   1926-1938   550.00   600.00

HN 1242
☐ Patchwork skirt, lilac shawl with yellow lining, height 10″, designer H. Tittensor.   1927-1938   550.00   600.00

HN 1356
☐ Skirt of white with stripes of red, blue and black at hemline, upper portion has orange spots, large green sleeves, red shawl and bonnet with black ribbon trim, large yellow sleeves, height 9¼″, designer H. Tittensor.   1929-1938   475.00   550.00

HN 2018
☐ Darker patchwork skirt, purple hat and cloak, height 9¾″, designer H. Tittensor.   1949-1953   250.00   300.00

PAST GLORY

HN 2484
☐ Older male figure seated on brown and grey trunk, black trousers, red long coat, black cap with yellow trim, holding yellow bugle, height 7½″, designer M. Nicoll.   1973-1979   200.00   250.00

	Date	Price Range	
PATCHWORK QUILT, The			

HN 1984

☐ Seated figure in brown skirt, green blouse, white scarf and head covering, holding multicoloured quilt on lap, height 6″, designer L. Harradine. .   1945-1959   **450.00**   **500.00**

PATRICIA

HN 1414

☐ Gown of yellow with green sleeves and belt, black bonnet with green trim and ribbons with black tassels, height 8½″, designer L. Harradine. . .   1930-1949   **550.00**   **650.00**

HN 1431

☐ Gown of shaded blue and red, blue sleeves, black belt, bonnet light coloured with dark blue ribbons and yellow tassels, height 8½″, designer L. Harradine.   1930-1949   **550.00**   **650.00**

HN 1462

☐ Gown of green with darker green top, shaded blue/green sleeves, bonnet pink with blue trim and ribbons and tassels, blue belt, height 8½″, designer L. Harradine.   1931-1938   **550.00**   **650.00**

HN 1567

☐ Gown of red with light green belt, bonnet of shaded red and blues, height 8½″, designer L. Harradine. . .   1933-1949   **650.00**   **750.00**

☐ **M 7** Made as a miniature, gown of cream and light green, red bodice and sleeves, bonnet light green, height 4″, designer L. Harradine.   1932-1945   **300.00**   **350.00**

☐ **M 8** Gown of green, yellow, red, bonnet and ribbons of black, height 4″, designer L. Harradine.   1932-1938   **300.00**   **350.00**

☐ **M 28** Gown of shaded blues with dark blue sleeves, bonnet light with black trim, height 4″, designer L. Harradine.   1932-1945   **325.00**   **375.00**

PAULA

HN 2906

☐ Gown of yellow with green trim, green shoes, holding small brown box in one hand, height 7″, designer P. Parsons.   1980-   **185.00**

	Date	Price Range	
PAULINE			
HN 1444			
☐ Gown of mottled blues with green ribbon at bodice, green bonnet with darker green trim, height 6″, designer L. Harradine.	1931-1938	400.00	450.00
PAVLOVA			
HN 487			
☐ Small figure in ballet position on brown base, white ballet costume with very light colouring, white headdress, height 4¼″, designer C. J. Noke.	1921-1938	1500.00	1700.00
HN 676			
☐ Green base, height 4¼″, designer C. J. Noke.	1924-1938	1500.00	1700.00
PEARLY BOY			
HN 1482			
☐ Small figure of boy on cream coloured base, brown trousers, brown coat, red vest, green scarf with black dots, black cap with white trim (1st version), height 5½″, designer L. Harradine.	1931-1949	350.00	400.00
HN 1547			
☐ Green jacket, purple trousers (1st version), height 5½″, designer L. Harradine.	1933-1949	400.00	450.00
HN 2035			
☐ Trousers of brown and red, jacket of red and brown, vest of red, neck scarf with black dots, black hat with white trim, standing on reddish tint base (2nd version), height 5½″, designer L. Harradine.	1949-1959	225.00	250.00
PEARLY GIRL			
HN 1483			
☐ Small girl on light coloured base with pedestal, skirt of reds and greens, jacket of browns, reds and greens, large hat of brown with red and green feathers (1st version), height 5½″, designer L. Harradine.	1931-1949	350.00	400.00

Pearly Girl, HN1483, **350.00 — 400.00**

PEARLY GIRL (cont.)	Date	Price Range	
HN 1548			
☐ Purple bodice, green skirt (1st version), height 5½", designer L. Harradine.	1933-1949	**375.00**	**425.00**
HN 2036			
☐ Skirt of red and brown, jacket red, brown and green, green scarf with black dots, dark hat with red and green feathers, black shoes, white stockings, on light coloured base (2nd version), height 5½", designer L. Harradine.	1949-1959	**225.00**	**250.00**

PECKSNIFF
HN 535
☐ A character of Dicken's "Martin Chuzzlewit" (1st version), height 3¾", designer L. Harradine. 1922-   **45.00**   **60.00**

☐ **M 43** Renumbered as a miniature, height 4¼", designer L. Harradine. .. 1932-   **29.95**

	Date	Price Range	
PECKSNIFF (cont.)			
HN 553			
☐ Black trousers, also black long coat, yellow vest, white cravat, brown base with green bush (2nd version), height 7″, designer L. Harradine.	1923-1939	400.00	500.00
HN 1891			
☐ Very minor colour changes (2nd version), height 7″, designer L. Harradine.	1938-1952	400.00	450.00
HN 2098			
☐ Green base, brown trousers, black coat, orange vest, white cravat with blue tint, gold watch with chain (3rd version), height 7″, designer L. Harradine.	1952-1967	300.00	350.00
PEDLAR WOLF			
HN 7			
☐ Figure of wolf completely covered by robe of grey/white, height 5½″, designer C. J. Noke.	1913-1938	2000.00	2500.00
PEGGY			
HN 1941			
☐ HN 2038, minor glaze differences, height 5″, designer L. Harradine.	1940-1949	150.00	200.00
HN 2038			
☐ Gown of red, overdress of darker red trimmed in white, white head covering with ribbon, height 5″, designer L. Harradine.	1949-1979	75.00	125.00
PENELOPE			
HN 1901			
☐ Figure seated on multicoloured bench, gown of red with blue bows and trimmed in white, head covering is white with blue ribbon, small basket on bench, holding embroidering hoop and etc. in one hand, height 7″, designer L. Harradine.	1939-1975	350.00	400.00
HN 1902			
☐ Green petticoat, blue bodice, mauve and blue striped skirt, height 7″, designer L. Harradine.	1939-1949	550.00	600.00

Penny, HN2338, **65.00**

PENNY	Date	Price Range
HN 2338		
☐ Small figure in gown of white with overdress of green, height 4½ ", designer M. Davies.	1968-	**65.00**
HN 2424		
☐ Beautiful blond figure with undergown of delicate yellow, bodice and overgown are rich yellow, gown has layered frilled sleeves (2nd version), height 4¾ ", designer M. Davies.	1983-	**65.00**

PENSIVE MOMENTS

HN 2704

	Date	Price Range	
☐ Figure seated with large open parasol behind, gown of blue with white and black designs on hemline, light coloured hat with black ribbon trim and white flower lying on skirt, parasol is lavender and yellow, height 4⅞", designer M. Davies.	1975-1981	**150.00**	**200.00**

	Date	Price Range
PERFECT PAIR, The		

HN 581
☐ Two 18th century figures on single brown base, man's costume is black pants, long red coat trimmed in black, black shoes, white stockings, lady's costume is pink gown trimmed in lavender, red shoes, height 7″, designer L. Harradine.   1923-1938   1000.00   1100.00

PHILIPPA OF HAINAULT

HN 2008
☐ Gown of mottled reds and blues, red sleeves with white fur trim, belt of green with red designs, height 9¾″, designer M. Davies.   1948-1953   650.00   725.00

PHYLLIS

HN 1420
☐ 18th century style gown of shaded reds and greens, overlay of white with red and green designs, shawl lavender with spots of darker purples, light coloured hat with flower trim, single red flower in hand, basket of flowers on light coloured base, height 9″, designer L. Harradine.   1930-1949   550.00   650.00

HN 1430
☐ Dark blue shawl, striped pink skirt, height 9″, designer L. Harradine.   1930-1938   700.00   800.00

HN 1486
☐ Blue shawl, spotted pink overskirt, pink base, height 9″, designer L. Harradine.   1931-1949   650.00   750.00

HN 1698
☐ Blue/green gown with darker green overskirt, shawl white with red and black flower designs, green hat with red flower trim, flower basket green/brown, light green base, height 9″, designer L. Harradine.   1935-1949   750.00   850.00

PICARDY PEASANT (Female)

HN 4
☐ HN 351, white hat and blue skirt, height 9½″, designer P. Stabler.   1913-1938   1500.00   2000.00

HN 5
☐ Dove grey costume, height 9½″, designer P. Stabler.   1913-1938   1500.00   2000.00

	Date	Price Range

PICARDY PEASANT (Female) (cont.)

HN 17A
☐ Green hat and green costume, height
9½ ", designer P. Stabler. 1913-1938 1850.00 2000.00

HN 351
☐ Blue striped skirt, lighter blue blouse
with trim of blue and pink, apron,
white with blue stripes, hat, light blue
with darker blue dots, seated on light
pedestal type base, height 9½ ",
designer P. Stabler. 1919-1938 3000.00 3250.00

HN 513
☐ Blue blouse, spotted skirt, height
9½ ", designer P. Stabler. 1921-1938 1750.00 2000.00

PICARDY PEASANT (Male)

HN 13
☐ Blue costume with apron of lighter
blue, white cap, seated on pedestal
style blue base, height 9½ ", designer
P. Stabler. 1913-1938 1950.00 2000.00

HN 17
☐ Green hat and green trousers, height
9½ ", designer P. Stabler. 1912-1939 1850.00 2000.00

HN 19
☐ Green costume, height 9½ ", designer
P. Stabler. 1913-1938 1600.00 1850.00

PIED PIPER, The

HN 1215
☐ Dark brown base, costume of red leggings, red cloak with yellow lining,
red hat, black costume, height 8¾ ",
designer L. Harradine. 1926-1938 800.00 900.00

HN 2102
☐ Light brown base, beige costume,
cloak is black with red lining, blue hat
and shoes, height 8½ ", designer
L. Harradine. 1953-1976 250.00 300.00

PIERRETTE

HN 642
☐ Blue dress (1st version), height 7¼ ",
designer L. Harradine. 1924-1938 900.00 1000.00

HN 643
☐ Black pedestal style base, red tights,
costume is black, white and red
squares, black bodice, red sleeves,
white and red collar, white hat with
black balls (1st version), height 7¼ ",
designer L. Harradine. 1924-1938 900.00 1000.00

PIERRETTE (cont.)	Date	Price Range	

HN 644

☐ White tights, costume of white with a very few black squares, collar has black trim, hat white with black balls (1st version), height 7¼", designer L. Harradine..................... 1924-1938 **800.00 900.00**

HN 691

☐ HN 643, gold costume (1st version), height 7¼", designer L. Harradine. .. 1925-1938 **1250.00 1500.00**

HN 721

☐ Black and white striped skirt (1st version), height 7¼", designer L. Harradine......................... 1925-1938 **900.00 1000.00**

HN 731

☐ Spotted black and white skirt (1st version), height 7¼", designer L. Harradine......................... 1925-1938 **900.00 1000.00**

HN 732

☐ Black and white dress with petalled border (1st version), height 7¼", designer L. Harradine............. 1925-1938 **900.00 1000.00**

HN 784

☐ Jazzy markings, on pink costume with black muff (1st version), height 7¼", designer L. Harradine........ 1926-1938 **900.00 1000.00**

HN 795

☐ This figure is a miniature — pink roses on skirt, also made in colour schemes not recorded in pattern books (2nd version), height 3½", designer L. Harradine............. 1926-1938 **650.00 750.00**

HN 796

☐ Also miniature — white skirt with silver spots (2nd version), height 3½", designer L. Harradine............. 1926-1938 **650.00 750.00**

HN 1391

☐ Black pedestal style base, costume of red with tiny black, green and yellow blocks, collar is white with red and green trim, black hat with yellow balls, this figure is holding a black half mask (3rd version), height 8½", designer L. Harradine............. 1930-1938 **1000.00 1100.00**

HN 1749

☐ HN 643, pink and blue costume with playing card patterns (3rd version), height 8½", designer L. Harradine. .. 1936-1949 **1000.00 1100.00**

	Date	Price Range

PICNIC

HN 2308

☐ Small female figure seated on green/ yellow base, gown of yellow with white trim, blue scarf, brown shoes, brown basket, white cloth and white cups on base, height 3¾", designer M. Davies. 1965-   100.00

PILLOW FIGHT

HN 2270

☐ Small girl figure in pink nightgown with tiny design with white collar, holding white pillow over shoulder, height 5¼", designer M. Davies. 1965-1969   200.00   250.00

PINKIE

HN 1552

☐ Small figure on pedestal style light base, tiered gown of shaded reds, blue and red sash, white pantalettes, white hat with blue ribbon trim, holding small bouquet of blue flowers, height 5", designer L. Harradine. 1933-1938   450.00   500.00

HN 1553

☐ Yellow and blue dress, height 5", designer L. Harradine. 1933-1938   450.00   500.00

PIPER, The

HN 2907

☐ Scottish figure seated on green stone-like base, skirt of blue with black stripes, white shirt, brown vest, tam of dark blue, green stockings, brown shoes, bagpipe is brown, black and white, height 8", designer M. Abberley 1980-   250.00

PIRATE KING, The

HN 2901

☐ Character seated on black and white pirate flag on light tan base, costume of green shirt, white lace ruff, blue boots and blue braided jacket with plumed captain's hat, his belt holds dagger and pistol, height 10", designer W. K. Harper. 1981-   750.00

Pirouette, HN2216, 225.00 — 275.00

	Date	Price Range	
PIROUETTE			
HN 2216			
☐ Gown of cream with blue tint, with trim of red at waist and shoulder, height 5¾", designer M. Davies.	1959-1967	**225.00**	**275.00**
POACHER, The			
HN 2043			
☐ Character figure kneeling on one knee, brown trousers, blue/black coat, brown/orange vest and hat, red scarf with white dots, height 6", designer L. Harradine.	1949-1959	**325.00**	**375.00**
POKE BONNET			
HN 612			
☐ See classification "LILAC SHAWL, A," height 9½", designer C. J. Noke. .	1924-1938	**1350.00**	**1500.00**
HN 765			
☐ See classification "LILAC SHAWL, A," height 9½", designer C. J. Noke. .	1925-1938	**1500.00**	**1600.00**

POLKA, The	Date	Price Range	

POLKA, The
HN 2156
☐ Pink gown with white trim and yellow rose, height 7½ ", designer M. Davies.   1955-1969   **250.00   300.00**

POLLY PEACHUM
HN 463
☐ Character from "The Beggar's Opera," black base, gown of white with blue ribbon trim, white cap with blue ribbon (1st version), height 6¼ ", designer L. Harradine.   1921-1949   **600.00   700.00**
HN 465
☐ Red dress (1st version), height 6½ ", designer L. Harradine.   1921-1949   **500.00   600.00**
HN 489
☐ This figure in curtsey position, light green gown with white cap and green ribbon trim (2nd version), height 4¼ ", designer L. Harradine.   1921-1938   **400.00   500.00**
HN 549
☐ Gown is red (2nd version), height 4¼ ", designer L. Harradine.   1922-1949   **450.00   500.00**
HN 550
☐ Gown is pink (1st version), height 6½ ", designer L. Harradine.   1922-1949   **500.00   600.00**
HN 589
☐ HN 463, pink dress, yellow underskirt (1st version), height 6½ ", designer L. Harradine.   1924-1949   **500.00   600.00**
HN 614
☐ Pale pink dress, blue bows (1st version), height 6½ ", designer L. Harradine.   1924-1949   **600.00   700.00**
HN 620
☐ HN 489, Rose dress, cream underskirt (2nd version), height 4¼ ", designer L. Harradine.   1924-1938   **450.00   500.00**
HN 680
☐ HN 463, White dress with black, yellow and blue spots (1st version), height 6½ ", designer L. Harradine. . .   1924-1949   **600.00   700.00**
HN 693
☐ Deep rose pink dress with green bows (1st version), height 6½ ", designer L. Harradine.   1925-1949   **600.00   700.00**

POLLY PEACHUM (cont.)	Date	Price Range	
HN 694			
☐ HN 489, deep rose pink dress, green bows (2nd version), height 4¼", designer L. Harradine.	1925-1949	400.00	500.00
HN 698			
☐ This figure is miniature in curtsey position, pink gown (3rd version), height 2¼", designer L. Harradine. . .	1925-1949	400.00	500.00
HN 699			
☐ Blue dress (3rd version), height 2¼", designer L. Harradine.	1925-1949	400.00	500.00
HN 734			
☐ HN 489, black bodice, white skirt, black spots (2nd version), height 4¼", designer L. Harradine.	1925-1949	450.00	500.00
HN 757			
☐ HN 698, red bodice, spotted skirt and holding coloured streamers (3rd version), height 2¼", designer L. Harradine.	1925-1949	350.00	400.00
HN 758			
☐ Pink skirt with orange stripes (3rd version), height 2¼", designer L. Harradine.	1925-1949	350.00	400.00
HN 759			
☐ Yellow and white skirt with black spots (3rd version), height 2¼", designer L. Harradine.	1925-1949	350.00	400.00
HN 760			
☐ Mottled multicoloured skirt (3rd version), height 2¼", designer L. Harradine.	1925-1949	350.00	400.00
HN 761			
☐ Blue and purple skirt (3rd version), height 2¼", designer L. Harradine. . .	1925-1949	350.00	400.00
HN 762			
☐ Pink roses on skirt (3rd version), height 2¼", designer L. Harradine. . .	1925-1949	350.00	400.00
☐ **M 21** Miniature figures in curtsey position, deep red gown, height 2¼", designer L. Harradine.	1932-1945	325.00	375.00
☐ **M 22** Blue spotted gown, height 2¼", designer L. Harradine.	1932-1938	325.00	375.00
☐ **M 23** White gown with red and green stripes and with overlay of red with red and blue dots, height 2¼", designer L. Harradine.	1932-1938	325.00	375.00

	Date	Price Range	
POTTER, The			
HN 1493			
☐ Character figure seated on purple rug on brown base, robe and hood of dark brown and red, jugs and jars on base are multicoloured, height 7", designer C. J. Noke.	1932-	325.00	
HN 1518			
☐ Green cloak, height 7", designer C. J. Noke.	1932-1949	425.00	475.00
HN 1522			
☐ Dark blue and green cloak, height 7", designer C. J. Noke.	1932-1949	425.00	475.00
PREMIERE			
HN 2343			
☐ Gown of blue/white, cloak of darker green with white design on edge with yellow lining, black opera glasses, height 7½", designer M. Davies.	1969-1979	175.00	225.00
PRETTY LADY			
HN 69			
☐ HN 70, flowered blue dress, height 9½", designer H. Tittensor.	1916-1938	1250.00	1500.00
HN 70			
☐ Gown of very pale grey with raise white dots, height 9½", designer H. Tittensor.	1916-1938	1250.00	1500.00
HN 302			
☐ Patterned lilac dress, height 9½", designer H. Tittensor.	1918-1938	1350.00	1600.00
HN 330			
☐ Patterned blue dress, height 9½", designer H. Tittensor.	1918-1938	1450.00	1600.00
HN 361			
☐ Blue/green dress, height 9½", designer H. Tittensor.	1919-1938	1450.00	1600.00
HN 384			
☐ Red dress with striped skirt, height 9½", designer H. Tittensor.	1920-1938	1450.00	1600.00
HN 565			
☐ Orange dress, white sleeves with green spots, height 9½", designer H. Tittensor.	1923-1938	1450.00	1600.00
HN 700			
☐ Yellow dress with black spots, height 9½", designer H. Tittensor.	1925-1938	1500.00	1750.00

	Date	Price Range
PRETTY LADY (cont.)		
HN 763		
☐ Orange gown with sleeves of blue with black design, waistband of white with red spots and stripes, orange ribbon in hair, height 9½", designer H. Tittensor.	1925-1938	1450.00 1600.00
HN 783		
☐ HN 70, blue dress, height 9½", designer H. Tittensor.	1926-1938	1450.00 1600.00
PRIMROSES		
HN 1617		
☐ Character figure seated with brown basket at her side, red dress, white apron, shawl dark mottled with orange fringe, hat black with flower trim and black ribbons, height 6½", designer L. Harradine.	1935-1949	525.00 575.00
PRINCE OF WALES, The		
HN 1217		
☐ Riding costume of white trousers, black and red boots, red jacket, yellow vest, white cravat, black hat, dark brown base, height 7½", designer L. Harradine.	1926-1938	1450.00 1600.00
PRINCESS, A		
HN 391		
☐ Skirt of purple with green and yellow designs, green blouse, green cloak with orange round designs, has yellow lining, black rope type belt, height unknown, designer unknown.	1920-1938	2750.00 3000.00
HN 392		
☐ Multicoloured costume, striped skirt, height unknown, designer unknown.	1920-1938	2750.00 3000.00
HN 420		
☐ Pink and green striped skirt, blue cloak, height unknown, designer unknown.	1920-1938	2750.00 3000.00
HN 430		
☐ Green flowered dress, blue-green striped cloak, height unknown, designer unknown.	1921-1938	2750.00 3000.00

PRINCESS, A. (cont.)	Date	Price Range	

HN 431
☐ Pink dress, blue-green cloak, height unknown, designer unknown. 1921-1938 **2750.00 3000.00**

HN 633
☐ Black and white dress, height unknown, designer unknown. 1924-1938 **2750.00 3000.00**

PRISCILLA

HN 1337
☐ Gown of tiers of shaded reds, yellows, blues, pantalettes of same colour, hat and jacket of darker mottled colours, parasol also of same colours, base is black, height 8″, designer L. Harradine. 1929-1938 **500.00 600.00**

HN 1340
☐ Tiered gown of red with dark blue collar, bonnet and parasol are blue with darker blue trim, red shoe, black base, height 8″, designer L. Harradine. 1929-1949 **325.00 375.00**

HN 1495
☐ Gown of shaded blues with pink collar, bonnet, and parasol are green, pantalettes are white, height 8″, designer L. Harradine. 1932-1949 **500.00 600.00**

HN 1501
☐ Gown of shaded yellows, bonnet and parasol are green, shoes light red, base black, height 8″, designer L. Harradine. 1932-1938 **500.00 600.00**

HN 1559
☐ HN 1337, pink and yellow skirt, height 8″, designer L. Harradine. 1932-1949 **400.00 500.00**

☐ **M 13** Made as a miniature, gown of green and yellow, height 3¾″, designer L. Harradine. 1932-1938 **400.00 500.00**

☐ **M 14** Gown of shaded blue, height 3¾″, designer L. Harradine. 1932-1945 **275.00 325.00**

☐ **M 24** Gown of red with green bonnet, height 3¾″, designer L. Harradine. . . 1932-1945 **300.00 350.00**

	Date	Price Range
PROFESSOR, The		
HN 2281		
☐ Character figure seated on brown chair, brown suit, black robe with wine lining, white shirt with black bow tie holding open book, with books stacked beside chair, glasses on head and also on knee, height 7¼ ", designer M. Nicoll.	1965-1980	150.00 200.00
PROMENADE		
HN 2076		
☐ Two figures on black base, lady has shaded red skirt with blue overskirt trimmed in black, has high head piece of white and blue, male has red shoes, white stockings, white long coat with red, blue and black designs, multicoloured long vest, red sash and with black curly hair, height 8", designer M. Davies.	1951-1953	1150.00 1350.00
PROPOSAL (Lady)		
HN 715		
☐ Lady seated in brown and cream love-seat on black base, gown of red with shades of black, white cap with red and black ribbon, height 5¾ ", designer unknown.	1925-1938	950.00 1000.00
HN 716		
☐ Gown of white with a few black squares, white cap with black, height 5¾ ", designer unknown.	1925-1938	950.00 1000.00
HN 788		
☐ Gown of pink, height 5¾ ", designer unknown.	1926-1938	900.00 1000.00
PROPOSAL (Male)		
HN 725		
☐ Male on knee on black base, black shoes, white stockings, black trousers, black and white chequered long vest, coat of red with black and white trim, white with black trim at wrist and neck, holding black hat with red feathers, dark curly hair, height 5½ ", designer unknown.	1925-1938	950.00 1000.00
HN 1209		
☐ Blue coat, flowered pink waistcoat, height 5½ ", designer unknown.	1926-1938	900.00 1000.00

	Date	Price Range

PRUDENCE
HN 1883
☐ Seated figure in gown of shaded blues with lining of darker blue with red design, white collar and small close bonnet of white, height 6¾", designer L. Harradine. 1938-1949   750.00   800.00

HN 1884
☐ Gown of shaded reds with lining of white with blue designs, height 6¾", designer L. Harradine. 1938-1949   750.00   800.00

PRUE
HN 1996
☐ Gown of red with white apron and collar, darker red waistband, white cap with blue ribbon, carrying basket with fruit, height 6¾", designer L. Harradine. 1947-1955   325.00   375.00

PUFF AND POWDER
HN 397
☐ HN 398, yellow skirt, brown bodice, height unknown, designer L. Harradine. 1920-1938   2000.00   2200.00

HN 398
☐ Gown of lavender with black and white designs, bodice of purple, overskirt of yellow with black and white designs, height unknown, designer L. Harradine. 1920-1938   2000.00   2200.00

HN 400
☐ Green and blue bodice, yellow skirt, height unknown, designer L. Harradine. 1920-1938   2000.00   2200.00

HN 432
☐ Lilac skirt with orange spots, height unknown, designer L. Harradine. 1921-1938   2000.00   2200.00

HN 433
☐ Yellow skirt with blue spots, height unknown, designer L. Harradine. 1921-1938   2000.00   2200.00

	Date	Price Range	
PUNCH AND JUDY MAN			

HN 2765

☐ Light tan base, costume of elderly man in yellow trousers, green sweater, black shoes, puppets are male with costumes of red, yellow and black, lady's costume blue dress, green shawl and white hat, height 9″, designer W. K. Harper.   1981-   **295.00**

PUPPETMAKER, The

HN 2253

☐ Brown trousers, green vest, white shirt, small cap of brown and tan, boy puppet costume of red and green and girl puppet dress of green and overdress of light and dark blue, height 8″, designer M. Nicoll.   1962-1973   **425.00   475.00**

PUSSY

HN   18

☐ Barefooted girl seated holding black cat in lap, gown of light blue, height 7½ ″, designer F. C. Stone.   1913-1938   **2400.00   2600.00**

HN   325

☐ White dress with black patterning, height 7½ ″, designer F. C. Stone. . . .   1918-1938   **2450.00   2650.00**

HN   507

☐ Spotted blue dress, height 7½ ″, designer F. C. Stone.   1921-1938   **2400.00   2600.00**

PYJAMS

HN 1942

☐ Small figure on white base wearing light red pajamas trimmed in white and blue stripe, holding blue ball, height 5¼ ″, designer L. Harradine. . .   1940-1949   **325.00   375.00**

QUALITY STREET

HN 1211

☐ Gown of red with blue and red long scarf, bonnet light coloured with red feathers and red ribbons, height 7¼ ″, designer unknown.   1926-1938   **1100.00   1200.00**

	Date	Price Range

RACHEL
HN 2919
☐ Green gown, yellow ochre hooded coat trimmed with brown fur, height 7½ ", designer P. Gee.   1981-   185.00

RAG DOLL
HN 2142
☐ Small figure in blue gown with bibbed white apron, white cap, holding doll wrapped in red, height 4¾ ", designer M. Davies.   1954-   75.00

REBECCA
HN 2805
☐ Gown of pink with floral design at hemline, overskirt of blue with darker blue trim, pink ribbon in hair, holding single red flower, height 7¼ ", designer M. Davies.   1980-   325.00

REFLECTIONS
HN 1820
☐ HN 1821, red dress, lilac sofa, height 5", designer L. Harradine.   1937-1938   1000.00 1100.00

HN 1821
☐ Orange and green sofa, gown of green with trim of white, large white cap with red trim, multicoloured pillow on sofa, height 5", designer L. Harradine.   1937-1938   1000.00 1100.00

HN 1847
☐ Green sofa, shaded red gown with white trim, red bonnet with blue ribbons, blue shoes, light green pillow on sofa, height 5", designer L. Harradine.   1938-1949   1000.00 1100.00

HN 1848
☐ Green skirt, height 5", designer L. Harradine.   1938-1949   1000.00 1100.00

REGAL LADY
HN 2709
☐ Cream with yellow shadings skirt with gold trim on hemline, dark blue overdress, height 7⅝", designer M. Davies.   1975-   170.00

REGENCY	Date	Price Range	

HN 1752

☐ Skirt of shaded green with red, green and purple stripes at hemline, long jacket of purple with green and red trim, white cravat, triangular hat of green with red trim, holding white and brown riding crop, height 8″, designer L. Harradine.   1936-1949   600.00   700.00

REGENCY BEAU

HN 1972

☐ 18th century costume of red with black buttons, cloak of green, black triangular hat, black shoes, white with black trim at wrist and neck, white stockings, on light coloured base, height 8″, designer H. Fenton. .   1941-1949   850.00   950.00

RENDEZVOUS

HN 2212

☐ Gown of light green with overdress of shaded reds standing beside pedestal of white with red roses on top, height 7¼″, designer M. Davies.   1962-1971   350.00   400.00

REPOSE

HN 2272

☐ Chaise lounge of green and brown, barefoot figure in gown of rose with blue trim, green ribbon in hair, holding small book, height 5¼″, designer M. Davies.   1972-1979   150.00   200.00

REST AWHILE

HN 2728

☐ Older lady figure seated on brown stile on green base, gown of grey/blue with white apron, purple jacket, bonnet is grey/blue with red flowers and grey/blue ribbons, holding brown basket with a green and white striped cover, height 8″, designer W. K. Harper.   1981-   200.00

	Date	Price Range	

RETURN OF PERSEPHONE, The
HN 31
☐ This is a large two figure on one base (16″), one costume in robes of grey, second figure has cream coloured gown, base is green with bush on one end, height 16″, designer C. Vyse. ...   1913-1938   **4000.00 5000.00**

REVERIE
HN 2306
☐ Figure seated on chaise lounge of brown and white, gown of peach and yellow with white trim, holding open book on lap, pillow of grey and pillow of purple, height 6½″, designer M. Davies.   1964-1981   **250.00 300.00**

RHAPSODY
HN 2267
☐ Gown of blue/green, long yellow scarf, holding small white fan in one hand, height 6¾″, designer M. Davies   1961-1973   **200.00 250.00**

RHODA
HN 1573
☐ Skirt of muted yellow and blue, bodice of red, shawl is red with colours of green, yellow and red trimmed in dark red and blue, bonnet green with green feather and purple ribbons, height 10¼″, designer L. Harradine.   1933-1949   **575.00 650.00**

HN 1574
☐ Gown of purple with red bow trim, shawl of red with shaded greens, bonnet green with light green feather and purple ribbons, height 10¼″, designer L. Harradine.   1933-1938   **500.00 550.00**

HN 1688
☐ Gown of orange with purple bodice, shawl of red with large green and black flower design with green fringe, bonnet black with green feather and dark ribbons, height 10¼″, designer L. Harradine.   1935-1949   **550.00 650.00**

RHYTHM
HN 1903
☐ HN 1904, pink dress, height 6¾″, designer L. Harradine.   1939-1949   **575.00 625.00**

	Date	Price Range	
RHYTHM (cont.)			

HN 1904

☐ Blue gown with overskirt of blue with darker blue and gold flower designs, height 6¾", designer L. Harradine. . .   1939-1949   575.00   625.00

RITA

HN 1448

☐ HN 1450, yellow and pink dress, height 7", designer L. Harradine.   1931-1938   600.00   700.00

HN 1450

☐ Blue patterned tiered gown with shawl of brown, bonnet is brown with green ribbons, parasol is green, white and yellow, height 7", designer L. Harradine.   1931-1938   600.00   700.00

RIVER BOY

HN 2128

☐ Small figure of boy kneeling on green base, dark blue trousers, very light green shirt, cream coloured hat holding black frying pan over fire, height 4", designer M. Davies.   1962-1975   150.00   200.00

ROBERT BURNS

HN   42

☐ Scottish figure on black base, brown trousers, green coat, orange vest, white cravat, brown tam with green ball trim, scarf of yellow with brown stripes, height 18", designer E. W. Light.   1914-1938   3000.00   3500.00

ROBIN

Girl on hands and knees
Issued only as a miniature

☐ **M 38** Red shirt with blue collar, blue shorts on green stand, height 2½", designer unknown.   1933-1945   275.00   325.00

☐ **M 39** Blue shirt with red collar, green shorts on tan stand, height 2½", designer unknown.   1933-1945   275.00   325.00

Rocking Horse, HN2072, **1450.00 — 1750.00**

ROCKING HORSE, The	Date	Price Range
HN 2072			
☐ Rocking horse on brown base, horse is light blue-grey with red cloth and red straps, rocking base is cream with red and yellow trim, boy figure in blue pants, lighter blue shirt, black shoes, height 7″, designer L. Harradine.	1951-1953	**1450.00** **1750.00**

ROMANCE		
HN 2430		
☐ Figure seated in green chair, gown of yellow with brown trim at hemline, black shoe, holding open book on lap, height 5¼″, designer M. Davies.	1972-1979	**125.00** **175.00**

	Date	Price Range	
ROMANY SUE			
HN 1757			
☐ Green gown with white apron which has pink stripes, shawl of red and blue with fringe of green, black hat with blue/red feather, carrying basket of vegetables and flowers on each arm, height 9½″, designer L. Harradine.	1936-1949	650.00	750.00
HN 1758			
☐ Gown of lavender with apron, also lavender with darker stripe shawl of cream with blue designs and green fringe, hat dark green with blue/red feather, two baskets are of darker brown, height 9½″, designer L. Harradine.	1936-1949	650.00	750.00
ROSABELL			
HN 1620			
☐ Seated figure with skirt of muted blue/red, red bodice, red hat with blue/red feather, shawl is multicoloured, height 6¾″, designer L. Harradine.	1934-1938	900.00	1000.00
ROSALIND			
HN 2393			
☐ Gown of dark blue with white flower design and large white cuffs, dark hair, holding white fan in one hand, flower in other, height 5½″, designer M. Davies.	1970-1975	150.00	200.00
ROSAMUND			
HN 1320			
☐ Skirt shaded green, jacket light red, long scarf of purple white, green and red, tall crown hat of green with black feather and red band (1st version), height 7½″, designer L. Harradine.	1929-1938	1500.00	2000.00
HN 1497			
☐ Full skirted gown of red with ligher red trim, green hat, long necklace with cross, small bouquet of flowers in hand (2nd version), height 8½″, designer L. Harradine.	1932-1938	800.00	1000.00

	Date	Price Range	

ROSAMUND (cont.)

HN 1551
☐ Gown of blue trimmed in ligher blue, hat is of shaded reds and blues, necklace and cross is of white, height 8½", designer L. Harradine. . . . . | 1932-1938 | 450.00 | 500.00
☐ **M 32** Made as a miniature, gown of shaded yellows and blue, also hat, height 4¼", designer L. Harradine. . . | 1932-1945 | 250.00 | 375.00
☐ **M 33** Gown of shaded reds and blues, red hat, height 4¼", designer L. Harradine. . . . . | 1932-1945 | 325.00 | 375.00

ROSE

HN 1368
☐ Small figure in tiered red gown, height 4⅝", designer L. Harradine. . . . | 1930- | 65.00 |
HN 1387
☐ Flowered blue and pink dress, orange roses, height 4½", designer L. Harradine. . . . . | 1930-1938 | 250.00 | 300.00
HN 1416
☐ Tiered gown of shaded blues, height 4½", designer L. Harradine. . . . . | 1930-1949 | 150.00 | 200.00
HN 1506
☐ Yellow dress, height 4½", designer L. Harradine. . . . . | 1932-1938 | 250.00 | 300.00
HN 1654
☐ Green bodice, flowered skirt, height 4½", designer L. Harradine. . . . . | 1934-1938 | 250.00 | 300.00
HN 2123
☐ Gown is layers of flounces, color is mauve, height 4½", designer L. Harradine. . . . . | 1983- | 65.00 |

ROSEANNA

HN 1921
☐ HN 1926, green dress, height 8", designer L. Harradine. . . . . | 1940-1949 | 400.00 | 450.00
HN 1926
☐ Gown of shaded red with blue/red hemline, with blue/green bow trim on bodice, dark bows in hairs, standing with hands on bowl of flowers on pedestal, height 8", designer L. Harradine. . . . . | 1940-1959 | 300.00 | 350.00

	Date	Price Range	
ROSEBUD			

HN 1580

☐ Very small figure, seated, in wide ruffled and pleated gown of pink (1st version), height 3″, designer L. Harradine. 1933-1938   **600.00   700.00**

HN 1581

☐ Pale dress with flower sprays (1st version), height 3″, designer L. Harradine. 1933-1938   **600.00   700.00**

HN 1983

☐ This is larger figure, gown of shaded reds, with light green cross design as trim, darker red shawl, green bonnet with white trim, carrying small basket of flowers with flowers in other arm (2nd version), height 7½″, designer L. Harradine. 1945-1952   **450.00   500.00**

ROSEMARY

HN 2091

☐ Gown of red with shawl of blue with red designs, dark blue bonnet with white scarf, carrying basket of flowers, height 7″, designer L. Harradine. 1952-1959   **450.00   500.00**

ROSINA

HN 1358

☐ Seated figure, gown of red with cape of red with white fur trim, red bonnet with purple ribbons, height 5½″, designer L. Harradine. 1929-1938   **750.00   850.00**

HN 1364

☐ Gown and cape of purple with red wide stripe as trim, which has dark dots, bonnet red with purple trim and red ribbons, height 5½″, designer L. Harradine. 1929-1938   **750.00   850.00**

HN 1556

☐ Gown of cream with shaded blues and reds, bonnet shaded reds and blues with red trim and ribbons, height 5½″, designer L. Harradine. . . 1933-1938   **500.00   600.00**

	Date	Price Range

ROWENA
HN 2077
☐ Underskirt is shaded green and red, overskirt is red, next overlay is dark red with blue and black designs, muff is brown, bonnet is green with shaded blue ribbons, height 7½", designer L. Harradine. 1951-1955   550.00   650.00

ROYAL GOVERNOR'S COOK
HN 2233
☐ Seated coloured figure, gown of dark blue with white apron and crossed white scarf, white head covering, holding pink bowl on lap, height 6", designer M. Davies. 1960-   200.00

RUBY
HN 1724
☐ Tiered gown of shaded red and white, dark flowers on blue ribbons in hair, holding small bouquet in hand, height 5¼", designer L. Harradine. 1935-1949   300.00   350.00
HN 1725
☐ Tiered gown of shaded blues, flowers on ribbon in hair are red on red ribbon, height 5¼", designer L. Harradine. 1935-1949   300.00   350.00

RUSTIC SWAIN, The
HN 1745
☐ Two figures on brown couch, lady's gown of white with red and blue flower design, overlay of green, bonnet and shoes green, man's costume of brown and white, dark brown hat, brown shoes, pillow on couch is red and white stripes, height 5¼", designer L. Harradine. 1935-1949   1750.00   2250.00
HN 1746
☐ Man's costume of green, height 5¼", designer L. Harradine. 1935-1949   1850.00   2350.00

	Date	Price Range

RUTH (Kate Greenaway)
HN 2799
☐ Green gown with red and yellow flowers at hemline, white waistband and collar, large white cap with red ribbon, holding single flower in one hand, on white base, height 6⅛″, designer M. Davies. 1976-1982   100.00

RUTH THE PIRATE MAID
HN 2900
☐ Costume of brown striped skirt, blue blouse with gold and black trim, white apron, black captains hat with trim of gold and white skull and cross bones, on mottled brown base, height 11¾″, designer W. K. Harper. 1981-   750.00

SABBATH MORN
HN 1982
☐ Gown of red, shawl and parasol of mottled green and yellow, bonnet red with green and white trim with blue ribbons, height 7¼″, designer L. Harradine. 1945-1959   300.00   350.00

SAILOR'S HOLIDAY
HN 2442
☐ Kneeling character figure on dark brown and purple base, purple trousers, yellow coat, green coloured sweater, black cap, black tie, light purple shirt, holding small sail boat of blue, tan and white, height 6¼″, designer M. Nicoll. 1972-1979   200.00   250.00

SAIREY GAMP
HN 533
☐ This figure is miniature — A character from Dicken's "Martin Chuzzlewit" (1st version), height 4″, designer L. Harradine. 1922-   45.00   60.00
☐ **M 46** Renumbered as a miniature. Gown of light green, black cloak, white, pink head cap with black ribbons, red small round cloth with black dots in one hand, height 4″, designer L. Harradine. 1932-   29.95

	Date	Price Range	

SAIRY (cont.)

HN 558

☐ Larger figure, dressed in black on black base, black bonnet with white trim, blue round cloth bag with white dots, umbrella of green and blue (2nd version), height 7″, designer L. Harradine. 1923-1939   400.00   500.00

HN 1896

☐ Very minor colour changes (2nd version), height 7″, designer L. Harradine. 1938-1952   325.00   375.00

HN 2100

☐ Gown of very light green, darker green cloak, black bonnet with white trim, red round cloth bag with white dots, umbrella of black, black shoes, on black base (3rd version), height 7¼″, designer L. Harradine. 1952-1967   275.00   325.00

SALOME

HN 1828

☐ Tinted finish, height unknown, designer R. Garbe. 1937-1949   4500.00   5000.00

SAM WELLER

HN 531

☐ A character in Dicken's "Pickwick Papers" (1st version), height 4″, designer L. Harradine. 1922-   45.00   60.00

☐ **M 48** Renumbered as a miniature, brown trousers, yellow vest with red stripes, red neck scarf, black hat, seated on black base, height 4″, designer L. Harradine. 1932-   29.95

SANDRA

HN 2275

☐ Gown of tan, with trim and petticoat of white with brown dots, brown hat to match gown, height 7¾″, designer M. Davies. 1969-   155.00

Santa Claus, HN2725, **195.00**

SANTA CLAUS	Date	Price Range	
HN 2725			
☐ Character figure in brilliant red suit with white fur, black boots, holding aloft a teddy bear in one hand and a sack of toys in the other, height 9½ ", designer W. K. Harper.	1982-	**195.00**	
SARA			
HN 2265			
☐ Gown of white with red bodice and overskirt, collar is white with blue flowers design, height 7½ ", designer M. Davies.	1981-	**215.00**	
SAUCY NYMPH, A			
HN 1539			
☐ Small white nude figure seated on mottled green, red, brown base, height 4½ ", designer unknown.	1933-1949	**275.00**	**325.00**

	Date	Price Range

SCHOOLMARM
HN 2223

☐ Character figure seated at brown bench type desk, gown of grey, shawl of purple, white head cap with black ribbon, desk has red and grey inkwell, dunce hat of white beside desk, world globe under desk of white, black, orange and brown, height 6¾", designer M. Davies.   1958-1980   150.00   200.00

SCOTCH GIRL
HN 1269

☐ Costume of red with dark brown and black stripes, jacket dark brown with white trim, stockings red with black stripes, on pedestal style black base, height 7½", designer L. Harradine. . .   1928-1938   1350.00   1500.00

SCOTTIES
HN 1281

☐ Figure seated on cream coloured bench, dress of red, red shoes, one black scottie on bench, the other at side of bench, height 5¼", designer L. Harradine.   1928-1938   1100.00   1200.00

HN 1349

☐ Pale multicoloured costume, white dogs, height 5¼", designer L. Harradine.   1929-1949   1500.00   1600.00

SCRIBE, A
HN 305

☐ Figure seated on blue and gold cushion, robes of green, costume of yellow, turban of blue, light purple shoes, height 6", designer C. J. Noke.   1918-1936   1100.00   1200.00

HN 324

☐ Cushion of dark green and orange, costume and robes of shades of brown, green and blue turban, green shoes, height 6", designer C. J. Noke.   1918-1938   1100.00   1200.00

HN 1235

☐ Brown coat, blue hat, height 6", designer C. J. Noke.   1927-1938   1100.00   1200.00

	Date	Price Range	

SCROOGE
Issued only as a miniature
☐ **M 87** White cap, brown coat, black
money bag in hands, tan shoes, black
stand, height 4″, designer L. Harradine   1949-   29.95

SEAFARER, The
HN 2455
☐ Character figure seated on light blue
pedestal on blue base, blue trousers,
black boots with red trim, yellow zip-
pered sweater, blue shirt, black cap,
base has bird on it, height 8½″,
designer M. Nicoll.   1972-1976   225.00   275.00

SEA HARVEST
HN 2257
☐ Blue coat, brown trousers, black
boots, black rain hat, holding large
brown net, height 7½″, designer
M. Nicoll.   1969-1976   150.00   200.00

SEASHORE
HN 2263
☐ Small boy figure in red swim trunks,
on light brown base, height 3½″,
designer M. Davies.   1961-1965   250.00   300.00

SEA SPRITE
HN 1261
☐ Small white nude figure standing on
black rock style base with long red
and black scarf behind figure (1st version), height 5″, designer L. Har-
radine.   1927-1938   600.00   650.00
HN 2191
☐ Barefooted figure in blue and white
shell, pink gown (2nd version), height
7″, designer M. Davies.   1958-1962   475.00   525.00

SECRET THOUGHTS
HN 2382
☐ Seated figure, gown of shaded greens
and yellow, blue bow in hair, holding
two pink roses, leaning on cream coloured pedestal, height 6¼″, designer
M. Davies.   1971-   215.00

	Date	Price Range

SENTIMENTAL PIERROT, The
HN 36
☐ HN 307, dove grey costume, height 13½ ", designer C. J. Noke. 1914-1938 1750.00 1900.00
HN 307
☐ Seated male figure in costume of black and white, height 13½ ", designer C. J. Noke. 1918-1938 1750.00 1900.00

SENTINEL
HN 523
☐ Figure in knight's costume on black base, costume is of grey and red, shield has three golden lion's heads, height 17½ ", designer unknown. 1921-1938 4500.00 5000.00

SERENA
HN 1868
☐ Gown of red with blue ruffle trim, undergown of light red with design of red, yellow and blue, red shoe, height 11", designer L. Harradine. 1938-1949 1100.00 1200.00

SHE LOVES ME NOT
HN 2045
☐ Small boy figure on yellow/green base, blue suit with white straps, barefooted, red hair, height 5½ ", designer L. Harradine. 1949-1962 150.00 200.00

SHEPHERD, A
HN 81
☐ Black base, blue/grey trousers, brown coat, brown hat with light coloured scarf tied around it, holding lantern in one hand and small lamb in other arm. Made in earthenware (1st version), height 13¼ ", designer C. J. Noke. 1918-1938 2250.00 2500.00
HN 617
☐ China body and purple-blue trousers and coat (1st version), height 13¼ ", designer C. J. Noke. 1924-1938 1750.00 2000.00
HN 632
☐ China body and white smock, blue trousers (1st version), height 13¼ ", designer C. J. Noke. 1924-1938 1750.00 2000.00

SHEPHERD, A (cont.)	Date	Price Range	
HN 709			
☐ This is a miniature figure, green jacket, red cloak and black trousers (1st version), height 3½", designer unknown..........................	1925-1938	550.00	650.00
HN 751			
☐ Yellow and brown base, costume of black trousers, green coat, red cloak, white shirt, black hat, black cane, single flower in hand (3rd version), height 7", designer unknown.............	1925-1938	1500.00	1750.00
HN 1975			
☐ Green base, brown trousers, tan long coat, red scarf, brown hat, carrying lantern and staff (4th version), height 8½", designer H. Fenton...........	1945-1975	150.00	200.00
☐ **M 17** Made as a miniature, in the style of HN 751, brown trousers, blue coat, red cloak, height 3¾", designer unknown...........................	1932-1938	550.00	700.00
☐ **M 19** Brown trousers, blue coat and blue cloak, height 3¾", designer unknown...........................	1932-1938	550.00	700.00
SHEPHERDESS			
HN 708			
☐ This is a miniature, on yellow/brown base, red overskirt with yellow and pink striped skirt (1st version), height 3½", designer unknown............	1925-1948	650.00	750.00
☐ **M 18** Made as a miniature, green bodice, pink overskirt. height 3½", designer unknown................	1932-1938	600.00	700.00
☐ **M 20** Yellow bodice, flowered dress, height 3¾", designer unknown......	1932-1938	600.00	700.00
HN 735			
☐ Yellow/green base, black shoes with red bows, multicoloured skirt with overlay of purple, yellow trim on sleeves, dark bow in hair (2nd version), height 7", designer unknown...	1925-1938	1500.00	1750.00
HN 750			
☐ Pink bodice, yellow skirt (2nd version), height 7", designer unknown...	1925-1938	1500.00	1750.00

	Date	Price Range

SHORE LEAVE
HN 2254
☐ Character figure seated on grey stone-line wall, black suit, black cap, grey sweater, green parrot on shoulder, bag between feet, wicker basket at side, height 8″, designer M. Nicoll.   1965-1979   **200.00   250.00**

SHY ANNE
HN 60
☐ HN 64, flowered blue dress, height 7¾″, designer L. Perugini.   1916-1938   **1500.00 1600.00**

HN 64
☐ Light coloured base, girl figure with white dress with raised white design, white large bow in hair, says Shy Anne on base, height 7¾″, designer L. Perugini.   1916-1938   **1500.00 1600.00**

HN 65
☐ Spotted blue dress with dark blue hem, height 7¾″, designer Perugini. .   1916-1938   **1550.00 1800.00**

HN 568
☐ Black base, dress of shaded green with darker dots, yellow ribbon around waist, bow in hair is dark blue and pink squares, stockings are pink and dark blue stripes, height 7¾″, designer L. Perugini.   1923-1938   **1450.00 1600.00**

SHYLOCK
HN 79
☐ HN 317, multicoloured cloak, yellow sleeves, height unknown, designer C. J. Noke.   1917-1938   **2500.00 2750.00**

HN 317
☐ Shaded robes of blue and purple, head cap of same, height unknown, designer C. J. Noke.   1918-1938   **2500.00 2750.00**

SIBELL
HN 1668
☐ 18th century gown of light green with blue bow trim, overskirt is red with white trim, hat is black with red trim, height 6½″, designer L. Harradine. . .   1934-1949   **600.00   700.00**

HN 1695
☐ Gown of green with blue bows, overskirt is orange with multicoloured designs, height 6½″, designer L. Harradine.   1935-1949   **600.00   700.00**

	Date	Price Range	

SIBELL (cont.)

HN 1735

☐ HN 1668, blue and green gown, height 6½ ", designer L. Harradine.   1935-1949   800.00   850.00

SIESTA

HN 1305

☐ White nude figure lying on couch of dark red with shaded reds and blues in cloth covering couch, height 4¾ ", designer L. Harradine.   1928-1938   1350.00   1500.00

SILK AND RIBBONS

HN 2017

☐ Character figure seated on wooden bench, dark green dress, shawl dark green with black stripes, black bonnet with red ribbons, box of different coloured ribbons on lap, white apron, brown wicker basket, height 6", designer L. Harradine.   1949-   150.00

SILVERSMITH OF WILLIAMSBURG

HN 2208

☐ White coloured base with brown pedestal which contains grey object, brown trousers, blue long vest, white shirt, brown head covering, black shoes, white stockings, height 6¼ ", designer M. Davies.   1960-   200.00

SIMONE

HN 2378

☐ Shaded green gown with white cuffs and black trim around top, blue/yellow ribbons in hair, holding small fan in one hand, height 7¼ ", designer M. Davies.   1971-1981   135.00   185.00

SIR THOMAS LOVELL

HN 356

☐ Brown base, costume of browns and red, sleeves green with yellow and red design, brown hat with orange feather, brown stockings and black shoes, height 7¾ ", designer C. J. Noke.   1919-1938   1500.00   1700.00

Sir Walter Raleigh, HN2015, **750.00 — 850.00**

SIR WALTER RALEIGH	Date	Price Range	
HN 1742			
☐ Black base, costume of red stockings, red and white costume of purple vest, cloak of dark green, hat is black, height 10½ ", designer L. Harradine. .	1935-1949	**700.00**	**800.00**
HN 1751			
☐ Earthenware model, with minor glaze differences, height 11½ ", designer L. Harradine.	1936-1949	**1000.00**	**1100.00**
HN 2015			
☐ Green base, brown stockings, costume of orange with brown designs and stipes, black cloak with blue and red, hat black, height 11½ ", designer L. Harradine.	1948-1955	**750.00**	**850.00**

	Date	Price Range
SKATER, The		
HN 2117		
☐ Skirt of red, white jacket with brown collar, brown sash, bonnet light yellow with blue ribbons, brown muff on cords, height 7¼ ", designer M. Davies	1953-1971	350.00 400.00
SLEEPYHEAD		
HN 2114		
☐ Over-stuffed chair with red, orange, yellow and blue, girl in dress of white with black trim, teddy bear brown, dunce style hat of black and white, cushion blue, height 5", designer M. Davies.	1953-1955	800.00 900.00
SLEEP		
HN 24		
☐ Light blue gown and hood, holding naked baby to shoulder on light blue base, height 8", designer P. Stabler. .	1913-1938	2000.00 2250.00
HN 24A		
☐ Dark blue dress, height 8", designer P. Stabler.	1913-1938	2200.00 2400.00
HN 25		
☐ Blue-green dress, height 8", designer P. Stabler.	1913-1938	2500.00 2800.00
HN 25A		
☐ Fewer firings, height 8", designer P. Stabler.	1913-1938	2500.00 2800.00
HN 424		
☐ HN 24, smaller figure with blue dress, height 8", designer P. Stabler.	1921-1938	2000.00 2200.00
HN 692		
☐ Smaller figure with gold dress, height 8", designer P. Stabler.	1925-1938	2050.00 2200.00
HN 710		
☐ Smaller figure with matt vellum finish, height 8", designer P. Stabler. .	1925-1938	2050.00 2200.00
SLEEPY SCHOLAR, The		
HN 15		
☐ HN 16, blue costume, height 6¾ ", designer W. White.	1913-1938	1650.00 1800.00

	Date	Price Range

SLEEPY SCHOLAR, THE (cont.)
HN 16
- ☐ Seated figure on blue/grey basket on light green base, dress of shaded yellow and green with narrow green trim on hemline, black shoes with gold trim, height 6¾", designer W. White. . 1913-1938   1550.00   1700.00

HN 29
- ☐ Brown costume, height 6¾", designer W. White. 1913-1938   1450.00   1600.00

SMILING BUDDHA, The
HN 454
- ☐ Rotune seated figure of blue/green, costume is patterned blue, very tiny Chinese figure on one knee, height 6¼", designer C. J. Noke. 1921-1938   1250.00   1400.00

SNAKE CHARMER, The
HN 1317
- ☐ Seated figure on multicoloured base which has small snake on it, costume of black, green and red, figure is brown, turban is green with black and red, basket is brown and red, pipe is yellow and brown, height 4", designer unknown. 1929-1938   1000.00   1100.00

SOIREE
HN 2312
- ☐ Gown of white with gold design at hemline, overskirt of green, holding small white fan in one hand, height 7½", designer M. Davies. 1967-   170.00

SOLITUDE
HN 2810
- ☐ Figure seated on chaise lounge of brown and yellow, gown of white with mottled yellow, green, blue halfway up skirt, pillow multicoloured, holding open book on pillow, height 5½", designer M. Davies. 1977-   215.00

Song Of The Sea, HN2729, **150.00**

	Date	Price Range
SONG OF THE SEA		

HN 2729

☐ Depicts a weather beaten man with blue turtle neck sweater, denim trousers, black boots with white socks. Young boy at his feet. Man seated on fishbasket, holding shell in his hand. Boy has green short trousers, light blue shirt, height 7¼ ", designer W. K. Harper. 1983- **150.00**

SONIA

HN 1692

☐ Figure seated on arm of brown and green chair, white tiered gown with red bodice and sleeves, small red hat with white trim, red shoes, black small purse on chair, flowers also, height 6¼ ", designer L. Harradine. .. 1935-1949 **650.00** **750.00**

	Date	Price Range	

SONIA (cont.)
HN 1738
☐ Green dress, height 6½", designer
L. Harradine. 1935-1949   750.00   850.00

SONNY
HN 1313
☐ Seated barefoot figure in red cos-
tume, top has white dots, height 3½",
designer L. Harradine. 1929-1938   600.00   700.00
HN 1314
☐ Blue costume, height 3½", designer
L. Harradine. 1929-1938   600.00   700.00

SOPHIE (Kate Greenaway)
HN 2833
☐ Small figure on white base, mauve
coat with white fur trim, white fur
muff, large bonnet of light red, holding single flower, height 6", designer
M. Davies. 1977-   100.00

SOUTHERN BELLE
HN 2229
☐ Gown of shaded yellows with overskirt of red with blue bow, trim on
sleeves, blue shoe, height 7½", de-
signer M. Davies. 1958-   185.00

SPANISH LADY
HN 1262
☐ Brown base, gown of patterned purple with large red rose design, bodice
patterned purple with small red design, mantilla of brown, blue and
black, necklace of dark grey, height
8½", designer L. Harradine. 1927-1938   900.00   1000.00
HN 1290
☐ Yellow dress, height 8¼", designer
L. Harradine. 1928-1938   900.00   1000.00
HN 1293
☐ Skirt of patterned purple with large
yellow rose design, bodice with small
red design, mantille brown and blue,
necklace green, height 8¼", designer
L. Harradine. 1928-1938   900.00   1000.00

	Date	Price Range
SPANISH LADY (cont.)		
HN 1294		
☐ Tiered gown of red, mantilla of brown, green and black, necklace white, light brown base, height 8¼", designer L. Harradine.	1928-1938	900.00 1000.00
HN 1309		
☐ HN 1262, black bodice, multicoloured skirt, height 8¼", designer L. Harradine.	1929-1938	900.00 1000.00
SPIRIT OF THE WIND		
☐ Entire figure and base is of green, beginning at the head it is a very light green, lower torso and gown is a darker green, base and flowers on base of still another green, height unknown, designer R. Garbe.	1937-1949	3500.00 4000.00
SPOOK, A		
HN 50		
☐ Figure wrapped entirely in robe of blue, black cap, height 7", designer H. Tittensor.	1916-1938	1100.00 1200.00
HN 51		
☐ Robe of green with red cap, height 7", designer H. Tittensor.	1916-1938	1250.00 1400.00
HN 51A		
☐ Black cap, height 7", designer H. Tittensor.	1916-1938	1250.00 1400.00
HN 51B		
☐ Blue cloak, height 7", designer H. Tittensor.	1916-1938	1250.00 1400.00
HN 58		
☐ Colour not recorded, height 7", designer H. Tittensor.	1916-1938	1250.00 1400.00
HN 512		
☐ Spotted blue costume, height 7", designer H. Tittensor.	1921-1938	1250.00 1400.00
HN 625		
☐ Yellow robe, height 7", designer H. Tittensor.	1924-1938	1250.00 1400.00
HN 1218		
☐ Multicoloured costume, blue cap, height 7", designer H. Tittensor.	1926-1938	1250.00 1400.00

	Date	Price Range

SPOOKS

HN   88

☐ Two figures wrapped in shaded blue robes, dark blue caps, height 7″, designer H. Tittensor.   1918-1936   **1400.00 1650.00**

HN   89

☐ Red caps, height 7″, designer H. Tittensor.   1918-1936   **1400.00 1650.00**

HN 372

☐ Patterned green costume, brown caps, height 7″, designer H. Tittensor.   1920-1936   **1400.00 1650.00**

SPRING

HN 312

☐ Blue/grey base, long narrow gown of yellow, holds small bird in hands (1st version), height 7½″, designer unknown.   1918-1938   **1500.00 1800.00**

HN 472

☐ Patterned robes (1st version), height 7½″, designer unknown.   1921-1938   **1500.00 1800.00**

HN 1827

☐ White base, barefooted figure in very light yellow robe with gold flowers held with both hands (2nd version), height 21″, designer R. Garbe.   1937-1949   **2500.00 3000.00**

HN 2085

☐ Cream/green base, gown of shaded blues and reds, bodice is darker blue, blouse white, tiny blue/red cap, small white lamb on base (3rd version), height 7¾″, designer M. Davies.   1952-1959   **450.00   500.00**

SPRING FLOWERS

HN 1807

☐ Gown of light green, overskirt of shaded blue, white apron and white collar, bonnet blue with green lining and dark ribbons, holding flower in one hand and small basket of flowers in other arm, light coloured basket of flowers on light coloured base, height 7¼″, designer L. Harradine.   1937-1959   **325.00   375.00**

HN 1945

☐ Green skirt, pink overskirt, height 7¼″, designer L. Harradine.   1940-1949   **500.00   550.00**

	Date	Price Range	

SPRING MORNING

HN 1922

☐ Gown of very light blue, long pink coat, scarf of blue and green, bonnet has white feather and dark blue ribbons, height 7½″, designer L. Harradine.   1940-1973   **225.00**   **275.00**

HN 1923

☐ Gown of green, long coat of red, scarf of green and yellow, bonnet blue with white feather and darker blue ribbons, height 7½″, designer L. Harradine.   1940-1949   **300.00**   **350.00**

SPRINGTIME

HN 1971

☐ Small girl figure in blue gown, peach coat, green bonnet hanging head on green ribbons, holding single flower in hand, height 6″, designer L. Harradine.   1941-1949   **900.00**   **950.00**

SQUIRE, The

HN 1814

☐ This figure is made of earthenware, figure seated on blue and white horse mounted on black base, red jacket, white trousers, black boots, black hat, height 9¾″, designer unknown. .   1937-1949   **2100.00**   **2600.00**

ST GEORGE

HN 385

☐ HN 386, blue-green multicoloured costume (1st version), height 16″, designer S. Thorogood.   1920-1938   **4500.00**   **5000.00**

HN 386

☐ Horse and base dark coloured, cloth over horse is white with dark blue, yellow and red designs, armor in blue/grey, shield is white with blue design, figure has dark hair (1st version), height 16″, designer S. Thorogood. . .   1920-1938   **4500.00**   **5000.00**

HN 1800

☐ White horse with white robe green overlay with crosses as a design. Knight has blue/grey armor, hair dark, robe is red with gold lion and purple border, (1st version), height 16″, designer S. Thorogood.   1934-1950   **3000.00**   **3500.00**

	Date	Price Range

HN 2051
☐ Yellow and green base, white horse with gold straps, figure has green/blue armor with white overskirt with red cross, green dragon alson base (2nd version), height 7½", designer M. Davies. 1950-   475.00

HN 2067
☐ Multicoloured base, horse is light coloured with cloth of purple with gold lions and red lining, figure has grey/blue armor with shield of white with red stripes, figure has blonde hair (1st version), height 15¾", designer S. Torogood. 1950-1976   3750.00   4500.00

STAYED AT HOME
HN 2207
☐ Green gown with darker green collar, white apron, holding white pig in arms, green head ribbon, height 5", designer M. Davies. 1958-1969   150.00   200.00

STEPHANIE
HN 2807
☐ Gown of yellow with brown trim near hemline, white trim on sleeves, height 7¼", designer M. Davies. 1977-   170.00

HN 2811
☐ Gown crimson red and off white, dark brown hair, height 7½", designer M. Davies. 1983-

STIGGINS
HN 536
☐ A character of Dicken's "Pickwick Papers," 3¾", designer L. Harradine. 1922-   45.00   60.00
☐ **M 50** Renumbered as a miniature, height 4", designer L. Harradine. 1932-   29.95

STITCH IN TIME, A
HN 2352
☐ Character figure seated in brown rocking chair, with brown and red foot stool, gown of dark grey, brown shawl, green suit for child on lap, coloured threads on chair arm, height 6¼", designer M. Nicoll. 1966-1980   150.00   200.00

	Date	Price Range

STOP PRESS
HN 2683
☐ Character figure seated on wooden box, blue trousers, brown coat, beige vest, light green hat with dark band, reading newspaper and eating roll, newspapers on stand next to figure, height 7½ ", designer M. Nicoll.   1977-1980   **200.00   250.00**

SUITOR, The
HN 2132
☐ Two figures, male kneeling has beige trousers, dark brown coat, yellow vest, white cravat, female has cream coloured gown with overskirt of shadedblues, height 7¼ ", designer M. Davies.   1962-1971   **400.00   475.00**

SUMMER
HN 313
☐ Long slender gown of light green, bouquet of flowers in left arm on blue/grey base (1st version), height 7½ ", designer unknown.   1918-1938   **1650.00   1800.00**

HN 473
☐ Patterned gown (1st version), height 7½ ", designer unknown.   1921-1938   **1650.00   1800.00**

HN 2086
☐ Green/yellow base with brown wooden fence, gown of red with blue designs, blue waistband, blue shoes, white scarf (2nd version), height 7¼ ", designer M. Davies.   1952-1959   **450.00   500.00**

SUMMER'S DAY
HN 2181
☐ Seated figure on white wicker trunk, gown of white with gold designs, white bonnet with gold trim beside trunk, height 5¾ ", designer M. Davies   1957-1962   **375.00   450.00**

SUNDAY BEST
HN 2206
☐ Gown of yellow with large white and red flower design in skirt, bonnet of yellow with red ribbons and flowers, height 7½ ", designer M. Davies.   1979-   **295.00**

	Date	Price Range
SUNDAY MORNING		
HN 2184		
☐ Cloak of red with darker red yoke with yellow bow trim and sleeves, bonnet with dark red ribbons and black and white feather, height 7½ ", designer M. Davies.	1963-1969	265.00 325.00
SUNSHINE GIRL		
HN 1344		
☐ Green/yellow base with red and white towel, figure seated on towel is in green and black bathing suit, bathing cap of green with black dots, black and red open parasol, height 5", designer L. Harradine.	1929-1938	1400.00 1500.00
HN 1348		
☐ Black and orange costume, height 5", designer L. Harradine.	1929-1938	1400.00 1500.00
SUSAN		
HN 2056		
☐ Skirt of blue, blouse darker blue with white collar, apron very light red with small blue design, little white cap, height 7", designer L. Harradine.	1950-1959	325.00 375.00
HN 2952		
☐ Young lady with blonde hair, gown is gold with an overdress of pale blue, black jacket with blue belt, holding a white kitten aloft (2nd version), height 8½ ", designer P. Parsons.	1982-	175.00
SUSANNA		
HN 1233		
☐ White nude figure on red coloured base, long red robe hanging down back from hands, has white designs, height 6½ ", designer L. Harradine. . .	1927-1938	1100.00 1200.00
HN 1288		
☐ Yellow/green base, white nude figure with robe hanging down back which is reds and blues, height 6", designer L. Harradine.	1928-1938	1100.00 1200.00
HN 1299		
☐ HN 1233, black-red and blue robe, height 6", designer L. Harradine.	1928-1938	1100.00 1200.00

SUZETTE

	Date	Price Range	

HN 1487

☐ Light green gown with patterned red overgown, solid blue/red bodice, green/blue head cap with green ribbons, blue/white apron, height 7½″, designer L. Harradine.   1931-1950   **325.00**   **375.00**

HN 1577

☐ Light red gown with patterned blue overgown, blue/red bodice, white apron, light red head cap with red ribbons, height 7½″, designer L. Harradine.   1933-1949   **500.00**   **550.00**

HN 1585

☐ HN 1487, green and yellow dress, height 7½″, designer L. Harradine. . .   1933-1938   **500.00**   **600.00**

HN 1696

☐ Gown of blue with small red flower designs, blue shoes, small blue head cap with dark blue ribbons, height 7½″, designer L. Harradine.   1935-1949   **400.00**   **450.00**

HN 2026

☐ HN 1487, minor colour differences, height 7¼″, designer L. Harradine. . .   1949-1959   **325.00**   **375.00**

SWEET ANNE

HN 1318

☐ Skirt of shaded blues and greens, jacket dark blue with black trim, bonnet dark blue with dark red ribbons, height 7½″, designer L. Harradine. . .   1929-1949   **200.00**   **250.00**

HN 1330

☐ Skirt of shaded reds, jacket shaded blue and green, bonnet and ribbons of red, height 7¼″, designer L. Harradine.   1929-1949   **325.00**   **375.00**

HN 1331

☐ Skirt of shaded yellow and blue, jacket red with purple trim, bonnet red with purple ribbons, height 7¼″, designer L. Harradine.   1929-1949   **300.00**   **350.00**

HN 1453

☐ Skirt of light green, jacket shaded blues with darker blue trim, bonnet blue with purple ribbons, height 7″, designer L. Harradine.   1931-1949   **325.00**   **375.00**

	Date	Price Range
SWEET ANNE (cont.)		
HN 1496		
☐ Skirt of red with jacket of patterned red, bonnet is shaded red and blue, also ribbons, height 7", designer L. Harradine......................	1932-1967	**225.00** **275.00**
HN 1631		
☐ HN 1318, green bonnet, red jacket, pink and yellow skirt, height 7", designer L. Harradine...............	1934-1938	**300.00** **400.00**
HN 1701		
☐ Flowered yellow and pink dress, blue trim, height 7", designer L. Harradine.	1935-1938	**300.00** **400.00**
☐ **M 5** Made as a miniature, gown of cream with red shading, jacket of shaded red and blues, bonnet same with dark ribbons, height 4", designer L. Harradine......................	1932-1945	**300.00** **375.00**
☐ **M-6** Gown of light blue designs, jacket of darker blue, bonnet also, height 4", designer L. Harradine.	1932-1945	**300.00** **375.00**
☐ **M-27** Gown of cream with shaded blues, jacket of red with blue trim, bonnet red with blue ribbons, height 4", designer L. Harradine...........	1932-1945	**300.00** **375.00**
SWEET AND FAIR		
HN 1864		
☐ HN 1865, blue shawl with pink dress, height 7½", designer L. Harradine. ...	1938-1949	**650.00** **700.00**
HN 1865		
☐ Figure is seated on brown chair, skirt of light green, bodice darker green, sleeves have trim of blue, shawl draped on chair back is white with multicoloured flowers, open book in hand, height 7¼", designer L. Harradine..........................	1938-1949	**650.00** **700.00**
SWEET AND TWENTY		
HN 1298		
☐ Figure seated on small couch of shaded blues, gown of red, bonnet black with multicoloured ribbons, holding open fan, height 5¾", designer L. Harradine...............	1928-1969	**225.00** **275.00**

Sweet And Twenty, HN1298, **225.00 — 275.00**

SWEET AND TWENTY (cont.)

	Date	Price Range	
HN 1360			
☐ Couch of blue, gown of shaded reds and blues, bonnet dark blue with shaded red and blue ribbons, height 6″, designer L. Harradine.	1929-1938	450.00	500.00
HN 1437			
☐ HN 1298, dark sofa, shaded red dress, height 6″, designer L. Harradine.	1930-1938	400.00	450.00
HN 1438			
☐ Mottled multicoloured dress, height 6″, designer L. Harradine.	1930-1938	450.00	500.00
HN 1549			
☐ Couch of light multicoloured, gown is dark multicoloured in skirt and lighter at waist and bodice, bonnet of light multicolours, height 6″, designer L. Harradine.	1933-1949	350.00	400.00
HN 1563			
☐ HN 1298, black sofa, pale pink dress, height 6″, designer L. Harradine.	1933-1938	450.00	500.00

SWEET AND TWENTY (cont.)	Date	Price Range	

SWEET AND TWENTY (cont.)

HN 1589
- ☐ This figure is of small size, couch light green, gown red and blue, bonnet blue/red with blue ribbon, height 6″, designer L. Harradine. 1933-1949   225.00   275.00

HN 1610
- ☐ This figure is of small size, couch is blue/green, gown red, bonnet black with yellow ribbon, height 3½″, designer L. Harradine. 1933-1938   275.00   325.00

HN 1649
- ☐ HN 1298, couch of orange, gown of white with small red designs, green bodice, green bonnet with shaded red ribbons, height 6″, designer L. Harradine. 1934-1949   450.00   500.00

SWEET APRIL

HN 2215
- ☐ Gown of light red with blue/red collar, hat blue with green bow on top, height 7¼″, designer L. Harradine. . . 1965-1969   325.00   400.00

SWEET DREAMS

HN 2380
- ☐ Character figure seated in cream coloured chair with green skirt, head on brown pillow, foot on purple stool, gown of green with bibbed apron of white with red design, green shoes, holding small child on lap in blue and red sleeper, height 5″, designer M. Davies. 1971-   150.00

SWEETING

HN 1935
- ☐ Gown of red and shaded blues, blue bow in hair, height 6″, designer L. Harradine. 1940-1973   200.00   250.00

HN 1938
- ☐ Skirt multicoloured, bodice blue, bow in hair red, height 6″, designer L. Harradine. 1940-1949   325.00   375.00

	Date	Price Range	

SWEET LAVENDER

HN 1373

☐ Black base, skirt cream with red stripes, blouse green, shawl is black, red and light green, hat green with black feather and trim, basket brown, small baby in arm is dressed in red, red, necklace, lavender in basket, height 9″, designer L. Harradine. .... 1930-1949 — 650.00 — 750.00

SWEET MAID

HN 1504

☐ Gown of blue, cape darker blues, bonnet shaded red and blue with red ribbons, small round red purse, height 8″, designer L. Harradine. .... 1932-1938 — 900.00 — 1000.00

HN 1505

☐ Gown of shaded red and blue, cape dark red and blue, bonnet red with green ribbons, small purse is also green (1st version), height 8″, designer L. Harradine. .... 1932-1938 — 900.00 — 1000.00

HN 2092

☐ Light lavender gown, white headdress with white veil with small design and purple ribbons, holding small round bouquet of flowers in hands, height 7″, designer L. Harradine. .... 1952-1955 — 450.00 — 500.00

SWEET SEVENTEEN

HN 2734

☐ Gown of white with gold narrow trim, height 7½″, designer D. V. Tootle. ... 1975- — 185.00

SWEET SIXTEEN

HN 2231

☐ White base, light blue skirt, blouse white with small black design, black belt, black shoes, red bow in blonde hair, height 7¼″, designer M. Davies. 1958-1965 — 275.00 — 325.00

SWEET SUZY

HN 1918

☐ Light green gown, overdress of light red with dark green trim, black bonnet with green ribbon trim, height 6½″, designer L. Harradine. .... 1939-1949 — 650.00 — 750.00

Swimmer, HN1270, 1100.00 — 1200.00

SWIMMER, The	Date	Price Range	
HN 1270			
☐ Black base, swim suit black with red, green, purple spots, red bathing shoes with spots, robe of red with black design, height 7¼", designer L. Harradine.	1928-1938	1100.00	1200.00
HN 1326			
☐ Lilac and orange costume, height 7½", designer L. Harradine.	1929-1938	1300.00	1400.00
HN 1329			
☐ Pink costume, height 7½", designer L. Harradine.	1929-1938	1300.00	1400.00
SYLVIA			
HN 1478			
☐ Gown of mottled orange and brown, jacket blue/grey and brown, bonnet yellow with brown feather, scarf of shaded red and cream, small round orange and brown purse, height 10½", designer L. Harradine.	1931-1938	700.00	800.00

	Date	Price Range

SYMPHONY

HN 2287

☐ Light green skirt, brown bodice with light green bow, holding mandolin type instrument of brown and blue/grey on lap, height 5¼", designer D. B. Lovegrove. 1961-1965 **350.00 425.00**

TAILOR

HN 2174

☐ Seated character figure, red trousers, cream shirt, vest of orange, working or purple coat with orange buttons, bolts of different coloured cloth at side, height 5", designer M. Nicoll. . . . 1956-1959 **650.00 750.00**

TAKING THINGS EASY

HN 2677

☐ Male figure seated in brown wicker chair, white trousers and shoes, blue coat, grey hat with light trim, news-papers on lap, also black rimmed glasses, height 6¾", designer M. Nicoll 1975- **125.00**

TALL STORY

HN 2248

☐ Character figure seated on wooden bench, dark grey trousers, darker grey jacket, black cap with yellow trim, black boots with white cuff, tackle box beside bench, height 6½", de-signer M. Nicoll. 1968-1975 **200.00 250.00**

TEATIME

HN 2255

☐ Gown of brown with darker reddish brown jacket, beige blouse, holding white teapot and cup and saucer with blue design, height 7¼", designer M. Nicoll. 1972- **165.00**

TEENAGER

HN 2203

☐ Slender dress of white with red cape, height 7¼", designer M. Davies. 1957-1962 **275.00 325.00**

	Date	Price Range

TERESA
HN 1682
☐ Lady seated on loveseat of brown and multicolour, gown of red with red shoes and small white cap with green ribbon, the base is black with small brown table with flowers on table and base, height 5¾", designer L. Harradine. 1935-1949   800.00   900.00

HN 1683
☐ Pale blue dress, height 5¾", designer L. Harradine. 1935-1938   900.00   1000.00

TESS (Kate Greenaway)
HN 2865
☐ Small figure on white base, green gown with red flower trim at hemline, red waistband and single red flower in hand, height 5¾", designer M. Davies . 1978-   100.00

TETE-A-TETE
HN 798
☐ HN 799, gown of lady is pink with shades of very light blue with white stripes and blue/red bows on bodice. Male costume is brownish orange with a cravat of white with green, hat is black with orange design, couch is designed purple and yellow with brown, pillow is very bright blue with dark red and gold design, all on black base (1st version), height 5¾", designer L. Harradine. 1926-1938   1150.00   1300.00

HN 799
☐ Two figures on base of black, also couch of brown, gown of lady is lavender with red pattern, overskirt of purple, male has costume of red with white, black hat with red trim (1st version), height 5¾", designer L. Harradine. 1926-1938   1150.00   1300.00

HN 1236
☐ Colour and design same but in miniature size (2nd version), height 3", designer C. J. Noke. 1927-1938   650.00   750.00

HN 1237
☐ Pink dress (2nd version), height 3", designer C. J. Noke. 1927-1938   650.00   700.00

THANKS DOC	Date	Price Range

HN 2731

☐ Brown trousers, white long coat, white shirt, dark tie, dog is brown and white sitting on brown stand, white towel on side, height 8¾", designer W. K. Harper.............................. 1975-   **200.00**

THANK YOU

HN 2732

☐ Old lady standing at cottage gate waving goodbye to someone who has given her a bouquet of bluebells. Hair is grey, long brown skirt, white blouse with pink flowers, wearing cameo brooch, height 8¼", designer W. K. Harper. 1983-   **145.00**

This Little Pig, HN1793, **75.00**

	Date	Price Range	

THANKSGIVING

HN 2446

☐ Light brown base, character figure in blue overalls, red shirt, light coloured hat, turkey also on base, matt finish, height 8″, designer M. Nicoll. 1972-1976   200.00   250.00

THIS LITTLE PIG

HN 1793

☐ Small seated figure wrapped completely in red robe with small design of blue, height 4″, designer L. Harradine. 1936-   75.00

HN 1794

☐ Small figure wrapped completely in robe of blue with green, height 4″, designer L. Harradine. 1936-1949   300.00   350.00

TIBETIAN LADY

HN 582

☐ Formal name is "Grossmith's 'Tsang lhang' Perfume of Tibet, see that classification, height 11½″, designer unknown. 1923-Unknown   650.00   700.00

TILDY

HN 1576

☐ Seated figure in tiered goen of shaded colours, bodice of red, trimmed with blue bows, bonnet of shaded blue with darker blue ribbons, light blue shoes, white pantalettes, height 5″, designer L. Harradine. 1933-1938   700.00   800.00

HN 1859

☐ No details of colour available, height 5½″, designer L. Harradine. 1938-1949   800.00   900.00

TINKLE BELL

HN 1677

☐ Small figure in shaded red gown with darker red bodice, small white cap with red ribbons, small light coloured basket on one arm, height 4¾″, designer L. Harradine. 1935-   75.00

	Date	Price Range	

TINSMITH

HN 2146

☐ Character figure seated, brown trousers, mottled brown stockings, ligher brown shirt, green vest, white cravat, working on blue/grey material, tools in front of green/grey stump, height 6½ ", designer M. Nicoll.   1962-1967   450.00   500.00

TINY TIM

HN 539

☐ A character from Dicken's "Christmas Carol," height 3½ ", designer L. Harradine.   1922-   45.00   60.00

☐ **M 56** Renumbered as a miniature, height 3¾ ", designer L. Harradine. . .   1932-   29.95

TO BED

HN 1805

☐ Small figure on light blue coloured base, pulling light green shirt over head, light green shorts, barefooted, height 6", designer L. Harradine.   1937-1959   150.00   200.00

HN 1806

☐ Green base, shirt and shorts are very light blue and red, height 6", designer L. Harradine.   1937-1949   150.00   200.00

TOINETTE

HN 1940

☐ Full tiered red gown with darker red jacket, stole of black trimmed with white fur, green bonnet, open parasol in one hand, flowers in other, height 6¾ ", designer L. Harradine.   1940-1949   1450.00   1750.00

TOM (Kate Greenaway)

HN 2864

☐ Small male figure on white base, blue trousers, cream coloured shirt with red designs and white collar, holding single flower in one hand and toy horse of white and yellow with other hand, height 5¾ ", designer M. Davies   1978-1981   85.00   110.00

Tom, HN2864, **85.00 — 100.00**

TONY WELLER	Date	Price Range	
HN 346			
☐ HN 684, green coat, blue rug, brown base (1st version), height 10½", designer C. J. Noke.	1919-1938	1800.00	2000.00
HN 368			
☐ Blue coat, brown blanket (1st version), height 10½", designer C. J. Noke.	1920-1938	1800.00	2000.00
HN 544			
☐ This figure is miniature, green coat, dark brown suit, red vest, white shirt, yellow with dark spots cravat, black hat (2nd version), height 3½", designer L. Harradine.	1922-	45.00	60.00
☐ **M 47** Renumbered as a miniature, height 4", designer L. Harradine.	1932-	29.95	

	Date	Price Range

TONY WELLER (cont.)

HN 684

☐ Black base, long green coat, undercoat is orange with black buttons, rug is red with black stripes, hat black, scarf is orange with black dots (1st version), height 10½ ", designer L. Harradine. 1924-1938 1650.00 1800.00

TOOTLES

HN 1680

☐ Small figure, gown skirt is shaded reds with blue stripes, red bodice, green apron with green stripes, white bonnet with green ribbons, height 4¾ ", designer L. Harradine. 1935-1975 110.00 150.00

TOP 'O THE HILL

HN 1833

☐ Skirt of green, jacket shades of blue, dark blue large brim hat, scarf of blue/green with red designs, height 7 ", designer L. Harradine. 1937-1971 175.00 225.00

HN 1834

☐ Gown of red, hat red with light green lining, scarf is mottled yellow and green, height 7", designer L. Harradine. 1937- 170.00

HN 1849

☐ Gown of dark pink, hat black with blue ribbon and lining, scarf striped red and blue, height 7¼ ", designer L. Harradine. 1938-1975 225.00 275.00

TOWN CRIER

HN 2119

☐ Brown base, yellow trousers, red coat trimmed in yellow, black cloak with red colouring, vest green patterned, black hat trimmed in yellow, black boots with red tops ringing bell and holding white papers, height 8½ ", designer M. Davies. 1953-1976 250.00 300.00

	Date	Price Range	

TOYMAKER, The
HN 2250
☐ Character figure seated in dark grey rocker holding red engine, brown trousers, blue/green shirt, grey vest, green shoes, tools and toys at sides of rocker, height 6″, designer M. Nicoll . . 1959-1973 **425.00 475.00**

TOYS
HN 1316
☐ Skirt of green, white apron with blue stripes, red jacket, yellow scarf with green dots and red fringe, black hat with green feathers, holding small black tray with three male dolls, height unknown, designer L. Harradine. 1929-1938 **1200.00 1500.00**

TREASURE ISLAND
HN 2243
☐ Small barefooted boy seated on white base, purple shorts, light brown shirt, holding open book on lap, book shows printing, height 4¾″, designer M. Davies. 1962-1975 **150.00 200.00**

TROTTY VECK
Issued only as a miniature.

☐ **M 91** Orange vest, white apron, brown hat, black coat and stand, height 4¼″, designer L. Harradine. 1949- **29.95**

TULIPS
HN 466
☐ HN 747, green dress, height 9½″, designer unknown. 1921-1938 **1500.00 1700.00**
HN 488
☐ Ivory dress, height 9½″, designer unknown. 1921-1938 **1500.00 1700.00**
HN 672
☐ Green shawl and cream dress, height 9½″, designer unknown. 1924-1938 **1550.00 1700.00**

	Date	Price Range	
TULIPS (cont.)			
HN 747			
☐ Purple dress with small black designs, shawl is green with red thin stripes, holding bouquet of flowers in one hand, height 9½ ", designer unknown.	1925-1938	1550.00	1700.00
HN 1334			
☐ Pink and blue shawl and green dress, height 9½ ", designer unknown.	1929-1938	1550.00	1700.00
TUPPENCE A BAG			
HN 2320			
☐ Seated character figure on blue/green bricks, basket beside figure, green gown, blue shawl, black brimmed hat, one bird on shoulder and one on basket handle, height 5½ ", designer M. Nicoll.	1968-	165.00	
TWILIGHT			
HN 2256			
☐ Character figure seated in brown rocker with purple pad and purple foot stool, knitting with black kitten playing with yarn, gown of dark green, shawl black, small white headcap, height 5", designer M. Nicoll.	1971-1976	200.00	250.00
TWO-A-PENNY			
HN 1359			
☐ Green and yellow shaded skirt, red jacket with black collar and buttons, shawl yellow with green stripes, black hat with green and black feathers, white apron, holding black tray with green and black objects, height 8¼ ", designer L. Harradine.	1929-1938	1200.00	1500.00
UNCLE NED			
HN 2094			
☐ Character figure seated in brown and beige chair, green trousers, long brown coat and leggings, yellow and green scarf, holding blue mug, black and white dog sitting at feet, height 6¾ ", designer H. Fenton.	1952-1965	400.00	450.00

Under The Goosberry Bush, HN49, **1250.00 — 1500.00**

UNDER THE GOOSEBERRY BUSH	Date	Price Range

UNDER THE GOOSEBERRY BUSH
HN   49
☐ Small nude child laying on bed of flowers with black, green and brown bush over figure, height 3½", designer C. J. Noke.   1916-1938   1250.00 1500.00

'UPON HER CHEEKS SHE WEPT'
HN   59
☐ Figure of young girl, shaded blue dress, headband of green and white checks, barefooted, standing on light coloured base which has flowers, also printing on front of base, height 9", designer L. Perugini.   1916-1938   1500.00 1600.00
HN 511
☐ Lilac dress with large spots, height 9", designer L. Perugini.   1921-1938   1500.00 1600.00
HN 522
☐ Lilac dress with small spots, height 9", designer L. Perugini.   1921-1938   1500.00 1600.00

URIAH HEEP	Date	Price Range	
HN 545			
☐ A character from Dicken's "David Copperfield" (1st version), height 4", designer L. Harradine.	1922-	**45.00**	**60.00**
☐ **M 45** Renumbered as a miniature, height 4", designer L. Harradine.	1932-	**29.95**	
HN 554			
☐ Black base, complete black suit with white cravat, a stack of books also on base, red hair (2nd version), height 7¼", designer L. Harradine.	1923-1939	**400.00**	**500.00**
HN 1892			
☐ Very minor colour changes (2nd version), height 7", designer L. Harradine.	1938-1952	**275.00**	**325.00**
HN 2101			
☐ Green base, green trousers, black coat, yellow vest, white shirt, scarf white/blue with blue dots, red hair, books on base are browns and blacks (3rd version), height 7½", designer L. Harradine.	1952-1967	**300.00**	**350.00**
VALERIE			
HN 2107			
☐ Small figure, light red gown with white apron, darker red overskirt, white headcap with blue ribbons, holding single flower of yellow with green leaves, height 4¾", designer M. Davies.	1953-	**100.00**	
VANESSA			
HN 1836			
☐ Skirt of green, bodice of dark blue with trim of green and white, green bonnet with red ribbons, height 7½", designer L. Harradine.	1938-1949	**600.00**	**700.00**
HN 1838			
☐ Red skirt with bodice of green with red and white trim, bonnet is green with red lining, height 7½", designer L. Harradine.	1938-1949	**600.00**	**700.00**

Valerie, HN2107, **100.00**

	Date	Price Range	
VANITY			
HN 2475			
☐ Small figure, red gown with white waistband, white bow in dark hair, holding small yellow mirror, height 5¼ ", designer M. Davies.	1973-	**100.00**	
VENETA			
HN 2722			
☐ White gown with yellow and black design, overdress of green holding small white bird in hands, height 8", designer W. K. Harper.	1974-1980	**150.00**	**200.00**
VERA			
HN 1729			
☐ Head and shoulders only on cream coloured base, pink dress, height 4¼ ", designer L. Harradine.	1935-1938	**500.00**	**600.00**

Vera, HN1729, **500.00 — 600.00**

VERA (cont.)	Date	Price Range	
HN 1730			
☐ Green dress, height 4¼", designer L. Harradine.	1935-1938	**500.00**	**600.00**
VERENA			
HN 1835			
☐ Green gown with overdress of orange with yellow flower design, white ruffles on sleeves, green hat with white and black feathers, height 8¼", designer L. Harradine.	1938-1949	**750.00**	**850.00**
HN 1854			
☐ Green dress, height 8¼", designer L. Harradine.	1938-1949	**750.00**	**850.00**

	Date	Price Range

VERONICA

HN 1517

☐ Tiered gown of shaded red with green ribbon trim, bodice is darker red with green ribbon trim, large brim hat is shadded blues and reds with feathers of green, white and shaded red (1st version), height 8″, desinger L. Harradine   1932-1951   300.00   350.00

HN 1519

☐ Gown of shaded blues and cream, hat shaded red with feathers of cream and red (1st version), height 8″, designer L. Harradine   1932-1938   400.00   450.00

HN 1650

☐ HN 1517, green dress (1st version), height 8″, designer L. Harradine.   1934-1949   500.00   550.00

HN 1915

☐ Smaller version with gown of shaded reds and green ribbon trim, bodice of darker red with blue ribbon trim, hat is green with blue ribbon and blue and white feathers (2nd version), height 5¾″, designer L. Harradine. ..   1939-1949   400.00   450.00

☐ **M 64** Made as a miniature, gown of shaded reds with bodice of darker red, with green ribbons, hat is blue, height 4½″, designer L. Harradine. ..   1934-1949   325.00   375.00

☐ **M 70** Gown of green, height 4¼″, designer L. Harradine.   1936-1949   325.00   375.00

HN 1943

☐ Pink dress and blue hat (1st version), height 8″, designer L. Harradine.   1940-1949   400.00   450.00

VICTORIA

HN 2471

☐ Large full gown of red with white and green flower design, gown trimmed in white, holding open white fan, height 6½″, designer M. Davies.   1973-   170.00

VICTORIAN LADY, A

HN 726

☐ Tiered patterned gown of purple, cream, red and black, shawl is of a very dark plain colour, bonnet black with light lining and red ribbons, also red feather trim, height 7½″, designer L. Harradine.   1925-1938   350.00   400.00

	Date	Price Range	

HN 727
☐ Gown of shaded yellows, shawl red, bonnet black with light red lining and red feather with red ribbons, height 7½ ", designer L. Harradine. 1925-1938   **350.00**   **400.00**

HN 728
☐ Gown of shaded reds, shawl shaded blues and reds, bonnet is blue/red with feather and ribbons to match, height 7¾ ", designer L. Harradine. . . 1925-1952   **300.00**   **350.00**

HN 736
☐ Gown of purple with patterned white trim, shawl red, bonnet is black with red feather and ribbons, height 7¾ ", designer L. Harradine. 1925-1938   **450.00**   **500.00**

HN 739
☐ HN 726, mottled red, blue and yellow skirt, yellow scarf, height 7¾ ", designer L. Harradine. 1925-1938   **650.00**   **750.00**

HN 740
☐ Gown of shaded red, shawl red with black, red and blue spots, bonnet black with red feather and ribbons, height 7¾ ", designer L. Harradine. . . 1925-1938   **450.00**   **500.00**

HN 742
☐ HN 726, black with white chequered shawl, white dress with blue spots, height 7¾ ", designer L. Harradine. . . 1925-1938   **450.00**   **500.00**

HN 745
☐ Dress patterned with pink roses, height 7¾ ", designer L. Harradine. . . 1925-1938   **450.00**   **500.00**

HN 1208
☐ Gown of cream and green, shawl shaded dark reds, bonnet is dark with red feather and dark ribbons, height 7¾ ", designer L. Harradine. 1926-1938   **450.00**   **500.00**

HN 1258
☐ HN 726, mottled purple shawl, mottled blue dress, height 7¾ ", designer L. Harradine. 1927-1938   **450.00**   **500.00**

HN 1276
☐ Gown of cream and green with large red spots, bodice is solid red, shawl purple, bonnet dark with red feather and red ribbons, height 7½ ", designer L. Harradine. 1928-1938   **350.00**   **400.00**

	Date	Price Range	

HN 1277
☐ HN 726, red shawl, yellow and blue tiered dress, height 7¾", designer L. Harradine. 1928-1938 **350.00 400.00**

HN 1345
☐ Gown of shaded greens and blues, shawl shaded lavender and red, bonnet dark with red feather and ribbons, height 7¾", designer L. Harradine. . . 1929-1949 **250.00 300.00**

HN 1452
☐ HN 726, green dress and shawl, height 7¾", designer L. Harradine. . . 1931-1949 **250.00 300.00**

HN 1529
☐ Gown of shaded greens and reds, shawl shaded greens, bonnet is light coloured with shaded red ribbons and feather, height 7¾", designer L. Harradine. 1932-1938 **400.00 450.00**
☐ **M 1** Made as a miniature, gown of red and cream, shawl green, bonnet blue/red with feather and ribbons to match, height 3¾", designer L. Harradine. 1932-1945 **300.00 325.00**
☐ **M 2** Gown of blue, purple shawl, green bonnet with red feather and ribbons, height 3¾", designer L. Harradine. . . 1932-1945 **300.00 325.00**
☐ **M 25** Gown of shaded reds, shawl is shaded blue and reds, bonnet also shaded red/blue with dark ribbons and feather, height 3¾", designer L. Harradine. 1932-1945 **300.00 325.00**

VIKING, The

HN 2375
☐ Base is beige and light blue, costume is blue shirt, cape in brown fur like colour, red belt and red straps on legs, light green leggings, helmet of blue/grey with white and black horns, height 8¾", designer J. Bromley. 1973-1976 **250.00 300.00**

The Viking, Bisque, HN2375, **250.00 — 300.00**

	Date	Price Range	
VIRGINIA			
HN 1693			
☐ Light coloured base, gown of yellow with flower design and light red bows, underskirt is red, red shoes, small red scarf around neck, height 7½ ", designer L. Harradine.	1935-1949	**650.00**	**750.00**
HN 1694			
☐ Green gown with small red bows on bodice, undergown is white with green dots, shoes green, red scarf around neck and held by each hand, light coloured base, height 7½ ", designer L. Harradine.	1935-1949	**650.00**	**750.00**
VIVIENNE			
HN 2073			
☐ Full gown of red with white at sleeves, black hat with white and pink feathers with blue ribbons, height 7¾ ", designer L. Harradine.	1951-1967	**300.00**	**350.00**

	Date	Price Range	

VOTES FOR WOMEN
HN 2816
☐ White base, green gown, long brown coat, black hat tied with white scarf, holding placard of white with black printing, height 9¾", designer W. K. Harper. 1978-1981   200.00   250.00

WANDERING MINSTREL, The
HN 1224
☐ Costume of chequered black and red, black stockings, red shoes, jester type hat of black, red and green, holding small instrument of black and shaded red, also small head on stick, seated on green/white brick wall, height 7", designer L. Harradine. 1927-1938   1350.00   1500.00

WARDROBE MISTRESS
HN 2145
☐ Character figure seated, gown of black and white overdress, beside her are hats of yellow, black and yellow, blue and red gown, height 5¾", designer M. Davies. 1954-1967   475.00   525.00

WAYFARER, The
HN 2362
☐ Character figure seated on brown base, blue/grey trousers, green jacket, red vest, chequered black and white cap, holding white bottle and white pipe, height 5½", designer M. Nicoll. 1970-1976   200.00   250.00

WEDDING MORN
HN 1866
☐ HN 1867, cream dress, height 10½", designer L. Harradine. 1938-1949   1200.00   1300.00
HN 1867
☐ Red gown with white veil and long white train, holding white lilies, height 10½", designer L. Harradine. . 1938-1949   1200.00   1300.00

WEE WILLIE WINKIE
HN 2050
☐ Small figure on light blue/red base, long blue nightshirt carrying lantern of brown, red and yellow, height 5¼", designer M. Davies. 1949-1953   225.00   250.00

WELSH GIRL, The

	Date	Price Range	
HN 39			
☐ Light brown base with MYFANWY JONES printed on base, skirt is purple with red flower design, blouse red with white tie collar, apron white, cape black with cram lining, broad brim black hat, height 12″, designer E. W. Light.	1914-1938	2500.00	2750.00
HN 92			
☐ Blue/grey costume, height 12″, designer E. W. Light.	1918-1938	2500.00	2750.00
HN 456			
☐ Green blouse and brown skirt, height 12″, designer E. W. Light.	1921-1938	2500.00	2700.00
HN 514			
☐ Green skirt, spotted apron, height 12″, designer E. W. Light.	1921-1938	2500.00	2700.00
HN 516			
☐ Chequered lilac dress, black spotted cloak, height 12″, designer E. W. Light.	1921-1938	2500.00	2700.00
HN 519			
☐ Blue skirt, chequered lilac skirt, height 12″, designer E. W. Light.	1921-1938	2500.00	2700.00
HN 520			
☐ Spotted lilac dress, height 12″, designer E. W. Light.	1921-1938	2500.00	2700.00
HN 660			
☐ Spotted white costume, blue-lined cloak, height 12″, designer E. W. Light.	1924-1938	2500.00	2750.00
HN 668			
☐ Chequered yellow costume, pink lined cloak, height 12″, designer E. W. Light.	1924-1938	2500.00	2700.00
HN 669			
☐ Spotted yellow costume, chequered green lined cloak, height 12″, designer E. W. Light.	1924-1938	2500.00	2700.00
HN 701			
☐ Striped costume, chequered blue lined cloak, height 12″, designer E. W. Light.	1925-1938	2500.00	2700.00
HN 792			
☐ Pink chequered costume, blue cloak, height 12″, designer E. W. Light.	1926-1938	2550.00	2700.00

	Date	Price Range

WENDY

HN 2109

☐ Small figure in blue gown with shades of red, blue bonnet with dark pink ribbons, light coloured basket with flowers in one hand, height 5", designer L. Harradine. . . . . — 1953- — 75.00

WEST WIND

HN 1826

☐ Tinted finish, height 14½", designer R. Garbe. . . . . — 1937-1949 — 4500.00 5000.00

WIGMAKER OF WILLIAMSBURG

HN 2239

☐ White base, has brown pedestal with head form on it, costume of brown trousers, white stockings, black shoes, cream coloured coat with black trim, white shirt, height 7½", designer M. Davies. . . . . — 1960- — 200.00

WILLY-WON'T HE

HN 1561

☐ HN 1584, blue jacket and pink trousers, height 6", designer L. Harradine. — 1933-1949 — 500.00 550.00

HN 1584

☐ Two figures, Dutch costumes, boy's blue/brown trousers, shirt red, cap blue, girl's costume, blue dress, white apron and collar, white Dutch cap, both wearing wooden shoes, height 6", designer L. Harradine. . . . . — 1933-1949 — 350.00 400.00

HN 2150

☐ Minor glaze changes, height 5½", designer L. Harradine. . . . . — 1955-1959 — 300.00 325.00

WINDFLOWER

HN 1763

☐ Pale yellow skirt with red flower design, red blouse, hat is shaded reds and blues with black ribbon, on green base (1st version), height 7¼", designer L. Harradine. . . . . — 1936-1949 — 350.00 400.00

HN 1764

☐ White skirt with blue flower design, blouse blue, hat is shaded blues and reds with green ribbon, green base (1st version), height 7¼", designer L. Harradine. . . . . — 1936-1949 — 425.00 475.00

	Date	Price Range	

HN 1920
☐ Multicoloured skirt, red bodice, black base (2nd version), height 11″, designer L. Harradine.   1939-1949   **500.00   550.00**

HN 1939
☐ Flowered pink skirt, blue hat and gloves (2nd version), height 11″, designer L. Harradine.   1940-1949   **500.00   550.00**

☐ **M 78** Made as a miniature, light coloured base, white skirt with red flower designs, red blouse, blue hat, height 4″, designer L. Harradine.   1939-1949   **400.00   450.00**

☐ **M 79** Green skirt, height 4″, designer L. Harradine.   1939-1938   **500.00   550.00**

HN 2029
☐ Skirt is very light red with red flower designs, blouse is red, hat is green with black ribbon, base is blue/green (1st version), height 7¼″, designer L. Harradine.   1949-1952   **400.00   450.00**

WINDMILL LADY, The
HN 1400
☐ Character figure seated on brown base, green skirt, black jacket, shawl is chequered red, yellow and green, black hat, dark brown basket with green cloth at side, brown and white dog on other side, holding a ring of multicoloured toy windmills, height 8½″, designer L. Harradine.   1930-1938   **1550.00   1700.00**

WINNER, The
HN 1407
☐ Green base with white fence, horse of grey and white, rider in white trousers, dark red jacket with purple and white sleeves, purple cap, height 6¾″, designer unknown.   1930-1938   **3000.00   3500.00**

WINSOME
HN 2220
☐ Red gown, holding white bonnet with white ribbons over one arm, height 8″, designer M. Davies.   1960-   **155.00**

	Date	Price Range

WINTER

HN 315

☐ Light coloured base, figure completely wrapped in robe of shaded blues (1st version), height 7½", designer unknown........................ 1918-1938 1500.00 1800.00

HN 475

☐ Patterned robe (1st version), height 7½", designer unknown........... 1921-1938 1500.00 1800.00

HN 2088

☐ Blue/grey base, skirt shaded blues, jacket shaded green, cloak dark green with red lining, hood trimmed in brown fur, holding brown lantern (2nd version), height 6¼", designer M. Davies. 1952-1959 450.00 500.00

WISTFUL

HN 2396

☐ Gown of cream with light yellow shading with red flower design at hemline, overdress of red with shaded blue and green design, white sleeves with green and yellow shading, holding purple mask in one hand, height 6½", designer M. Davies. 1979- 325.00

WIZARD, The

HN 2877

☐ Blue robe with beige coloured rope belt, black coned hat with white designs, open book in hand, black cat at feet, brown and white owl on shoulder, height 9¾", designer A. Maslankowski. 1979- 215.00

WOMAN HOLDING CHILD

HN 462

☐ Green dress, white apron and blanket, height 9¼", designer unknown........................ 1921-1938 2000.00 2200.00

HN 570

☐ Pink and green striped skirt, pink and red striped blanket, height 9¼", designer unknown.................. 1923-1938 2000.00 2200.00

HN 703

☐ Purple cloak, black and red chequered skirt, height 9¼", designer unknown. 1925-1938 2000.00 2200.00

WOMAN HOLDING CHILD (cont.)	Date	Price Range	

HN 743

☐ Blue and yellow striped apron, height
9¼ ", designer unknown.   1925-1938   **2050.00 2200.00**

WOOD NYMPH

HN 2192

☐ Base is white with grey stripes and
leaf design, costume is blue/green
with white waist straps, same colour
ribbon in hair, barefooted figure,
height 7¼ ", designer M. Davies.   1958-1962   **300.00   350.00**

YEOMAN OF THE GUARD, A

HN 688

☐ Brown/green base which has brown
chest, figure seated, costume of
orange/red with stripes of gold and
black, white ruffled collar, white design on front of jacket, black shoes
with red and white trim, height 5¾ ",
designer L. Harradine.   1924-1938   **950.00 1050.00**

HN 2122

☐ Very minor glaze differences, height
5¾ ", designer L. Harradine.   1954-1959   **650.00   750.00**

YOUNG KNIGHT, The

HN 94

☐ Young man kneeling, hands holding a
scepter, gown is purple to maroon
color, robe dark brown, armor headdress at his knees. Figurine is on a
black base, height 9½ ", designer C.
J. Noke.   1918-1936   **2750.00 3250.00**

YOUNG LOVE

HN 2735

☐ Two figures on white base with gold
trim, girl's gown is white with light
shades of green, skirt with red flower
design, bodice is shaded green,
male's costume is grey trousers,
white stockings, black shoes, purple
long coat, vest of blue , height 10",
designer D. V. Tootle.   1975-   **695.00**

	Date	Price Range	

YOUNG MASTER
HN 2872
☐ Shaded green base, young man with blue trousers, purple jacket trimmed in black, white shirt, holding yellow and black violin, tan dog at his feet, a sheet of music and books also on base, height 7″, designer M. Davies. . 1980-   325.00

YOUNG MISS NIGHTINGALE, The
HN 2010
☐ Gown of yellow and green with green overdress, red long jacket, green/yellow hat with red feathers, carrying parasol and round bag, height 9¼″, designer M. Davies. 1948-1953   700.00   800.00

YOUNG WIDOW, The
HN 1399
☐ Quickly withdrawn and renamed 'THE LITTLE MOTHER'. See that classification, height 8″, designer L. Harradine. 1930-   1250.00   1500.00

YUM-YUM
HN 1268
☐ Chinese figure on yellow/green base, costume of shaded reds and cream, large fan behind head is black and red, height 5″, designer L. Harradine. 1928-1938   650.00   750.00
HN 1287
☐ Base of shaded browns, costume of shaded reds, yellows and blues, large fan is dark blue and red, height 5″, designer L. Harradine. 1928-1939   650.00   750.00
HN 2899
☐ Round light coloured base, costume of green and yellow with waistband of blue and gold, white flowers in black hair, holding white fan in one hand (2nd version), height 10¾″, designer W. K. Harper. 1980-   750.00

IMAGES

This series of modernistic figures, a fresh step taken by Doulton in 1980, combines old and new. "Images" features designs that are unmistakably 20th century, but in a concept that dates to the 18th. In Georgian England, it was popular to exhibit black basalt or white marble busts and other sculptures in fashionable homes. The "Images" series recalls this tradition as each piece is available in both black basalt (matte finish) or white bone china, suggesting marble. Subjects are inspired by the works of sculptors Henry Moore and Barbara Hepworth.

	Price
AWAKENING	
☐ **HN 2837** Black	50.00
☐ **HN 2875** White	50.00

Contemplation, HN2213 75.00

CONTEMPLATION	
☐ **HN 2241** Black	75.00
☐ **HN 2213** White	75.00

FAMILY	Price
☐ **HN 2721** Black	95.00
☐ **HN 2720** White	95.00

LOVERS
☐ **HN 2763** Black	95.00
☐ **HN 2762** White	95.00

MOTHER AND DAUGHTER
☐ **HN 2843** Black	95.00
☐ **HN 2841** White	95.00

PEACE
☐ **HN 2433** Black	50.00
☐ **HN 2470** White	50.00

SYMPATHY
☐ **HN 2838** Black	75.00
☐ **HN 2876** White	75.00

TENDERNESS
☐ **HN 2714** Black	75.00
☐ **HN 2713** White	75.00

TRANQUILITY
☐ **HN 2426** Black	75.00
☐ **HN 2469** White	75.00

YEARNING
☐ **HN 2921** Black	75.00
☐ **HN 2920** White	75.00

IMAGES OF NATURE

An exciting new approach has been introduced in the Animal and Bird Models. These figures present a streamlined and modernistic style, each conveying an animal in action. This new Image Collection was introduced in 1982.

THE LEAP
HN 3522
☐ Dolphin rising from the water, designer A. Hughes................	75.00

GOING HOME
HN 3527
☐ A pair of flying geese, designer A. Hughes........................	50.00

Going Home, HN3527, **50.00**

CAPRICORN   Price
HN 3523
☐ Mountain goat poised on a precipice,
   designer A. Hughes. **50.00**

THE GIFT OF LIFE
HN 3524
☐ A mare with her new born foal,
   designer R. Willis. **175.00**

COURTSHIP
HN 3525
☐ Dramatic mating display of two terns,
   designer R. Willis. **250.00**

SHADOWPLAY
HN 3526
☐ A playful cat sitting erect, designer
   R. Willis. **75.00**

LIMITED EDITIONS

The Doulton Company has on numerous occasions issued a series in a limited edition. Limited edition, of course, being a pre-determined number of a given item. Each piece, normally, is sequentially numbered and accompanied with a certificate of authenticity, and beautifully boxed.

DANCERS OF THE WORLD. This series, begun in 1977, was created by Royal Doulton's premier modeler of feminine figurines, Peggy Davies. The concept is to show folk dancers from various parts of the world, garbed in native costume. The series is noteworthy for the attention given to small detailing and coloration. As the costumes are "traditional," they cannot be assigned to any given time-period. Many other porcelain makers have attempted works of this kind, but the Doulton Dancers of the World is generally acknowledged to be the outstanding series of the type.

FEMME FATALE SERIES. A new series begun in 1979. Each figure is limited to 750 pieces. These are large and rather elaborate works. To date only two have been issued, both on historical themes, but it would seem as though the "femme fatale" concept could lend itself to inclusion of fictional or modern types as well — these may be added in the future. Those who wish to get in "at the ground floor" of a series should have a good opportunity with the Femme Fatales.

HEIRLOOM DOLLS. In 1981 Royal Doulton combined with the talents of the House of Nisbet introduced their first limited edition dolls. The heads and hands are fine bone china each hand painted with each doll having a different face. The costumes are created to perfection through the skills of the House of Nisbet, whose dolls have long been collected throughout the world. Each carries the Royal Doulton stamp on the nape of the neck, the costumes have a sewn-in label bearing the wording "Royal Doulton and Nisbet".

LADY MUSICIANS. Instituted in 1970. Each has been limited to 750 pieces and at this writing all are entirely sold out (that is, obtainable now only from retail dealers — not obtainable from the factory). Each figure shows a female musician playing a different instrument. Some collectors like to group them together as a "band," in the spirit of early porcelain sets that were intended to be displayed in that manner (Staffordshire put out many "bands").

MISCELLANEOUS FIGURINES. These are individually issued Limited Editions, not part of any sub-series. All carry numbering in the standard HN prefix series for Fancy and Character figures. These very desirable works have all been completely sold out and have definite investment appeal. The variety in subject matter adds to their interest.

MYTHS AND MAIDENS. A new collection introduced in 1982 these fine bone china figures have been inspired by ancient myths and legends. Each figure will be limited to 300, and a subject will be offered each year until 1986.

SHIPS' FIGUREHEADS. This series, introduced in 1980, has limited figures of 950 each. These are ceramic reproductions of colorful ship figureheads of olden time, from the days of sailing vessels. The originals were made of sculptured wood, but porcelain faithfully captures their line and color. Interest in this series comes not only from Doulton collectors but hobbyists in the field of nautical art. Possibilities in this series would be almost limitless, as historical and fictional characters of all types were the models for figurehead makers.

SOLDIERS OF THE REVOLUTION. This limited edition series was issued in conjunction with the U.S. Bicentennial. Most of the figures were released in 1975 on the eve of the celebration, but an additional figure (George Washington at Prayer), appeared two years later.

CHILDHOOD DAYS SERIES

An exciting new figure collection introduced in 1982. As the title suggests these pieces capture the memorable moments of children. Handmade and hand-decorated.

	Date	Price
IT WON'T HURT		
HN 2963		
☐ Little girl in nurse outfit tending to a dog which is sitting on top of a brown woven basket. Both characters on a white base. height 7½", designer P. Parsons.	1982-	75.00
DRESSING UP		
HN 2964		
☐ Young lady in Mother's dress which is white with blue trim, high heel black slippers, carrying gold purse, her light brown hair showing under a white hat trimmed in blue ribbons, height 7½", designer P. Parsons.	1982-	75.00
AND SO TO BED		
HN 2966		
☐ Little girl with black hair clad in nightgown, clutching her teddy bear, ready for bed, height 7½", designer P. Parsons.	1983-	75.00
SAVE SOME FOR ME		
HN 2959		
☐ Little girl mixing cake in bowl while cat at her feet watches patiently, height 7¼", designer P. Parsons. ...	1983-	75.00

Save Some For Me, HN2959, **75.00**

	Date	Price
PLEASE KEEP STILL		
HN 2967		
☐ Little boy on his knees bathing his dog, dog is standing in a tub patiently waiting for the boy to finish, height 4½ ", designer A. Hughes.	1983-	**75.00**
AND ONE FOR YOU		
HN 2970		
☐ Teddy bear sitting on a table with little girl bent over trying to feed him from the bowl which sits alongside the teddy bear, height 6½ ", designer A. Hughes.	1982-	**75.00**

	Date	Price

AS GOOD AS NEW
HN 2971
☐ Dog in doghouse sitting on a white
  base, little boy sitting on top of doghouse with paint brush and bucket in
  hand painting the doghouse to make
  it "look as good as new," height 6½ ",
  designer A. Hughes................ 1982-　　　**75.00**

CHARACTERS FROM CHILDREN'S LITERATURE

This exciting new series begun in 1982 features favorite characters
from children's literature. Each figure has been designed from the story-
book originals. Each is hand-made and hand-decorated, thus making no two
exactly the same.

TOM SAWYER
HN 2926
☐ Height 5¼ ", designer D. Littleton. ... 1982-　　　**50.00**

Huckleberry Finn, HN2927, **50.00**

HUCKLEBERRY FINN
HN 2927
☐ Height 7 ", designer D. Littleton. ..... 1982-　　　**50.00**

	Date	Price

TOM BROWN
HN 2941
☐ Height 7″, designer R. Tabbenor. 1983- **50.00**

POLLYANNA
HN 2965
☐ Height 6¾″, designer P. Parsons. . . . 1982- **50.00**

LITTLE LORD FAUNTLEROY
HN 2972
☐ Height 6¼″, designer A. Hughes. 1982- **50.00**

HEIDI
HN 2975
☐ Height 4½″, designer A. Hughes. 1983- **50.00**

DANCERS OF THE WORLD

BALINESE DANCER
HN 2808
☐ Delicate in her gown of green with gold design, overskirts of yellow and pink, sleeveless bodice of multicolours, highlighted with a beautiful black belt. Gold necklace, gold and jeweled crown. Limited edition of 750, height 8¾″, designer M. Davies. 1982- **950.00**

BRETON DANCER
HN 2410
☐ Cream coloured headdress in lace, black and green bodice over royal blue striped full dress, creamy pink apron, decoration on cuffs and skirt hem are as lace, matt finish. Limited edition of 750, height 8¾″, designer M. Davies 1981- **850.00**

CHINESE DANCER
HN 2840
☐ Costume is of blue with over-blouse of orange and blue, green skirt, purple sash which is long and extending almost to feet, base is white, height 9″, designer M. Davies. 1980- **750.00**

	Date	Price Range	

INDIAN TEMPLE DANCER
HN 2830
☐ Costume of yellow with trim of green and gold design. Limited edition of 750, figure on white base, height 9¼ ", designer M. Davies. 1977-   800.00   850.00

KURDISH DANCER
HN 2867
☐ Base is light blue, costume is purple trousers, gown of dark blue with trim of white with black design and red and yellow dots, purple head covering trimmed with gold dots, gold necklace. Limited edition of 750, height 8¼ ", designer M. Davies. 1979-   550.00

MEXICAN DANCER
HN 2866
☐ Light brown base, group of orange with shaded browns, trimmed at hem line in designs of black on yellow, waistband of dark brown, hat light yellow with very light red/blue ribbons, long white cloth falls from under hat, figure base footed. Limited edition of 750, height 8¼ ", designer M. Davies. 1979-   550.00

NORTH AMERICAN INDIAN DANCER
HN 2809
☐ Beautiful young Indian maiden in traditional dress, holding a bouquet of wildflowers. Hair is raven black with headband of white with red design and white feather. Limited edition of 750, height 8¼ ", designer M. Davies. 1982-   950.00

PHILIPPINE DANCER
HN 2439
☐ Skirt of light blue with red shading with darker blue and yellow trim, blouse peach with leaf design of red and green, open fan of white in each hand, head-covering is yellow with white trim with long light blue cloth, red shoes, base is blue with cream. Limited edition of 750, height 9½ ", designer M. Davies. 1978-   550.00   650.00

	Date	Price Range

POLISH DANCER
HN 2836
☐ Green base, red boots, skirt white with blue design and coloured flowers, white apron with red flowers, black and gold bodice, blue/white blouse, headdress of red, blue and yellow flowers, several strands of coloured beads, height 9½ ", designer M. Davies............................ 1980-   750.00

SCOTTISH HIGHLAND DANCER
HN 2436
☐ Green base, skirt of red with black stripes and squares, red vest trimmed in yellow, white blouse, red and white chequered stockings, black shoes. Limited edition of 750, height 9½ ", designer M. Davies. 1978-   600.00   650.00

Spanish Flemenco Dancer, HN2831, **800.00 — 850.00**

	Date	Price Range

SPANISH FLEMENCO DANCER
HN 2831
☐ Gown of red with large blue/white ruffles trimmed in black, single red flower in hair, red shoes on white/blue base. Limited edition of 750, height 9½", designer M. Davies.   1977-   800.00   850.00

WEST INDIAN DANCER
HN 2384
☐ Costume is a long sleeved dress of buttercup yellow decorated with a reddish design, a long white petticoat decorated around hem, figure is brown colour on multicoloured base, semi-matt finish. Limited edition of 750, height 9", designer M. Davies . . .   1981-   800.00   850.00

FEMME FATALE SERIES

CLEOPATRA & SLAVE
HN 2868
☐ Large light brown base, blue chair, gown of white with shaded blues and reds, necklace of blue, red, black and gold, head band gold and blue, mirror blue and gold, black slave holding gold and red bowl, fan is white feathers and red design with blue/red handle, chest of white and black, two bowls, one of gold and blue, the other gold and black. Limited edition of 750, height 7¼", designer M. Davies.   1979-   900.00   1000.00

HELEN OF TROY
HN 2387
☐ Figure is standing on base which contains a marble pillar which holds a peacock, his tail flows to base, costume of figure is pale pink dress and saga green cloak. Limited edition of 750, height 12", designer M. Davies . .   1981-   1250.00

Tz 'U-Hsi, Empress Dowager, HN2391, **1250.00**

	Date	Price Range

QUEEN OF SHEBA
HN 2328
☐ Regal lady she is. Tall in stature,
gown is gold and blue with yellow
draping sash at waist, lilac cloak
draped over her shoulder trimmed in
gold, gold neckband, gold crown over
her auburn hair. Cheetah at her side.
Both figures on a green base, height
9″, designer M. Davies. 1982- **1250.00**

TZ'U-HSI EMPRESS DOWAGER
HN 2391
☐ Beautiful figure sitting on a dragon
throne green in color with a marble
like effect. The Empress Dowager is
cooling herself with a fan. Pekingese
dog stands on a black laquered stool.
Figure is dressed in red cloak with a
deep blue dragon decorated cloak,
height 8″, designer M. Davies. 1983- **1250.00**

Koko, HN2898, **750.00**

GILBERT & SULLIVAN SERIES

KO-KO	Date	Price Range
HN 2898		
☐ Japanese figure from "The Mikado." Black hair on light brown base, costume of orange, blue, green, black, red, holding scroll, with large ax-like weapon on stand (2nd version), height 11½", designer W. K. Harper.	1980-	**650.00 750.00**
YUM-YUM		
HN 2899		
☐ Japanese figure from "The Mikado." Round light coloured base, costume of green and yellow with waistband of blue and gold, white flowers in black hair, holding white fan in one hand (2nd version), height 10¾", designer W. K. Harper.	1980-	**650.00 750.00**

	Date	Price Range

RUTH, THE PIRATE MAID
HN 2900
☐ Figure from "The Pirates of Penzance." Costume of brown, striped skirt, blue blouse with gold and black trim, white apron, black captain's hat with trim of gold and white skull and crossbones on mottled brown base, height 11¾", designer W. K. Harper. . 1981- 750.00

THE PIRATE KING
HN 2901
☐ Figure from "The Pirates of Penzance." Character seated on black and white pirate flag on light tan base, costume of green shirt, white lace ruff, blue boots and blue braided jacket with plumed captain's hat, his belt hold dagger and pistol, height 10", designer W. K. Harper. 1981- 750.00

ELSIE MAYNARD
HN 2902
☐ Figure from "The Yeomen of the Guard." Dancing girl with flowing red hair topped with a cap of blue, green skirt with white blouse, holding a tambourine aloft, height 11¼", designer W. K. Harper. 1982- 750.00

COLONEL FAIRFAX
HN 2903
☐ Figure from "The Yeomen of the Guard." Man in traditional Beefeater uniform standing on base of mottled greys, height 11½", designer W. K. Harper. 1982- 750.00

HEIRLOOM DOLLS

KATE GREENAWAY SERIES
LITTLE MODEL
☐ Gown is light beige with blue ribbon at waist, hat is blue matching ribbon on dress with deep maroon ties, cape is maroon. Limited edition of 5,000, height 12". 1981- 175.00

	Date	Price Range

VERA

☐ Beautiful deep beige dress with matching color overdress, hat matches dress, light auburn hair, carrying basket of pink flowers. Limited edition of 5,000, height 12″. 1981- **175.00**

WINTER

☐ Costume is scarlet red trimmed with black fur, carrying fur muff, beautiful black hat showing underneath is her red hair, black shoes. Limited edition of 5,000, height 12″. 1981- **175.00**

BIG SISTER

☐ Beautiful white dress with lacey underskirt, royal blue ribbon at the waist, hat is white trimmed in same color blue, slippers white, carrying dark brown basket with white and red flowers. Limited edition of 5,000, height 12″...................... 1981- **175.00**

SMALL SISTER

☐ Small child has all white dress with white shoes tied with pink ribbons, bonnet is white with pink bows over dark blonde hair. Limited edition of 5,000, height 8″ 1981- **125.00**

PINK RIBBON

☐ Dress is white taffeta line with pink underskirt, hat white with pink satin ribbon and white feathers, carrying a miniature bouquet of silk rosebuds. Limited edition of 5,000, height 12″... 1982- **195.00**

WAITING

☐ Simple white gown of silk with frilled neckline and cuff. Wide sash of orange satin ribbon at waistline, matching the lining of her dark brown lace and feather hat, under the hat is a white linen cap trimmed in lace. Limited edition of 5,000, height 12″... 1982- **195.00**

The Muff, Kate Greenaway Series, **195.00**

	Date	Price Range
THE MUFF		
☐ Dressed in tailored full length coat with a fur cape collar and carrying a fur muff, the coat has a pink lining, dress is maroon satin, hat is plum colored and trimmed with chocolate and pink feathers, hair is auburn. Limited edition of 5,000, height 12″	1982-	**195.00**
SWANSDOWN		
☐ Dressed in a white figured satin fur trimmed coat over a white satin dress, she carries a white fur muff and wears a lace trimmed hat over her blonde curly hair, decorated with Swansdown and yellow ribbons. Limited edition of 5,000, height 12″. . .	1982-	**195.00**

PINK SASH	Date	Price Range
☐ Dressed in white taffeta over a pink underskirt, wearing white hat decorated with feathers and pink ribbon, over blonde hair, carrying a miniature bouquet of silk rosebuds. Limited edition of 5,000, height 10"	1982-	**150.00**

VICTORIAN BIRTHDAY DOLLS

The well remembered nursery rhyme inspired this charming new collection. While each Day's child is represented by a boy and girl doll, each girl has a hairpiece while the boys hair is sculptured in the ceramic. Their costumes follow the 19th century tradition. This is a non-limited edition. Each retails for **$125.00.**

Monday's Child, Victorian Series, **145.00**

☐ **Monday's Child** is fair of face.		145.00
☐ **Tuesday's Child** is full of grace.		145.00
☐ **Wedneday's Child** is full of woe.		145.00

	Date	Price Range
☐ **Thursday's Child** has far to go.		145.00
☐ **Friday's Child** is loving and giving.		145.00
☐ **Saturday's Child** works hard for a living.		145.00
☐ **Sunday's Child,** a child that is born on the Sabbath Day is bonny and blithe and good and gay.		145.00

OTHER HEIRLOOM DOLLS

WEDDING DAY

☐ Bride wears a wedding dress of ivory silk which is almost entirely covered with ivory lace, the veil is matching lace and pink and cream flowers accentuate her brunette real hair, she carries a miniature bouquet of yellow, orange and white flowers, height 14″.   1982   225.00

LITTLE BRIDESMAID

☐ Dressed in cream satin, trimmed with cream lace which matches the lace on the bride (Wedding Day), flowers are yellow, orange and white, hair is light auburn, and headdress is a ringlet of similar flowers. 175.00

ROYAL BABY DOLL

☐ To commemorate the birth of His Royal Highness Prince William of Wales, born June 21, 1982. Baby wears a dress and bonnet of cream lace and net over taffeta, underneath are cream cotton bloomers, Bonnet is cream trimmed in matching lace and ribbons, the canopied crib is draped with a white and cream figured cotton, trimmed with baby blue, the face, hands and feet are a delicate baby tone. Limited edition of 2,500.   1982-   295.00

First Born, 195.00

	Date	Price Range
FIRSTBORN		
☐ This baby doll is a beautiful blue-eyed infant in a basket crib trimmed in lace, the infant is dressed in a traditional christening robe of white figured cotton with a lace front panel, bonnet is of white satin and lace.....	1982	**195.00**

LADY MUSICIANS

	Date	Price Range	
CELLO			
HN 2331			
☐ Seated lady in gown of yellow with white bow trim, darker brown bodice, white ribbon in hair, playing brown cello. Limited edition of 750, now sold out, height 6″, designer M. Davies....	1970-	**750.00**	**800.00**

Chitarrone, HN2700, **650.00 — 700.00**

CHITARRONE	Date	Price Range	
HN 2700			
☐ Standing figure in gown of dark blue and light blue with trim of roses on bodice, holding very long neck instrument. Limited edition of 750, now sold out, height 7½", designer M. Davies..........................	1974-	**650.00**	**700.00**
CYMBALS			
HN 2699			
☐ Green and orange gown, standing figure holding cymbals. Limited edition of 750, now sold out, height 7½", designer M. Davies.	1974-	**650.00**	**700.00**

	Date	Price Range	

DULCIMER
HN 2798
☐ Seated lady at table holding instrument, round box at side, gown of lavenders and white. Limited edition of 750, now sold out, height 6½″, designer M. Davies. 1975-   **650.00 700.00**

FLUTE
HN 2483
☐ Seated figure in red and white gown playing flute. Limited edition of 750, now sold out, height 6¼″, designer M. Davies 1973-   **750.00 800.00**

FRENCH HORN
HN 2795
☐ Seated lady holding french horn, gown of light green with darker green design, overlay of purple with white design. Limited edition of 750, now sold out, height 6″, designer M. Davies. 1976-   **650.00 700.00**

HARP
HN 2482
☐ Lady seated in chair with hands on golden harp, blue gown with purple overlay. Limited edition of 750, now sold out, height 8¾″, designer M. Davies. 1973-   **750.00 800.00**

HURDY GURDY
HN 2796
☐ Lady seated in chair with instrument on lap, white gown with blue overlay, roses as trim on skirt, red hair. Limited edition of 750, which are now sold out, height 6″, designer M. Davies. 1975-   **650.00 750.00**

LUTE
HN 2431
☐ Figure seated before a marble top table, holding lute on table, gown of blue and white, white ribbon in hair, open book on table. Limited edition of 750, now sold out, height 6½″, designer M. Davies. 1972-   **750.00 800.00**

	Date	Price Range	

VIOLA d'AMORE
HN 2797
☐ Seated figure on brown and green chair, gown of yellow with red roses around hemline, overdress is blue with flower designs of red and green, holding viola under chin (viola is brown). Limited edition of 750 which is now sold out, height 6″, designer M. Davies.   1976-   650.00   700.00

VIOLIN
HN 2432
☐ Figure seated, gown of yellow with shaded brown overdress holding brown violin under chin. Limited edition of 750 which is now sold out, height 6½″, designer M. Davies.   1972-   750.00   800.00

VIRGINALS
HN 2427
☐ Figure seated at brown and white top table with instrument of brown colour, gown of yellow with white bows, overdress of green with white bows, open book on instrument top. Limited edition of 750 which is now sold out, height 6½″, designer M. Davies.   1971-   750.00   800.00

MISCELLANEOUS FIGURINES

BEETHOVEN
HN 1778
☐ Bust style of Beethoven with figures of women around what appears to be hair, matte ivory glaze. Limited edition of 25, sold out, height 22″, designer R. Garbe.   1933-1939   6000.00   6500.00

HENRY VIII
HN 370
☐ Robe of red, blue and black trimmed in fur, beige coloured stockings, red shoes, standing on small base which has his name on it. Limited edition of 200, sold out, height unknown, designer C. J. Noke.   1933-1939   1750.00   2000.00

HER MAJESTY QUEEN ELIZABETH II
HN 2878

☐ Designed as a tribute to Her Majesty, Queen of England to commemmorate her 30th Anniversary of the Coronattion. Figure has gown of white over which is a blue and crimson robe, badge of order is worn on the left, chain has the initials of the order 22 kt. gold trimmed with white crosses, white ribbons on the shoulder. Limited edition of 2,500, height 10½ ", designed E.J. Griffiths   1983-

His Holiness Pope John Paul II, HN2888, **150.00**

	Date	Price Range

HIS HOLINESS POPE JOHN PAUL II
HN2888
☐ Beautiful likeness of His Holiness inspired by his visit to the United Kingdom. Height 10″, designer E.J. Griffiths 1982   **150.00**

H.R.H. THE PRINCE OF WALES
HN 2883
☐ Beautiful figure in black suit with red trim, cloak is purple and white with gold trim, gold sword in hand. Limited edition of 15,000, height 8″, designer E. J. Griffiths 1982-   **750.00**

INDIAN BRAVE
HN 2376
☐ Indian mounted on black and white horse, costume of beige, dark blue, red and white, holding lance and shield of light brown with darker brown figures, headdress has yellow feathers. Limited edition of 500, which are now sold out, height 15½″, designer M. Davies. 1967-   **4000.00 5000.00**

LADY DIANA SPENCER
HN 2885
☐ Sleeveless gown of blue with white polka dots, white ruffle at bust line, white shawl over her bare shoulders, carrying beautiful bouquet of flowers, blonde hair. Limited edition of 1,500, height 7¾″, designer E. J. Griffiths... 1982-   **750.00**

MARRIAGE OF ART AND INDUSTRY
HN 2261
☐ Two bronze coloured figures on base of bronze with tints of green, base has figures of birds, flowers, etc. Limited edition of 12 — was never put on sale, height 18″, designer M. Davies......................... 1958-   **7000.00 8000.00**

	Date	Price Range

PALIO, The

HN 2428

☐ Knight mounted on horse on walnut base, armor of dark blue and light blue with gold design, light brown footwear, horse costume of light blue with gold design, light blue with white design, black, gold and red stripes, dark brown color for animal. Limited edition of 500, height 18″, designer M. Davies.......................... 1971-1973

PRINCE PHILIP, DUKE OF EDINBURG

HN 2386

☐ Limited edition of 750, height 8¼″, designer M. Davies. 1981-   750.00

QUEEN ELIZABETH II

HN 2502

☐ Gown of light blue with blue designs, purple ribbon over shoulder and front. Limited edition of 750, now sold out, height 7¾″, designer M. Davies 1973-   2000.00   2500.00

QUEEN ELIZABETH, The QUEEN MOTHER

HN 2882

☐ Figure is mounted on dark wooden base, gown is pink with white designs, dark blue ribbons across shoulder down to waist, wearing crown and necklace, holding white gloves. Limited edition of 1500, height 11¾″, desinger, unknown 1980-   1250.00

ROYAL CANADIAN MOUNTED POLICE

HN 2547

☐ Bust figure of a Royal Canadian Policeman showing red coat and brown hat mounted on a black base. Limited edition of 1,500, height 8″, designer unknown.................. 1973-   150.00   200.00

SALOME

HN 1775

☐ Matt ivory finish. Limited edition of 100, sold out by 1939, height unknown, designer R. Garbe. 1933-   4500.00   5000.00

	Date	Price Range

SPIRIT OF THE WIND
HN 1777
☐ HN 1825, matte ivory finish. Limited edition of 40, sold out in 1939, height 14½", designer R. Garbe.   1933-   3500.00 4000.00

SPRING
HN 1774
☐ As 1827 but with matte ivory finish. Limited edition of 100, sold out by 1939, height 21", designer R. Garbe. .   1933-   2500.00 3000.00

WEST WIND
HN 1776
☐ Large figure (14½") of two, head and shoulders only, each has wings, matte ivory finish. Limited edition of 25 sold out in 1939, height 14½", designer R. Garbe.   1933-   4500.00 5000.00

Leda And The Swan, HN2826, **2500.00**

MYTHS & MAIDENS

LADY AND THE UNICORN	Date	Price Range

HN 2825

☐ White Unicorn lying on a blue and gold base, lady's dress blue, gold flowers, red bodice with white ties, she is holding a gold mirror to reflect the unicorn to itself, beautiful fleurs de lis emphasis on the base, height 8¾", designer R. Jefferson. 1982-   **2500.00**

LEDA AND THE SWAN

HN 2826

☐ Seated figure within the wingspan of a white swan, barefooted, gown is pale and gold, trimming is black and white, dark brown hair with red headband, base is decorated in blues, greens and reds, banded in blue and gold, height 9¾", designer R. Jefferson 1983   **2500.00**

SHIPS FIGUREHEADS

All are Limited Editions of 950. Designed by Sharon Keenan

AJAX
☐ HN 2908 1980   **750.00**

BENMORE
☐ HN 2909 1980   **750.00**

CHIEFTAN
☐ HN 2929 1982   **950.00**

HIBERNIA
☐ HN 2932 1983   **950.00**

LALLA ROOKH
☐ HN 2910 1981   **950.00**

MARY QUEEN OF SCOTS
☐ HN 2931 1983   **950.00**

NELSON
☐ HN 2928 1981   **950.00**

POCAHONTAS
☐ HN 2930 1982   **950.00**

Ajax,
HN2908, **750.00**

Hibernia,
HN2932, **950.00**

Mary Queen Of Scots,
HN2931, **950.00**

SOLDIERS OF REVOLUTION

	Date	Price Range
CAPTAIN, 2nd NEW YORK REGIMENT		
HN 2755		
☐ Brown base, beige trousers, darker beige coat with blue trim, holding lance. Limited edition of 350	1975-1980	**750.00**
CORPORAL, 1st NEW HAMPSHIRE REGIMENT 1778		
HN 2780		
☐ Brown base, green trousers, lighter green coat with red trim, white cross straps, green vest, black hat, white stockings, brown shoes. Limited edition of 350	1975-1980	**750.00**
GEORGE WASHINGTON AT PRAYER		
HN 2861		
☐ George Washington in full uniform, kneeling on white base. Limited edition of 750, created by Laszlo Ispansky and available by subscription only from Limited Editions Collectors Society of America	1977-	**1800.00 2000.00**
MAJOR, 3rd NEW JERSEY REGIMENT 1776		
HN 2752		
☐ Brown base, seated on wooden fence, light blue costume with darker blue trim, hat black with white trim. Limited edition of 350	1975-1980	**750.00**
PRIVATE, CONNECTICUT REGIMENT, 1777		
HN 2845		
☐ Yellow/green base, beige trousers, brown coat, white cross straps, red trim on coat, black hat with blue/white trim, small cannon on base. Limited edition of 350	1975-1980	**750.00**

	Date	Price Range

PRIVATE, DELAWARE REGIMENT 1776

HN 2761

☐ Yellow/green base, beige trousers, coat dark blue with red and white trim, cross strap of white, hat dark blue with white trim, small black box at waist, white vest. Limited edition of 350   1975-1980   **750.00**

PRIVATE, 1st GEORGIA REGIMENT 1777

HN 2779

☐ Brown base, white leggings, brown long coat, white shirt, white cross straps, has a tomahawk attached to base. Limited edition of 350   1975-1980   **750.00**

PRIVATE, MASSACHUSETTS REGIMENT 1778

HN 2760

☐ Dark coloured figure in blue/white uniform, dark blue hat, cross straps of dark blue, base contains blue/black barrel, brown box and cream coloured box, base is yellow/green. Limited edition of 350   1975-1980   **750.00**

PRIVATE, PENNSYLVANIA RIFLE BATTALION, 1776

HN 2846

☐ Kneeling figure on yellow/green base, costume of blue/grey, large brimmed hat of same colour, powder horn, knife holder and small pouch of brown. Limited edition of 350   1975-1980   **750.00**

PRIVATE, RHODE ISLAND REGIMENT 1781

HN 2759

☐ Costume of beige trousers, white stockings, black shoes, blue coat with red trim, white crossed straps, black hat with yellow trim, holding ram pole for cannon. Limited edition of 350   1975-1980   **750.00**

	Date	Price Range

PRIVATE, 2nd SOUTH CAROLINA REGIMENT 1781

HN 2717
☐ Brown base, light coloured trousers, blue coat with red lining, dark brown hat. Limited edition of 350   1975-1980   **750.00**

PRIVATE, 3rd NORTH CAROLINA REGIMENT 1778

HN 2754
☐ Brown base, costume of beige with green rolled bundle around shoulder. Limited edition of 350   1975-1980   **750.00**

SERGEANT, 6th MARYLAND REGIMENT 1777

HN 2815
☐ Brown base, blue trousers, lighter blue coat and vest trimmed in green, waistband blue with red trim, hat black with white trim. Limited edition of 350   1975-1980   **750.00**

SERGEANT, VIRGINIA 1st REGIMENT CONTINENTAL LIGHT DRAGOON 1777

HN 2844
☐ Light yellow/green base which contains tree trunk with posted white sign, horse is brown and black, trappings on horse are green and yellow, costume of soldier is white trousers, brown coat with green trim, blue/white gloves, black hat with green ribbon trim. Limited edition of 350   1975-1980   **1750.00**

MIDDLE EARTH FIGURINES (J. R. R. TOLKIEN SERIES)

Inspired by the great work of J. J. R. Tolkien's fiction "The Lord of the Rings" and created by the artists of Royal Doulton is this new series of figures featuring new lands and new creatures. All are created from the vivid characters envisioned in the mind of Tolkien and portrayed in this book.

ARAGORN
☐ **HN 2916**
   Tan Costume   1980   **45.00**

Barliman Butterbur, HN2923, **45.00**

BARLIMAN BUTTERBUR	Date	Price Range
☐ HN 2923	1982	45.00
BILBO		
☐ HN 2914		
Brown shorts, tan vest	1980	35.00
BOROMIR		
☐ HN 2918	1981	50.00
FRODO		
☐ HN 2912		
Dark blue shorts and vest	1980	35.00
GALADRIAL		
☐ HN 2915		
Ivory dress	1981	45.00
GANDALF		
☐ HN 2911		
Blue cloak	1980	50.00

	Date	Price Range
GIMLI		
☐ HN 2922	1981	**45.00**
GOLLUM		
☐ HN 2913		
Green	1980	**35.00**
LEGOLAS		
☐ HN 2917	1981	**45.00**

Samwise, HN2925, **35.00**   **Tom Bombadil,** HN2924, **50.00**

	Date	Price Range
SAMWISE		
☐ HN 2925	1982	**35.00**
TOM BOMBADIL		
☐ HN 2924	1982	**50.00**

PRESTIGE FIGURES

These are large-size figures, in some cases extremely large (Matador and Bull measures a huge 28″). While not actually limited editions, it is obvious that the Prestige Figures, because of their high retail prices, are produced in smaller edition sizes than the regular HN pieces. The concept for this series dates to 1952. Additions have been made to it only occasionally. Apparently the feeling, among directors of the factory, was that wealthy collectors might welcome deluxe figures. In general the series has been well received. It would be difficult to predict the prices that might be reached by Princess Badoura and Matador and Bull (the two most spectacular Prestige Figures) if they were taken out of production.

Columbine, HN2738, 750.00

COLUMBINE	Date	Price Range
HN 2738		
☐ Subject from the famous "Commedia dell'Arte." Swirling gown of pink, floral bodice, on a rococo style base of white with gold trim, height 12½″, designer D. Tootle.	1982-	**750.00**

	Date	Price Range

ELEPHANT
HN 2640
☐ Fighting, 12″ **1350.00**

FOX
HN 2634
☐ Sitting, 10⅜″ **650.00**

HARLEQUIN
HN 2737
☐ Subject from the famous "Commedia
dell'Arte." Brightly coloured chequered suit, on a rococo style base of
white with gold trim, height 12½″,
designer D. Tootle.   1982-   **750.00**

JACK POINT
HN 2080
☐ Costume of red, purple, green with
gold lion and leaf trim, has instrument slung over shoulder, base light
beige   1952-   **1350.00**

KING CHARLES
HN 2084
☐ Figure is on light beige base, 17″   1952-   **1500.00**

LEOPARD ON ROCK
HN 2638
☐ 9″ **1500.00**

LION ON ROCK
HN 2641
☐ 12″ **1500.00**

MATADOR AND BULL
HN 2324
☐ Bull is dark grey with brown shadings, matador costume of green and
yellow, cape is blue/red with pale
yellow lining, 28″   1964-   **10500.00**

THE MOOR
HN 2082
☐ Red with shaded greens costume
with multicoloured waistband, deep
brown cloak with shades of dark
green, on dark brown base, 17½″   1952-   **1350.00**

	Date	Price Range

PHEASANT
HN 2632
☐ (Cock) **495.00**

PRINCESS BADOURA
HN 2081
☐ This is a 20″ figure, on black base, large elephant is dark grey with coverings of reds, blues, golds and brown, lady is seated in gold coloured chair with pink gown and gold head piece and necklace, male figure is seated on head of elephant costume of blue and gold with green trousers   1952-   **14000.00 15000.00**

ST. GEORGE AND THE DRAGON
HN 2856
☐ Blue/grey base with dragon head and brown treen trunk, horse is white with cloth of cream with gold designs, red lining, figure in blue/grey armor and helmet with white feather, 16″   1978-   **6500.00**

TIGER
HN 2646
☐ **850.00**

TIGER ON ROCK
HN 2639
☐ 12″ **1500.00**

VANITY FAIR SERIES

This collection of figurines was introduced in 1982, and is becoming extremely popular.

Vanity Fair ladies are individually hand-made and hand-decorated so each will be an original, each different from the other. Subtle matte skin tones are complemented by highly glazed white clothes, most with a small touch of color.

ANGELA
HN 2389
☐ White gown, flowing skirt with elbow length sleeves, dark brown hair highlighted with golden colour, height 7⅜″, designer M. Davies.   1982-   **95.00**

	Date	Price Range

BARBARA
HN 2962
☐ White gown, white hat hanging at the neckline tied in front with white ribbons, auburn hair, height 8″, designer P. Parsons   1982-   **95.00**

CAROL
HN 2961
☐ Regal figure with white gown accented with pale pink, embroidering in hand with design on work of red flowers, green stems and leaves, reddish hair, height 7½″, designer P. Parsons.   1982-   **95.00**

Joanne, HN2373, **95.00**

	Date	Price Range

JOANNE
HN 2373
☐ Seated figure with legs tucked up revealing ruffled petticoats, gown is white, hair blonde, height 5¼", designer E.J. Griffiths 1982-   95.00

HEATHER
HN 2956
☐ Seated figure, white gown, white purse on arm, blonde hair, height 6", designer P. Parsons. 1982-   95.00

NANCY
HN 2955
☐ White gown, white flower in light brown hair, height 7½", designer P. Parsons. 1982-   95.00

PATRICIA
HN 2715
☐ Beautiful dark haired figure with ball gown of white satin, height 7½", designer J. Bromley 1982-   95.00

MARGARET
HN 2397
☐ Gown is white accented at waistline with blue ribbon, hat is white with blue ribbon, dark hair, height 7½", designer M. Davies. 1982-   95.00

SAMANTHA
HN 2954
☐ Beautiful blonde lady, white gown, white hat, height 7", designer P. Parsons. 1982-   95.00

TRACY
HN 2736
☐ Gown white with tight fitting bodice and plunging neckline with flowing skirt, rose in the folds of the skirt, blonde hair, height 7⅜", designer D. Tootle. 1983-   95.00

NUMERICAL LISTINGS OF "D" MODEL NUMBERS

The following is a NUMERICAL listing of all Royal Doulton products bearing the prefix letter D. Mostly these are Character or Toby Jugs, for which the D prefix was instituted. However, over the years the factory has occasionally issued other items bearing the D prefix. In all cases, these non-jug articles with D prefix are directly associated with the company's jugs, as the motifs they carry are adapted *from* Character or Toby Jugs. Since this is a NUMERICAL listing, all objects bearing the same motif are not necessarily grouped together. Missing numbers were, mostly, used for miscellaneous items bearing jug-type motifs. See next section.

	Date	Price Range	
D 5327			
☐ John Barleycorn, large............	1934-1960	125.00	150.00
D 5327			
☐ John Barleycorn, large............	1978-	125.00	150.00
D 5420			
☐ Old Charley, large................	1934-	75.00	
D 5451			
☐ Sairey Gamp, large...............	1935-	75.00	
D 5486			
☐ Parson Brown, large.............	1935-1960	95.00	115.00
D 5495			
☐ Dick Turpin (1st version), large	1935-1960	100.00	125.00
D 5504			
☐ Simon the Cellarer, large..........	1935-1960	100.00	125.00
D 5521			
☐ Granny, large	1935-	75.00	
D 5527			
☐ Old Charley, small	1935-	50.00	
D 5528			
☐ Sairey Gamp, small	1935-	50.00	
D 5529			
☐ Parson Brown, small	1935-1960	60.00	70.00
D 5530			
☐ Tony Weller, small	1936-1960	50.00	60.00
D 5531			
☐ Tony Weller, large	1936-1960	100.00	125.00
D 5556			
☐ Jester, small	1936-	115.00	135.00
D 5584			
☐ Old Curiosity Shop Jug (Miscellaneous, Dickens Jug)	1935-1960	125.00	175.00
D 5599			
☐ Old Charley (Ash Tray)	1936-1960	75.00	100.00
D 5600			
☐ Parson Brown (Ash Tray)	1936-1960	85.00	125.00
D 5601			
☐ Dick Turpin (Ash Tray)	1936-1960	75.00	100.00

D 5602	Date	Price Range	
☐ John Barleycorn (Ash Tray)	1936-1960	85.00	125.00
D 5610			
☐ Clown, red hair	1937-1942	4750.00	5000.00
D 5612			
☐ John Peel, large	1936-1960	110.00	125.00
D 5613			
☐ Touchstone, large	1936-1960	300.00	350.00
D 5614			
☐ Cardinal, large	1936-1960	110.00	135.00
D 5615			
☐ The Vicar of Bray, large	1936-1960	160.00	180.00
D 5616			
☐ Simon the Cellarer, small	1936-1960	60.00	75.00
D 5617			
☐ Oliver Twist Jug (Miscellaneous Dickens Jugs)	1937-1960	125.00	175.00
D 5618			
☐ Dick Turpin (1st version), small	1935-1960	55.00	70.00
D 5731			
☐ John Peel, small	1937-1960	60.00	70.00
D 5735			
☐ John Barleycorn, small	1937-1960	60.00	75.00
D 5736			
☐ Toby Philpots, large	1937-1969	90.00	110.00
D 5737			
☐ Toby Philpots, small	1937-1969	50.00	60.00
D 5753			
☐ Paddy, large	1937-1960	100.00	125.00
D 5756			
☐ Pickwick Papers Jug (Miscellaneous Dickens Jugs)	1937-1960	150.00	225.00
D 5757			
☐ Mephistopheles, large	1937-1948	2000.00	2500.00
D 5758			
☐ Mephistopheles, small	1937-1948	775.00	850.00
D 5768			
☐ Paddy, small	1937-1960	55.00	65.00
D 5788			
☐ Farmer John, large	1938-1960	125.00	150.00
D 5789			
☐ Farmer John, small	1938-1960	60.00	70.00
D 5823			
☐ Owd Mac, large..................	1938-1945	100.00	125.00
D 5823			
☐ Auld Mac, large..................	1938-	75.00	
D 5824			
☐ Auld Mac, small	1938-	50.00	
D 5838			
☐ Buz Fuz, intermediate size	1938-1948	110.00	125.00

	Date	Price Range	
D 5838			
☐ Buz Fuz, intermediate size	1948-1960	**100.00**	**115.00**
D 5839			
☐ Mr. Pickwick, special size	1938-1948	**125.00**	**150.00**
D 5839			
☐ Mr. Pickwick, small	1948-1960	**50.00**	**60.00**
D 5840			
☐ Fat Boy, special size	1938-1948	**110.00**	**125.00**
D 5840			
☐ Fat Boy, small...................	1948-1960	**55.00**	**65.00**
D 5841			
☐ Sam Weller, special size	1938-1948	**100.00**	**125.00**
D 5841			
☐ Sam Weller, small	1948-1960	**60.00**	**75.00**
D 5842			
☐ Cap'n Cuttle, special size	1938-1949	**120.00**	**135.00**
D 5842			
☐ Cap'n Cuttle, special size	1948-1960	**85.00**	**95.00**
D 5843			
☐ Mr. Micawber, special size	1938-1948	**125.00**	**150.00**
D 5843			
☐ Mr. Micawber, small..............	1948-1960	**75.00**	**100.00**
D 5925			
☐ Old Charley (Ash Bowl)	1938-1960	**100.00**	**125.00**
D 5926			
☐ Paddy (Ash Bowl)	1938-1960	**100.00**	**125.00**
D 6006			
☐ Auld Mac (Ash Bowl)	1939-1960	**115.00**	**135.00**
D 6007			
☐ Farmer John (Ash Bowl)...........	1939-1960	**100.00**	**125.00**
D 6008			
☐ Parson Brown (Ash Bowl)	1939-1960	**100.00**	**125.00**
D 6009			
☐ Sairey Gamp (Ash Bowl)	1939-1960	**100.00**	**125.00**
D 6030			
☐ Old Charley (Toby Jug)............	1939-1960	**150.00**	**175.00**
D 6031			
☐ Happy John (Toby Jug)	1939-	**95.00**	
D 6033			
☐ Cardinal, small	1939-1960	**65.00**	**80.00**
D 6036			
☐ Old King Cole, large	1939-1960	**150.00**	**175.00**
D 6037			
☐ Old King Cole, small	1939-1960	**75.00**	**100.00**
D 6041			
☐ John Barleycorn, miniature	1939-1960	**50.00**	**60.00**
D 6042			
☐ Paddy, miniature	1939-1960	**50.00**	**65.00**
D 6043			
☐ Toby Philpots, miniature	1939-1969	**35.00**	**50.00**

D 6044	Date	Price Range	
☐ Tony Weller, miniature............	1939-1960	40.00	50.00
D 6045			
☐ Sairey Gamp, miniature...........	1939-	29.95	
D 6046			
☐ Old Charley, miniature...........	1939-	29.95	
D 6047			
☐ Sairey Gamp (Bust)	1939-1960	65.00	85.00
D 6048			
☐ Buz Fuz (Bust)..................	1939-1960	75.00	100.00
D 6049			
☐ Mr. Pickwick (Bust)..............	1939-1960	75.00	100.00
D 6050			
☐ Mr. Micawber (Bust).............	1939-1960	65.00	85.00
D 6051			
☐ Tony Weller (Bust)	1939-1960	65.00	85.00
D 6052			
☐ Sam Weller (Bust)...............	1939-1960	65.00	85.00
D 6060			
☐ Mr. Pickwick, large	1940-1960	125.00	150.00
D 6062			
☐ Falstaff (Toby Jug)	1939-	95.00	
D 6063			
☐ Falstaff (Toby Jug)	1939-	50.00	
D 6064			
☐ Sam Weller, large	1940-1960	100.00	125.00
D 6069			
☐ Old Charley (Toby Jug)...........	1939-1960	100.00	125.00
D 6070			
☐ Happy John (Toby Jug)	1939-	45.00	
D 6088			
☐ Double XX or The Man on the Barrell (Toby Jug)	1939-1969	325.00	375.00
D 6107			
☐ The Best is Not Too Good (Toby Jug) .	1939-1960	225.00	275.00
D 6108			
☐ Honest Measure (Toby Jug).........	1939-	45.00	
D 6109			
☐ Jolly Toby (Toby Jug)	1939-	65.00	
D 6114			
☐ The Cavalier, large	1940-1960	125.00	150.00
D 6115			
☐ Drake (2nd version), large	1940-1960	125.00	150.00
D 6128			
☐ Dick Turpin (1st version), miniature ..	1940-1960	50.00	65.00
D 6129			
☐ Cardinal, miniature	1940-1960	50.00	65.00
D 6130			
☐ John Peel, miniature	1940-1960	45.00	55.00

	Date	Price Range	
D 6138			
☐ Mr. Micawber, miniature	1940-1960	45.00	55.00
D 6139			
☐ Fat Boy, miniature	1940-1960	60.00	70.00
D 6140			
☐ Sam Weller, miniature	1940-1960	50.00	60.00
D 6142			
☐ Fat Boy, tiny	1940-1960	110.00	135.00
D 6143			
☐ Mr. Micawber, tiny	—	110.00	135.00
D 6144			
☐ Old Charley, tiny	1940-1960	100.00	125.00
D 6145			
☐ Paddy, tiny	1940-1960	100.00	125.00
D 6146			
☐ Sairey Gamp, tiny	1940-1960	45.00	60.00
D 6147			
☐ Sam Weller, tiny	1940-1960	100.00	125.00
D 6170			
☐ Churchill, large	1940-	8500.00	10000.00
D 6171			
☐ Sir Winston Churchill, large (Toby Jug)	1941-	95.00	
D 6172			
☐ Sir Winston Churchill, small (Toby Jug)	1941-	65.00	
D 6173			
☐ The Cavalier, small	1940-1960	75.00	85.00
D 6174			
☐ Drake (2nd version), small	1941-1960	80.00	100.00
D 6175			
☐ Sir Winston Churchill, miniature (Toby Jug)	1941-	45.00	
D 6198			
☐ Smuts, large	1946-1948	1750.00	2000.00
D 6202			
☐ Monty, large	1946-	75.00	
D 6205			
☐ Robin Hood (1st version), large	1947-1960	125.00	150.00
D 6206			
☐ Beefeater, large	1947-	75.00	
D 6207			
☐ 'Arry, large	1947-1960	175.00	200.00
D 6207			
☐ Pearly Boy, large	—	950.00	1050.00
D 6208			
☐ 'Arriet, large	1947-1960	175.00	200.00
D 6208			
☐ Pearly Girl, large	—	1050.00	1150.00
D 6233			
☐ Beefeater, small	1947-	50.00	

	Date	Price Range	
D 6234			
☐ Robin Hood (1st version), small	1947-1960	70.00	90.00
D 6235			
☐ 'Arry, small	1947-1960	60.00	65.00
D 6235			
☐ Pearly Boy, small	—	600.00	700.00
D 6236			
☐ 'Arriet, small	1947-1960	60.00	65.00
D 6236			
☐ Pearly Girl, small	—	625.00	725.00
D 6245			
☐ Mr. Pickwick, miniature	1947-1960	45.00	55.00
D 6249			
☐ 'Arry, miniature..................	1947-1960	70.00	80.00
D 6250			
☐ 'Arriet, miniature	1947-1960	50.00	60.00
D 6250			
☐ Pearly Girl, miniature	—	500.00	600.00
D 6251			
☐ Beefeater, miniature	1947-	29.95	
D 6252			
☐ Robin Hood (1st version), miniature ..	1947-1960	50.00	60.00
D 6253			
☐ Auld Mac, miniature..............	1946-	29.95	
D 6255			
☐ 'Arry, tiny......................	1947-1960	200.00	225.00
D 6256			
☐ 'Arriet, tiny	1947-1960	175.00	225.00
D 6257			
☐ Auld Mac, tiny...................	1946-1960	185.00	225.00
D 6258			
☐ Cardinal, tiny	1947-1960	220.00	250.00
D 6259			
☐ John Peel, tiny	1947-1960	225.00	250.00
D 6260			
☐ Mr. Pickwick, tiny	1947-1960	180.00	215.00
D 6261			
☐ Mr. Pickwick (Toby Jug)	1948-1960	200.00	225.00
D 6262			
☐ Mr. Micawber (Toby Jug)	1948-1960	200.00	225.00
D 6263			
☐ Sairey Gamp (Toby Jug)	1948-1960	200.00	225.00
D 6264			
☐ The Fat Boy (Toby Jug)	1948-1960	200.00	225.00
D 6265			
☐ Sam Weller (Toby Jug)	1948-1960	200.00	225.00
D 6266			
☐ Cap'n Cuttle (Toby Jug)	1948-1960	200.00	250.00

D 6285	Date	Price Range	
☐ Oliver Twist Jug (Miscellaneous Dickens Jugs)	1936-1960	**225.00**	**275.00**
D 6286			
☐ Oliver Twist Tankard	1949-1960	**200.00**	**250.00**
D 6287			
☐ Falstaff, large	1950-	**75.00**	
D 6288			
☐ Jarge, large	1950-1960	**275.00**	**300.00**
D 6289			
☐ Samuel Johnson, large	1950-1960	**225.00**	**250.00**
D 6291			
☐ Old London Jug (Miscellaneous Dickens Jugs)	1949-1960	**200.00**	**275.00**
D 6292			
☐ Peggotty Jug (Miscellaneous Dickens Jugs)	1949-1960	**275.00**	**350.00**
D 6295			
☐ Jarge, large	1950-1960	**150.00**	**185.00**
D 6296			
☐ Samuel Johnson, small	1950-1960	**150.00**	**175.00**
D 6319			
☐ The Squire (Toby Jug)	1950-1969	**250.00**	**300.00**
D 6320			
☐ The Hunstman (Toby Jug)	1950-	**95.00**	
D 6321			
☐ Friar Tuck, large	1951-1960	**350.00**	**400.00**
D 6322			
☐ Clown, white hair, large	1951-1955	**900.00**	**1000.00**
D 6335			
☐ Long John Silver, large	1952-	**75.00**	
D 6336			
☐ Lord Nelson, large	1952-1969	**235.00**	**285.00**
D 6337			
☐ Uncle Tom Cobbleigh, large	1952-1960	**350.00**	**400.00**
D 6372			
☐ Johnny Appleseed, large	1935-1969	**235.00**	**260.00**
D 6374			
☐ Simple Simon, large	1953-1960	**525.00**	**575.00**
D 6375			
☐ Dick Whittington, large	1953-1960	**325.00**	**375.00**
D 6384			
☐ Granny, small	1953-	**50.00**	
D 6385			
☐ Falstaff, small	1950-	**50.00**	
D 6386			
☐ Long John Silver, small	1952-	**50.00**	

	Date	Price Range	
D 6403			
☐ The Pied Piper, large	1954-1980	**75.00**	
D 6404			
☐ Issac Walton, large	1953-	**75.00**	
D 6429			
☐ Poacher, large	1955-	**75.00**	
D 6438			
☐ Rip Van Winkle, large.............	1955-	**75.00**	
D 6439			
☐ Athos, large....................	1960-	**75.00**	
D 6440			
☐ Porthos, large	1956-	**75.00**	
D 6441			
☐ Aramis, large	1956-	**75.00**	
D 6452			
☐ Athos, small	1960-	**50.00**	
D 6453			
☐ Porthos, small	1956-	**50.00**	
D 6454			
☐ Aramis, small	1956-	**50.00**	
D 6455			
☐ Don Quixote, large	1957-	**75.00**	
D 6456			
☐ Sancho Panza, large	1960-1982	**65.00**	**85.00**
D 6460			
☐ Don Quixote, small...............	1957-	**50.00**	
D 6461			
☐ Sancho Panza, small	1960-1982	**40.00**	**60.00**
D 6462			
☐ The Pied Piper, small	1957-1980	**50.00**	
D 6463			
☐ Rip Van Winkle, small	1957-	**50.00**	
D 6464			
☐ Poacher, small	1957-	**50.00**	
D 6467			
☐ Captain Henry Morgan, large	1958-1981	**65.00**	**95.00**
D 6469			
☐ Captain Henry Morgan, small	1958-1981	**40.00**	**60.00**
D 6470			
☐ Mine Host, small	1958-1981	**35.00**	**55.00**
D 6488			
☐ Mine Host, large	1958-1981	**60.00**	**80.00**
D 6496			
☐ Viking, large	1959-1975	**85.00**	**115.00**
D 6497			
☐ The Fortune Teller, large	1959-1967	**400.00**	**450.00**
D 6498			
☐ The Lawyer, large	1959-	**75.00**	

D 6499	Date	Price Range	
☐ Bacchus, large	1959-	75.00	
D 6500			
☐ Captain Ahab, large	1959-	75.00	
D 6501			
☐ The Mikado, large	1959-1969	325.00	375.00
D 6502			
☐ Viking, small	1959-1975	55.00	70.00
D 6503			
☐ The Fortune Teller, small	1959-1967	350.00	400.00
D 6504			
☐ The Lawyer, small	1959-	50.00	
D 6505			
☐ Bacchus, small	1959-	50.00	
D 6506			
☐ Captain Ahab, small	1959-	50.00	
D 6507			
☐ The Mikado, small	1959-1969	300.00	350.00
D 6508			
☐ Aramis, miniature	1960-	29.95	
D 6509			
☐ Athos, miniature	1960-	75.00	
D 6510			
☐ Captain Henry Morgan	1960-1981	25.00	35.00
D 6511			
☐ Don Quixote, miniature	1960-	29.95	
D 6512			
☐ Long John Silver	1960-	29.95	
D 6513			
☐ Mine Host, miniature	1960-1981	20.00	30.00
D 6514			
☐ The Pied Piper, miniature	1960-1980	29.95	
D 6515			
☐ Poacher, miniature	1960-	29.95	
D 6516			
☐ Porthos, miniature	1960-	29.95	
D 6517			
☐ Rip Van Winkle, miniature	1960-	29.95	
D 6518			
☐ Sancho Panza, miniature	1960-1982	25.00	35.00
D 6519			
☐ Falstaff, miniature	1960-	29.95	
D 6520			
☐ Granny, miniature	1960-	29.95	
D 6521			
☐ Bacchus, miniature	1960-	29.95	
D 6522			
☐ Captain Ahab, miniature	1960-	29.95	

	Date	Price Range	
D 6523			
☐ The Fortune Teller, miniature	1960-1967	350.00	400.00
D 6524			
☐ The Lawyer, miniature	1960-	29.95	
D 6525			
☐ The Mikado, miniature	1960-1969	350.00	385.00
D 6526			
☐ Viking, miniature	1960-1975	30.00	45.00
D 6527			
☐ Robin Hood (2nd version), large	1960-	75.00	
D 6528			
☐ Dick Turpin (2nd version), large	1960-	75.00	
D 6529			
☐ Merlin, large	1960-	75.00	
D 6530			
☐ Town Crier, large	1960-1973	150.00	175.00
D 6531			
☐ Gone Away, large	1960-1981	65.00	95.00
D 6532			
☐ Robinson Crusoe, large	1960-1982	60.00	80.00
D 6533			
☐ Falconer, large	1960-	75.00	
D 6534			
☐ Robin Hood (2nd version), small	1960-	50.00	
D 6535			
☐ Dick Turpin (2nd version), small	1960-	50.00	
D 6536			
☐ Merlin, small	1960-	50.00	
D 6537			
☐ Town Crier, small	1960-1973	100.00	125.00
D 6538			
☐ Gone Away, small	1960-	40.00	60.00
D 6539			
☐ Robinson Crusoe, small	1960-1982	35.00	55.00
D 6540			
☐ Falconer, small	1960-	50.00	
D 6541			
☐ Robin Hood (2nd version), miniature .	1960-	29.95	
D 6542			
☐ Dick Turpin (2nd version), miniature . .	1960-	29.95	
D 6543			
☐ Merlin, miniature	1960-	29.95	
D 6544			
☐ Town Crier, miniature	1960-1973	125.00	150.00
D 6545			
☐ Gone Away, miniature	1960-	25.00	35.00
D 6546			
☐ Robinson Crusoe, miniature	1960-	25.00	35.00

	Date	Price Range	
D 6547			
☐ Falconer, miniature	1960-	**29.95**	
D 6548			
☐ Neptune, large	1961-	**75.00**	
D 6374			
☐ Simple Simon, large	1953-1960	**525.00**	**575.00**
D 6550			
☐ Gladiator, large.	1961-1967	**450.00**	**500.00**
D 6551			
☐ Old Salt, large	1961-	**75.00**	
D 6552			
☐ Neptune, small	1961-	**50.00**	
D 6553			
☐ Gladiator, small	1952-	**50.00**	
D 6554			
☐ Old Salt, small	1961-	**50.00**	
D 6555			
☐ Neptune, miniature	1961-	**29.95**	
D 6556			
☐ Gladiator, miniature.	1961-1967	**275.00**	**325.00**
D 6558			
☐ Scarmouche, large	1962-1967	**425.00**	**475.00**
D 6559			
☐ Regency Beau, large	1962-1967	**500.00**	**550.00**
D 6560			
☐ Gulliver, large	1962-1967	**450.00**	**500.00**
D 6561			
☐ Scarmouche, small	1962-1967	**325.00**	**375.00**
D 6562			
☐ Regency Beau, small	1962-1967	**325.00**	**375.00**
D 6563			
☐ Gulliver, small.	1962-1967	**350.00**	**400.00**
D 6564			
☐ Scarmouche, miniature	1962-1967	**300.00**	**325.00**
D 6565			
☐ Regency Beau, miniature	1962-1967	**375.00**	**425.00**
D 6566			
☐ Gulliver, miniature	1962-1967	**350.00**	**400.00**
D 6567			
☐ The Apothecary, large	1963-	**75.00**	
D 6568			
☐ Guardsman, large.	1963-	**75.00**	
D 6569			
☐ Night Watchman, large	1963-	**75.00**	
D 6570			
☐ Goaler, large	1963-	**75.00**	
D 6571			
☐ Blacksmith, large	1963-	**75.00**	
D 6572			
☐ Bootmaker, large	1963-	**75.00**	

	Date	Price Range	
D 6573			
☐ Gunsmith, large	1963-	**75.00**	
D 6574			
☐ The Apothecary, small	1963-	**50.00**	
D 6575			
☐ Guardsman, small	1963-	**50.00**	
D 6576			
☐ Night Watchman, small	1963-	**50.00**	
D 6577			
☐ Goaler, small	1963-	**50.00**	
D 6578			
☐ Blacksmith, small	1963-	**50.00**	
D 6579			
☐ Bootmaker, small	1963-	**50.00**	
D 6580			
☐ Gunsmith, small	1963-	**50.00**	
D 6581			
☐ The Apothecary, miniature	1963-	**29.95**	
D 6582			
☐ Guardsman, miniature	1963-	**29.95**	
D 6583			
☐ Night Watchman, miniature	1963-	**29.95**	
D 6584			
☐ Goaler, miniature	1963-	**29.95**	
D 6585			
☐ Blacksmith, miniature	1963-	**29.95**	
D 6586			
☐ Bootmaker, miniature	1963-	**29.95**	
D 6587			
☐ Gunsmith, miniature	1963-	**29.95**	
D 6588			
☐ 'Ard of 'Earing, large	1964-1967	**850.00**	**900.00**
D 6589			
☐ Gondolier, large	1964-1969	**375.00**	**425.00**
D 6590			
☐ Punch and Judy Man, large	1964-1969	**475.00**	**525.00**
D 6591			
☐ 'Ard of 'Earing, small	1964-1967	**650.00**	**700.00**
D 6592			
☐ Gondolier, small	1964-1969	**275.00**	**325.00**
D 6593			
☐ Punch and Judy Man, small	1964-1969	**350.00**	**400.00**
D 6594			
☐ 'Ard of 'Earing, miniature...........	1964-1967	**1300.00**	**1500.00**
D 6595			
☐ Gondolier, miniature	1964-1969	**400.00**	**450.00**
D 6596			
☐ Punch and Judy Man, miniature	1964-1969	**325.00**	**375.00**

	Date	Price Range	
D 6597			
☐ Captain Hook, large	1965-1971	**250.00**	**300.00**
D 6598			
☐ Mad Hatter, large	1965-	**75.00**	
D 6599			
☐ Ugly Duchess, large	1965-1973	**230.00**	**260.00**
D 6600			
☐ Walrus and Carpenter, large	1965-1979	**75.00**	**100.00**
D 6601			
☐ Captain Hook, small	1965-1971	**235.00**	**275.00**
D 6602			
☐ Mad Hatter, small.................	1965-	**50.00**	
D 6603			
☐ Ugly Duchess, small	1965-1973	**225.00**	**250.00**
D 6604			
☐ Walrus and Carpenter, small	1965-1969	**55.00**	**70.00**
D 6605			
☐ Captain Hook, miniature	1965-1971	**270.00**	**315.00**
D 6606			
☐ Mad Hatter, miniature	1965-	**29.95**	
D 6607			
☐ Ugly Duchess, miniature	1965-1973	**225.00**	**275.00**
D 6608			
☐ Walrus and Carpenter, miniature	1965-1979	**35.00**	**50.00**
D 6609			
☐ Trapper, large	1967-	**75.00**	
D 6610			
☐ Lumberjack, large	1967-1982	**60.00**	**80.00**
D 6611			
☐ North American Indian, large	1967-	**75.00**	
D 6612			
☐ Trapper, small...................	1967-	**50.00**	
D 6613			
☐ Lumberjack, small	1967-1982	**35.00**	**55.00**
D 6614			
☐ North American Indian, small	1967-	**50.00**	
D 6616			
☐ Smuggler, large	1968-1980	**75.00**	
D 6617			
☐ Lobster Man, large	1968-	**75.00**	
D 6618			
☐ St. George, large.................	1968-1975	**90.00**	**110.00**
D 6619			
☐ Smuggler, small	1968-1980	**60.00**	
D 6620			
☐ Lobster Man, small	1968-	**50.00**	
D 6621			
☐ St. George, small	1968-1975	**60.00**	**75.00**
D 6622			
☐ Yachtsman, large	1971-1979	**100.00**	**125.00**

	Date	Price Range	
D 6623			
☐ Golfer, large	1971-	**75.00**	
D 6625			
☐ Jockey, large.	1971-1975	**175.00**	**200.00**
D 6630			
☐ Gardener, large.	1973-1980	**75.00**	
D 6631			
☐ Sleuth, large	1973-	**75.00**	
D 6632			
☐ Tam O'Shanter, large	1975-1979	**80.00**	**100.00**
D 6633			
☐ Veteran Motorist, large	1973-	**75.00**	
D 6634			
☐ Gardener, small	1973-1980	**50.00**	
D 6635			
☐ Sleuth, small	1973-	**50.00**	
D 6636			
☐ Tam O'Shanter, small	1973-1979	**60.00**	**75.00**
D 6637			
☐ Veteran Motorist, small	1973-	**50.00**	
D 6638			
☐ Gardener, miniature.	1973-1980	**29.95**	
D 6639			
☐ Sleuth, miniature	1973-	**29.95**	
D 6640			
☐ Tam O'Shanter, miniature	1973-1979	**30.00**	**45.00**
D 6641			
☐ Veteran Motorist, miniature	1973-	**29.95**	
D 6642			
☐ Henry VIII, large	1975-	**75.00**	
D 6643			
☐ Catherine of Aragon, large	1975-	**75.00**	
D 6644			
☐ Anne Boleyn, large	1975-	**75.00**	
D 6645			
☐ Catherine Howard, large	1978-	**75.00**	
D 6646			
☐ Jane Seymour, large	1979-	**75.00**	
D 6647			
☐ Henry VIII, small	1979-	**50.00**	
D 6648			
☐ Henry VIII, miniature	1979-	**29.95**	
D 6650			
☐ Anne Boleyn, small	1975-	**50.00**	
D 6651			
☐ Anne Boleyn, miniature	1981-	**29.95**	
D 6652			
☐ Lobster Man, miniature	1981-	**29.95**	
D 6653			
☐ Anne of Cleves, large	1980-	**75.00**	

D 6654	Date	Price Range
☐ Mark Twain, large	1980-	75.00
D 6657		
☐ Catherine of Aragon, small	1981-	50.00
D 6658		
☐ Catherine of Aragon, miniature	1981-	29.95
D 6659		
☐ The Cabinetmaker, large	1981-	75.00
D 6660		
☐ Sir Frances Drake (Toby Jug)	1981-	95.00
D 6661		
☐ Sherlock Holmes (Toby Jug)	1981-	95.00
D 6664		
☐ Catherine Parr, large	1981-	75.00
D 6665		
☐ North American Indian, miniature . . .	1981-	29.95
D 6669		
☐ George Washington, large	1982-	75.00
D 6667		
☐ Macbeth, large	1982-	75.00
D 6672		
☐ Hamlet, large	1982-	75.00
D 6673		
☐ Othello, large	1982-	75.00
D 6671		
☐ Henry V, large	1982-	75.00
D 6668		
☐ Santa Claus, large	1981 only	75.00
D		
☐ Santa Claus, large	1982 only	75.00
D 6690		
☐ Santa Claus, large	1983-	75.00
D 6670		
☐ Romeo, large.	1983-	75.00
D 6689		
☐ Shakespeare, large	1983-	75.00
D 6691		
☐ D'Artagnan, large	1983-	75.00
D 6694		
☐ Mark Twain, small	1983-	39.95
D 6695		
☐ Benjamin Franklin, small	1983-	39.95
D 6698		
☐ U.S. Civil War/Grand and Lee, large (limited edition)	1983-	95.00
D 6699		
☐ Mr. Litigate, The Lawyer	1983-	
D 6700		
☐ Miss Nostrum, The Nurse	1983-	

D 6701   Date   Price Range
☐ Mr. Furrow, The Farmer 1983-
D 6702
☐ Rev. Cassock, The Clergyman 1983-

CHARACTER AND TOBY JUGS

It is thought by most persons who are collectors of "Toby Jugs" and "Character Jugs" that the idea of a pitcher or jug depicting either a full figure or head was first designed and made early in the eighteenth century by some potter believed to be a Staffordshire potter. These drinking vessels and flasks soon became very popular, spreading from England to all parts of the world. Although we know from museums around the world can be found various forms of pitchers, jugs, flasks and etc., although very crude in form, do resemble a living being. However, it was not until the eighteenth century that there began to appear a series of jugs in a more decorative and distinctive design pattern.

The Toby jug, which over the period of years, has become one of the more popular items for collectors usually depicts a seated character with a peculiar type hat with three points, one of which is used for the pouring spout. It is believed that this jug has carried down the name "Toby" from a song popular in the mid-eighteenth century in which there was a character called "Toby Fillpot."

It was not until the early 1930's that Charles J. Noke, then Art Director for the Royal Doulton Company, decided to model a design he had been working on for some time in the form of a pitcher with a face. This was titled "John Barleycorn" an imaginary being representing whiskey. Secondly, there was Old Charley, a night watchman . . . Saurey Gamp, a Dickens character . . . Dick Turpin, a notorious highwayman, and Parson Brown, all accepted with widespread popularity. Some of the other Doulton modellers for the character jugs were Leslie Harradine (who also modelled a number of figurines), Max Henk, Harry Fenton and David Brian Biggs.

From the artist mind comes the sketch, and from this sketch a master mold is made. The master mold is then taken and a "working" mold is made from it . . . from this working mold there might be as many as thirty molds made for pouring. These are plaster of paris and when the liquid is poured into them it is allowed to sit for a while as the plaster of paris will absorb the liquid and the mixture becomes a hardened clay molded figure. After the figure is removed from the mold it is cleaned up, any seams erased and the handle which is cast separately is then applied. The figure is then fired at a very high degree causing a great deal of shinkage. When removed and carefully inspected it is sent to the decorating studios where specially prepared paints are used in colors selected from the original design. It is then fired a second time for the hardening of the colors. The third firing is for the glossy finish which appears on most all of the figurines and mugs. There was a span of a few years in the late 1960's and 1970's when the character jugs were made of fine china instead of earthenware, and these figures have the translucent appearance of fine china.

Each character jug is titled and the name appears on the bottom along with the Royal Doulton trademark and a "D" number. The name also is embedded into the back of the jug. It is widely recognized among collectors that a jug bearing an "A" mark is of more value because of this mark which supposedly signified an earlier issue. However, it appears there is no basis to this as this mark was apparently used for factory identification purposes. Nevertheless the jugs bearing the "A" mark command a higher price.

As with the figurines a few prototype jugs were made but to the authors knowledge were never marketed. Sometimes prototypes are made as samples for the factory's use in determining if the subject is a saleable item or perhaps even to test market in areas throughout the world but quite often or probably most often these figures never are available to the public or to the collector, such as the character jugs titled Buffalo Bill, Maori and the Baseball Player. It has been reported that these jugs do exist in collections, although to my knowledge they were not marketed in any manner, perhaps a few escaped from the factory in an unexplained manner. Since it is not known how many truly exist one cannot put a dollar value on such a piece.

A few jugs have experienced some design changes over the years of production such as Auld Mac was "Owd Mac" during production years of 1938 through 1945; Beefeater appears with both "GR" and "ER" on the handles . . . from 1947 through 1953 the handle bears "GR" for George Rex and in 1953 the initials "ER" for Elizabeth Regina were used and is still in current production; Cavalier experienced a color change (though very slight) and a change in the collar in 1950; Dick Turpin in the earlier version has a mask on his hat but was changed in 1960 with a mask covering his eyes, a horse for a handle and a complete different color version . . . a total reconstruction of this figure; Drake, the very early version did not have a hat . . . this figure was test marketed but never put into general production . . . a few do exist in collections today and are known as the "Hatless Drake" . . . the second version redesigned with a hat and different coloring was introduced in 1940; John Barleycorn jugs in the early versions bear a different handle than the later pieces. Handle is molded down into the pitcher itself rather than leaving the appearance of an attached handle; earlier versions of Lumberjack, North American Indian and The Trapper bear the words "Canadian Centennial Series 1867-1967" and were produced for sale in Canada in 1967, however, in 1968 they were issued for sale world-wide without the backstamp; four Dickens characters were changed to a smaller size in 1949 with the style remaining the same . . . they were Buz Fuz, Cap'n Cuttle, Fat Boy, Mr. Micawber, Mr. Pickwick and Sam Weller; an earlier version of Old King Cole shows the character with a yellow crown.

On the bottom of the jug may appear a copyright date, register number and a Royal Doulton trademark . . . sometimes one, two or all three may be on the jug, however, the date that appears does not necessarily mean the date the jug was placed in production, it is merely the date of copyright for that particular piece. Normally release is sometime within a twelve month period of the copyright date.

DICKENS TINIES

A new set of tinies will be introduced into the character jug line in the Spring of 1983 depicting characters from Dickens popular and best loved writings. This is the first tinies series issued for some time and should generate a great deal of interest. There were no prices available at the time of compilation of material for this book. The figures are as follows . . .

Mr. Bumble	**Fagin**
Bill Sykes	**Uriah Heep**
Betsy Trotwood	**Little Nell**
Artful Dodger	**David Copperfield**
Oliver	**Charles Dickens**
Scrooge	**Mrs. Bardell**

CHARACTER JUGS

	Date	Price Range
ANNE BOLEYN		
Second wife of Henry VIII.		
☐ **D 6644,** large	1975-	**75.00**
☐ **D 6650,** small	1975-	**50.00**
☐ **D 6651,** miniature	1981-	**29.95**
ANNE OF CLEVES		
Fourth wife of Henry VIII.		
☐ **D 6653,** large	1980-	**75.00**
available in large size only		
APOTHECARY, The		
A character from the Williamsburg series. Apothecary was the forerunner of what today is our drug store. The person who owned an Apothecary was allowed to dispense drugs for medicinal purposes, even going as far as treating a patient.		
☐ **D 6567,** large	1963-	**75.00**
☐ **D 6574,** small	1963-	**50.00**
☐ **D 6581,** miniature	1963-	**29.95**
ARAMIS		
A character from the book "The Three Musketeers".		
☐ **D 6441,** large	1956-	**75.00**
☐ **D 6454,** small	1956-	**50.00**
☐ **D 6508,** miniature	1960-	**29.95**

	Date	Price	Range
'ARD OF 'EARING			

A character with hand cupped to his
ear indicating he is partially deaf.

	Date	Price	Range
☐ **D 6588,** large	1964-1967	850.00	900.00
☐ **D 6591,** small	1964-1967	650.00	700.00
☐ **D 6594,** miniature	1964-1967	1300.00	1500.00

'ARRIET

Depicts a London Cockney street
trader or costermonger as they are
called in England.

☐ **D 6208,** large	1947-1960	175.00	200.00
☐ **D 6236,** small	1947-1960	60.00	65.00
☐ same jug with an "A" mark		65.00	70.00
☐ **D 6250,** miniature	1947-1960	50.00	60.00
☐ same jug with an "A" mark		70.00	80.00
☐ **D 6256,** tiny	1947-1960	175.00	225.00

'ARRY

Companion to 'Arriet; also depicts a
London Cockney street trader or costermonger.

☐ **D 6207,** large	1947-1960	175.00	200.00
☐ **D 6235,** small	1947-1960	60.00	65.00
☐ same jug with an "A" mark		75.00	85.00
☐ **D 6249,** miniature	1947-1960	70.00	80.00
☐ same jug with an "A" mark		80.00	90.00
☐ **D 6255,** tiny	1947-1960	200.00	225.00

ATHOS

A character from the book "The Three
Musketeers".

☐ **D 6439,** large	1960-	75.00	
☐ **D 6452,** small	1960-	50.00	
☐ **D 6509,** miniature	1960-	29.95	

AULD MAC

Depicts a thrift Scotsman. Also
known as "Owd Mac", note listing
under that title.

☐ **D 5823,** large	1938-	75.00	
☐ same jug with an "A" mark		85.00	95.00
☐ **D 5824,** small	1938-	50.00	
☐ same jug with an "A" mark		75.00	85.00
☐ **D 6253,** miniature	1946-	29.95	
☐ same jug with an "A" mark		45.00	60.00
☐ **D 6257,** tiny	1946-1960	185.00	225.00

BACCHUS	Date	Price Range	
The Greek "god of wine", this character has a wreath of greenery and grapes representing the grape harvest.			
☐ **D 6499,** large	1959-	75.00	
☐ **D 6505,** small	1959-	50.00	
☐ **D 6521,** miniature	1960-	29.95	

BEEFEATER	Date	Price Range	
A popular name for a member of the Yeoman of the Guard, bodyguards for the Queen.			
☐ **D 6206,** large	1947-	75.00	
☐ same jug with an "A" mark		100.00	125.00
☐ **D 6233,** small	1947-	50.00	
☐ same jug with an "A" mark		55.00	65.00
☐ **D 6251,** miniature	1947-	29.95	

Benjamin Franklin, D6695, large, **75.00**

BENJAMIN FRANKLIN

Depicting one of America's most famous statesmen in his famous experiment of flying a kite in a thunderstorm to demonstrate that lightning was a form of electricity. Handle is a kite in the clouds with a key at the base of the handle.

	Date	Price Range
☐ **D 6695,** small....................	1983-	**39.95**

BLACKSMITH

A character from the Williamsburg series. Blacksmith was an eighteenth century ironworker. These characters have been recreated in the restoration of the town of Williamsburg, the original capital of Virginia.

☐ **D 6571,** large.....................	1963-	**75.00**
☐ **D 6578,** small	1963-	**50.00**
☐ **D 6586,** miniature	1963-	**29.95**

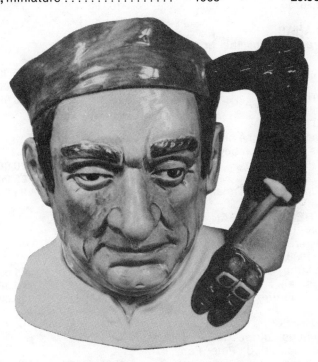

Bootmaker, D6572, large, **75.00**

	Date	Price Range	
BOOTMAKER			

A character from the Williamsburg series. Bootmaker was the gentleman who made shoes and boots in the eighteenth century.

	Date	Price Range	
☐ **D 6572,** large	1963-	75.00	
☐ **D 6579,** small	1963-	50.00	
☐ **D 6586,** miniature	1963-	29.95	

BUZ FUZ

A character from the book "Pickwick Papers" by Charles Dickens. Also note listing under Sergeant Buz Fuz.

☐ **D 5838,** intermediate size	1938-1948	110.00	125.00
☐ **D 5838,** same size	1948-1960	100.00	115.00
☐ **Same jug with an "A" mark**		125.00	150.00

CABINETMAKER, The

A character from the Williamburg series.

☐ **D 6659,** large	1981-	75.00	

CAPTAIN AHAB

A character from the book "Moby Dick".

☐ **D 6500,** large	1959-	75.00	
☐ **D 6506,** small	1959-	50.00	
☐ **D 6522,** miniature	1960-	29.95	

CAP'N CUTTLE

A character from the novel by Charles Dickens titled "Dombey and Sons".

☐ **D 5842,** special size	1938-1948	120.00	135.00
☐ **D 5842,** small size	1948-1960	85.00	95.00
☐ same jug with an "A" mark		95.00	100.00

CAPTAIN HENRY MORGAN

Probably the most famous British Buccaneer of his time. Born in 1635, died in 1688.

☐ **D 6467,** large	1958-1981	65.00	95.00
☐ **D 6469,** small	1958-1981	40.00	60.00
☐ **D 6510,** miniature	1960-1981	25.00	35.00

CAPTAIN HOOK

A villainous pirate in James M. Barrie's book titled "Peter Pan".

☐ **D 6597,** large	1965-1971	275.00	325.00
☐ **D 6601,** small	1965-1971	250.00	300.00
☐ **D 6605,** miniature	1965-1971	300.00	350.00

CARDINAL

A dignitary in the Catholic Church. This jug may represent a character from Shakespeare's Henry VIII known as Cardinal Woolsey.

	Date	Price Range	
☐ **D 5614**, large	1936-1960	110.00	135.00
☐ same jug with an "A" mark		120.00	145.00
☐ **D 6033**, small	1939-1960	65.00	80.00
☐ same jug with an "A" mark		75.00	90.00
☐ **D 6129**, miniature	1940-1960	50.00	65.00
☐ same jug with an "A" mark		60.00	75.00
☐ **D 6258**, tiny	1947-1960	220.00	250.00

CATHERINE HOWARD

Fifth wife of Henry VIII.

☐ **D 6645**, large	1978-	75.00	

CATHERINE OF ARAGON

First wife of Henry VIII.

☐ **D 6643**, large	1975-	75.00	
☐ **D 6657**, small	1981-	50.00	
☐ **D 6658**, miniature	1981-	29.95	

CATHERINE PARR

Sixth and final wife of Henry VIII.

☐ **D 6664**, large	1981-	75.00	

CAVALIER, The

During the reign of King Charles I his staunch supporters were given a title of honor and were known as "The Cavaliers".

☐ **D 6114**, large	1940-1960	125.00	150.00
☐ same jug with an "A" mark		160.00	175.00
☐ **D 6173**, small	1941-1960	75.00	85.00
☐ same jug with an "A" mark		75.00	90.00

CHURCHILL

Depicting the distinguished stateman Winston Churchill this jug is believed to have been in production for a short time only. It is not known the exact date it was withdrawn from the market. Considered extremely rare.

☐ **D 6170**, large	1940-	8500.00	10000.00

D'Artagnan, D6691, large, **75.00**

CLOWN, Red hair	Date	Price Range	
Depicting a character from the circus. Considered rare.			
☐ **D 5610,** large	1937-1942	**4750.00**	**5000.00**

CLOWN, White hair.			
☐ **D 6322,** large	1951-1955	**1000.00**	**1200.00**

D'ARTAGNAN
Depicting one of the colorful Dumas characters. Attired in costume of the period, plumed hat, lace trimmed collar.
☐ **D 6691,** large   1983-   **75.00**

DICK TURPIN
A notorious highwayman who was eventually hanged. Released in two versions.

DICK TURBIN (cont.)	Date	Price Range	
First version - mask up on hat			
☐ **D 5495,** large	1935-1960	125.00	150.00
☐ same jug with an "A" mark		140.00	180.00
☐ **D 5618,** small	1935-1960	60.00	80.00
☐ same jug with an "A" mark		70.00	90.00
☐ **D 6128,** miniature	1940-1960	55.00	70.00
☐ same jug with an "A" mark		70.00	85.00
Second version - Mask on face, horse handle.			
☐ **D 6528,** large	1960-	75.00	
☐ **D 6535,** small	1960-	50.00	
☐ **D 6542,** miniature	1960-	29.95	

DICK WHITTINGTON
Lord Mayor of London three times during the fifteenth century.

	Date	Price Range	
☐ **D 6375,** large	1953-1960	325.00	375.00

DON QUIXOTE
A character from the novel by Miguel de Cervantes' titled "Don Quixote".

	Date	Price Range	
☐ **D 6455,** large	1957-	75.00	
☐ **D 6460,** small	1957-	50.00	
☐ **D 6511,** miniature	1960-	29.95	

DRAKE
Depicting Sir Frances Drake, a distinguished figure in British sea power in the sixteenth century.

First version - Hatless Drake

	Date	Price Range	
☐		8000.00	8500.00

Second version - With hat and different collar.

	Date	Price Range	
☐ **D 6115,** large	1940-1960	125.00	150.00
☐ same jug with an "A" mark		140.00	175.00
☐ **D 6174,** small	1941-1960	80.00	100.00
☐ same jug with an "A" mark		90.00	115.00

FALCONER
Depicting a man who is trainer of birds. A falcon is the handle of this jug.

	Date	Price Range	
☐ **D 6533,** large	1960-	75.00	
☐ **D 6540,** small	1960-	50.00	
☐ **D 6547,** miniature	1960-	29.95	

	Date	Price Range	
FALSTAFF			

A character in the Shakespeare novel "Henry IV", Sir John Falstaff a fat and jolly character particularly liked for his wit and laughter.

	Date	Price Range	
☐ **D 6287**, large	1950-	75.00	
☐ **D 6385**, small	1950-	50.00	
☐ **D 6519**, miniature	1960-	29.95	

FARMER JOHN

Depicts the typical English farmer.

	Date	Price Range	
☐ **D 5788**, large	1938-1960	125.00	150.00
☐ same jug with an "A" mark		135.00	160.00
☐ **D 5789**, small	1938-1960	60.00	70.00
☐ same jug with an "A" mark		70.00	80.00

FAT BOY

Depicting a character from the Charles Dicken's novel "Pickwick Papers".

	Date	Price Range	
☐ **D 5840**, special size	1938-1948	110.00	125.00
☐ **D 5840**, small	1948-1960	55.00	65.00
☐ same jug with an "A" mark		75.00	85.00
☐ **D 6139**, miniature	1940-1960	60.00	70.00
☐ same jug with an "A" mark		65.00	75.00
☐ **D 6142**, tiny	1940-1960	110.00	135.00

FORTUNE TELLER, The

Depicts a gypsy woman who roams the countryside who for a "piece of silver" will reveal the future for you.

	Date	Price Range	
☐ **D 6497**, large	1959-1967	400.00	450.00
☐ **D 6503**, small	1959-1967	350.00	400.00
☐ **D 6523**, miniature	1960-1967	350.00	400.00

FRIAR TUCK

A member of Robin Hood's band, he was the chaplain. Also a character in Sir Walter Scott's book titled "Ivanhoe".

	Date	Price Range	
☐ **D 6321**, large	1951-1960	350.00	375.00

George Washington, D6669, large, **75.00**

	Date	Price Range	
GEORGE WASHINGTON			
Issued to commemorate the 250th anniversary of his birth. Designed by Stan Taylor this mug depicts the first President of the United States.			
☐ **D 6669,** large size	1982-	75.00	
GARDENER			
A character jug depicting the typical man who can be found working with the earth with the handle being a shovel and some vegetables.			
☐ **D 6630,** large	1973-1980	75.00	
☐ **D 6634,** small	1973-1980	50.00	
☐ **D 6638,** miniature	1973-1980	29.95	
GLADIATOR			
Depicting a warrior of the Roman Empire.			
☐ **D 6550,** large	1961-1967	500.00	600.00
☐ **D 6553,** small	1961-1967	375.00	425.00
☐ **D 6556,** miniature	1961-1967	300.00	350.00

	Date	Price Range	
GOALER			

A character from the Williamsburg series.

	Date	Price Range	
☐ **D 6570,** large	1963-	**75.00**	
☐ **D 6577,** small	1963-	**50.00**	
☐ **D 6584,** miniature	1963-	**29.95**	

GOLFER

Depicting an English gentleman out for a game of golf.

☐ **D 6623,** large	1971-	**75.00**	

Small and miniature sizes were test marketed but not produced.

GONDOLIER

Depicts the romantic singing boatman who guides his boat through the narrow canals of Venice singing his romantic songs.

☐ **D 6589,** large	1964-1969	**500.00**	**550.00**
☐ **D 6592,** small	1964-1969	**325.00**	**375.00**
☐ **D 6596,** miniature	1964-1969	**425.00**	**475.00**

GONE AWAY

Depicts an English huntsman with his typical red coat and black silk hat. Handle is a fox.

☐ **D 6531,** large	1960-1981	**65.00**	**95.00**
☐ **D 6538,** small	1960-1981	**40.00**	**60.00**
☐ **D 6545,** miniature	1960-1981	**25.00**	**35.00**

GRANNY

Depicts an aged woman.

☐ **D 5521,** large	1935-	**75.00**	
☐ same jug with an "A" mark		**90.00**	**100.00**
☐ **D 6384,** small	1953-	**50.00**	
☐ same jug with an "A" mark		**110.00**	**125.00**
☐ **D 6520,** miniature	1960-	**29.95**	

An early version of Granny shows the characters face without the front tooth which appears on the currently produced jugs. Usually found on older "A" marked pieces.

☐ **Granny** jug without tooth		**300.00**	**350.00**

The Civil War, Grant And Lee, D6698, **75.00**

	Date	Price Range
GRANT AND LEE — THE CIVIL WAR		

The first in a series titled "The Antagonists Collection" this mug represents the first double faced character jug since 1937. Both men wear the uniforms of their sides, navy blue for the Union and grey for the Confederacy. Their collars are embellished with bright golden stars of rank and the handle in their colourful flags. Limited edition of 9,500.

	Date	Price Range
☐ **D 6698,** large	1983-	**95.00**

GUARDSMAN

A character from the Williamsburg series.

	Date	Price Range
☐ **D 6568,** large	1963-	**75.00**
☐ **D 6575,** small	1963-	**50.00**
☐ **D 6582,** miniature	1963-	**29.95**

GULLIVER	**Date**	**Price Range**	
Depicting a character from the book "Gulliver's Travels", the handle is a castle with two Lilliputians on top.			
☐ **D 6560,** large	1962-1967	**450.00**	**500.00**
☐ **D 6563,** small	1962-1967	**350.00**	**400.00**
☐ **D 6566,** miniature	1962-1967	**350.00**	**400.00**

GUNSMITH			
A character from the Williamburg series.			
☐ **D 6573,** large	1963-	**75.00**	
☐ **D 6580,** small	1963-	**50.00**	
☐ **D 6587,** miniature	1963-	**29.95**	

Hamlet, D6672, large, **75.00**

HAMLET		
Depicting one of the characters from a Shakespearian play.		
☐ **D 6672,** large size	1982-	**75.00**

	Date	Price Range	

HENRY V
    Depicting one of the famous kings of
England.

☐ **D 6671**, large size   1982-   **75.00**

HENRY VIII
    Second son of Henry VII . . . he ruled
England from 1509 to 1547.

☐ **D 6642**, large   1975-   **75.00**
☐ **D 6647**, small   1979-   **50.00**
☐ **D 6648**, miniature   1979-   **29.95**

IZAAC WALTON
    An author who has endeared himself
to many , . . probably best known for
his work titled "The Compleat Angler".

☐ **D 6404**, large   1953-1982   **60.00**   **85.00**

JANE SEYMOUR
    Third wife of Henry VIII.

☐ **D 6646**, large   1979-   **75.00**

JARGE
    Depicts the original country boy, by
no means handsome and often ridi-
culed.

☐ **D 6288**, large   1950-1960   **300.00**   **350.00**
☐ **D 6295**, small   1950-1960   **175.00**   **200.00**

JESTER
    A character known for his wit, he was
often one who was instructed to use
his wit to entertain nobility.

☐ **D 5556**, small   1936-   **115.00**   **135.00**
☐ same jug with an "A" mark **125.00**   **150.00**

JOCKEY
    Depicting a character who rides thor-
oughbred horses.

☐ **D 6625**, large   1971-1975   **175.00**   **200.00**

JOHN BARLEYCORN
    Depicting a character in Old English
ballads, familiar to many as the per-
sonification of whiskey or malt liq-
uours. This jug was re-issued in 1978
as a limited edition of 7,500 for distribution in North America.

JOHN BARLEYCORN (cont.)

	Date	Price Range	
☐ **D 5327**, large	1934-1960	**125.00**	**150.00**
☐ same jug with an "A" mark		**135.00**	**160.00**
☐ **D 5327**, large signed by Doulton	1978-	**125.00**	**150.00**
☐ **D 5735**, small	1937-1960	**60.00**	**75.00**
☐ same jug with an "A" mark		**70.00**	**85.00**
☐ **D 6041**, miniature	1939-1960	**50.00**	**60.00**
☐ same jug with an "A" mark			

JOHN PEEL

Immortalized in song by John Woodcock Graves in a song titled "D'ye ken John Peel" a man who had a passion for fox-hunting.

	Date	Price Range	
☐ **D 5612**, large	1936-1960	**135.00**	**175.00**
☐ same jug with an "A" mark		**140.00**	**150.00**
☐ **D 5731**, small	1937-1960	**70.00**	**80.00**
☐ same jug with an "A" mark		**80.00**	**90.00**
☐ **D 6130**, miniature	1940-1960	**50.00**	**60.00**
☐ same jug with an "A" mark		**70.00**	**85.00**
☐ **D 6259**, tiny	1947-1960	**250.00**	**300.00**

JOHNNY APPLESEED

Depicts the man John Chapman, whose nickname was "Johnny Appleseed", because he traveled on foot all across the Midwestern United States planting apple seeds near the cabins of early settlers.

	Date	Price Range	
☐ **D 6372**, large	1935-1969	**250.00**	**300.00**

LAWYER, The

Depicts an English lawyer with a quill for a handle.

	Date	Price Range
☐ **D 6498**, large	1959-	**75.00**
☐ **D 6504**, small	1959-	**50.00**
☐ **D 6524**, miniature	1960-	**29.95**

LOBSTER MAN

Depicts a seaman, a jolly one, who sets out at night to set his pots for a lobster catch. Handle is a lobster.

	Date	Price Range
☐ **D 6617**, large	1968-	**75.00**
☐ **D 6620**, small	1968-	**50.00**
☐ **D 6652**, miniature	1981-	**29.95**

Long John Silver, D6335, large, **75.00**

LONG JOHN SILVER	Date	Price Range	
Depicts one of the most famous fictional buccaneers. A character from the book "Treasure Island" by Robert Louis Stevenson. Handle is a parrot.			
☐ **D 6335,** large	1952-	**75.00**	
☐ **D 6386,** small	1952-	**50.00**	
☐ **D 6512,** miniature	1960-	**29.95**	
LORD NELSON			
Depicts Admiral Lord Nelson, one of England's great naval heroes.			
☐ **D 6336,** large	1952-1969	**250.00**	**300.00**
LUMBERJACK			
Depicts the typical fellow who works in a lumber camp. His work was hard and often his only tool was an axe. Handle is a tree with an axe.			
☐ **D 6610,** large	1967-1982	**60.00**	**80.00**
☐ **D 6613,** small	1967-1982	**35.00**	**55.00**

Lumberjack, D6610, large, **60.00 — 80.00**

MACBETH	Date	Price Range
Depicting one of the characters from a Shakespearian play.		
☐ **D 6667,** large	1982-	**75.00**

MAD HATTER
Depicts a character from the book "Alice's Adventure in Wonderland" by Lewis Carroll. Handle is a mouse and a clock.

☐ **D 6598,** large	1965-	**75.00**
☐ **D 6602,** small	1965-	**50.00**
☐ **D 6606,** miniature	1965-	**29.95**

MARK TWAIN
Depicts the author of such well known classics as "The Adventures of Tom Sawyer" and "The Adventures of Huck Finn". His real name was Samuel Clemens, Mark Twain being a pen name.

☐ **D 6654,** large	1980-	**75.00**
☐ **D 6694,** small	1983-	**39.95**

MEPHISTOPHELES

A two faced jug showing a happy face and the sad face of the legendary figure most people associate with the devil to whom Faust sold his soul. It carries a verse on the bottom as shown in an illustration of this jug. Considered extremely rare.

	Date	Price Range	
☐ **D 5757,** large	1937-1948	2000.00	2500.00
☐ same jug with an "A" mark		2000.00	2500.00
☐ **D 5758,** small	1937-1948	900.00	1000.00

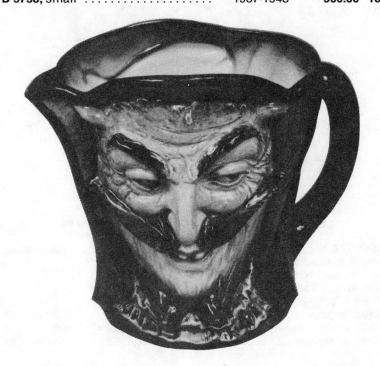

Mephistopheles, D5757, large, **2000.00 — 2500.00**

MERLIN

Depicting the magician from the tales of King Arthur and The Knights of the Round Table. Has an owl for a handle.

	Date	Price Range
☐ **D 6529,** large	1960-	75.00
☐ **D 6536,** small	1960-	50.00
☐ **D 6543,** miniature	1960-	29.95

The Mikado, D6501, large, **325.00 — 375.00**

MIKADO, The	Date	Price Range	
Depicts a Japanese Emperor. Probably most well remembered as a character in the opera "The Mikado" by Gilbert & Sullivan. Handle is a fan.			
☐ **D 6501,** large	1959-1969	325.00	375.00
☐ **D 6507,** small	1959-1969	300.00	350.00
☐ **D 6525,** miniature	1960-1969	350.00	385.00
MINE HOST			
Depicting a jovial and hospitable character from the nineteenth century.			
☐ **D 6488,** large	1958-1981	60.00	80.00
☐ **D 6470,** small	1958-1981	35.00	55.00
☐ **D 6513,** miniature	1960-1981	20.00	30.00

	Date	Price Range	
MONTY Depicting the popular Field-Marshal Montgomery commander of the British forces who achieved great respect for his command of the 8th Army in North Africa and during the Allied invasion of Europe.			
☐ **D 6202,** large	1946-	**75.00**	

	Date	Price Range	
MR. MICAWBER Depicting a character from the Charles Dicken's classic tale "David Copperfield".			
☐ **D 5843,** special size	1938-1948	**125.00**	**150.00**
☐ same jug with an "A" mark		**135.00**	**160.00**
☐ **D 5843,** small	1948-1960	**75.00**	**100.00**
☐ same jug with an "A" mark		**85.00**	**110.00**
☐ **D 6138,** miniature	1940-1960	**45.00**	**55.00**
☐ same jug with an "A" mark		**55.00**	**65.00**
☐ **D 6143,** tiny		**110.00**	**135.00**

	Date	Price Range	
MR. PICKWICK Depicting a character from another of Charles Dicken's classics "Pickwick Papers".			
☐ **D 6060,** large	1940-1960	**125.00**	**150.00**
☐ same jug with an "A" mark		**135.00**	**160.00**
☐ **D 5839,** special size	1938-1948	**125.00**	**150.00**
☐ same jug with an "A" mark		**135.00**	**160.00**
☐ **D 5839,** small	1948-1960	**50.00**	**60.00**
☐ same jug with an "A" mark		**65.00**	**75.00**
☐ **D 6245,** miniature	1947-1960	**45.00**	**55.00**
☐ same jug with an "A" mark		**55.00**	**65.00**
☐ **D 6260,** tiny	1947-1960	**180.00**	**215.00**

	Date	Price Range	
NEPTUNE Depicting the Roman God of the seas and rivers. Handle is a fish.			
☐ **D 6548,** large	1961-	**75.00**	
☐ **D 6552,** small	1961-	**50.00**	
☐ **D 6555,** miniature	1961-	**29.95**	

	Date	Price Range	
NIGHT WATCHMAN A character from the Williamburg series.			
☐ **D 6569,** large	1963-	**75.00**	
☐ **D 6576,** small	1963-	**50.00**	
☐ **D 6583,** miniature	1963-	**29.95**	

OLD CHARLEY
Depicting a night watchman of the eighteenth century.

	Date	Price Range	
☐ **D 5420,** large	1934-	75.00	
☐ same jug with an "A" mark		85.00	95.00
☐ **D 5527,** small	1935-	50.00	
☐ same jug with an "A" mark		75.00	85.00
☐ **D 6046,** miniature	1939-	29.95	
☐ same jug with an "A" mark		45.00	60.00
☐ **D 6144,** tiny	1940-1960	100.00	125.00

OLD KING COLE
Depicting the "merry old soul" from the familiar nursery rhyme Old King Cole.

☐ **D 6036,** large	1939-1960	200.00	250.00
☐ **D 6037,** small	1939-1960	100.00	150.00

Old Salt, D6551, large, **75.00**

OLD SALT   **Date**   **Price Range**

Depicting an old sailor whose face shows the many years he spent at sea, but smiling as he recalls the days he spend sailing. Handle is a mermaid.

	Date	Price Range
☐ **D 6551,** large	1961-	**75.00**
☐ **D 6554,** small	1961-	**50,00**

Othello, D6673, large, **75.00**

OTHELLO

The Moor who murdered his beautiful wife Desdemona in a jealous rage having been convinced she was an adultress.

☐ **D 6673,** large	1982-	**75.00**

OWD MAC

The earlier version of Auld Mac. This jug depicts a thirfty Scotsman.

☐ **D 5823,** large	1938-1945	**100.00**	**125.00**

	Date	Price Range	
PADDY			

Depicting a jolly Irish character. Paddy is the familiar nickname for Patrick. St. Patrick being the Patron Saint of Ireland.

	Date	Price Range	
☐ **D 5753**, large	1937-1960	100.00	125.00
☐ same jug with an "A" mark		115.00	140.00
☐ **D 5768**, small	1937-1960	55.00	65.00
☐ same jug with an "A" mark		65.00	75.00
☐ **D 6042**, miniature	1939-1960	50.00	65.00
☐ same jug with an "A" mark		60.00	75.00
☐ **D 6145**, tiny	1940-1960	100.00	125.00

PARSON BROWN

Depicting a typical Anglican parson of the eighteenth and nineteenth century.

	Date	Price Range	
☐ **D 5486**, large	1935-1960	95.00	115.00
☐ same jug with an "A" mark		110.00	135.00
☐ **D 5529**, small	1935-1960	60.00	70.00
☐ same jug with an "A" mark		65.00	75.00

PEARLY BOY

An early version of 'Arry except buttons are on the cap and around the collar. Known to be made in two colour variations.

	Date	Price Range	
☐ **D 6207**, large		950.00	1050.00
☐ **D 6235**, small		600.00	700.00

PEARLY GIRL

An early version of 'Arriet except as in Pearly Boy buttons appear on the hat and the collar.

	Date	Price Range	
☐ **D 6208**, large		1050.00	1150.00
☐ **D 6236**, small		625.00	725.00
☐ **D 6250**, miniature		500.00	600.00

PIED PIPER, The

Immortalized by Robert Browning he was a figure of medieval legend the Pied Piper of Hamelin.

	Date	Price Range	
☐ **D 6403**, large	1954-1980	75.00	
☐ **D 6462**, small	1957-1980	50.00	
☐ **D 6514**, miniature	1960-1980	29.95	

	Date	Price Range
POACHER		

Depicts a person who trespasses on other people's property illegally taking fish or game or personal property. Handle is a fish.

	Date	Price Range
☐ **D 6429,** large	1955-	**75.00**
☐ **D 6464,** small	1957-	**50.00**
☐ **D 6515,** miniature	1960-	**29.95**

PORTHOS

A character from "The Three Muskateers" by Alexandre Dumas.

	Date	Price Range
☐ **D 6440,** large	1956-	**75.00**
☐ **D 6453,** small	1956-	**50.00**
☐ **D 6516,** miniature	1960-	**29.95**

Punch And Judy Man, D6590, large, **575.00 — 650.00**

	Date	Price Range	

PUNCH AND JUDY MAN
Depicts the man who might resemble the original puppet showman. Handle is a puppet and the curtain.

	Date	Price Range	
☐ **D 6590**, large	1964-1969	575.00	650.00
☐ **D 6593**, small	1964-1969	400.00	450.00
☐ **D 6596**, miniature	1964-1969	375.00	425.00

REGENCY BEAU
Depicts a gentleman of the early nineteenth century who was instantly recognized for his fashionable clothes and elegant living.

☐ **D 6559**, large	1962-1967	500.00	550.00
☐ **D 6562**, small	1962-1967	325.00	375.00
☐ **D 6565**, miniature	1962-1967	375.00	425.00

RIP VAN WINKLE
Depicts a character from Washington Irving's "Sketch Book".

☐ **D 6438**, large	1955-	75.00	
☐ **D 6463**, small	1957-	50.00	
☐ **D 6517**, miniature	1960-	29.95	

ROBIN HOOD
Depicts the notorious outlaw who robbed the rich to feed the poor.

First Version

☐ **D 6205**, large	1947-1960	125.00	150.00
☐ **D 6234**, small	1947-1960	70.00	90.00
☐ same jug with an "A" mark		85.00	105.00
☐ **D 6252**, miniature	1947-1960	50.00	60.00
☐ same jug with an "A" mark		65.00	75.00

Second Version
Different jug than the first version. Shows acorns and oak leaves on the hat and bow/arrow for the handle.

☐ **D 6527**, large	1960-	75.00	
☐ **D 6534**, small	1960-	50.00	
☐ **D 6541**, miniature	1960-	29.95	

ROBINSON CRUSOE
Depicts a character from the book "Robinson Crusoe" by Daniel Defoe.

☐ **D 6532**, large	1960-1982	60.00	80.00
☐ **D 6539**, small	1960-1982	35.00	55.00
☐ **D 6546**, miniature	1960-1982	25.00	35.00

Romeo, D6670, large, **75.00**

ROMEO

Depicting the popular hero of centuries ago. Handle is the dagger which Juliet uses to stab herself on discovering her loved ones death.

☐ **D 6670,** large   1983-   75.00

SAIREY GAMP

Depicts the fat mid-wife from the Charles Dicken's book titled "The Life and Adventure of Martin Chuzzlewit".

☐ **D 5451,** large   1935-   75.00
☐ same jug with an "A" mark 80.00   100.00
☐ **D 5528,** small   1935-   50.00
☐ same jug with an "A" mark 60.00   75.00
☐ **D 6045,** miniature   1939-   29.95
☐ same jug with an "A" mark 45.00   60.00
☐ **D 6146,** tiny   1940-1960   95.00   115.00

	Date	Price Range	
SAMUEL JOHNSON			

Depicting the great English writer, most widely recognized for his writing "Dictionary of the English Language".

	Date	Price Range	
☐ **D 6289,** large	1950-1960	250.00	275.00
☐ **D 6296,** small	1950-1960	175.00	200.00
☐ same jug with an "A" mark		210.00	240.00

SAM WELLER

Depicting a character from Charles Dicken's "Pickwick Papers".

	Date	Price Range	
☐ **D 6064,** large	1940-1960	100.00	125.00
☐ same jug with an "A" mark		135.00	145.00
☐ **D 5841,** special size	1938-1948	100.00	125.00
☐ **D 5841,** small	1948-1960	60.00	75.00
☐ same jug with an "A" mark		70.00	85.00
☐ **D 6140,** miniature	1940-1960	50.00	60.00
☐ same jug with an "A" mark		60.00	70.00
☐ **D 6147,** tiny	1940-1960	100.00	125.00

SANCHO PANZA

Depicting a character from Miguel de Cervantes book "Don Quixote".

	Date	Price Range	
☐ **D 6456,** large	1960-1982	65.00	85.00
☐ **D 6461,** small	1960-1982	40.00	60.00
☐ **D 6518,** miniature	1960-1982	25.00	35.00

SANTA CLAUS

Depicting the jovial character with his twinkling eyes and jolly expression. Handle is Rag doll.

	Date	Price Range	
☐ **D 6668,** large	1981 only	75.00	
☐ **D** , large, handle is reindeer.	1982 only	75.00	
☐ **D 6690,** large, handle is Christmas stocking filled with toys.	1983-	75.00	

SCARMOUCHE

Depicting a character probably from an Italian comedy, a buffoon.

	Date	Price Range	
☐ **D 6558,** large	1962-1967	500.00	600.00
☐ **D 6561,** small	1962-1967	375.00	425.00
☐ **D 6564,** miniature	1962-1967	400.00	450.00

SIMPLE SIMON

Depicting the character in the well known nursey rhyme "Simple Simon".

	Date	Price Range	
☐ **D 6374,** large	1953-1960	525.00	575.00

	Date	Price Range	
SLEUTH			

SLEUTH

Depicting a character similar to the famous detective "Sherlock Holmes" from the books by Sir Arthur Conan Doyle. Handle is a pipe and magnifying glass.

	Date	Price Range	
☐ **D 6631,** large	1973-	75.00	
☐ **D 6635,** small	1973-	50.00	
☐ **D 6639,** miniature	1973-	29.95	

SMUGGLER

Depicting a member of a gang who smuggled goods into the country without paying duty, and whom dwellers along the coast feared.

☐ **D 6616,** large	1968-1980	75.00	
☐ **D 6619,** small	1968-1980	50.00	

SMUTS

Depicting Field Marshal Jan Christian Smuts.

☐ **D 6198,** large	1946-1948	1750.00	2000.00

TAM O'SHANTER

Depicting the character from the Robert Burns' poem "Tam O'Shanter". He was a farmer who barely escaped the witches.

☐ **D 6632,** large	1975-1979	80.00	100.00
☐ **D 6636,** small	1973-1979	60.00	75.00
☐ **D 6640,** miniature	1973-1979	30.00	45.00

TOBY PHILPOTS

Depicting the familiar character from a mid-eighteenth century song. He has always been pictured as a seated male with a three cornered hat with the points being used as pouring spouts.

☐ **D 5736,** large	1937-1969	90.00	110.00
☐ same jug with an "A" mark		115.00	130.00
☐ **D 5737,** small	1937-1969	50.00	60.00
☐ same jug with an "A" mark		60.00	70.00
☐ **D 6043,** miniature	1939-1969	35.00	50.00
☐ same jug with an "A" mark		50.00	65.00

	Date	Price Range	
TONY WELLER			

The father of Sam Weller, he was a coach driver.

	Date	Price Range	
☐ **D 5531,** large	1936-1960	100.00	125.00
☐ same jug with an "A" mark		125.00	150.00
☐ **D 5530,** small	1936-1960	50.00	60.00
☐ same jug with an "A" mark		60.00	75.00
☐ **D 6044,** miniature	1939-1960	40.00	50.00
☐ same jug with an "A" mark		50.00	60.00

TOUCHSTONE

Depicting the clown in Shakespeare's play "As You Like It".

	Date	Price Range	
☐ **D 5613,** large	1936-1960	300.00	350.00

TOWN CRIER

Depicts the eighteenth century man who called to the townspeople all the latest news, coming events, and meetings taking place plus many other important events before the event of newspapers.

	Date	Price Range	
☐ **D 6530,** large	1960-1973	150.00	175.00
☐ **D 6537,** small	1960-1973	100.00	125.00
☐ **D 6544,** miniature	1960-1973	125.00	150.00

TRAPPER

Depicting the northwoodsman of North America who trapped for fur bearing animals. Handle is a horn and snowshoes.

	Date	Price Range	
☐ **D 6609,** large	1967-	75.00	
☐ **D 6612,** small	1967-	50.00	

UGLY DUCHESS

A character from the Lewis Carroll book "Alice in Wonderland". Handle is a flamingo.

	Date	Price Range	
☐ **D 6599,** large	1965-1973	300.00	350.00
☐ **D 6603,** small	1965-1973	275.00	325.00
☐ **D 6607,** miniature	1965-1973	250.00	300.00

UNCLE TOM COBBLEIGH

Depicting a character from a nineteenth century song. Uncle Tom and others rode a horse to the Widdecombe Fair.

	Date	Price Range	
☐ **D 6337,** large	1952-1960	350.00	400.00

VETERAN MOTORIST

Depciting a driver in the Veteran Car Run held each year from London to Brighton.

	Date	Price Range	
☐ **D 6633**, large	1973-	75.00	
☐ **D 6637**, small	1973-	50.00	
☐ **D 6641**, miniature	1973-	29.95	

VICAR OF BRAY, The

Depicting a country parson from an eighteenth century song.

☐ **D 5615**, large	1936-1960	160.00	180.00
☐ same jug with an "A" mark		180.00	200.00

VIKING

Depicting one of a band of Scandinavian seafarers and explorers.

☐ **D 6496**, large	1959-1975	100.00	150.00
☐ **D 6502**, small	1959-1975	65.00	80.00
☐ **D 6526**, miniature	1960-1975	35.00	50.00

Walrus And Carpenter, D6600, large, **75.00 — 100.00**

WALRUS AND CARPENTER   **Date**   **Price Range**

A character from the Lewis Carroll classic "Through The Looking Glass". Handle is a walrus.

	Date	Price Range	
☐ **D 6600,** large	1965-1979	75.00	100.00
☐ **D 6604,** small	1965-1979	55.00	70.00
☐ **D 6608,** miniature . . . . : .	1965-1979	35.00	50.00

William Shakespeare, D6689, large, **75.00**

WILLIAM SHAKESPEARE

Very recognizable with his Vandyke beard and bald head. Collar has the masks of comedy and tragedy. Handle is pen and quill.

☐ **D 6689,** large	1983-	75.00

YACHTSMAN

Depicting a modern English sailing man. Handle is a sailboat.

☐ **D 6622,** large	1971-1979	100.00	125.00

The Best Is Not Too Good, D6107, **225.00 — 275.00**

TOBY JUGS

	Date	Price Range	
THE BEST IS NOT TOO GOOD Depicts a jovial character who loves his brew. ☐ **D 6107**	1939-1960	**225.00**	**275.00**
CAP'N CUTTLE A character from the Charles Dicken's book "Dombey and Son". ☐ **D 6266**	1948-1960	**200.00**	**250.00**
DOUBLE XX or THE MAN ON THE BARREL Depicts a person astride a barrell of brew yet still demanding another drink. ☐ **D 6088**	1939-1969	**325.00**	**375.00**

Falstaff, D6062, **95.00**

FALSTAFF	Date	Price Range	
Depicts a character in the Shakesperean plays "Henry VIII" and "The Merry Wives of Windsor".			
☐ D 6062	1939-	95.00	
☐ D 6063	1939-	50.00	
FAT BOY, The			
Depicts a character from Charles Dicken's "Pickwick Papers".			
☐ D 6264	1948-1960	200.00	225.00
HAPPY JOHN			
Depicts a seated character with a pitcher of ale in one hand and a glass full of ale in the other.			
☐ D 6031	1939-	95.00	
☐ D 6070	1939-	45.00	

Honest Measure, D6108, **45.00**

	Date	Price Range
HONEST MEASURE Inscription reads "Honest Measure: Drink at Leisure". Sitting on the base and approximate 4½" tall this character is doing just that "taking it easy". ☐ **D 6108**	1939-	**45.00**
THE HUNTSMAN Depicts an English huntsman. ☐ **D 6320**	1950-	**95.00**
JOLLY TOBY Seated toby with a warm smile. ☐ **D 6109**	1939-	**65.00**

	Date	Price Range

MISS NOSTRUM, THE NURSE
Jolly lady with rosy cheeks. Wearing
blue/black uniform with white apron.
Hat same colour as uniform, grey
hair. Fob watch on the bib of her
apron.
☐ **D 6700** 1983-

MR. FURROW, THE FARMER
Depicting a man with weatherbeaten
face indicating much time spent in the
outdoors. Wears an old battered hat.
He carries in one hand a riding crop
and in the other corn. Coat is brown,
his waistcoat yellow, green bow tie.
☐ **D 6701** 1983-

MR. LITIGATE, THE LAWYER
Figure has long black coat, grey trou-
sers, yellow vest. Gold watch chain.
Traditional powdered wig.
☐ **D 6699** 1983-

MR. MICAWBER
Depicts a character from Charles
Dicken's book "David Copperfield".
☐ **D 6262** 1948-1960   250.00   300.00

MR. PICKWICK
A character from Charles Dicken's
book "Pickwick Papers".
☐ **D 6261** 1948-1960   250.00   300.00

OLD CHARLEY
Seated character depicting an early
nineteenth century nightwatchman.
☐ **D 6030** 1939-1960   150.00   175.00
☐ **D 6069** 1939-1960   100.00   125.00

REV. CASSOCK, THE CLERGYMAN
Dressed in a black jacket, wearing a
clerical collar, grey uniform under
jacket. Carrying an open bible.
☐ **D 6702** 1983-

SAIREY GAMP
A character from Charles Dicken's
book "Martin Chuzzlewit".
☐ **D 6263** 1948-1960   200.00   225.00

	Date	Price Range	

SAM WELLER
  Depicts a character from Charles Dicken's "Pickwick Papers".

☐ **D 6265** 1948-1960   **200.00   225.00**

SHERLOCK HOLMES
  Depicting the famous sleuth from Sir Arthur Conan Doyle's many mystery books. Released to commemorate the fiftieth anniversary of the death of Sir Arthur.

☐ **D 6661** 1981-   **95.00**

THE SQUIRE
  Depicts a character known to exist in early medieval times He was all around assistant to a knight and often accompanied him into battle. In later years this title was given to young men of good family training who would later become knights themselves.

☐ **D 6319** 1950-1969   **250.00   300.00**

Sir Francis Drake, D6660, large, **95.00**

	Date	Price Range

SIR FRANCES DRAKE
  Depicts this famous nobleman kneeling as if to bow before the queen. Released to commemorate the 400th anniversary of the arrival of Sir Frances Drake and his ship's landing at Plymouth.

☐ **D 6660** 1981- **95.00**

Winston Churchill, D6171, 9", **95.00**

SIR WINSTON CHURCHILL
  Depicting the statesman and Prime Minister of Great Britain. Earlier models bear the inscription "Winston Churchill Prime Minister of Great Britain 1940".

☐ **D 6171,** large 1941- **95.00**
☐ **D 6172,** small 1941- **65.00**
☐ **D 6175,** miniature 1941- **45.00**

MISCELLANEOUS ITEMS

Royal Doulton has produced a number of miscellaneous items which do not fall into any of the major categories. These have mostly been in the class of novelties or novelty giftware, with adaptations of characters from its jugs. The Ash Trays and Ash Bowls (ash bowls are large receptacles for emptying pipe ashes) bear a variety of characters, following no special theme. All of the Busts feature Dickens characters, and these are supplemented by the Dickens Jugs and Tankards. The characters of Charles Dickens seem ideally suited to Doultonware; although fictional, they seem to typify traditional British "types" known all over the world. All the works listed in this section are out of production and have acquired solid collector status.

Left to Right: **John Barleycorn**, D5602, **85.00 — 125.00**
Dick Turpin, D5601, **75.00 — 100.00**

ASH TRAYS

	Date	Price Range	
DICK TURPIN			
☐ D 5601	1936-1960	75.00	100.00
JOHN BARLEYCORN			
☐ D 5602	1936-1960	85.00	125.00
OLD CHARLEY			
☐ D 5599	1936-1960	75.00	100.00
PARSON BROWN			
☐ D 5600	1936-1960	85.00	125.00

ASH BOWLS

	Date	Price Range	
AULD MAC			
☐ D 6006	1939-1960	115.00	135.00

FARMER JOHN	Date	Price Range	
☐ D 6007	1939-1960	100.00	125.00

OLD CHARLEY			
☐ D 5925	1938-1960	100.00	125.00

PADDY			
☐ D 5926	1938-1960	100.00	125.00

Left to Right: **Sairy Gamp,** D6009, **100.00 — 125.00**
Parson Brown, D6008, **100.00 — 125.00**

PARSON BROWN			
☐ D 6008	1939-1960	100.00	125.00

SAIREY GAMP			
☐ D 6009	1939-1960	100.00	125.00

BUSTS

BUZ FUZ			
☐ D 6048	1939-1960	75.00	100.00

MR. MICAWBER			
☐ D 6050	1939-1960	65.00	85.00
MR. PICKWICK			
☐ D 6049	1939-1960	75.00	100.00

SAIREY GAMP			
☐ D 6047	1939-1960	65.00	85.00

SAM WELLER			
☐ D 6052	1939-1960	65.00	85.00

TONY WELLER			
☐ D 6051	1939-1960	65.00	85.00

DICKENS JUGS AND TANKARDS

	Date	Price Range	

OLD CURIOSITY SHOP JUG
Figures in relief of Little Nell and her grandfather on one side, and the Marchioness on the other.
☐ **D 5584** 1935-1960   **125.00**   **175.00**

OLD LONDON JUG
Depicts London during the time of Charles Dickens with Old Charley on one side and Sairey Gamp on the other.
☐ **D 6291** 1949-1960   **200.00**   **275.00**

OLIVER TWIST JUG.
☐ **D 5617** 1937-1960   **125.00**   **175.00**

OLIVER TWIST JUG
Oliver asking for more.
☐ **D 6285** 1936-1960   **225.00**   **275.00**

OLIVER TWIST TANKARD
Oliver watching the Artful Dodger picking a pocket.
☐ **D 6286** 1949-1960   **200.00**   **250.00**

PEGGOTTY JUG
Depicting a scene from David Copperfield.
☐ **D 6292** 1949-1960   **275.00**   **350.00**

PICKWICK PAPERS JUGS
Depicts the characters from Dickens book "The Pickwick Papers" outside the White Hart Inn.
☐ **D 5756** 1937-1960   **150.00**   **225.00**

PLATES

This terminology is strictly British and is often misunderstood by Americans. A "head rack plate" is a plate designed to be displayed on a wall or in a cabinet ("rack"), rather than used as tableware. *Head* rack means that the plate carries a human likeness. Royal Doulton's Head Rack Plates have borne portraits of characters from the novels of Charles Dickens, as well as miscellaneous types both historical and fictional. In addition to Head Rack Plates, the factory has also made Scenic Rack Plates, which have landscape views, often including colorful wildlife.

Though we live in an age of plate collecting and might think decorative plates to be something new, the concept of Head Rack and Scenic Rack Plates dates back very far. Beautifully enameled majolica plates, with painted scenes, were made in Italy in the 15th century. English porcelain factories began putting them out in the 1700's, for use on elegant tables. But many were in fact purchased to use as wall decorations. In the early Victorian era (1840's) a vogue developed in England for encircling whole rooms with these plates, on upper walls near the ceiling. This gave further impetus to the manufacturers. Royal Doulton has been making decorative plates for many years. Interested collectors might want to seek out some of the early issues, in addition to the modern ones listed here.

These plates are issued without serial numbers.

Back in the early 1970's when the collector plate market was in somewhat of a turmoil, plaques with poor examples of what was supposed to be quality plates at high prices, and a seemingly get-rich quick attitude of many persons the Doulton Company conceived the idea of transferring quality works of art by good artists, some well-known, some not, on to plates of highest quality with great emphasis on the finished product being as near the artists original work as possible.

After considerable thought the Collectors International was established to issue products of Fine Art on Fine China. The first plate being introduced in 1973 with a series of Mothers Day plates by artist, Edna Hibel. Following is the entire series offered since 1973 bearing the secondary market prices as of the current date.

HEAD RACK PLATES

CHARLES DICKENS SERIES

	Size	Price	Range
☐ Artful Dodger	10¼″	50.00	65.00
☐ Barkis	10¼″	65.00	80.00
☐ Cap'n Cuttle	10¼″	65.00	80.00
☐ Fagin	9½″	45.00	55.00
☐ Fat Boy	10¼″	50.00	65.00
☐ Mr. Micawber	10¼″	50.00	65.00
☐ Mr. Pickwick	10¼″	65.00	80.00
☐ Old Peggoty	10¼″	65.00	80.00
☐ Poor Jo	10¼″	50.00	65.00
☐ Sairey Gamp	10¼″	65.00	80.00
☐ Sam Weller	10¼″	50.00	65.00
☐ Serjeant Buzfuz	10¼″	65.00	80.00
☐ Tony Weller	10¼″	50.00	65.00

HISTORICAL BRITAIN SERIES

English Translucent China plates

	Size	Price	Range
☐ Anne Hathaway's Cottage Shottery Near Stratford-on-Avon	10½″	40.00	50.00
☐ Clovelly, North Devon	10½″	35.00	45.00
☐ House of Parliament, London	10½″	35.00	45.00
☐ Tower of London	10½″	45.00	55.00
☐ Tudor Mansion	10½″	50.00	60.00

MISCELLANEOUS

	Size	Price	Range
☐ The Admiral	10¼″	55.00	70.00
☐ Arabian Knights	10¼″	70.00	85.00
☐ Bradley Golfers Pictures of men golfing with sayings printed around the plate very early 1900 era	10¼″	150.00	200.00
☐ Charles Dickens	10¼″	70.00	85.00
☐ The Cobbler	10¼″	40.00	55.00
☐ The Doctor	10¼″	40.00	55.00
☐ Don Quixote	10¼″	50.00	65.00
☐ The Falconer	10¼″	45.00	60.00
☐ Falstaff	10¼″	50.00	65.00
☐ Gaffers	10¼″	50.00	65.00
☐ The Hunting Man	10¼″	70.00	85.00
☐ Jackdaw of Reims	10¼″	50.00	65.00
☐ The Jester	10¼″	60.00	75.00
☐ The Mayor	10¼″	70.00	85.00
☐ Omar Khayyam	10¼″	65.00	80.00
☐ Ophelia, Shakespeare	10¼″	65.00	80.00
☐ Othelo, The Moor of Venice Act IV	10¼″	70.00	85.00
☐ The Parson	10¼″	40.00	55.00

	Size	Price Range	
☐ Robert Burns	10¼ "	40.00	55.00
☐ Shakespeare	10¼ "	40.00	50.00
☐ The Squire	10¼ "	40.00	55.00

SCENIC RACK PLATES

	Size	Price Range	
☐ African Elephants	10¼ "	25.00	35.00
☐ Australian Aborigine	10¼ "	20.00	25.00
☐ Bow Valley	10¼ "	30.00	40.00
☐ Giraffes	10¼ "	25.00	35.00
☐ Koala Bears	10¼ "	35.00	45.00
☐ Lake Louise and Victoria Glacier	10¼ "	22.50	35.00
☐ Lioness	10¼ "	35.00	45.00
☐ Maritime Provinces	10¼ "	25.00	35.00
☐ Mother Kangaroo with Joey	10¼ "	30.00	40.00
☐ Mount Egmont	10¼ "	20.00	30.00
☐ Murray River Gums	10¼ "	20.00	30.00
☐ Niagara Falls	10¼ "	25.00	35.00
☐ Vermilion Lake and Mount Rundle	10¼ "	20.00	30.00
☐ Young Kookaburras	10¼ "	30.00	40.00

SERIES PLATES

	Year	Edition Size	Issue Price
"BEHIND THE PAINTED MASQUE" by Ben Black			
☐ Painted Feelings	1982	10000	95.00
"AMERICAN TAPESTRIES" by C. A. Brown			
☐ Sleigh Bells	1978	15000	70.00
☐ Pumpkin Patch	1979	15000	70.00
☐ General Store	1981	10000	95.00
☐ Fourth of July	1982	10000	95.00
"REFLECTIONS OF CHINA" by Chen Chi			
☐ Garden of Tranquility	1976	15000	90.00
☐ Imperial Palace	1977	15000	80.00
☐ Temple of Heaven	1978	15000	75.00
☐ Lake of Mists	1980	15000	85.00
"ALL GOD'S CHILDREN" by Lisette DeWinne			
☐ A Brighter Day	1978	10000	75.00
☐ Village Children	1980	10000	65.00
☐ Noble Heritage	1981	10000	85.00
☐ Buddies	1982	10000	85.00
"MOTHER AND CHILD" by Edna Hibel			
☐ Colette and Child	1973	15000	500.00
☐ Sayuri and Child	1974	15000	175.00

"Painted Feelings"
Artist: Ben Black
95.00

"Sleigh Bells"
Artist: C.A. Brown
70.00

"Pumpkin Patch"
Artist: C.A. Brown
70.00

"General Store"
Artist: C.A. Brown
95.00

"4th Of July"
Artist: C.A. Brown
95.00

"Garden Of Tranquility"
Artist: Chen Chi
90.00

"Imperial Palace"
Artist: Chen Chi
80.00

"Temple Of Heaven"
Artist: Chen Chi
75.00

"Lake Of Mists"
Artist: Chen Chi
85.00

"A Brighter Day"
Artist: Lisette DeWinne
75.00

"Village Children"
Artist: Lisette DeWinne
65.00

"Nobel Heritage"
Artist: Lisette DeWinne
85.00

"Buddies"
Artist: Lisette DeWinne
85.00

"Colette And Child"
Artist: Edna Hibel
500.00

"Sayuri And Child"
Artist: Edna Hibel
175.00

	Date	Edition Size	Issue Price
☐ Kristina and Child	1975	15000	125.00
☐ Marilyn and Child	1976	15000	110.00
☐ Lucia and Child	1977	15000	90.00
☐ Kathleen and Child	1981	15000	85.00

"PORTS OF CALL" by Doug Kingman

☐ San Francisco, Fisherman's Wharf	1975	15000	90.00
☐ New Orleans, Royal Street	1976	15000	80.00
☐ Venice, Grand Canal	1977	15000	65.00
☐ Paris, Montmartre	1978	15000	70.00

"PORTRAITS OF INNOCENCE" by Francisco Masseria

☐ Panchito	1980	15000	200.00
☐ Adrien	1981	15000	85.00
☐ Angelica	1982	15000	95.00

"COMMEDIA DELL'ARTE" by LeRoy Neiman

☐ Harlequin	1974	15000	100.00
☐ Pierrot	1975	15000	90.00
☐ Columbine	1977	15000	80.00
☐ Punchinello	1978	15000	75.00
☐ Winning Colors. Although not part of the Commedia Dell'Arte Series, this plate was offered in recognition of the vast popularity of LeRoy Neiman's most notable subject matter	1980	10000	85.00

"JUNGLE FANTASY" by Gustavo Novoa

☐ The Ark	1979	10000	75.00
☐ Compassion	1981	10000	95.00
☐ Patience	1982	10000	95.00

"I REMEMBER AMERICA" by Eric Sloane

☐ Pennsylvania Pastorale	1977	15000	90.00
☐ Lovejoy Bridge	1978	15000	80.00
☐ Four Corners	1979	15000	75.00
☐ Marshlands	1981	15000	95.00

"LOG OF THE DASHING WAVE" by John Stobart

☐ Sailing with the Tide	1976	15000	115.00
☐ Running Free	1977	15000	110.00
☐ Rounding the Horn	1978	15000	85.00
☐ Hong Kong	1979	15000	75.00
☐ Bora Bora	1981	15000	95.00

"FLOWER GARDEN" by Hahn Vidal

☐ Spring Harmony	1975	15000	80.00
☐ Dreaming Lotus	1976	15000	90.00

"Kristina And Child"
Artist: Edna Hibel
125.00

"Marilyn And Child"
Artist: Edna Hibel
110.00

"Lucia And Child"
Artist: Edna Hibel
90.00

"Kathleen And Child"
Artist: Edna Hibel
85.00

"New Orleans"
Artist: Doug Kingman
90.00

"Venice"
Artist: Doug Kingman
65.00

"Panchito"
Artist: Fransisco Masseria
200.00

"Adrien"
Artist: Fransisco Masseria
85.00

"Angelica"
Artist: Francisco Masseria
95.00

"Columbine"
Artist: LeRoy Neiman
80.00

"Punchinello"
Artist: LeRoy Neiman
75.00

"The Ark"
Artist: Gustavo Novoa
75.00

"Compassion"
Artist: Gustavo Novoa
95.00

"Patience"
Artist: Gustavo Novoa
95.00

"Pennsylvania Pastorale"
Artist: Eric Sloane
90.00

"Lovejoy Bridge"
Artist: Eric Sloane
80.00

"Four Corners"
Artist: Eric Sloane
75.00

"Marshlands"
Artist: Eric Sloane
95.00

"Sailing With The Tide"
Artist: John Stobart
115.00

"Rounding The Horn"
Artist: John Stobart
85.00

"Hong Kong"
Artist: John Stobart
75.00

"Bora Bora"
Artist: John Stobart
95.00

"Spring Harmony"
Artist: Hahn Vidal
80.00

"Dreaming Lotus"
Artist: Hahn Vidal
90.00

	Date	Edition Size	Issue Price
☐ From the Poet's Garden	1977	15000	75.00
☐ Country Bouquet	1978	15000	75.00
☐ From My Mother's Garden	1980	15000	85.00

"CELEBRATION OF FAITH" by James Woods

	Date	Edition Size	Issue Price
☐ Rosh Hoshanah	1982	N/A	250.00

"CHARACTER" PLATES
Series limited to the period of issue each year.

	Date	Edition Size	Issue Price
☐ Old Balloon Seller	1979	year	85.00
☐ Balloon Man	1980	year	100.00
☐ Silk and Ribbons	1981	year	100.00
☐ Biddy Penny Farthing	1982	year	100.00

"AROUND THE WORLD SERIES"
Beswick Christmas Plates

	Date	Edition Size	Issue Price
☐ Christmas in Old England	1972	15000	35.00
☐ Christmas in Mexico	1973	15000	37.50
☐ Christmas in Bulgaria	1974	15000	37.50
☐ Christmas in Norway	1975	15000	45.00
☐ Christmas in Holland	1976	15000	50.00
☐ Christmas in Poland	1977	15000	50.00
☐ Christmas in America	1978	15000	55.00

"VICTORIAN ERA" CHRISTMAS PLATES
Series limited to the period of issue each year.

	Date	Edition Size	Issue Price
☐ Winter Fun	1977	year	55.00
☐ Christmas Day	1978	year	25.00
☐ Christmas	1979	year	30.00
☐ Santa's Visit	1980	year	33.00
☐ Christmas Carolers	1981	year	37.50
☐ Santa on Bicycle	1982	year	39.95

"VICTORIAN ERA" VALENTINE PLATES
Series limited to the period of issue each year.

	Date	Edition Size	Issue Price
☐ Victorian Boy and Girl	1976	year	65.00
☐ My Sweetest Friend	1977	year	40.00
☐ If I Loved You	1978	year	40.00
☐ My Valentine	1979	year	35.00
☐ Valentine	1980	year	33.00
☐ Valentine Boy and Girl	1981	year	35.00
☐ Angel with Mandolin	1982	year	39.95

"From The Poet's Garden"
Artist: Hahn Vidal
75.00

"Country Bouquet"
Artist: Hahn Vidal
75.00

"From My Mother's Garden"
Artist: Hahn Vidal
85.00

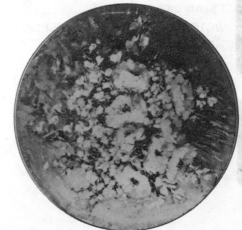

"Rosh Hashanah"
Artist: James Woods
250.00

"Old Balloon Seller"
Artist: William Harper
Royal Doulton Group
85.00

"Balloon Man"
Artist: William Harper
Royal Doulton Group
100.00

"Silk And Ribbons"
Artist: William Harper
Royal Doulton Group
100.00

"Biddy Penny Farthing"
Artist: William Harper
Royal Doulton Group
100.00

"Christmas In Old England"
By John Beswick
Studios Of
The Royal Doulton Group
35.00

"Christmas In Mexico"
By John Beswick
Studios Of
The Royal Doulton Group
37.50

"Christmas In Bulgaria"
By John Beswick
Studios Of
The Royal Doulton Group
37.50

"Christmas In Norway"
By John Beswick
Studios Of
The Royal Doulton Group
45.00

"Christmas In America"
By John Beswick
Studios Of
The Royal Doulton Group
55.00

"Winter Fun"
Artist Unknown
55.00

"Christmas Day"
Artist Unknown
25.00

"Santa's Visit"
Artist Unknown
33.00

"Christmas Sleigh Ride"
Artist Unknown
25.00

"Christmas Carolers"
Artist Unknown
37.50

"Santa On Bicycle"
Artist Unknown
39.95

"Victorian Boy And Gril"
Artist Unknown
65.00

"My Valentine"
Artist Unknown
35.00

"Valentine Boy And Girl"
Artist Unknown
35.00

"Valentine"
Artist Unknown
33.00

"Angel With Mandolin"
Artist Unknown
39.95

MISCELLANEOUS ITEMS

Royal Doulton certainly ranks as one of the pace-setters in the Limited Editions field. It was experimenting — very successfully — with limited editions as long ago as the 1930's, to which decade the first issues in its Jugs and Loving Cups date. Since there was no plan to issue such items on a regular basis, they were not given serial numbers; and this practice, once adopted, was continued even after the issues became more profuse. The majority of issues have had very limited editions indeed, even including those of recent date which went into a greatly expanded market.

CHERUB BELLS. Royal Doulton instituted its still-young series of Cherub Bells in 1979. To date, one has been issued each year, in an edition limited to 5,000 specimens. The name derives from the fact that cherubs (youthful angels) are always included in the motif.

CIGARETTE LIGHTERS. This series was introduced in 1958, when 11 designs were placed on the market, some of which were manufactured in that year only. The last year in which new additions was made was 1964. Royal Doulton's cigarette lighters feature "character" portraits, similar to those on its jugs. A number of the types are drawn from Dickens' novels but Shakespeare is also represented (Falstaff) as well as the creation of an American author (Rip Van Winkle, a character of Washington Irving). The scarcest are Musketeer and Rip Van Winkle, made in 1958 only.

EGG SERIES. In 1980 the factory began issuing decorative porcelain eggs, in editions of 3,500. The tradition for decorative porcelain eggs is very old, as they were a favorite at European royal courts and especially at St. Petersburg in Russia more than 100 years ago.

GOBLET SERIES.

JUG SERIES. This series goes back to the 1930's and includes some highly sought-after items.

JUGS. These include the "Cliff Cornell Jugs," made in the 1950's for an American business executive as a special order. Royal Doulton has very seldom, in modern times, created "special order" items. Thus the Cliff Cornell jugs have a definite collector appeal.

LIQUOR CONTAINERS. Apparently made for a commercial liquor dealer.

LOVING CUPS. The company began issuing limited edition Loving Cups in 1933 and has added periodically to the series. Originally, loving cups were awarded as prizes in British sporting events, usually made of silver. The Royal Doulton versions are in porcelain with attractive enameling.

MUSICAL JUGS.

NAPKIN RINGS.

NATIVITY CUP AND SAUCER SERIES.

TABLE LAMPS. These have never been a really significant part of the factory line, but some are quite old (from the '30's) and very attractive. They probably suffered destruction at a heavier rate than figurines and may be scarcer than many collectors realize.

TANKARD SERIES. Begun in 1971, this consists of decorative tankards with motifs from Dickens' "A Christmas Carol." Editions have run from 13,000 to 15,000 pieces.

TEAPOTS.

TOBACCO JARS.

WALL MASKS. Porcelain portaits in small size, to mount on the wall.

"SPEECH OF ANGELS" CHERUB BELL SERIES (LIMITED EDITION)

	Number	Date	Edition Size	Issue Price
☐ **Glad Tidings** (Clarion) . . . . No. 1		1979	5000	**95.00**
☐ **Peace** (Harp) . . . . No. 2		1980	5000	**95.00**
☐ **Joy** (Cymbals) . . . . No. 3		1981	5000	**100.00**

"TWELVE DAYS OF CHRISTMAS" GOBLET SERIES (LIMITED EDITION)

	Number	Date	Edition Size	Issue Price
☐ **Partridge in a Pear Tree** . . . . No. 1		1980	10000	**55.00**
☐ **Two Turtle Doves** . . . . No. 2		1981	10000	**60.00**
☐ **Three French Hens** . . . . No. 3		1982	10000	**60.00**

"JOY TO THE WORLD" NATIVITY CUP AND SAUCER SERIES (LIMITED EDITION)

Shepherds In The Fields, 60.00

	Number	Date	Edition Size	Issue Price
☐ **The Annunciation** . . . . No. 1		1980	10000	**55.00**
☐ **Journey to Bethlehem** . . . . No. 2		1981	10000	**60.00**
☐ **Shepherds In The Fields** . . . . No. 3		1982	10000	**60.00**

CIGARETTE LIGHTERS

Left to Right: **Long John Silver**, 1958-1973, **75.00 — 125.00**
Rip Van Winkle, 1958 only, **350.00 — 400.00**

	Date	Price Range	
☐ Bacchus	1964-1973	100.00	125.00
☐ Beefeater	1958-1973	75.00	90.00
☐ Buz Fuz	1958 only	155.00	175.00
☐ Captain Ahab	1964-1973	100.00	125.00
☐ Cap 'N Cuttle	1958 only	155.00	175.00
☐ Falstaff	1958-1973	75.00	90.00
☐ Lawyer	1962-1973	85.00	100.00
☐ Long John Silver	1958-1973	75.00	90.00
☐ Mr. Micawber	1958 only	155.00	175.00
☐ Mr. Pickwick	1958-1961	125.00	150.00
☐ Musketeer (Porthos)	1958 only	375.00	425.00
☐ Old Charley	1958 only	75.00	90.00
☐ Poacher	1958-1973	75.00	90.00
☐ Rip Van Winkle	1958 only	375.00	425.00

EGG SERIES

	Date	Edition Size	Issue Price
☐ Rouge Flambé Egg	1980	3500	100.00
☐ Royal Crown Derby Paradise Cobalt	1981	3500	175.00
☐ Minton 19th Century Egg	1979	3500	75.00
☐ Minton Emperors Garden Egg	1982	3500	95.00

The Emperor's Garden, 95.00

JUGS

	Date	Edition Size	Price Range	
☐ Captain Cook Jug	1933	350	650.00	700.00
☐ Captain Phillip Jug	1938	350	2000.00	2500.00
☐ Charles Dickens Jug	1936	1000	700.00	800.00
☐ Dickens Dream Jug			700.00	800.00
☐ George Washington Jug	1932	-150	2500.00	3000.00
☐ Guy Fawkes Jug	1934	600	600.00	650.00
☐ Master of Fox Hounds MFH Presentation Jug	1930	500	650.00	700.00
☐ Pied Piper Jug	1934	600	700.00	750.00
☐ Regency Coach Jug	1931	500	650.00	700.00
☐ Sir Frances Drake Jug	1933	500	750.00	850.00
☐ Tower of London Jug	1933	500	600.00	700.00
☐ Treasure Island Jug	1934	600	625.00	700.00
☐ Village Blacksmith Jug	1936	600	600.00	700.00
☐ William Shakespeare Jug	1933	1000	700.00	800.00

JUGS (LIMITED EDITION)

	Date	Price Range

CHARRINGTON TOBY

☐ Made in the mid to late 1950's this jug which is about 9¼″ high was produced for Charrington, well known brewers, for advertising purposes. One version reads "Toby Ales", and the second version reads "One Toby Leads to Another." 275.00 325.00

Cliff Cornell, large, **275.00**

CLIFF CORNELL

Special design produced in the late 1950's for Cliff Cornell, an American businessman for presentation to friends and as gifts. Jug depicts Mr. Cornell.

☐ Large size, 9″, brown suit. 275.00 325.00
☐ Large size, 9″, blue suit. 325.00 400.00

	Date	Price Range	
☐ Medium size, 5½ ", brown suit.		**150.00**	**200.00**
☐ Medium size, 5½ ", blue suit.	1939-	**175.00**	**225.00**

In recent years it has been brought to the attention of collectors that some Cornell jugs have appeared in a tan finish which apparently are in the same sizes as shown above.

CHARLIE CHAPLIN

☐ Seated Toby.		3000.00	3500.00

GEORGE ROBEY

☐ Seated Toby.		1500.00	1800.00

LIQUOR CONTAINERS

Left to Right:
Rib Van Winkle, Poacher, Falstaff, 65.00 — 85.00 each

	Price Range	
☐ **Falstaff**	65.00	85.00
☐ **Poacher**	65.00	85.00
☐ **Rip Van Winkle**	65.00	85.00

LOVING CUPS

	Date	Edition Size	Price Range	
☐ **Admiral Lord Nelson**	1935	600	850.00	950.00
☐ **The Apothecary**	1934	600	500.00	600.00
☐ **Captain Cook**	1933	350	2500.00	3000.00
☐ **Captain Cook** (Black Basalt)	1970	500	250.00	300.00
☐ **Charles Dickens**	1970	500	250.00	350.00
☐ **Jan Van Riebeeck**	1935	300	1500.00	1750.00
☐ **John Peel**	1933	500	650.00	750.00
☐ **King Edward VIII Coronation** (large) . .	1937	1080	550.00	600.00
☐ **King Edward VIII Coronation** (small) .	1937	464	550.00	600.00

	Date	Edition Size	Price Range	
☐ King George VI and Queen Elizabeth Coronation (large)	1937	2000	475.00	550.00
☐ King George VI and Queen Elizabeth Coronation (small)	1937	2000	500.00	550.00
☐ King George and Queen Mary Silver Wedding	1935	1000	600.00	700.00
☐ Mayflower (Black Basalt)...........	1970	500	250.00	350.00
☐ Queen Elizabeth II Silver Jubilee	1977	250	850.00	950.00
☐ Robin Hood.....................	1938	600	550.00	650.00
☐ The Wandering Minstrel	1934	600	500.00	600.00
☐ Three Musketeers.................	1936	600	650.00	750.00
☐ Wm. Wordsworth, unlimited but rare .			500.00	600.00

MUSICAL JUGS

	Price Range	
☐ Paddy	400.00	500.00
☐ Auld Mac	400.00	500.00
☐ Tony Weller	400.00	500.00
☐ Old Charley	400.00	500.00
☐ Old King Cole	700.00	800.00

NAPKIN RINGS

☐ Mr. Pickwick M 57	400.00	500.00
☐ Mr. Micawber M 58	400.00	500.00
☐ Fat Boy M 59	400.00	500.00
☐ Tony Weller M 60..............................	400.00	500.00
☐ Sam Weller M 61	400.00	500.00
☐ Sairey Gamp M 62	400.00	500.00

These came in a set and were given numbers for record purposes, however, it does not always appear on the napkin rings. Introduced about 1939 and withdrawn in 1960.

TABLE LAMPS

☐ Arabian Horse	450.00	500.00
☐ Autumn Breezes	600.00	700.00
☐ Alice	250.00	300.00
☐ Balloon Man	250.00	300.00
☐ Barnaby	375.00	425.00
☐ Captain, The	300.00	350.00
☐ Carmen......................................	200.00	250.00
☐ Celeste	250.00	300.00
☐ Clotilde......................................	575.00	650.00
☐ Fair Lady	250.00	300.00
☐ Falstaff	400.00	450.00
☐ Foaming Quart	300.00	350.00

	Price Range	
☐ Friar Tuck..	700.00	750.00
☐ Gay Morning	225.00	275.00
☐ Good Catch	250.00	300.00
☐ Huntsman Fox.....................................	200.00	250.00
☐ Immortal (The), sitting green mandarin, 12″..........	900.00	1000.00
☐ Jemima Puddleduck	250.00	300.00
☐ Judge, The	500.00	600.00
☐ Old Balloon Seller...............................	250.00	300.00
☐ Peter Rabbit......................................	250.00	300.00
☐ Polly Peachum	275.00	325.00
☐ Top Of The Hill...................................	250.00	300.00
☐ Town Crier	300.00	400.00
☐ Uriah Heep..	375.00	425.00
☐ Winston Churchill	250.00	300.00

"BESWICK" CHRISTMAS TANKARDS SERIES

Christmas At Bob Crachets', 65.00

	Date	Edition Size	Price
☐ Bob Crachit and Scrooge	1971	13000	50.00
☐ Christmas Carolers at Scrooge's Door	1972	13000	40.00
☐ Ghost of Christmas Future	1979	15000	60.00

	Date	Edition Size	Issue Price
☐ Marley's Ghost Visits Scrooge	1974	15000	45.00
☐ Scrooge is Asked to Aid the Poor	1973	13000	40.00
☐ Scrooge is Visited by Ghost of Christmas Past	1975	15000	50.00
☐ Scrooge is Visited by Ghost of Christmas Present	1976	15000	60.00
☐ Scrooge with Ghost of Christmas Present	1977	15000	50.00
☐ Scrooge with Ghost of Christmas Present	1978	15000	55.00
☐ Scrooge Going to Church	1981	15000	70.00
☐ Scrooge Visits His Own Grave	1980	15000	65.00
☐ Christmas at Bob Crachits	1982	15000	

TOBACCO JARS

	Price Range	
☐ Paddy	450.00	500.00
☐ Old Charley	450.00	500.00

TEAPOTS

☐ Sairey Gamp	450.00	500.00
☐ Old Charley	450.00	500.00
☐ Tony Weller	450.00	500.00

WALL MASKS

☐ Baby	450.00	550.00
☐ Blue Lady, mini	300.00	350.00
☐ Fate	1000.00	1200.00
☐ Friar Of Orders	750.00	850.00
☐ Green Lady, mini	300.00	350.00
☐ Greta Garbo	700.00	800.00
☐ Jester, large	450.00	550.00
☐ Jester, small	450.00	550.00
☐ Jester, mini	425.00	500.00
☐ Marlene Dietrich	700.00	800.00
☐ Pink Lady, mini	300.00	350.00
☐ Pompadour, large	700.00	800.00
☐ Pompadour, small	500.00	600.00
☐ St. Agnes	1000.00	1200.00
☐ Sweet Anne	450.00	550.00

WALL POCKETS

☐ Jester	650.00	750.00
☐ Old Charley	650.00	750.00

ROUGE FLAMBÉ

Back in the late 1880's Charles J. Noke, always fascinated with the glazes of the wares produced by the Chinese, began to experiment with the production of high-temperature transmutation glazes. His experiments were in the range of trying to duplicate the blood red color which the Chinese called "rouge flambé". Not meeting with much success, however, with the addition of Cuthbert Bailey in 1900 he brought with him a knowledge of the technical aspects of pottery making plus improvements in the design of the kiln. Since flambé was known for its inconsistencies Bailey became fascinated with the challenge and was determined to make it work. In 1902 Bernard Moore was appointed consultant to Doulton & Company. Bailey and Moore along with the assistance of Noke proceeded combining all their knowledge and financial resources of the company to finally produce with success the Royal Doulton Flambé Wares.

With their success Doulton Company increased their production to include animals, wares with landscape scenes, and some tableware. The tablewares were produced for only a brief period because of the difficulties of matching the red color. Introduced in 1920 was the Sung range of flambé wares, now considered the most prized of all flambé because of its beautiful designs and artistic value. Due to the extreme variations in firing the red color no two pieces are the exact coloring.

The following tradmarks may be found on the Rouge Flambé Wares.

BOWL	Price Range	
☐ Veined Sung, 8″ round	700.00	750.00
BUDDHA		
☐ Veined Sung, 7″	1100.00	1200.00
CAT		
☐ Rouge, No. 9, 4¾″	75.00	85.00
☐ Rouge, No. 2259, 12″	300.00	350.00
DRAGON		
☐ Veined Sung, No. 2085, 8″	500.00	550.00

DRAKE

	Price Range	
☐ Rouge, No. 137, 6″...............................	85.00	95.00
☐ Rouge, No. 806, 6″...............................	500.00	550.00

DUCK

☐ Rouge, No. 112, 1½″...........................	55.00	60.00
☐ Rouge, No. 395, 2½″...........................	55.00	60.00

Flambé Elephant, No. 489A, **115.00 — 150.00**

ELEPHANT

☐ Rouge, 9″, tusks down	300.00	350.00
☐ Rouge, No. 489, white tusks, 7″...................	300.00	350.00
☐ Rouge, No. 489A, 5½″	115.00	150.00

FISH

☐ Veined Sung, 12″................................	1000.00	1100.00

FOX, LYING

☐ Rouge, No. 29, 12″..............................	550.00	600.00
☐ Rouge 29B, 1″	60.00	75.00

FOX, SITTING

Price Range

☐ Rouge, No. 12, (Head pointed down), 5″ 75.00   95.00
☐ Rouge, No. 14, 4″. 85.00   100.00

HARE, LYING

☐ Rouge, No. 656A, 1¾″ 60.00   75.00
☐ Rouge, No. 1157, 2¾″. 85.00   100.00

LADY SEATED WITH FLOWING CLOAK

☐ Veined, rare, 5½″ 1200.00   1300.00

LEAPING SALMON

☐ Rouge, No. 666, 12″. 450.00   550.00

MONKEY

☐ Seated, arms folded, HN 118, 2¾″ 200.00   250.00

MONKEYS

☐ Rouge, No. 486, two in embrace 250.00   300.00

MOUSE ON A CUBE

☐ Rouge, HN 255. . . . .   250.00   300.00

NUDE ON A ROCK

☐ HN 604, 4½″ (considered rare) 700.00   800.00

OWL

☐ Veined, No. 2249, 12″ 300.00   350.00

PENGUIN

☐ Rouge, No. 84, 6″. 95.00   115.00
☐ Rouge, No. 585, 9″. 700.00   800.00

PIPER MINSTREL

☐ 16″ 1350.00   1500.00

PUPPY SITTING

☐ Rouge, HN 128, 4″. 250.00   300.00

RABBIT, EAR UP

☐ Rouge, No. 113, 2½″. 85.00   100.00

RHINOCEROS

☐ Veined, No. 615, 12″ 800.00   850.00

SOW

	Price Range	
☐ 2½″ x 5″	300.00	350.00

TIGER

☐ Rouge, No. 809, 6″	650.00	700.00

TRAY

☐ Veined, No. 1620, 4″	45.00	55.00
☐ Veined, No. 1621, 6″	75.00	85.00
☐ Woodcut, No. 1620, 4⅛″	45.00	55.00
☐ Woodcut, No. 1621, 7½″	100.00	125.00

Left to Right:
Veined Sung, No. 1618, No. 1619, **300.00 — 350.00 each**

VASE

☐ Landscape, 14″ high, 7″ round, old mark	750.00	900.00
☐ Landscape, No. 3879, 5¼″, signed O.C.K.	175.00	225.00
☐ No. 1622, large size	1100.00	1200.00
☐ No. 1623, large size	1100.00	1200.00
☐ No. 1624, large size	1100.00	1200.00

	Price Range	
☐ Veined, No. 1605, 4¼ "	85.00	100.00
☐ Veined, No. 1612, 8"	125.00	150.00
☐ Veined, No. 1614, 5¾ "	75.00	85.00
☐ Veined, No. 1616, 8¾ "	300.00	350.00
☐ Veined, No. 7798, artist signed, 11"	550.00	600.00
☐ Veined Sung, fish design, artist signed, 8½ "	1000.00	1250.00
☐ Veined Sung, Pumpkin shape, 6"	550.00	600.00
☐ Veined Sung, No. 925, 7"	125.00	150.00
☐ Woodcut, Deer Scene, old mark, 11".	600.00	700.00
☐ Woodcut, Desert Scene, 8½ "	500.00	550.00
☐ Woodcut, No. 1603, 7¼ "	75.00	85.00
☐ Woodcut, No. 1613, 6½ "	85.00	100.00
☐ Woodcut, No. 1617, 13¼ "	300.00	350.00
☐ Woodcut, No. 1619, 11"	300.00	350.00
☐ Woodcut, boat scene, No. 7203, 7½ "	225.00	275.00
☐ Woodcut, landscape, No. 7754, 8"	275.00	325.00

Left to Right:
Woodcut, No. 1618, No. 1619, **300.00 — 350.00 each**

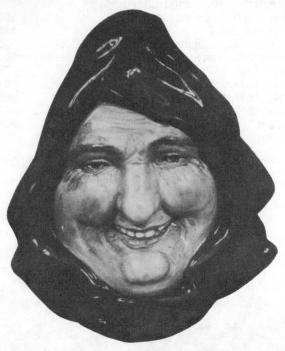

THE ROYAL DOULTON
INTERNATIONAL
COLLECTORS CLUB

U.S. Branch, Box 1815 Somerset, New Jersey 08873
Phone: 201-351-7880

☐ Please send me one John Doulton Character Jug, commemorating the founding of the Club, for $50. I understand that with my purchase I will automatically be enrolled for one year, at no extra charge, in the Royal Doulton International Collectors Club with full membership privileges. NJ residents add 5% sales tax.

☐ I wish to become a member of the Royal Doulton International Collectors Club, with all its privileges for one-year membership fee of $15.

Enclosed is my check _____ money order _____ for $ _____

SIGNATURE _____

Please Print
NAME _____

ADDRESS _____

CITY _____

STATE _____ ZIP _____
Please allow 4-6 weeks for delivery.

PRICE GUIDE SERIES

American Silver & Silver Plate

Today's silver market offers excellent opportunities *to gain big profits* — if you are well informed. *Over 15,000 current market values* are listed for 19th and 20th century American made Sterling, Coin and Silverplated flatware and holloware. Special souvenir spoon section. *ILLUSTRATED.*
$9.95-2nd Edition, 544 pgs., 5⅜" x 8", paperback, Order #: 184-5

Antique & Modern Firearms

This unique book is an encyclopedia of gun lore featuring over *21,000 listings with histories* of American and foreign manufacturers *plus a special section on collector cartridges values.* *ILLUSTRATED.*
$9.95-3rd Edition, 544 pgs., 5⅜" x 8", paperback, Order #: 363-5

Antiques & Other Collectibles

Introduces TODAY'S world of antiques with *over 62,000 current market values* for the most complete listing of antiques and collectibles IN PRINT! In this *new — 768 PAGE edition, many new categories have been added to keep fully up-to-date with the latest collecting trends.* *ILLUSTRATED.*
$9.95-3rd Edition, 768 pgs., 5⅜" x 8", paperback, Order #: 172-1

Antique Jewelry

Over *10,000 current collector values* for the most extensive listing of antique jewelry ever published, Georgian, Victorian, Art Nouveau, Art Deco. *Plus a special full color gem identification guide. ILLUSTRATED.*
$9.95-2nd Edition, 640 pgs., 5⅜" x 8", paperback, Order #: 354-6

Bottles Old & New

Over *22,000 current buying and selling prices* of both common and rare collectible bottles . . . ale, soda, bitters, flasks, medicine, perfume, poison, milk and more. *Plus expanded sections on Avon and Jim Beam. ILLUSTRATED.*
$9.95-6th Edition, 640 pgs., 5⅜" x 8", paperback, Order #: 350-3

Collector Cars

Over *36,000 actual current prices* for 4000 models of antique and classic automobiles — U.S. and foreign. Complete with engine specifications. *Special sections on auto memorabilia values and restoration techniques. ILLUSTRATED.*
$9.95-3rd Edition, 544 pgs., 5⅜" x 8", paperback, Order #: 181-0

Collector Knives

Over *14,000 buying and selling prices* on U.S. and foreign pocket and sheath knives. *Special sections on bicentennial, commemorative, limited edition, and handmade knives.* By J. Parker & B. Voyles. *ILLUSTRATED.*
$9.95-5th Edition, 640 pgs., 5⅜" x 8", paperback, Order #: 324-4

Collector Plates

Destined to become the ''PLATE COLLECTORS' BIBLE.'' This unique price guide offers the most comprehensive listing of collector plate values — *in Print! Special information includes: company histories; artist backgrounds; and helpful tips on buying, selling and storing a collection.* *ILLUSTRATED.*
$9.95-1st Edition, 640 pgs., 5⅜" x 8", paperback, Order #: 349-X

Collector Prints

Over *14,750 detailed listings* representing over 400 of the most famous collector print artists from Audubon and Currier & Ives, to modern day artists. *Special feature includes gallery/artist reference chart. ILLUSTRATED.*
$9.95-4th Edition, 544 pgs., 5⅜" x 8", paperback, Order #: 189-6

PUBLISHED BY: *THE HOUSE OF COLLECTIBLES, INC.*
1900 PREMIER ROW, ORLANDO, FL 32809   PHONE: (305) 857-9095

PRICE GUIDE SERIES

Comic & Science Fiction Books
Over *31,000 listings with current values* for comic and science fiction publications *from 1903-to-date. Special sections on Tarzan, Big Little Books, Science Fiction publications and paperbacks.* *ILLUSTRATED.*
$9.95-6th Edition, 544 pgs., 5⅜" x 8", paperback, Order #: 353-8

Hummel Figurines & Plates
The most complete guide ever published on every type of Hummel — including the most recent trademarks and size variations, with *4,500 up-to-date prices. Plus tips on buying, selling and investing. ILLUSTRATED.*
$9.95-3rd Edition, 448 pgs., 5⅜" x 8", paperback, Order #: 325-X

Military Collectibles
This detailed historical reference price guide covers the largest accumulation of military objects — 15th century-to-date — listing over *12,000 accurate prices. Special expanded Samuri sword and headdress sections. ILLUSTRATED.*
$9.95-2nd Edition, 544 pgs., 5⅜" x 8", paperback, Order #: 191-8

Music Machines
Virtually every music related collectible is included in this guide — over *11,000 current prices. 78 recordings, mechanical musical machines, and instruments. ILLUSTRATED.*
$9.95-2nd Edition, 544 pgs., 5⅜" x 8", paperback, Order #: 187-X

Old Books & Autographs
Descriptions of the finest literary collectibles available, with over *11,000 prices for all types of books:* Americana, bibles, medicine, cookbooks and more. *Plus an updated autograph section.* *ILLUSTRATED.*
$9.95-4th Edition, 510 pgs., 5⅜" x 8", paperback, Order #: 351-1

Paper Collectibles
Old Checks, Invoices, Books, Magazines, Newspapers, Ticket Stubs and even Matchbooks — any paper items that reflects America's past — are gaining collector value. This book contains *over 25,000 current values* and descriptions for all types of paper collectibles. *ILLUSTRATED.*
$9.95-2nd Edition, 608 pgs., 5⅜" x 8", paperback, Order #: 186-1

Pottery & Porcelain
Over *10,000 current prices and listings* of fine pottery and porcelain, plus an extensive Lenox china section. *Special sections on identifying china trademarks and company histories.* *ILLUSTRATED.*
$9.95-2nd Edition, 544 pgs., 5⅜" x 8", paperback, Order #: 188-8

Records
Over *31,000 current prices* of collectible singles, EPs, albums, plus 20,000 memorable song titles recorded by over 1100 artists. *Rare biographies and photos are provided for many well known artists. ILLUSTRATED.*
$9.95-4th Edition, 544 pgs., 5⅜" x 8", paperback, Order #: 356-2

Royal Doulton
This authoritative guide to Royal Doulton porcelains contains over *3,500 detailed listings* on figurines, plates and Toby jugs. Includes tips on buying, selling and displaying. *Plus an exclusive numerical reference index. ILLUSTRATED.*
$9.95-2nd Edition, 544 pgs., 5⅜" x 8", paperback, Order #: 355-4

Wicker
You could be sitting on a *fortune!* Decorators and collectors are driving wicker values to unbelievable highs! This pictorial price guide *positively identifies all types* of Victorian, Turn of the century and Art Deco wicker furniture. *A special illustrated section on wicker repair is included.* *ILLUSTRATED.*
$9.95-1st Edition, 416 pgs., 5⅜" x 8", paperback, Order #: 348-1

PUBLISHED BY: *THE HOUSE OF COLLECTIBLES, INC.*
1900 PREMIER ROW, ORLANDO, FL 32809   PHONE: (305) 857-9095

MINI PRICE GUIDE SERIES

Antiques & Flea Markets

Discover the fun and profit of collecting antiques with this handy pocket reference to *over 15,000 types of collectibles.* Avoid counterfeits and learn the secrets to successful buying and selling. *ILLUSTRATED.*
$2.50-1st Edition, 240 pgs., 4" x 5½", paperback, Order #: 308-2

Pete Rose Baseball Cards

This guide lists *over 44,000 current market values* for baseball cards – Bowman, Burger King, Donruss, Fleer, O-Pee-Chee and Topps. *Includes a full color PETE ROSE limited edition collector card. ILLUSTRATED.*
$2.50-2nd Edition, 288 pgs., 4" x 5½", paperback, Order #: 322-8

Comic Books

Young and Old are collecting old comic books for fun *and Profit!* This handy ''pocket-sized'' price guide lists current market values and detailed descriptions for the most sought-after ''collectible'' comic books. *Buying, selling and storing tips are provided for the beginning collector. ILLUSTRATED.*
$2.50-1st Edition, 240 pgs., 4" x 5½", paperback, Order #: 345-7

Dolls

Doll collecting is one of America's favorite hobbies and this guide lists *over 3,000 actual market values* for all the manufacturers! Kewpies, Howdy Doody, Shirley Temple, GI Joe plus comprehensive listings of Barbies. *ILLUSTRATED.*
$2.95-1st Edition, 240 pgs., 4" x 5½", paperback, Order #: 316-3

O.J. Simpson Football Cards

The world famous O.J. Simpson highlights this comprehensive guide to football card values. *Over 21,000 current collector prices* are listed for: Topps, Bowman, Fleer, Philadelphia and O-Pee-Chee. *Includes a full color O.J. SIMPSON limited edition collector card. ILLUSTRATED.*
$2.50-2nd Edition, 256 pgs., 4" x 5½", paperback, Order #: 323-6

Hummels

How much are your Hummels worth? You can become an expert on these lovely figurines with this complete guide, *FULLY ILLUSTRATED,* with a handy numerical index that puts descriptions and market prices at your fingertips. Learn why the slightest variation could mean hundreds in value.
$2.95-1st Edition, 240 pgs., 4" x 5½", paperback, Order #:318-X

Paperbacks & Magazines

Old discarded paperbacks and magazines could be worth 50-100 times their original cover price. Learn how to identify them. *Thousands* of descriptions and prices show which issues are rare. *ILLUSTRATED.*
$2.50-1st Edition, 240 pgs., 4" x 5½", paperback, Order #: 315-5

Scouting Collectibles

Discover the colorful history behind scouting, relive childhood memories and profit from those old family heirlooms. *Thousands of prices* are listed for all types of Boy and Girl Scout memorabilia. *ILLUSTRATED.*
$2.50-1st Edition, 240 pgs., 4" x 5½", paperback, Order #: 314-7

Toys

Kids from eight to eighty enjoy collecting toys and this comprehensive guide has them all! Trains, trucks, comic and movie character, space toys, boats and **MORE.** *Over 5,000 current market values* of toys, old and new, plus investment tips and histories. *ILLUSTRATED.*
$2.95-1st Edition, 240 pgs., 4" x 5½", paperback, Order #: 317-1

PUBLISHED BY: *THE HOUSE OF COLLECTIBLES, INC.*
1900 PREMIER ROW, ORLANDO, FL 32809   PHONE: (305) 857-9095